GROUPWARE AND AUTHORING

GROUPWARE AND AUTHORING

Edited by
Roy Rada
School of Electrical Engineering and Computer Science
Washington State University
Pullman, Washington, USA

ACADEMIC PRESS
Harcourt Brace & Company, Publishers
London San Diego New York
Boston Sydney Tokyo Toronto

ACADEMIC PRESS LIMITED
24–28 Oval Road
LONDON NWI 7DX

U.S. Edition Published by
ACADEMIC PRESS INC.
San Diego, CA 92101

This book is printed on acid free paper

A catalogue record for this book is available from the British Library.

ISBN 0-12-575005-6

Typeset by Mathematical Composition Setters Ltd, Salisbury, Wiltshire.
Printed in Great Britain by the University Printing House, Cambridge.

Contents

List of Contributors

Toyoko Abe,
Terminal System Research Laboratory,
NEC Corporation,
1-1 Miyazaki – 4 chrome,
Miyamae-ku, Kawasaki – city,
Kanagawa 216,
Japan

Ronald M. Baecker,
Dynamic Graphics Project,
University of Toronto,
10 King's College Road,
Toronto,
ON M5S 1A1,
Canada

Michael Capron,
Xerox Corporation,
1387 Fairpoint Road,
Bldg 1100,
Fairpoint,
NY 14450,
USA

Ravinder Chandhok,
Carnegie Mellon University,
Pittsburgh,
PA 15213,
USA

Chaomei Chen,
Department of Computer Studies,
Glasgow Caledonian University,
Cowcaddens Road,
Glasgow G4 OBA,
UK

Dominique Decouchant,
INRIA-IMAG,
Opera Project,
2 rue Vignate,
F-38610 Gieres,
France

Jacqueline Desimone,
Xerox Corporation,
1387 Fairpoint Road,
Bldg 1100,
Fairpoint,
NY 14450,
USA

Prasun Dewan,
Computer Science Collaboratory,
University of North Carolina,
Chapel Hill,
NC 27599-3175,
USA

Paul Erion,
Carnegie Mellon University,
Pittsburgh,
PA 15213,
USA

Hiromi Fukuoka,
Terminal System Research Laboratory,
NEC Corporation,
1-1 Miyazaki – 4 chrome,
Miyamae-ku, Kawasaki – city,
Kanagawa 216,
Japan

Jolene Galagher,
Department of English,
Carnegie Mellon University,
Pittsburgh,
PS 15213,
USA

Jörg Haake,
Integrated Publication and Information Systems Institute,
Gesellschaft fur Mathematik und Datenverargeitung,
Dolivostr. 15,
D-6100 Darmstadt,
Germany

Mark James Handley,
Department of Computer Science,
University College London,
Gower Street,
London, WC1E 6BT,
UK

Jörg Hannemann,
Integrated Publication and Information Systems Institute,
Gesellschaft fur Mathematik und Datenverargeitung,
Dolivostr. 15,
D-6100 Darmstadt,
Germany

David S. Kaufer,
Carnegie Mellon University,
Pittsburgh,
PA 15213,
USA

Robert E. Kraut,
School of Computer Science,
Carnegie Mellon University,
Pittsburgh,
PS 15213,
USA

Karen Lacomis-Cote,
Xerox Corporation,
1387 Fairpoint Road,
Bldg 1100,
Fairpoint,
NY 14450,
USA

Andreas Lemke,
Integrated Publication and Information Systems Institute,
Gesellschaft fur Mathematik und Datenverargeitung,
Dolivostr. 15,
D-6100 Darmstadt,
Germany

Kazutoshi Maeno,
Terminal System Research Laboratory,
NEC Corporation,
1-1 Miyazaki – 4 chrome,
Miyamae-ku, Kawasaki – city,
Kanagawa 216,
Japan

Antonios Michailidis,
27 Parnithas Street,
Kato Toumba,
54453 Thessaloniki,
Greece

Dale Miller,
Carnegie Mellon University,
Pittsburgh,
PA 15213,
USA

Alex Mitchell,
Dynamic Graphics Project,
University of Toronto,
10 King's College Road,
Toronto,
ON M5S 1A1,
Canada

Hiromi Mizuno,
Terminal System Research Laboratory,
NEC Corporation,
1-1 Miyazaki – 4 chrome,
Miyamae-ku, Kawasaki – city,
Kanagawa 216,
Japan

James Morris,
Carnegie Mellon University,
Pittsburgh,
PA 15213,
USA

Jonathan Munson,
Computer Science Collaboratory,
University of North Carolina,
Chapel Hill,
NC 27599-3175,
USA

Jaime Navon
Computer Science Collaboratory,
University of North Carolina,
Chapel Hill,
NC 27599-3175,
USA

Christine M. Neuwirth,
Department of English,
Carnegie Mellon University,
Pittsburgh,
PA 15213,
USA

Gary M. Olson,
Cognitive Science and Machine Intelligence Laboratory,
University of Michigan,
701 Tappan St,
Ann Arbor,
MI 48109–1234,
USA

Judith S. Olson,
Cognitive Science and Machine Intelligence Laboratory,
University of Michigan,
701 Tappan St,
Ann Arbor,
MI 48109–1234,
USA

Jo Ann Oravec,
Baruch College
City University of New York,
School of Public Affairs,
17 Lexington Avenue,
Box F-1228, New York,
NY 10010,
USA

Vincent Quint
INRIA-IMAG,
Opera Project,
2 rue Vignate,
F-38610 Gieres,
France

Ilona R. Posner,
Dynamic Graphics Project,
University of Toronto,
10 King's College Road,
Toronto,
ON M5S 1A1,
Canada

Roy Rada,
School of Electrical Engineering and Computer Science,
Washington State University,
Pullman,
WA 99164–2752,
USA

Shiro Sakata,
Terminal System Research Laboratory,
NEC Corporation,
1-1 Miyazaki – 4 chrome,
Miyamae-ku, Kawasaki – city,
Kanagawa 216,
Japan

Manuel Romero Salcedo,
INRIA-IMAG,
Opera Project,
2 rue Vignate,
F-38610 Gieres,
France

A. Santos,
Electronic Data Systems Deutschland GmbH,
Eisenstr. 56,
65428 Russelsheim,
Germany

Martina Angela Sasse,
Department of Computer Science,
University College London,
Gower Street,
London, WC1E 6BT,
UK

Wolfgang Schuler,
Integrated Publication and Information Systems Institute,
Gesellschaft fur Mathematik und Datenverargeitung,
Dolivostr. 15,
D-6100 Darmstadt,
Germany

Helge Schütt,
Integrated Publication and Information Systems Institute,
Gesellschaft fur Mathematik und Datenverargeitung,
Dolivostr. 15,
D-6100 Darmstadt,
Germany

David Stotts,
Computer Science Collaboratory,
University of North Carolina,
Chapel Hill,
NC 27599-3175,
USA

Norbert Streitz,
Integrated Publication and Information Systems Institute,
Gesellschaft fur Mathematik und Datenverargeitung,
Dolivostr. 15,
D-6100 Darmstadt,
Germany

Manfred Thüring,
Integrated Publication and Information Systems Institute,
Gesellschaft fur Mathematik und Datenverargeitung,
Dolivostr. 15,
D-6100 Darmstadt,
Germany

B. Tritsch,
Fraunhofer Institute for Computer Graphics,
Wilhelminenstr. 7,
64283 Darmstadt,
Germany

Preface

Authoring is a fundamental activity of people, particularly people who are either learning to play useful roles in society or people who already have important roles in society. Working in teams to author is commonplace. The maintenance manual for an airplane engine is not written by one person. At schools, teachers are discovering that students authoring together can learn effectively from one another. This importance of writing and writing together is stimulated by the new information technologies which support networking and multimedia.

This book had its inception at a workshop organized by Saul Greenberg and Stephen Hayne. The workshop was entitled 'Real-Time Group Drawing and Writing Tools' and occurred in the Fall of 1992. Although a number of the contributors to this book were present at that workshop, the editor asked additional people not present but working in the field of groupware and authoring to contribute. Thus, some time elapsed from the original idea to this book as presented now. By the same token, the book reflects a change in the concepts and technology since 1992, although it does not attempt to provide a history.

Other books have recently appeared on topics related to groupware and authoring. The book edited by Mike Sharples entitled *Computer-Supported Collaborative Writing* emphasizes user-oriented studies by British groups through 1993 and is excellent. However, no other book has this book's particular breadth and depth.

This book covers work from the major centers related to groupware and authoring from many countries including Canada, England, France, Germany, Japan and the USA (in alphabetical order). The latest developments in new collaborative authoring. The overwhelming success of the World Wide Web is acknowledged in the adaptations that some of the tools have made to work with the World Wide Web. The book's commercial concerns are supported in Part 5, Commercial Systems and Experiences.

Similar to the diversity of backgrounds of the contributors to this book is the diversity of targeted audiences. The audiences for this book could come from many disciplines, such as business, communications, computer science, information systems, psychology, rhetoric, sociology, and more. The book has a scholarly tone which might particularly appeal to students and academics, but people from industry and government will also find the book useful.

The editor and the authors of the chapters believe that the topics of groupware and authoring are vitally important and that the emphasis on the intersection of these two topics is growing daily. The chapters in this book represent some of the finest work on the topic and this collection is offered in the expectation that members of the audience will not only use such tools but might contribute to the development of better tools.

1 Introduction

ROY RADA

Writing is the most frequent task which computers help people to accomplish. What kind of technological support is appropriate for what aspects of the authoring task when people work together? Group work is always mediated by some form of communication. Without communication people could not coordinate their efforts. Technology can play a paradoxical role in coordinating collaboration: it can severely limit communication or it can enhance the scope for meaningful communication. This book is about computer-based support for collaborative authoring. Information technology for groups may be called groupware and hence the title of the book, *Groupware and Authoring*.

BACKGROUND

In the late 1980s, the near ubiquity of networked computers in organizations created a paradigm shift in the way human–computer interaction is viewed. Instead of creating applications that allowed a person to pursue only individual work, researchers and developers started thinking about systems that let people work together. The discipline of 'Computer-supported cooperative work' arose, collecting researchers interested in the study and theory of how people work together, and how the computer and related technologies affect group behavior. There was a strong applied component to such work as well, and 'groupware' systems were designed and built to support and augment group work.

Text processing programs, very popular as single user applications, became the natural target application for groupware for several reasons. First, groupware for writing could benefit many users. These systems were seen as a valuable medium for people to share on-line work with each other. Second, the area is a rich research domain. Researchers in psychology and sociology could study how people write together in non-computer settings, and extract principles that could be applied to groupware design. They could also investigate how groups react to novel facilities that groupware could offer. Third, groupware is full of challenging technical problems and innovative potential. Computer scientists and developers could grapple with many issues, such as distributed systems, multimedia, communications, and toolkit

GROUPWARE AND AUTHORING
ISBN 0-12-575005-6

development. Finally, groupware for writing is attractive because of its commercial possibilities. If marketers could attract people already using single-user versions of these tools into the fold, then the potential market of groupware users could be enormous.

GENERAL ISSUES

Initial technological breakthroughs of building computer-based group writing tools were made several years ago, and many researchers are now constructing their own group tools as well as pursuing human factors issues. While new ideas are plentiful, there is also a great deal of unnecessary overlap and replication of effort. Lessons must be drawn from the communal research experiences and empirical design rules formulated. This book documents this process for collaborative writing.

The emphases of this book are placed on:

- the human factors research behind the design of shared writing tools;
- the technical innovations involved in building these systems;
- specific applications of these tools;
- empirical validation with people using shared work spaces;
- the factors involved in the adoption of these tools by groups and organizations; and
- the factors involved in making such groupware a commercial product.

Much writing occurs both inside and outside meetings, but for quite different purposes. Face-to-face meetings, for example, often require sharing document notes. Collaborative writing continues outside meetings through report generation and revision, exchange of notes and memos, and so on. One might suppose that writing on the computer can facilitate collaboration, because the computer has great potential as a shared interactive workspace and as a medium to facilitate document exchange and revision. Experience already suggests that, in spite of the variety of writing applications, simple tools can allow people to interact comfortably with minimal interference from the technology.

CHAPTER-BY-CHAPTER PREVIEW

This book contains 14 chapters within five major parts covering:

- Reviews and views
- Studying users
- New tools and users
- New tools
- Commercial systems and experiences

Several chapters describe a special groupware authoring tool and then focus on the impact of this tool. Two to four chapters appear in each major section and those chapters are next previewed in order of appearance.

Part 1, Reviews and Views, includes two review chapters. 'Review of Collaborative Authoring Tools' by Antonios Michailidis and Roy Rada begins with a framework for characterizing groupware authoring tools. Then many groupware authoring tools are described in terms of this framework. 'Collaborative Authoring Dynamics' by Chaomei Chen and Roy Rada reviews user studies of collaborative authoring and also includes a brief user study to illustrate one method for studying authoring dynamics.

The chapter of by Jo Ann Oravec is entitled 'A Portrait of the Author as an Interacting Group'. The genres of documents produced collaborative writing are different from those produced by solo writing. The relationships between the people and the tools reflects itself in the character of the resultant document. A charismatic speaker will use one tool for a brainstorming session, whereas a careful negotiator with good correspondence skills will use a different tool to manage the frequent reports of a large, long-term authoring task. With the heavy cultural emphasis on the notion of the individual author, there has been far less attention on development of vocabularies and imageries associated with group production and composition.

'Coordination and Reuse' by Roy Rada views the authoring of documents from the perspective of coordination theory. Building libraries of reusable material and guiding people so that they effectively reuse information is a coordination problem. Industry approaches coordination in a very systematic way and defines clear life cycles of documents and roles for people to fulfil in producing documents. Academics tend to operate in non-systematic ways but might benefit by adopting some of the methods of industry.

The next three chapters belong in Part 2, Studying Users. Gary and Judith Olson in 'The Effectiveness of Simple Shared Electronic Workspaces' have studied the support offered by a groupware editor ShrEdit for real-time meetings. Their paper shows how shared electronic workspaces can support the synchronous work of small, task-oriented groups. ShrEdit supports simple authoring of text through which authors can track what other authors are writing. Experiments were done with computer screens embedded in a table and with people seated around the table. Surprisingly, the groups supported by ShrEdit explored fewer options than those working without technological tools but also produced a higher quality and more focused result.

One of the longest chapters in the book also presents the most experimental detail. Jolene Galegher and Robert Kraut in 'Computer-Mediated Communication for Intellectual Teamwork: An Experiment in Group Writing' present a large study of collaborative authoring. Over 100 university students were subjects in the study. The chapter establishes and refutes possible criticisms of its methodology. Fairly complicated statistics are presented in an understandable manner.

In 'Learning to Write Together', Ilona Posner *et al.* describe an ethnographic study of collaborative writing by two groups of sixth-grade students using synchronous collaborative writing software for one hour per week over a 12-week period. Each group produced several, short documents. Analysis of the ethnographic data demonstrated the importance of concepts such as awareness, ownership, and control in the writing process, and highlighted many examples of strengths and weaknesses in the writing software.

Part 3 contains two chapters; each chapter describes in some detail a prototype system and also presents the results of user studies on the system. Christine Neuwirth *et al.* in 'Flexible Diff-ing in a Collaborative Writing System' have methodologically studied the differences which people want to see between two versions of a document. The types of differences that people want to see were found to depend on their role in the group, the phase of the group work, and the type of text being created. If many differences have recently been created, a high-level view of them might help; whereas when very few changes have occurred, seeing each change may be important.

Martina Angela Sasse and Mark Handley in their chapter 'Collaborative Writing with Synchronous and Asynchronous Support Environments' describe a group authoring system for large-scale documents prepared by teams of geographically distributed authors. The synchronous part of the system was good for the initial and reviewing stages of writing, but a different tool was more appropriate for intermediate production and management tasks. Furthermore, for this kind of asynchronous multi-site authoring, users should be able to work with their own tools as much as possible. The system integrates automatically answered electronic mail, shared file store administration, and a version control tool.

Part 4, New Tools, contains four chapters. Adelinos Santos and B. Tritsch in 'Using Multimedia to Support Cooperative Editing' describe a sophisticated, multimedia collaborative work system, called CoMedia, which is specifically tailored to collaborative authoring. The requirements for the system were based on observations of group performance and on the belief that multimedia groupware could both support group communication and enhance the expressiveness of the edited information. The video and audio support is intended to create a seamless environment between synchronized group work and asynchronous solo work.

Norbert Streitz *et al.* in 'SEPIA: A Cooperative Hypermedia Authoring Environment' report on the design, development, and implementation of SEPIA. Using interacting problem spaces as the vehicle for modelling the dynamic aspects of authoring, Streitz *et al.* arrive at a set of requirements based on the concept of activity spaces. Based on these requirements, SEPIA's architecture supports a hypermedia data model, authoring functionality, and human–human cooperative rhetoric.

Dominique Decouchant *et al.* in 'Structured and Distributed Cooperative Editing in a Large Scale Network' describe a new system, called Alliance, to help collaborating authors exploit structure in documents. In addition to the local editing functions made available on each site by a structured editor, the application provides such basic functionalities, as management of document storage and remote access to distributed documents. It offers services for managing user interaction and cooperation, for dynamically distributing roles to users, for showing documents through multiple views, and for controlling the consistency of modifications. The extensions for Alliance that permit it to be run on the World Wide Web are described.

In 'A Three-Level Binding for Collaborative Editing Semantics' David Stotts *et al.* present a new groupware authoring tool called Sui'tre. The chapter begins with a model of three levels of binding of collaboration semantics to a groupware tool. 'Sui'tre embodies one example of such a three-level binding. The interpreted component of Sui'tre provides maximum flexibility in defining group behavior, allowing users to alter their interactions while a collaboration is taking place. The Sui'tre efforts have been extended to provide World Wide Web interfaces.

The final part of the book looks at 'Commercial Systems and Experiences'. A system and experiences with its use are described both from NEC and from Xerox. The chapter 'Multimedia and Multiparty Desk-Top Conference System MERMAID as Groupwares Platform' is written by Shiro Sakata *et al.* from NEC. The Multimedia Environment for Remote Multiple-Attendee Interactive Decision-making (MERMAID) System was developed as a groupware platform in 1989 through the integration of computer and communications technologies. MERMAID is a widely sold multimedia and multi-party system. This chapter describes the MERMAID functionalities, and experience with its use.

Michael Capron *et al.* describe a commercial tool which is used at Xerox Corporation in practical business meetings. The authors suggest that simple systems which fit into the work flow are what people need for synchronous writing. Xerox has a corporate policy on how meetings should be handled to increase efficiency and effectiveness. The Xerox system prompts a single meeting facilitator in taking minutes on the computer and has proven attractive for several reasons. For one, the members of the group can work comfortably without having to type at the computer; and the equipment costs are low as just one stand-alone computer is needed. In meetings the majority of interaction continues to be face-to-face but the computer acts as a structuring device, a kind of electronic, structured whiteboard and fits into the workflow.

Multimedia, networked computers are sometimes seen as necessary for adequate support of group meetings. But as years of frustrating experience at fitting systems into the work flow have suggested, the problem is not sophistication but workability. The chapter by Jo Ann Oravec discusses a model of collaborative writing without a specific tool or experiments with it. The chapter by Capron *et al.* is just the opposite – it presents a commercial writing tool which has been used at Xerox Corporation to improve the efficiency of note-taking in meetings. The range of tools addressed in the intervening chapters vary from the email tool of Sasse *et al.*, to the tool for sharing a text database of Olson *et al.*, to the audio-video groupware of Santos *et al.*

DIRECTIONS

Document authoring is the most common activity to be exercised on computers. The group aspect of authoring has traditionally been handled asynchronously and on paper. As computer networks are becoming commonplace and software supports multi-person work, the work of groups in writing may be supported in new ways.

The enormous popularity of the World Wide Web (WWW) has led to a revolution in electronic publishing. The ease with which people can use the WWW to contribute to the evolving world information space has stimulated a large, popular front for groupware and authoring. Two technical chapters of this book have explicitly noted how authoring groupware can be developed for the WWW, namely the chapters of Decouchant *et al.* and Stotts *et al.* One can expect the WWW to influence the direction of groupware and authoring over the coming years.

Despite the book's focus on technology, the book's authors know and demonstrate that people are the principal players in collaborative authoring – the intellectual activities are far from mechanized – and the needs are not so much for sophisticated tools as for reliable human–human relations, clear and agreed plans, and constructive feedback. One of the major lessons of the modern information ages is actually as old as time – namely, the tool should fit the job. In the complex activity of collaborative authoring many tasks, some requiring intense human–human interaction and others not, must be performed, and no single tool is best for all of these tasks. In matching technology and task, some have noted that synchronous tools, such as the telephone, go with interactive tasks such as brainstorming, while asynchronous tools, such as electronic mail, suit less interactive tasks such as revising. Much remains to be learned about the kind of technology to support a specific group in a specific writing task.

Part 1

Reviews and Views

2 A Review of Collaborative Authoring Tools

ANTONIOS MICHAILIDIS and ROY RADA

INTRODUCTION

Group authoring systems are designed to support multiple users who jointly create, edit, annotate and revise a shared document. The goal of group authoring systems is to improve the efficiency and quality of group writing (Johansen, 1989) and support the cooperation processes between collaborating authors (Rodden, 1991). Group writing systems may support the forms, social interactions and cognitive processes of collaborative writing (Streitz, 1993). Co-authoring systems provide support to a group of authors during the phases of writing (e.g. brainstorming, information gathering, planning, drafting and revising). They allow users to work either asynchronously or at the same time. They offer mechanisms for separating comments from text, defining roles, and notification of the group members' actions. Some systems focus on the facilities for physical sharing of information, while others focus on the logical structure of the information.

Some group authoring systems are built with collaborative authoring in mind, while others are extensions to single author systems (Rada, 1991). The design of group writing systems has been influenced by advances in three kinds of technologies: hypertext, computer networks, and database management systems (Haake and Wilson, 1992). The use of hypertext technology in collaborative writing focuses on information structuring and document representation. Computer networks and recent advances in multimedia conferencing provide rich communication channels that can be utilized as an alternative to face-to-face communications and informal social interactions. Database management systems facilitate multi-user access control to stored documents, information sharing, and transaction management.

The framework of analysis provided by Peng (1993) is adopted here to perform a comparative analysis among group writing systems. This framework can be summarized as follows:

1. The salient conceptual aspects of collaborative writing in the computer-supported cooperative work (CSCW) field are identified. These aspects reflect the current state of understanding of collaborative writing in CSCW research.

GROUPWARE AND AUTHORING
ISBN 0-12-575005-6

2. The design issues that are raised in response to the research issues in computer-supported collaborative writing are identified. The design issues indicate how CSCW research approached the problem of designing systems to support collaborative writing.
3. The different ways in which group writing systems address each design issue are presented.

This framework is considered to be appropriate for a comparative analysis among group writing systems because it allows comparison of the systems at three levels of system design:

1. The conceptual aspects of collaboration supported by each system;
2. The design issues addressed by each group writing system;
3. The technological approaches followed to tackle each design issue.

In the following sections, first the research issues for collaborative writing studied within the CSCW field are presented. Design issues and system features are then described. Next, a classification of group authoring tools is presented followed by concluding remarks.

	Issues \ Systems	AUGMENT	InSynch	CAR	MESSIE	NSF EXPRESS	Quilt	Grove	ShrEdit	Aspects	MULE	SASSE	SASE	MMM	DistEdit	Timbuktu	COeX	NoteCards	MILO	Intermedia	InterNote	CoAuthor	CoMEdiA	KMS	Contexts	SEPIA	CES	CompareRite	PREP	MarkUp	BibDb	GroupWrite	ForComment	Shared Books	MUCH	DOLPHIN	Duplex	IRIS	Alliance	MultimETH	Mjolner project	COOPerator
Task	substantive	■		■		■	■	■	■	■	■	■	■	■	■			■	■	■		■	■	■	■	■	■	■	■			■	■	■	■		■	■	■	■	■	■
	procedural			■			■															■				■								■		■				■		■
	annotative			■	■		■	■				■						■	■	■	■	■	■	■		■			■		■	■	■	■	■	■				■	■	■
	asynchronous			■	■		■					■						■	■	■	■	■	■	■	■	■		■	■	■		■	■		■		■	■	■		■	■
	synchronous	■	■	■				■	■	■	■	■	■	■	■	■	■							■			■					■					■		■				
	semi-(a)synchronous					■													■		■	■			■	■	■	■							■	■					■	■	
	group awareness	■					■	■	■	■	■	■	■	■			■			■	■					■								■	■		■	■	■	■	■
	mutual intelligibility																							■		■			■							■				■		
	individual writing						■					■	■						■	■	■	■	■		■	■	■			■		■	■	■		■	■	■			■	■	■
	forms/strategies			■															■							■				■		■	■	■		■						
	transition						■					■	■		■					■		■				■			■							■						
	document access			■	■		■	■		■								■					■						■				■	■					■	■		■
	version control	■		■	■		■					■								■					■	■	■		■	■	■		■		■					■		■	
	undo						■								■														■															
Group	identities						■	■				■	■	■										■			■			■				■		■	■		■			■	
	social complexity						■	■	■										■				■			■			■															
	membership																■																										
	authority						■		■	■																																■		■
	roles						■			■	■				■									■						■	■			■						■	■		■
	conflict management																					■				■																	
	sub-groups							■				■	■												■	■																
	collocated	■						■	■	■		■	■	■										■			■			■					■	■	■					
	distributed	■	■	■	■	■	■	■		■	■	■	■		■	■	■		■			■	■	■	■	■		■	■	■		■	■	■	■	■	■	■	■	■	■	■
Comm.	synchronous	■	■	■				■		■	■		■	■	■	■	■					■	■			■											■	■	■		■		
	asynchronous	■		■													■	■	■	■	■	■	■		■	■		■						■		■	■	■	■		■
Tools	basic word-processing		■			■			■	■									■	■										■			■		■	■		■					
	mixed media				■	■	■			■		■	■		■		■		■						■										■		■		■		■
	document interchange					■				■																		■			■			■			■		■		

Figure 2.1 Research issues that have been addressed in group writing system design. The symbol ■ indicates that a research issue has been addressed in system design.

RESEARCH ISSUES IN COMPUTER-SUPPORTED COLLABORATIVE WRITING

This section presents the main research issues and conceptual aspects of collaborative writing that have been investigated within CSCW. The purpose is to present the current state of understanding of the collaborative writing process which informed the design and development of computer-based systems for collaborative writing. This section can be viewed as a precursor to understanding the main design issues and system features presented in the next section.

The studies described in Appendix A (see Tables A.1 to A.4 and Figure A.1) served as the basis for classifying research issues into four main categories: task, group, communication and tools. These categories are discussed briefly in the sub-sections below.

Figure 2.1 shows the research issues that have been addressed in group writing system design. In Figure 2.1 (as well as in Figure 2.2) only the issues and system features which are explicitly reported in the literature are marked. The fact that most of the systems found in the literature were not described in every single detail poses a restriction in identifying all research issues that have been addressed in system design or all system features. So, unmarked entries in Figures 2.1 and 2.2 do not necessarily mean that they are not addressed or supported by the systems, but that support was not evident from the system's description in the literature.

Task

Task refers to the activities that co-authors perform during their collaboration. Several dimensions of collaborative writing activities have been identified and are presented here. These dimensions include: content, time, collaboration mode, and form of collaboration.

Three types of activities have been identified based on their content:

- Substantive: refers to the actual writing activities, such as brainstorming, planning, writing, editing and revising, that people perform.
- Procedural: refers to the activities that people perform to coordinate their work. Such activities include decision making, discussions about the procedures of the collaboration.
- Annotative: activities focus on annotating the products of substantive activities using comments, questions, critiques, and suggestions for revision. Three types of annotations have been identified: public, directed to a subgroup, and private.

Writing activities are distributed in time. Synchronous collaboration occurs when multiple authors work on the same document at the same time. Two modes of synchronous collaboration have been identified: loosely-coupled (LC) and tightly-

	Issues \ Systems	AUGMENT	InSynch	CAR	MESSIE	NSF EXPRESS	Quilt	Grove	ShrEdit	Aspects	MULE	SASSE	SASE	MMM	DistEdit	Timbuktu	COeX	NoteCards	MILO	Intermedia	InterNote	CoAuthor	CoMEdiA	KMS	Contexts	SEPIA	CES	CompareRite	PREP	MarkUp	BibDb	GroupWrite	ForComment	Shared Books	MUCH	DOLPHIN	Duplex	IRIS	Alliance	MultimETH	Mjolner project	COOPerator
Shared-screen / cursor	telepointer									■			■		■	■							■			■										■						
	multiple cursors									■				■									■			■										■				■		
	WYSIWIS	■		■				■	■	■				■									■			■										■				■		
	relaxed WYSIWIS							■			■	■	■										■			■								■				■				
	WYSIWITYS								■																																	
	handles													■																												
	teleportation																						■																			
	snapshots							■																														■				
	sound											■														■																
	change bars											■																														
	multiple scroll bars											■	■																													
	screen refresh																									■	■									■				■			
	icons																																						■			
Storage and retrieval	single file			■	■	■	■	■	■	■	■	■	■	■	■	■	■		■												■	■	■	■				■	■	■	■	■	■
	semantic network	■					■											■	■	■	■	■	■	■	■	■	■	■	■			■		■	■	■						
	contexts																								■	■										■						
	meta-information				■		■					■						■	■	■	■	■	■	■	■	■	■		■		■	■	■	■	■	■		■		■	■	■
	following links																	■	■	■	■	■	■	■	■	■									■	■						
	string search										■							■	■				■	■					■		■	■			■					■		
	graphical browsing																	■		■	■		■			■						■				■	■			■	■	■
	content search																		■						■																	
	structure search																								■																	
	index																																		■							
Communication	audio			■		■	■			■			■										■			■										■		■		■		
	video	■		■									■													■										■						
	off-document / email	■		■	■	■	■			■									■			■	■			■				■		■			■	■	■	■		■		■
	computer conferencing	■	■				■			■												■																		■		
	shared workspace	■	■					■	■	■	■	■	■	■	■	■	■					■	■			■										■		■	■	■	■	■
	annotations				■		■					■						■	■	■	■	■	■	■	■	■			■	■		■	■	■	■	■				■	■	■
	discussion																	■				■	■			■							■		■	■				■		■
Collaboration	awareness lists								■			■						■		■			■			■								■	■	■		■		■		■
	history		■	■	■		■											■	■		■	■					■							■	■		■	■	■	■		
	triggering mechanisms				■		■										■				■																					
	activity spaces									■				■				■		■	■	■	■		■	■			■						■	■						■
	information exchange	■	■	■	■		■	■			■							■	■	■	■	■	■			■						■	■		■	■						
	discussion	■																■				■	■			■									■	■				■		■
	structuring																					■				■										■						■
Doc. represent.	age							■																																		
	identity									■	■	■	■	■												■																
	trace							■																																		
	WYSIWYG																							■											■	■						
	fonts																	■											■						■			■				
Doc. view	miniatures																									■																
	alternate views	■							■			■						■	■							■	■								■			■	■		■	■
	gestalt view											■																														
	observation view											■																														
	localisation																																									
Network	centralised			■	■		■			■	■	■					■	■							■	■			■					■	■			■		■		
	replicated							■	■				■		■								■				■				■					■		■			■	
	hybrid									■																											■		■			■
Concurrency	locking			■	■				■	■	■	■	■		■			■			■					■	■				■			■	■	■	■	■		■		
	transactions																	■		■					■	■	■									■						
	serialisation							■	■														■													■	■					
	version management		■	■															■							■			■			■						■			■	

Figure 2.2 Design issues and system features.

coupled (TC). In LC mode a user can observe her/his partner's actions but is allowed to act independently. In TC mode users' interfaces are closely coupled so that all users are forced to observe any action taken by an individual user.

Two important requirements for synchronous writing are maintaining group awareness and notifying presence. Co-authors need to be aware of the identities of others working on the same document and of their actions. Furthermore, collaborators need to maintain mutual intelligibility, that is to understand the intentions and actions taken by other people.

Asynchronous collaboration occurs when co-authors work on the same document at different times. Systems that support asynchronous collaborative writing allow only one author to modify a shared document. Some systems may allow access to other authors but only for reading the document. In asynchronous collaborative writing co-authors need to know what has changed in the document since the last time they visited it, who made the changes, and the rationale of such modifications. Version control and annotation facilities could support the requirements for asynchronous writing.

System design should not be restricted to supporting one of the above modes of collaboration. In order to support real-life collaborative writing, system design should focus on supporting the transitions from asynchronous to synchronous writing and back again. Furthermore, the system should be capable of supporting both group writing and single author writing. A single author should be able to use the system and join or leave a collaborative situation without the need to use different writing tools.

The issue of undoing co-authors' actions has been raised recently (Prakash and Knister, 1992; Abowd and Dix, 1992). This basic functionality of single-user writing systems has been largely ignored in the development of computer systems for collaborative writing. The main requirement is to allow individual writers to reverse their actions without affecting other users. Undoing actions in a collaborative writing requires the selection of actions to be reversed on criteria such as the identity of people performing an action and the location of such actions within a document.

Another task-related issue is the forms or strategies for collaboration that co-authors employ. A group writing system should be flexible enough to support different forms of collaboration and transitions between these forms. Four general forms of the collaborative writing process have been identified (Stratton, 1989; Sharples, 1993):

1. *Horizontal division*

   This form of collaboration is carried out in three stages: planning, executing and integrating. First, people plan the work. They set the goals, partition the work and allocate tasks to individuals. The second stage is the execution stage where people perform the work individually and in parallel. At the third stage the collaborators determine how the individual contributions can be integrated into a consistent final product.

2. *Turn Taking*
   In this form, a member of the team may start working on the project. That author produces an intermediate product which is passed to the next member and so on. Each member acts as an editor and revises each intermediate product. This circuit is repeated until all members either are satisfied with the product or agree that there is no need for further modification. The turn-taking strategy seems to be applicable in work situations where computer support for collaboration is not available. With the advent of groupware it will probably fade.
3. *Stratification*
   The stratification form refers to vertical division of work. People are assigned certain roles and they work in parallel. Role definition and assignment is done according to people's expertise. Each person contributes one or more specialisms to the work. A manager coordinates the collaboration. Each person has a strong sense of involvement. The identification of a number of different roles does not imply that each role is filled in by a different person (the fewer the number of people, the better) but a person could be charged with more than one role or a role could be filled in by more than one person. It is important to assign precise roles to people, since without a clear definition and sharing of responsibilities, at a given moment some team remembers could be repeating other people's work. It is important to note that to the extent that the roles are not filled in by people with appropriate skills, the product will suffer. In such a case, it is essential for people to be flexible and to be able to exchange roles.
4. *Discourse interaction*
   It has been observed that collaborative writing practice in industry does not have the form of group writing as it has been claimed by researchers in academia. In contrast, collaborative writing in industry takes the form of interaction between the writer and others. Discourse interaction is characterized by limited planning. Single writers have the authority for the document and the decision-making based on feedback that they receive from others (Pelt and Gillam, 1991). Quite often discourse interaction may lead to inefficient collaboration because of its dependence on interaction. Ineffective communication of ideas, perspectives or problems may cause inefficiencies (Coutoure and Rymer, 1991).

Group

An important dimension that characterizes collaborative writing situations is the degree of social complexity. Social complexity refers to the range of interactions within a group. For instance, a co-author may interact with one or more persons, or interact only with a subset of group members by forming subgroups. One approach towards supporting subgroups in hypermedia systems is the definition of composite nodes or partitions of the hypermedia structure.

Recent research indicates that group membership changes over time (Beck, 1993). The issue of supporting groups with changing membership has not been addressed yet in the design of computer systems for collaborative writing. Support for this issue requires that substitutes or other group members should be able to trace back progress and have access to information repositories used by the group member who resigned.

Because of the social interactions that take place in any collaboration the issue of authority in performing actions (e.g. decision-making) and in accessing and modifying information is raised. Authority on actions may span from autonomous to regulated. Access to information may vary as well. Depending on participant's authority different types of access, such as write, read and comment, may be allowed. The definition of roles and actions associated with roles is one approach to manage the authority and social complexity of collaborative writing.

In any kind of group work, members' behavior varies from competitive to cooperative. Conflicts in group interactions are likely to occur – about the substance of the writing process, working procedures, and interpersonal relationships. Conflicts may arise from different interpretations of the document, different perceptions of the target audience, and different intentions. Mechanisms for conflict resolution are necessary. Such mechanisms should support discussion representation, communication of beliefs, knowledge, intentions and voting procedures.

Finally, a central group issue in collaborative writing is the place where co-authors perform their activities. Co-authors may be colocated (e.g. working in the same room) or geographically distributed in remote locations.

Communication

Communication is required to perform substantive, procedural and annotative activities during collaborative writing. Communication in collaborative writing may occur in synchronous and asynchronous mode. Face-to-face is the most preferable means for synchronous communication. For distributed groups, however, voice and video links are used as alternative means of communication. Because synchronous communication within a group may occur with some members colocated and others at remote locations, computer systems should be designed to provide multiple communication channels that fit different types of interaction.

Asynchronous communication is mainly text-based (e.g. email) although some systems employ voice messages (Rice and Shook, 1990) for commenting. Two issues have been raised about text-based communication:

- the need to make a distinction between communication content and writing product since both are based on language;
- the need to communicate intentions and context in order to facilitate understanding of text-based messages.

Tools

The use of tools for collaborative writing is another issue that has been addressed in CSCW research. Today, most group writing systems remain experimental. Few commercial systems exist (e.g. Aspects, MarkUp, ForComment). Writing groups, especially distributed ones, use a variety of heterogeneous computer-based systems, conventional word-processors, and off-line media. Furthermore, such groups may not always have access to networked technology. To bridge the gap between different writing technologies a group writing system should support seamless transitions between different writing tools. Support for multiple file formats, document interchange, basic word-processing capabilities, and the use of mixed media (Diaper, 1993), such as graphical scanners, OCR readers and fax, would increase the functionality of collaborative writing tools.

DESIGN ISSUES

In the previous section research efforts within the CSCW field towards understanding collaborative writing have been presented. In this section specific design issues (see Figure 2.2), that have been raised in the process of developing systems that satisfy the requirements as given above, and system features are presented.

The design issues and corresponding system features are grouped into the following categories:

- concurrency control and data sharing
- communication networks
- multi-user interfaces
- document representation
- document view
- communication channels
- information storage and retrieval
- collaboration.

Each one of these categories is described in the sub-sections below.

Concurrency control and data sharing

In collaborative writing multiple users issue commands to access (read and write) a shared document. Concurrency control mechanisms are needed to ensure data consistency. Consistency should be maintained at two levels: (a) all users share and view the same information, and (b) information is consistent with users' requests. Existing group writing systems use either simple locking, transaction mechanisms, or serialization techniques such as optimistic concurrency control (Ellis and Gibbs, 1989; Greenberg and Marwood, 1994 give detailed discussions of concurrency control mechanisms).

Simple locking (data is locked before it is modified – for instance, in the MUCH system a node is locked by the first user selecting the node; the lock is released when the user leaves the node) and transaction mechanisms are appropriate for asynchronous or loosely-coupled groupware systems.

Real-time groupware writing systems require short response and notification times. New command serialization techniques have been developed to meet these requirements (Brinck *et al.*, 1993). In optimistic concurrency control each command is processed by the server as soon as it arrives. If another command arrives with an earlier time stamp then the server performs an undo operation to fix the problem. For synchronous groupware, command serialization can occur at two levels that allow users to maintain awareness of others' actions: (a) at the level of user actions (e.g. keystroke), and (b) at the user-interface level (e.g. selecting text).

In asynchronous collaborative writing a document may undergo a number of changes. The system should make sure that, each time, co-authors use the current version of the document. Version control is needed to manage multiple versions. Sometimes co-authors may wish to maintain multiple parallel versions of the same document. The system should allow users to trace back the evolution of different versions of the same document and also compare them to highlight differences (Malcom and Gaines, 1993). Recently tools gave control to users on how changes are reported, what changes are reported, and how the user interface displays the reported changes (Neuwirth *et al.*, 1992).

Communication networks

Designers of group writing systems have to make a choice on the network architecture that is most appropriate for the collaborative writing process. The following network architecture requirements need to be considered (Brinck *et al.*, 1993):

- Simplicity: the communication network should be simple to design, implement, maintain and extend.
- Responsiveness: response and notification times should be short. Response time is the time required for a user's operation to be reflected on her/his own interface. Notification time is the time required for her/his actions to be propagated to other users' interfaces (Ellis *et al.*, 1991).
- Robustness: the system should be able to recover from network breakdowns or unpredicted user actions.
- Scalability: the application should work well with any number of users.
- Transitions: the system should allow transitions between individual and group writing modes.

- Concurrency control: the architecture should be able to support traditional multi-user database concurrency control mechanisms and also groupware-oriented serialization techniques.

Three general types of network architecture exist:

- Centralized: each user has a workstation connected to a central server which runs the application and stores all information. User commands are sent to the server which processes them and display the results on users displays.
- Replicated: all information is replicated on each user's workstation which runs a copy of the application process. Each copy of the application process communicates directly with processes running on other users' processors.
- Hybrid: any combination between centralized and replicated architecture.

In addition to the physical network architecture designers need to make decisions on how software applications are connected (the logical network topology). There are several types of logical network topology: star, ring, mesh, hierarchy and *ad hoc* connectivity. Typically, star topology is suitable for centralized architecture, while mesh topology fits replicated architectures.

Communication

Co-authors need to communicate to initiate and coordinate their work, and exchange information. Some group writing systems (e.g. multi-user real-time editors) assume that co-authors work at the same time at the same place and communicate face-to-face. For distributed collaborative writing, however, it is expensive and difficult to arrange and attend frequent face-to-face meetings. Systems designers have considered the development of alternative channels of communication. Five types of communication media have been used for collaborative writing:

- Audio: voice links have been used for direct communication. Some systems allow asynchronous exchange of voice messages while others support voice annotations of written messages or documents. Although it is easy to follow instructions recorded in a voice message it remains an open issue whether one can extract from a voice message the same amount of task-related information included in a typical e-mail message (Holleran and Haller, 1990).
- Video: video communication provides a rich channel but it cannot manipulate computer stored data. At present video conferencing facilities fit pairwise interactions better. When multiple participants occupy a single screen then aspects of interaction such as gaze direction, attention focus, awareness and eye contact are limited (Sellen, 1992).
- Message-based: these channels include electronic mail and computer conferencing. Several design issues such as reliability, security, connectivity capabilities, information overload and seamless integration with work

surface need to be considered. Information overload can be reduced by using message filtering techniques, forms to produce semi-structured messages to help receivers locate information easily (Malone *et al.*, 1987), and by forming discussion groups in conferencing systems. Email should not be restricted to textual information. A variety of media types (drawings, fonts, text styles, animation, pictures, video) should be supported.
- Shared workspaces: shared workspaces allow multiple participants to work, view, and share the same data in real-time.
- Asynchronous annotation/discussions: This channel is provided by MUCH. That is, users are able to create annotations and hierarchically structured discussions asynchronously. Both annotations and discussions are attached to the relevant document parts.

Another important issue is that of transitions between asynchronous and synchronous communication. New communication channels need to be developed to support such transitions (Patel and Kalter, 1993).

Multi-user interfaces

In supporting multiple authors working on the same document, interface design issues are raised which are different from the ones in single-author writing tools. In this section design issues pertinent to multi-user interfaces in collaborative writing are presented at four levels of abstraction (Karsenty and Beaudouin-Lafon, 1993).

Cursor

Participants may use a variety of input devices. Cursors are used to represent them on the screen.

- Telepointer: a large cursor which shows where others are pointing with their mice on a shared screen. One user at a time controls the telepointer to direct group's attention to a particular area or object on the screen.
- Multiple cursors: multiple cursors are used to reflect the identities of multiple users by producing different colours or by representing the names of their users (Peng, 1993).

Shared screen

A shared screen allows multiple authors to work on the same document.

- WYSIWIS (What You See Is What I See) (Stefik, Foster *et al.* 1987): all users can view and type simultaneously into the same screen image.

Consistent images of shared information are presented to all users. It allows all participants to see work in progress. Synchronized scrolling may be used to make sure that all users are scrolled to the same place.

- Relaxed WYSIWIS: this alternative form allows some independent control of the screen, such as the position and size of shared windows. WYSIWIS can be in a relaxed form along four dimensions (Stefik, Bobrow *et al.*, 1987):
  - time (the time that displays are synchronized or not);
  - space (the windows or other objects to which WYSIWIS is applied);
  - subgroup (the set of users affected);
  - view congruence (a participant may want to scroll to a document section independently)
- WYSIWITYS (What You See is What I Think You See) (Brinck *et al.* 1993): this allows users to customize their displays, so that they share the same information which is presented in different ways.
- Handles: these allow simultaneous manipulation of the same object by multiple users (e.g. in MMM (Bier and Freeman, 1991) multiple users can simultaneously stretch a rectangle or other object).
- Teleportation: allows one user to teleport his screen view into another user's screen and thus synchronize their screens.
- Snapshots: are pictures of users currently working on the document. The pictures appear over the area where people working. Snapshots are used to facilitate group awareness.
- Sound: in SASSE (Baecker *et al.*, 1993) non-speech audio cues are used to signal users' actions.
- Change bars: in asynchronous writing change bars are used to indicate differences between revisions of the same document.
- Scroll bars: multiple coloured scroll bars are used to indicate the location in the shared document where other users are working. They allow the user to directly move to these locations.
- Icons: may be used to represent authors' roles and authority levels on segments of a co-edited document.

Systems like CES and MUCH, which support loosely coupled collaboration, allow one user to write a node and multiple other users to read the same node. If the writer updates the node then the modifications will be propagated to other users and their screen will be refreshed.

Document representation

Documents can be represented in a variety of ways on the screen. In heterogeneous environments users may share different representation of the same document.

- Age: use of colour to distinguish between old and recently typed text (e.g. new text appears in blue and gradually changes into black as time passes on).

- Identity: use of colour to represent the identity of different users and indicate the location where they are working.
- Trace: traces represent what has recently been done. For instance, a deleted word may leave a grey trace in its position or a cloudburst may appear over it.
- WYSIWYG (What You See Is What You Get): the information viewed on the screen appears exactly the same when it is printed out.
- Fonts: different fonts are used to distinguish meta-text (e.g. annotations in NoteCards).

Document view

Some systems allow users to view the same document in several ways.

- Miniatures: are used to shrink less important information or represent an condensed view of the network.
- Alternate document views: allow users to generate different alternate views of the same document (e.g. outline, table of contents, graphical representation of network).
- Gestalt view: in SASSE a gestalt view represents a condensed image of the whole document with the positions of other co-authors (Baecker *et al.*, 1993).
- Observation view: in SASSE an observational view allows a user to have an over-the-shoulder view of another user's screen.
- Localization: each user's front window is displayed in the document itself as a rectangle. It has been designed to give a sense of territory (Karsenty and Beaudouin-Lafon, 1993).

Information storage and retrieval

In this sub-section several metaphors to information storage and retrieval used in collaborative writing are presented. There are two main concepts that characterize document storage:

1. The concept of a single document file that is edited and communicated.
2. The concept of a hypermedia network. A hypermedia network can be stored in several ways:
   (a) each node in a separate file;
   (b) the entire network in a single file;
   (c) the hypermedia structure in a separate database from the actual document contents which may include text, images, drawings, digitized speech and audio;
   (d) the network distributed in multiple files.

The concept of partitioning hypertext into contexts (Delisle and Schwartz, 1987) has been proposed to support teams or subgroups. Contexts represent groupings of nodes and links with certain values. Modification of contexts do not affect the rest of the network and can be merged back into the original network.

In addition to the basic document, group writing systems may store document-related information such as: style rules, correspondence used by a publishing team, group discussions, author profile data, entire group sessions for replay, history of changes or other operations.

Several methods for accessing and retrieving information exist:

- Network browsing. There are three types of browsing: following links, keyword or string search, and graphical browsing (Irish and Trigg, 1989).
- Query-based search, which includes content search and structure search (Halasz, 1988).
- Index-based across.

Collaboration issues

In this section coordination and cognitive issues of collaborative writing are described. Support for coordination in group writing systems follows two approaches:

- Awareness lists: provide a history of events describing who performed particular actions on the document and when these actions took place.
- Triggering or notification mechanisms: a triggering mechanism allows the system to process automatically the content of messages and comments. Triggers are placed in particular parts of the document and when activated they cause a sequence of commands to be executed and notify users of their commitments (Fish *et al.*, 1988).

Little emphasis has been paid to the cognitive aspects of collaborative writing and the way that knowledge about these cognitive aspects can inform the system design. In the MUCH system an attempt has been made in the system design to reflect the following cognitive phases of writing: exploring ideas, organizing ideas, and encoding ideas into prose. Other attempts to use cognitive theories of writing in system design can be seen in CoAUTHOR (Hahn *et al.*, 1989) and SEPIA (Streitz *et al.*, 1992). All three approaches have a common design element: that is, the provision of activity spaces which correspond to cognitive tasks that collaborators perform. In SEPIA four activity spaces are provided for structuring, planning, arguing, and writing.

In addition to coordination and cognitive activity issues, one design issue that is closely related to the concept of efficiency of collaborative writing is the role of groupware on influencing the group's collective state of mind.

Groupsware technology can help co-authors reach a shared mental state (Watson, 1992) by:

- supporting information exchange;
- supporting discussion that evaluates and assesses communicated information (such as opinions, beliefs, arguments) and also by supporting representation of the main issues being discussed as a networked of linked items;
- supporting structuring of the network by making explicit the relationships between items to develop a map of the group's collective mind.

CLASSIFICATION OF COLLABORATIVE WRITING TOOLS

In this section the main approaches to the use of group authoring systems are described. Each approach represents a different perspective on the actual use of the systems and is accompanied by brief descriptions of group writing systems that adopted that particular perspective. The proposed classification is not exclusive in the sense that a particular system may fall in more than one category, but it is meant to be comprehensive. The following classes of systems have been identified in this study:

- conferencing systems and message-based systems
- group editors
- toolkits
- hypermedia systems
- task-oriented systems
- strategy-oriented systems.

Conferencing systems and message-based systems

This category includes systems that take advantage of developments in computer-based conferencing and message systems in order to provide alternative communication channels for geographically distributed groups of authors. Communication in collaborative writing is mediated through a variety of channels depending on the types of writing and communication tasks that collaborators perform. For ambiguous, creative writing tasks and for informal communication, rich communication channels (Gale, 1989) are required while for routine communication tasks asynchronous text-based message exchange may be sufficient. The integration of users' existing software applications with multimedia conferencing and electronic mail environments aimed at supporting the above forms of communication.

The Augmentation system (Engelbart and English, 1968) developed in the 1960s, is a precursor of current group writing systems and provided on-line conferencing by linking users displays to show the same view of the data. It also supported multiperson distributed conferencing/editing, allowing the images of collaborators to be superimposed on the display.

In-Synch (Dalton, 1987) is primarily a PC-to-PC conferencing tool. It allows geographically dispersed users to cooperate. Users are connected via modems and can trade files and run the same programs in real-time. It supports synchronous editing, since multiple users can run the same application program and the system propagates the changes simultaneously to all locations. The system also includes a messaging system that permits message exchange without affecting the files or other joint activities.

The CAR Multimedia Conferencing system (Baydere *et al.*, 1993) attempts to provide rich communication channels (e.g. via an audio, video and text data network) as alternative to face-to-face communication for distributed authors. The system allows users to run shared applications on their multimedia workstations. All changes to the shared applications are propagated and become visible to all users.

MESSIE (Sasse *et al.*, 1993) is an e-mail-based group-authoring system which allows collaborators distributed in space to create large documents using heterogeneous systems. Collaborators contribute via electronic mail their document material to a shared filestore which is installed and maintained at one site. The NSF Express (Olson and Atkins, 1990) project provides an interoperable multimedia electronic mail-based system that facilitates the creation and interchange of multimedia proposals.

Quilt (Leland *et al.*, 1988; Fish *et al.*, 1988) has been described as a 'hybrid of multi-user hypermedia system, a computer conferencing system, and multimedia electronic mail'. Quilt supports coordination and social aspects of group writing. It supports coordination through activity logging, notification and triggering mechanisms. Triggers are used for coordinating the work. They are placed in particular parts of the document and when activated they cause a sequence of commands to be executed. To support social aspects of the work Quilt allows the definition of roles for each group member and of the activities associated with a particular role. The document structure supported by Quilt is a simple tree structure. This structure imposes a particular kind of cooperation and interaction. The collaborators annotate a shared document and then structure the document to reflect their comments.

The MultimETH (Lubich and Plattner, 1990) prototype is a multimedia conferencing system which supports collaborative editing of both content and structure of hierarchically structured, following ODA, multimedia documents by small distributed groups. The system allows distributed authors to hold real-time meetings through a voice channel, a shared view of the workspace consisting of multimedia documents, and private communication channels. Asynchronous premeeting conferencing is also supported. MultimETH supports loosely coupled collaborative editing and annotating of different parts of the document content and structure. The ODA document model has been extended to fit the collaborative editing requirements of timing and synchronization dependencies between multimedia objects. For instance, a voice annotation providing the rationale for modifications in the document structure needs to be synchronized with the visualization of such modifications during the replay of an editing session.

Multi-user group editors

Group editors focus on issues of access and control to a shared document or information object by multiple users (Olson *et al.*, 1990). Synchronous group editors allow multiple users access a shared document concurrently. Editing of documents may occur at two levels: (a) at the actual content level, and (b) at the document structure level.

The GROVE editor (Ellis, Gibbs and Rein, 1991) allows simultaneous, at keystroke level, editing of an outline. Any changes in the outline are immediately seen by all users. The system provides shared and private workspaces and uses visual cues such as iconic images of participants to represent presence, and text colouring to indicate location of activity.

ShrEdit (Killey, 1991) also provides character level locking mechanisms to control synchronous access. It can be used with other word processors, drawing and painting applications. ShrEdit allows users to independently view any part of the work in a shared workspace and also allows infinite expansion of the shared workspace (Olson *et al.*, 1993). Aspects (Group Technologies Inc., 1990) provides similar functionality to ShrEdit and allows co-located or geographically distributed co-authors to work together at the same time. MULE (Pendergast and Vogel, 1990) allows synchronous editing of different parts of a document and provides locking control at the line level.

CES (Collaborative Editing System) (Greif and Sarin, 1987) supports loosely coupled collaboration. Multiple authors can have read and write access to a shared document but only one of them is granted a lock and is allowed to edit a section of the document. Other authors visiting the same section will be able to read the section which is periodically updated. Documents in CES are presented as a hierarchy of sections, each section has a caption and body.

SASE (Baecker *et al.*, 1993) uses multiple scroll bars and colour to give feedback on the locations of multiple activities. The extension of SASE into SASSE supports user awareness by providing in addition to visual cues non-speech audio cues about collaborators' actions. SASE provides a user-controlled locking mechanism. Users can negotiate locking at a text selection level. This approach offers flexibility and can fit different collaboration styles.

An interesting approach towards supporting synchronous collaboration is the one adopted by MMM (Multi-Device Multi-User Multi-Editor) (Bier and Freeman, 1991; Bier *et al.*, 1992). MMM is a multi-user editor that supports single-screen collaboration. It provides multiple pointing devices and each user has his/her own insertion points and home areas. MMM uses colour and graphic conventions to direct system feedback to appropriate users.

Alliance (Decouchant *et al.*, 1995) is an asynchronous multi-user editor that allow the creation and editing of structured documents. A structured document consists of a set of logical units (e.g. title, section, paragraph, bibliography, etc.) and a set of logical relations between these units. Alliance produces graphical representations of the document's logical structure. Authors are allowed to view on the screen such graphical representations and to interact with them. Concurrent access to the document is managed via the use of two techniques: dynamic sharing and fragmentation. Instead of using static predefined document fragments that other group editors such as CES (Greif and Sarin, 1987) and Mjølner project (Minör and Magnusson, 1993) use, in Alliance the application automatically assigns document variable document fragments to users. Furthermore, the group leader assigns access privileges to each fragment based on authors' roles (e.g. manager, writer, reader). Alliance supports group awareness through the use of icons which indicate the author's role for a fragment and the fragment's status.

IRIS (Borghoff and Teege, 1993) is another content-independent and media-independent editor that supports the creation and editing of structured documents which have the ODA form. IRIS distinguishes between document structure and content. It uses attributed links to connect structural units to their corresponding content. Link attributes are used to indicate the type of content and the time, state, and authorship of the edited part of the document. In IRIS link attributes are used to maintain group awareness. IRIS generates structure views of the document that serve as a notification mechanism indicating the location within a document where a user is working. Every time a user wishes to edit the content of the document, an appropriate content-dependent editor is invoked. Concurrent access to the document structure is managed through a locking mechanism that addresses the hierarchical dependencies between the structural elements of the document. Versioning and synchronous voice communication are also supported.

Duplex (Pacull *et al.*, 1994) is an asynchronous collaborative editing environment which has been designed to operate on large-scale networks such as the Internet. Document sharing in Duplex is achieved through document decomposition into independent parts. These parts are stored in a replicated kernel which is shared by all authors. Each author is also associated with a local environment which holds copies of the document parts that author is working on. Documents in Duplex are hierarchically structured and document decomposition is based on the formal structure. Concurrency control over the shared parts of the document stored in the kernel is achieved through a hybrid approach of serialization and direct author negotiation for conflict resolution. Duplex displays the document structure as a tree at the local environment level.

The Mjølner project editor (Minör and Magnusson, 1993) supports semi-(a)synchronous collaborative editing of documents which are decomposed into parts (e.g. chapters, sections, paragraphs) that are hierarchically organized in a tree structure. It also provides a version control mechanism for document parts and for the entire document. It is characterized as semi-(a)synchronous because although it does not allow multiple users to share the same part of the document, it provides group awareness that shared access would ensure. The system achieves group awareness through two mechanisms. First, by displaying the document evolution graph which is shared by all users. The evolution graph is a graphical representation of the document parts along with new versions of the edited parts. The users are able to see which parts of the document have been edited and by whom. Second, the system allows the users to be aware of what other users are currently doing through active diffs. Active diffs show the differences between two versions of the same part of the document that are edited synchronously by two other users.

Toolkits

Toolkits have been developed to allow instances of single-user editors to be extended to distributed groupware. The motivation for the development of such toolkits is that people use heterogeneous hardware and software platforms. Extending these platforms to support information sharing, communication, notification, and concurrency control may be uneconomical (e.g. different messaging and information sharing management mechanisms need to be implemented for different applications). Furthermore groupware systems require more effort to use than single-user systems and users are likely to reject a new system (Grudin, 1988). Groupware toolkits provide the services mentioned above independently of application and hardware platforms.

DistEdit (Knister and Prakash, 1990) is a toolkit for building applications that support collaboration between people in distributed environments. In particular, it allows one to build interactive group editors and has the ability to support different editors simultaneously. The DistEdit toolkit provides closely coupled real-time interaction. However, it does not give identical views of the text to all users but it guarantees the text's consistency.

Timbuktu (Ambayae, 1994; Malm, 1993) supports screen sharing, file transfer and remote session connections to PCs and Macs. With Timbuktu only one person controls the shared document while the other users can just observe it. COeX (Patel and Kalter, 1992) provides a framework for the development of a synchronous multi-user editor. COeX is application-neutral and platform independent.

Hypermedia systems

The systems in this category put emphasis on the organization, structuring, representation and communication (Conklin, 1987) of document material contributed by multiple authors to a document database. Hypermedia technology plays an important role in collaborative writing by allowing the non-sequential structuring of information, the maintenance of multiple organizations of that material, and the creation and linking of comments to the evolving document (Halasz, 1988).

NoteCards (Halasz, 1988; Trigg, 1988) is a collaborative hypermedia environment that has been designed to help people work with ideas. Its intended users are intellectual workers engaged in tasks involving analysis of ideas, formulation of arguments, and design of artifacts. The users work on a network of notecards interconnected by typed links. The system allows the users to display information, modify and manipulate the information stored in the system as well as navigate through the network. NoteCards provides record-keeping tools (Irish and Trigg, 1989) to support mutual intelligibility and group awareness.

The idea of using notecards as a basic document structural element has been adopted in the design of MILO (Jones, 1993). MILO supports distributed, asynchronous collaborative creation of structured documents. A document in MILO is a hierarchical structure of notecards. The system does not impose any constraints on the complexity of the network of notecards or on the size of each notecard. MILO provides two views of the underlying data network: (a) a graphical tree-like representation of the network, and (b) an outline view similar to the one used by MUCH. The idea of notecards is also considered valuable for supporting annotative collaboration (Neuwirth *et al.*, 1987) (see also Internote (Catlin *et al.*, 1989)). The system integrates email to support communication.

The design and development of the CoAUTHOR (Hahn *et al.*, 1989) system approaches the problem of producing hypermedia documents by multiple authors. The interactions among the members of the authoring team concerning idea processing, document design and generation, as well as group-specific activities such as critiquing issues, negotiating divergent opinions, and treating inconsistent or incomplete specifications, are shown to be fairly knowledge-intensive and thus require maintenance facilities provided by a sophisticated knowledge-base management system underlying the hypermedia surface. CoAUTHOR views all objects created during the document development and group interaction processes as parts of a carefully structured knowledge base. Consequently, formal relationships between such objects can be analysed and maintained in a much more flexible manner.

Intermedia (Landow, 1990) is a modeless system that supports natural transition from one writing activity to another without having to issue multiple commands before each switch. It allows multiple users to read and annotate a single document but only one user to write to the document at a time (Haan *et al.*, 1992).

CoMEdiA (Santos, 1992; Hornung *et al.*, 1992) is a hypermedia system that has been designed to encompass a wide range of features in order to support the varying needs of group writing. It supports both distributed and co-located collaborative authoring of hypermedia documents. It also support synchronous and asynchronous communication through textual and audio channels and allows collaborators to define social roles.

KMS (Akscyn *et al.*, 1988) is an early hypertext system that provides a standard format user interface in order to help collaborators interpret more easily others' actions. Contexts (Delisle and Schwartz, 1987) addresses the issue of conflicts that may arise when multiple authors modify a shared hypertext document. The system allows the partition of hypertext into independent sets of nodes and links that can be accessed and modified without affecting the rest of the document.

SEPIA (Structured Elicitation and Processing of Ideas for Authoring) (Haake and Wilson, 1992; Streitz *et al.*, 1992) is a hypermedia system that supports both synchronous and asynchronous collaboration. It supports writing activities by providing task-specific activity spaces for structuring, planning, writing and argumentation. Smooth transition between activities is supported by transferring and integrating design objects between activity spaces. SEPIA supports individual and group writing. In particular three forms of collaborative writing are supported: individual, loosely coupled and tightly coupled mode of work. Group awareness in loosely coupled mode is achieved through relaxed WYSIWIS, awareness lists, and highlighting of locked objects. In tightly coupled mode, group awareness is established through WYSIWIS and the use of telepointers both at the network and node editing level.

The MUCH (Many Using and Creating Hypermedia) system (Rada, Zeb *et al.*, 1991) has been developed to support the various phases of writing a document: *exploring, organizing* and encoding. In the exploration phase knowledge is acquired, brainstorming occurs, and unstructured notes are made. Next, the unstructured notes are organized into an outline. In the encoding phase the prose for the final document is written. The main functions of the MUCH system are accessing documents (which includes reading, browsing and searching), and creating documents which includes planning, writing and revising on one hand, and organizing, finding and reorganizing on the other hand (Rada, Wang and Strickland, 1991). Annotation and discussion are complementary features to support the writing process. Some other features to support and monitor collaboration among authors have also been added. The system also includes facilities for automatically importing and exporting documents marked up in a number of common formats. The user interface is primarily a split screen with outline in one window and detail or text block in another. The outline window provides a menu of functions. These functions include creation and modification of objects (link, annotation, etc.), a dynamic outline generator, word search facility, interface for drawing package 'xpic', linearization of documents using the UNIX document workbench. Access (who, when, where) to the network for the MUCH database is recorded and can be viewed on request.

Task-oriented systems

The systems in this category have been designed to support a particular set of writing tasks such brainstorming, planning, drafting, revising, annotating. The PREP editor (Neuwirth *et al.*, 1990) is an asynchronous collaborative writing tool. PREP documents are organized into columns. One author may create a document in a column and another author may annotate the document by placing annotations in an adjacent column. In traditional hypermedia systems annotations are stored in nodes and are separated from the text. Accessing an annotation involves a cognitive overhead of selecting the node. However, in writing people prefer to use visual cues and access annotations 'at a glance'. 'Flexible diff' is a software system embedded in the PREP editor to facilitate communication of changes and to track differences in two reports (Neuwirth *et al.*, 1992).

CompareRite (Dalton, 1987) supports revision tasks by simply showing the difference between two versions of a document, either on-screen or as a merged file that can be printed or loaded into a word processor for further revision. The feature of highlighted comparison is particularly useful to domains where subtle revisions are important and difficult to spot (e.g. law departments).

MarkUp (Ambaye, 1994) is designed to support the annotation phase of the reviewing process. It provides a set of editing tools that allow multiple authors to make their text annotations and marks on overlays on each page in the document and then merge the created overlays to integrate their comments. The distribution of comments is done via email. BIBDB (Musliner *et al.*, 1992) allows a group of authors to cooperatively create, maintain, and share a bibliographic database.

Strategy-oriented systems

The systems in this category have been designed to support a particular form of collaboration. GroupWrite (Malcolm and Gaines, 1993) was designed to support collaborative review between authors who are widely distributed and do not have access to communication networks. Collaborators communicate by exchanging word processor files that contain draft versions of the main document as well as annotations (both typed and sound) and a history of the changes in the main document. Instead of storing different versions of the document, the designers' goal was to provide a facility that would allow people keeping several versions of the document to bring them together, to relate and explore them in a simple and natural way in order to resolve possible inconsistencies. GroupWrite provides version management support at two levels of document detail: (a) entire document, and (b) paragraph level. Different versions are linked together as well as the paragraphs within a version.

ForComment (Dalton, 1987) is a word processor that allows up to 15 people to apply hypertext-like annotations to a document (and can operate over a local area network (LAN) in real-time). ForComment is used where precise documentation and management of group writing projects is important. It requires the designation of one person as the author, while others involved with the document (as many as 15 people) are reviewers. Only the author can make changes to the original text.

Shared Books (Lewis and Hodges, 1988) was designed to support collaborative publication management. In particular the system focuses on supporting three aspects of publication management: (a) storage and retrieval; (b) document binding; and (c) job management. Shared Books uses centralized storage of multi-part publications. In addition to the documents' contents, information relevant to each document, such as sample rules, contracts, correspondence, accounting data, schedules, and timestamps of revisions, is stored as well. Document binding functions supported by the system include pagination, table of contents generation, and index generation. Shared Books supports job management by providing revision numbers and timestamps and by indicating which parts of the document are currently locked, in order to help users keep track of the current state of publication.

DOLPHIN (Streitz *et al.*, 1994; Haake *et al.*, 1994) has been designed to support face-to-face and distributed meetings between co-authors during the phases of collaborative writing that require intense communication and negotiation (e.g. initiation of collaboration). The system allows pen-based gesture-driven interaction on an electronic whiteboard connected to local (in the same room) and remote networked computers. There are two styles of distributed meeting supported by DOLPHIN. First remote workstations can be connected to the meeting room and second the coupling of two remote meeting rooms. An audio/video channel is provided for distributed meetings. The personal workstations provide private workspaces to the participants and also present on a separate WYSIWIS window the shared whiteboard display. So, the participants can have access to and bring information into the meeting from their private information repositories. The system offers great flexibility in creating different types of content objects ranging from informal (drawings, scribbles, handwriting) to formal (typed nodes and links). The systems allows the coexistence and transformation of formal and informal objects. The users can also annotate and create structured relationships between content objects. Another important aspect of DOLPHIN's functionality is that it allows users to integrate the objects and structures created during a meeting into SEPIA in order to use them in subsequent phases of the collaborative writing process.

The COOPerator (Michels, 1995) supports asynchronous distributed collaborative writing and provides a group agenda for the organization and planning of group meetings. Co-authors communicate through annotations, email, and discussions. In COOPerator documents are organized in a tree-like structure and represented by a graph in a shared workspace. Access to the document is coordinated by the definition of social roles such as editor, author, and reviewer. A group agenda tool is provided to help co-authors organize face-to-face meetings.

CONCLUSIONS

In this study a comparative analysis of collaborative writing tools has been presented. Three levels of analysis were considered. First, the conceptual aspects of collaborative writing that are supported by collaborative writing tools have been identified. Second, the design issues that have been addressed in system design have been presented. Third, the systems' features that have been implemented in response to design issues have been described. A classification of collaborative writing tools based on their use has also been proposed.

Most of the systems reviewed here focus on supporting substantive and annotative writing activities. Little attention has been paid to the procedural aspects of group work. The issue of support for procedural activities such as coordination and organization (e.g. organizing meetings, setting up deadlines, setting up agendas, defining goals, negotiating partition of work) of the work needs to be addressed. Furthermore, the notions of group awareness and mutual intelligibility should be extended to cover procedural aspects of collaborative writing.

The support that some systems provide for the social roles is rather limited. Role support has been largely associated with different levels of document and shared workspace access control. However, roles have much wider scope: collaborators define roles to coordinate and organize their work. More research is needed to identify the dependencies between social roles, the communication needs between different types of roles, and information structures required by different roles.

The coexistence and transformation of formal and informal structures supported by DOLPHIN in synchronous meetings allows the immediacy of externalizing and expressing ideas and their integration into subsequent phases of collaborative writing. Such a functionality is required not only in face-to-face meetings but also during the phases of writing when idea generation and planning occurs. Collaborative writing systems should provide this functionality during asynchronous and individual writing modes.

References

Abowd, G. D. and Dix, A. J. (1992) Giving undo attention. *Interacting with Computers* **4** (3), 317–342.

Akscyn, R. M., McCracken, D. L. and Yoder, E. A. (1988) KMS: A distributed hypermedia system for managing knowledge in organizations. *Communications of the ACM*, **31** (7), 820–835.

Ambaye, D. (1994) Groupware: many hands. *MacUser*, **10** (4), 62–71.

Baecker, R. M., Nastos, D., Posner, R. and Mawby, K. L. (1993) The user-centred iterative design of collaborative writing software. *Proceedings of the ACM Conference on Human Factors in Computing Systems (INTERCHI'93)*, Amsterdam, The Netherlands, 24–29 April 1993, Addison-Wesley, Reading, MA, pp. 399–405.

Baydere, S., Casey, T., Chuang, S., Handley, M., Ismail, N. and Sasse, A. (1993) Multimedia conferencing as a tool for collaborative writing: a case study. *Computer Supported Collaborative Writing*, Sharples, M. (ed.), Springer-Verlag, pp. 113–135.

Beck, E. E. (1993) A survey of experiences of coauthoring. *Computer Supported Collaborative Writing*, Sharples, M. (ed.), Springer-Verlag, London, pp. 9–28.

Beck, E. E. and Bellotti, V. M. E. (1993) Informed opportunism as strategy: supporting coordination in distributed collaborative writing. *Proceedings of the Third European Conference on Computer-Supported Cooperative Work, ECSCW'93*, De Michelis, G., Simone, C. and Schmidt, K. (eds), Milan, Italy, 13–17 September, Kluwer Academic Publishers, pp. 233–248.

Bier, E. A. and Freeman, S. (1991) MMM: A user interface architecture for shared editors on a single screen. *Proceedings of the ACM Symposium on User Interface Software and Technology (UIST'91)*, South Carolina, USA, November 11–13, 1991, ACM Press, New York, 79–86.

Bier, E. A., Freeman, S. and Pier, K. (1992) MMM: The multi-device multi-user multi-editor. *Proceedings of ACM CHI'92 Conference on Human Factors in Computing Systems: Striking a Balance*, Bauersfeld P. (ed.) Association for Computing Machinery, pp. 645–646.

Borghoff, U. M. and Teege, G. (1993) Structure management in the collaborative multimedia editing system IRIS. *Proceedings of 1st International Conference on Multi-Media Modeling (MMM'93)*, Chua, T.S. and Letters Kunii, T. (eds), November 1993, World Scientific, Singapore, pp. 159–173.

Brinck, T., Hill, R. and Patterson, J. (1993) F2 tutorial notes – groupware for realtime collaboration, *Third European Conference on Computer Supported Cooperative Work ECSCW'93*, 13–17 September 1993, Milano, Italy.

Catlin, T., Bush, P. and Yankelovich, N. (1989) InterNote: extending a hypermedia framework to support annotative collaboration. *Hypertext '89 Proceedings*, pp. 365–378.

Conklin, J. (1987) Hypertext: An introduction and survey. *IEEE Computer*, **20** (9), 17–41.

Coutoure, B. and Rymer, J. (1991) Discourse interaction between writer and supervisor: a primary collaboration in workplace writing. *Collaborative Writing in Industry: Investigations in Theory and Practice*, Lay, M. M. and Karis, W. M. (eds), Baywood Publishing Company, pp. 87–108.

Dalton, R. (1987) Group-writing tools: four that connect. *Information WEEK*, March, 62–65.

Debs, M. B. (1991) Recent research on collaborative writing in industry. *Technical Communication*, **38** (4), 476–484.

Decouchant, D., Quint, V. and Salcedo, M. R. (1995) Structured cooperative editing and group awareness. *Proceedings HCI International '95, 6th International Conference on Human–Computer Interaction*, Yokohama, J., Anzai, Y. and Ogawa, K. (eds), July 1995, Elsevier Science.

Delisle, N. M. and Schwartz, M. D. (1989) Collaborative writing with hypertext. *IEE Transactions on Professional Communication*, **32** (3), 183–188.

Delisle, N. M. and Schwartz, M. D. (1987) Contexts – A partitioning concept for hypertext. *ACM Transactions on Office Information Systems*, **5** (2), 168–186.

Diaper, D. (1993) Small-scale collaborative writing using electronic mail. *CSCW in Practice: an Introduction and Case Studies*, Diaper, D. and Sanger, C. (eds), Springer-Verlag, pp. 69–92.

Ellis, C. A. and Gibbs, S. J. (1989) Concurrency control in groupware systems. *Proceedings of the ACM SIGMOD'89 Conference on the Management of Data*. Seattle, ACM Press, pp. 399–407.

Ellis, C. A., Gibbs, S. J. and Rein, G. L. (1991) Groupware: some issues and experiences, *Communications of the ACM*, **34** (1), 38–58.

Engelbart, D. E. and English, W. K. (1968) A research centre for augmenting human intellect. *American Federation of Information Processing Societies (AFIPS) Conference Proceedings of the Fall Joint Computer Conference*, **33** (1), San Francisco, California, Thompson Book Company, Washington, DC, pp. 395–410.

Fish, R. S., Kraut, R. E., Leland, D. P. and Cohen, M. (1988) Quilt: a collaborative tool for cooperative writing. *Proceedings Conference on Office Information Systems*, Allen, R. B. (ed.), ACM Press, pp. 30–37.

Floyd, B. D. and Turner, J. A. (1989) A method for evaluating work group productivity products. *Technological Support for Work Group Collaboration*, Olson, M. H. (ed.), LEA, Hillsdale, New Jersey, pp. 167–182.

Gale, S. (1989) Adding audio and video to an office environment. *Proceedings of the First European Conference on Computer Supported Cooperative Work EC-CSCW'89*, London, UK, pp. 121–130.

Greenberg, S. and Marwood, D. (1994) Real time groupware as a distributed system: concurrency control and its effect on the interface. *Proceedings of the ACM Conference on Computer-Supported Cooperative Work (CSCW'94)*, Chapel Hill, NC, October 22–26, pp. 207–217.

Greif, I. and Sarin, S. (1987) Data sharing in group work. *ACM Transactions on Office Information Systems*, **5** (2), 187–211.

Group Technologies Inc. (1990) *Aspects: The First Simultaneous Conference Software for the Macintosh*, Group Technologies, Inc. Arlington, VA.

Grudin, J. (1988) Why CSCW applications fail: problems in the design and evaluation of organization interfaces. *Proceedings of the Conference on Computer-Supported Cooperative Work – CSCW88*, Portland, Oregon, Association for Computing Machinery, pp. 85–93.

Haake, J., Neuwirth, C. and Streitz, N. (1994) Coexistence and transformation of informal and formal structures: Requirements for more flexible hypermedia systems. *Proceedings of the ACM European Conference on Hypermedia Technology (ECHT'94)*, Edinburgh, UK, September 18–23, pp. 1–12.

Haake, J. M. and Wilson, B. (1992) Supporting collaborative writing of hyperdocuments in SEPIA. *Proceedings of the ACM Conference on Computer Supported Cooperative Work (CSCW'92) – Sharing Perspectives*, Turner, J. and Kraut, R. (eds), ACM Press, pp. 138–146.

Haan, B. J., Kahn, P., Riley, A., Coombs, J. H. and Meyrowitz, N. K. (1992) IRIS hypermedia services. *Communications of the ACM*, **35** (1), 36–51.

Hahn, U., Jarke, M., Kreplin, K., Farusi, M. and Pimpinelli, F. (1989) CoAUTHOR: A hypermedia group authoring environment. *Proceedings of the First European Conference on Computer Supported Cooperative Work (EC-CSCW'89)*, September 13–15, Gatwick, London, UK, pp. 226–244.

Halasz, F. G. (1988) Reflections on NoteCards: seven issues for the next generation of hypermedia systems. *Communications of the ACM*, **31** (7), 836–852.

Holleran, P. A. and Haller, R. W. (1990) Characteristics of well-designed electronic communication systems, *Human–Computer Interaction – INTERACT'90*, Diaper, D. *et al.* (eds), Elsevier Publishers BV (North Holland), IFIP, pp. 841–847.

Hornung, C., Jäger, M., Santos, A. and Tritsch, B. (1992) Cooperative hypermedia – an enabling paradigm for cooperative work. *Proceedings of the Workshop on Real Time Group Drawing and Writing Tools*, Greenberg, S. and Hayne, S. (eds), held at CSCW'92, October 31, Toronto, Canada.

Irish, P. M. and Trigg, R. H. (1989) Supporting collaboration in hypermedia: issues and experiences. *Journal of the American Society for Information Science*, **40** (3), 192–199.

Johansen, R. (1989) User approaches to computer-supported teams. *Technological Support for Work Group Collaboration*, Olson, M. H. (ed.) LEA, pp. 1–31.

Jones, S. (1993) MILO: A computer based tool for (co)authoring structured documents. *Computer Supported Collaborative Writing*, Sharples, M. (ed.), Springer-Verlag.

Karsenty, A. and Beaudouin-Lafon, M. (1993) Slice: a logical model for shared editors. *Technical Report*, Laboratoire de Recherche en Informatique (CNRS URA 410), Universitè de Paris-Sud, Bâtiment 390, 91405 Orsay Cedex, France.

Killey, L. (1991) *ShrEdit 1.2: A Shared Editor for Apple Macintosh® – User's Guide and Technical Description*, Cognitive Science and Machine Intelligence Laboratory, University of Michigan, Ann Arbor, MI.

Knister, M. J. and Prakash, A. (1990) DistEdit: A distributed toolkit for supporting multiple group editors. *Proceedings of the Conference on Computer Supported Cooperative Work (CSCW'90)*, ACM Press, pp. 343–355.

Krasner, H., McInroy, J. and Walz, D. B. (1991) Groupware research and technology issues with application to software process management. *IEEE Transactions on Systems Management and Cybernetics*, **21** (4), 704–712.

Landow, G. P. (1990) Hypertext and collaborative work: the example of Intermedia. *Intellectual Teamwork: Social and Technological Bases of Cooperative Work*, Galegher, J., Kraut, R. E. and Egido, C. (eds), Lawrence Erlbaum, Inc., Hillsdale, NJ, pp. 407–428.

Leland, M. D. P., Fish, R. S. and Kraut, R. E. (1988) Collaborative document production using Quilt. *Proceedings of the Conference on Computer-Supported Cooperative Work – CSCW88*, Portland, Oregon, September 26–29, Association for Computing Machinery, pp. 206–215.

Lewis, B. T. and Hodges, J. D. (1988) Shared Books: collaborative publication management for an office information system. *Proceedings Conference on Office Information Systems*, Allen, R. B. (ed.), ACM Press, pp. 197–204.

Lubich, H. and Plattner, B. (1990) A proposed model and functionality definition for a collaborative editing and conferencing system. *Proceedings of the IFIP WG 8.4 Conference on Multi-User Interfaces and Applications*, Heraklion, Crete, Greece, Gibbs, S. and Verrijn-Stuart, A. A. (eds), Elsevier North-Holland, pp. 215–232.

Malcolm, N. and Gaines, B. R. (1993) Supporting collaboration in digital journal production. *Journal of Organizational Computing*, **3** (2), 195–213.

Malm, P. S. (1983) The unOfficial Yellow Pages of CSCW: groupware, prototypes, and projects, to appear in *Classification of Cooperative Systems from a Technological Perspective. Groupware in Local Government Administration*, thesis for the degree of Cand. Scient in Informatics, University of Tromso, Norway.

Malone, T. W., Grant, K. R., Lai, K.-Y., Rao, R. and Rosenblitt, D. (1987) Semistructured messages are surprisingly useful for computer-supported coordination. *ACM Transactions on Office Information Systems*, **5** (2), 115–131.

Michels, S. (1995) *Co-Writing, look and feel*, M.Sc. thesis, Infolab, Tilburg University, The Netherlands, (http://infolabwww.kub.nl:2080/w3thesis/).

Minör, S. and Magnusson, B. (1993) A model for semi-(a)synchronous collaborative editing. *Proceedings of the Third European Conference on Computer-Supported Cooperative Work, ECSCW'93*, De Michelis, G., Simone, C. and Schmidt, K. (eds), Kluwer Academic Publishers, pp. 219–231.

Musliner, D. J., Dolter, J. W. and Shin, K. G. (1992) BIBDB: a bibliographic database for collaboration. *Proceedings of the ACM Conference on Computer Supported Cooperative Work (CSCW'92)*, Toronto, Ontario, ACM Press, pp. 386–393.

Neuwirth, C. M., Chandhok, R., Kaufer, D. S., Erion, P., Morris, J. and Miller, D. (1992) Flexible diff-ing in a collaborative writing system. *Proceedings of the ACM Conference on Computer Supported Cooperative Work (CSCW'92)*, Toronto, Ontario, ACM Press, pp. 147–154.

Neuwirth, C. M., Kaufer, D. S., Chandhok, R. and Morris, J. H. (1990) Issues in the design of computer support for co-authoring and commenting. *Proceedings of the Conference on Computer-Supported Cooperative Work (CSCW'90)*, ACM Press, pp. 183–195.

Neuwirth, C. M., Kaufer, D. S., Chimera, R. and Gillespie, T. (1987) The Notes program: a hypertext application for writing from source texts. *Hypertext '87 Conference*, pp. 121–141.

Olson, G. M. and Atkins, D. W. (1990) Supporting collaboration with advanced multimedia electronic mail: the NSF EXPRES project. *Intellectual Teamwork: Social and Technological Bases of Cooperative Work*, Galegher, J., Kraut, R. E. and Egido, C. (eds), Lawrence Erlbaum, Inc., Hillsdale, NJ, pp. 429–451.

Olson, J. S., Olson, G. M., Mack, L. A. and Wellner, P. (1990) Concurrent editing: the group's interface. *Human–Computer Interaction – INTERACT'90*, Diaper, D. *et al.* (eds), Elsevier Publishers BV (North-Holland), IFIP, pp. 835–840.

Olson, J. S., Olson, G. M., Storrøsten, M. and Carter, M. (1992) How a group-editor changes the character of a design meeting as well as its outcome. *Proceedings of the ACM Conference on Computer Supported Cooperative Work (CSCW'92)*, Toronto, Ontario, ACM Press, pp. 91–98.

Olson, J. S., Olson, G. M., Storrøsten, M. and Carter, M. (1993) Groupwork close-up: a comparison of the group design process with and without a simple group editor. *ACM Transactions on Information Systems*, **11** (4), 321–348.

Pacull, F., Sandoz, A. and Schiper, A. (1994) Duplex: a distributed collaborative editing environment in large scale. *Proceedings of the ACM Conference on Computer-Supported Cooperative Work (CSCW'94)*, Chapel Hill, NC, October 22–26, pp. 165–173.

Patel, D. and Kalter, S. D. (1992) A toolkit for synchronous distributed groupware applications. *Proceedings of Groupware '92*, Colman, D. D. (ed.), San Jose, CA, Morgan Kaufman, pp. 225–227.

Patel, D. and Kalter, S. D. (1993) Low overhead, loosely coupled communication channels in collaboration. *Proceedings of the Third European Conference on Computer-Supported Cooperative Work ECSCW'93*, Milan, Italy, 13–17 September, De Michelis, G., Simone, C. and Schmidt, K. (eds), Kluwer Academic Publishers, pp. 203–218.

Pelt, W. and Gillam, A. (1991) Peer collaboration and the computer-assisted classroom: bridging the gap between academia and the workplace. *Collaborative Writing in Industry: Investigations in Theory and Practice*, Lay, M. M. and Karis, W. M. (eds), Baywood Publishing Company, pp. 170–205.

Pendergast, M. O. and Vogel, D. (1990) Design and implementation of a PC/LAN-based multi-user text editor. *Proceedings of the IFIP WG 8.4 Conference on Multi-User Interfaces and Applications*, Heraklion, Crete, Greece, Gibbs, S. and Verrijn-Stuart, A. A. (eds), Elsevier North-Holland, pp. 195–206.

Peng, C. (1993) Survey of collaborative drawing support tools: design perspectives and prototypes. *Computer Supported Cooperative Work (CSCW): An International Journal*, **1** (3), 197–228.

Posner, N. R. and Baecker, R. M. (1992) How people writer together. *Proceedings of the 25th Hawaii International Conference on System Sciences*, Kauai, Hawaii, January 7–10, IEEE Computer Society Press, **IV**, pp. 127–138.

Prakash, A. and Knister, M. J. (1992) Undoing actions in collaborative work. *Proceedings of the ACM Conference on Computer Supported Cooperative Work (CSCW'92)*, Toronto, Ontario, ACM Press, pp. 273–280.

Rada, R. (1991) *Hypertext: From Text to Expertext*, McGraw-Hill, London.

Rada, R., Wang, W. and Strickland, K. (1991) Groupware and hypertext for reuse. *Technical Report*, department of Computer Science, University of Liverpool, Liverpool, UK.

Rada, R., Zeb, A., You, G.-N., Michailidis, A. and Mhashi, M. (1991) Collaborative hypertext and the MUCH system. *Journal Information Science: Principles & Practice*, **17**, 191–196.

Rice, R. E. and Shook, D. E. (1990) Voice messaging, coordination, and communication. *Intellectual Teamwork: Social and Technological Bases of Cooperative Work*, Galegher, J., Kraut, R. E. and Egido, C. (eds), Lawrence Erlbaum, Inc., Hillsdale, NJ, pp. 327–350.

Rodden, T. (1991) A survey of CSCW systems. *Interacting with Computers*, **3** (3), 319–353.

Santos, A. (1992) A cooperative architecture for hypermedia editing – CoMEdiA. *Proceedings of the Workshop on Real Time Group Drawing and Writings Tools*, Greenberg, S. and Hayne, S. (eds), Held at CSCW'92, October 31, Toronto, Canada.

Sasse, M. A., Handley, M. J. and Chuang, S. C. (1993) Support for collaborative authoring via email: the MESSIE environment. *Proceedings of the Third European Conference on Computer-Supported Cooperative Work ECSCW'93*, De Michelis, G., Simone, C. and Schmidt, K. (eds), 13–17 September, Milan, Italy, Kluwer Academic Publishers, pp. 249–264.

Schlichter, J. and Borghoff, U. (1992) Concurrency control for multiuser editors. *Proceedings of the Workshop on CSCW Tools and Implementation*, Kaplan, S., Dewan, P., Rodden, T., Benford, S. and Johnson, P. (eds), held at CSCW'92, 31 October, Toronto, Canada.

Sellen, A. J. (1992) Speech patterns in video-mediated conversations. *CHI'92 Conference Proceedings: Striking a Balance*, Bauersfeld, P., Bennett, J. and Lynch, G. (eds), Addison-Wesley, 49–59.

Sharples, M. (1993) Adding a little structure to collaborative writing. *CSCW in Practice: an Introduction and Case Studies*, Diaper, D. and Sanger, C. (eds), Springer-Verlag, pp. 51–67.

Sharples, M., Goodlet, J. S., Beck, E., Wood, C. C., Easterbrook, S. M. and Plowman, L. (1993) Research issues in the study of computer supported collaborative writing. *Computer Supported Collaborative Writing*, Sharples, M. (ed.), Springer-Verlag.

Stefik, M., Bobrow, D. G., Foster, G., Lanning, S. and Tatar, D. (1987) WYSIWIS revised: early experiences with multiuser interfaces. *ACM Transactions on Office Information Systems*, **5** (2), 147–167.

Stefik, M., Foster, G., Bobrow, K., Kahn, K., Lanning, S. and Suchman, L. (1987) Beyond the chalkboard: computer support for collaboration and problem solving in meetings. *Communications of the ACM* **30** (1), 32–47.

Stratton, C. R. (1989) Collaborative writing in the workplace. *IEE Transactions on Professional Communication*, **32** (3), 178–182.

Streitz, N. (1993) The role of hypermedia for CSCW applications. *Hl Tutorial Notes – The Role of Hypermedia for CSCW Applications*, Third European Conference on Computer Supported Cooperative Work ECSW'93, 13–17 September, Milano, Italy.

Streitz, N., Geissler, J., Haake, J. and Hol, J. (1994) DOLPHIN: Integrated meeting support across Live Board, local and remote desktop environments. *Proceedings of the ACM Conference on Computer-Supported Cooperative Work (CSCW'94)*, Chapel Hill, NC, 22–26 October, pp. 345–358.

Streitz, N., Haake, J., Hannemann, J., Lemke, A., Schuler, W., Schütt, H. and Thüring, M. (1992) SEPIA: a cooperative hypermedia authoring environment. *Proceedings of the 4th ACM European Conference on Hypertext (ECHT'92)*, Milan, Italy, 30 November–4 December, pp. 11–22.

Trigg, R. H. (1988) Guided tours and tabletops: tools for communicating in a hypertext environment. *Proceedings of the Conference on Computer-Supported Cooperative Work – CSCW88*, Portland, Oregon, Association for Computing Machinery, pp. 216–226.

Watson, R. (1992) Grouping groupware. *Groupware Report*, Preview Issue, 4–5.

Whittaker, S. and Geelhoed, E. (1993) Shared workspaces: how do they work and when are they useful. *International Journal of Man–Machine Studies*, **39**, 813–842.

APPENDIX

Tables A.1 to A.4 summarize the research studies which have been reviewed in order to derive major research issues in computer supported collaborative writing that have been presented in this chapter. Figure A.1 indicates which research issues have been addressed by each study.

	Issues \ Study	1	2	3	4	5	6	7	8	9	10	11	12	13	14	15	16	17	18	19
Task	substantive				■	■	■				■			■	■	■		■	■	■
	procedural					■		■	■			■	■	■	■	■			■	■
	annotative			■	■	■			■		■		■	■		■		■	■	■
	asynchronous			■	■						■	■				■	■	■		
	synchronous		■	■	■		■	■		■	■	■			■		■			■
	semi-(a)synchronous																■			
	group awareness						■	■			■		■	■			■			■
	mutual intelligibility																			■
	individual writing					■	■		■		■			■						■
	forms/strategies				■	■					■					■	■			
	transition				■	■		■			■						■			■
	document access				■		■	■		■	■		■	■	■					■
	version control				■	■					■						■	■		■
	undo						■				■									
Group	identities				■		■				■									
	social complexity	■		■	■						■									
	membership			■		■							■			■				
	authority	■									■		■			■				
	roles			■	■	■		■	■		■		■							
	conflict management	■				■	■		■										■	
	sub-groups					■								■						
	collocated			■				■				■						■		
	distributed			■				■		■		■	■					■		
Comm.	synchronous		■	■	■			■	■		■				■				■	
	asynchronous			■	■				■		■		■			■			■	
	intentions					■										■				
	context					■							■							
Tools	basic word-processing								■		■									
	mixed media		■	■							■		■			■		■		
	document interchange										■		■							

Figure A.1 Research aspects in computer-supported collaborative writing. The research issues addressed by a particular study are marked with the symbol ■.

Table A.1 Survey of research on computer supported collaborative writing.

Study	Code #	Field	Method	Group size	Sample	Setting	Data sources	Major conceptual model	Tools	Research questions	Major findings
Debs (1991)	1	Research and theory of collaborative writing	Review	–	–	Industry	Interdisciplinary research literature	–	–	Understanding the concept of collaborative writing	Two common aspects: authority and interaction
Whittaker & Geelhoed (1993)	2	Pairs engaged in text-editing and graphic design with audio link and/or shared workspace	Experimental cost/benefit analysis	2	8 groups 5 judges	Laboratory	Observations Transcripts	Theory of common ground	Audio link Wscrawl Annotator	What are the benefits of shared workspace over audio on time, communication effectiveness and quality of output	For demanding complex tasks adding visual channel (workspace) beneficial
Krasner *et al.* (1991)	3	Research in software process management	Theoretical	–	–	–	Research literature	–	–	Conceptual framework for groupware	Set of key parameters Groupware research issues
Posner & Baecker (1992)	4	Computer supported collaborative writing	Interviews	–	10	Various fields	Tape recordings	–	–	How people write together	Writing process taxonomy System requirements
Sharples *et al.* (1993)	5	Computer supported collaborative writing	Theoretical	–	–	–	–	Extended single author writing model	–	Research issues for computer supported collaborative writing	Task, group, communication and representation research issues central to collaborative writing

Table A.2 Survey of research on computer supported collaborative writing.

Study	Code #	Field	Method	Group size	Sample	Setting	Data sources	Major conceptual model	Tools	Research questions	Major findings
Olson *et al.* (1990)	6	Real-time group editing	Review	–	–	–	Research literature	–	ShrEdit, Grove, Timbuktu, Capture Lab Rapport, MMconf	Evaluation of design alternatives	List of usability principles
Ellis *et al.* (1991)	7	Groupware	Overview of research and development	2–6	Several groups	–	Research literature Grove use experiences	–	Grove	Exploring groupware applications	Groupware taxonomy Research and development issues
Floyd & Turner (1989)	8	Groupware	Evaluation	–	–	–	Research literature	–	METAPHOR InSynch InBox Coordinator CoAuthor	Criteria for evaluating and selecting groupware by management	Evaluation framework
Schlichter & Borghoff (1992)	9	Multi-user editors	Review	–	–	–	Research literature	–	Various group editors	Concurrency control methods	Summary of available methods
Baecker *et al.* (1993)	10	User-centred design for collaborative writing	Interviews Lab experiment	2	4 groups under each of 4 conditions	Lab	Audio, video, recordings fax, email copies	–	SASE SASSE	How people write together using a variety of media	System design requirements

Table A.3 Survey of research on computer supported collaborative writing.

Study	Code #	Field	Method	Group size	Sample	Setting	Data sources	Major conceptual model	Tools	Research questions	Major findings
Watson (1992)	11	Groupware	Evaluation	–	–	–	Research literature	–	Several groupware systems	How can one identify products of interest?	Taxonomy of groupware
Beck & Bellotti (1993)	12	Collaborative writing	Case studies	2–3	3 groups	Academia and industry	Audio recording of interviews Direct observation Email and paper copies	–	Various conventional tools	How documents evolve and coordination and decision making	Informed opportunism as coordination strategy
Delisle & Schwartz (1989)	13	Hypertext	Survey	–	–	–	Research literature		NoteCards Intermedia, Neptune	Hypertext support for collaborative writing	Hypertext valuable for creation of complex documents
Olson *et al.* (1992)	14	Concurrent editing	experiment	3	38 groups 6 raters	Meeting room	Typed output Questionnaires Meeting transcripts	–	ShrEdit Whiteboard Pen-Paper	Technology effects of process and quality of output	Groupware produced output of higher quality
Diaper (1993)	15	Collaborative writing	Case study	3	1 group	Academia	Email messages	–	Email	How people write together	Email could/ may support collaborative writing but that depends on social relations

Table A.4 Survey of research on computer supported collaborative writing.

Study	Code #	Field	Method	Group size	Sample	Setting	Data sources	Major conceptual model	Tools	Research questions	Major findings
Minör & Magnasson (1993)	16	Collaborative editing	Model, development	–	–	–	–	Synchronous and asynchronous collaborative editing	–	Asynchronous or synchronous editing	Model for semi- (a) synchronous collaborative editing
Sasse *et al.* (1993)	17	Collaborative writing	Development case study	3–10	3 groups	Academia	Log files	–	MESSIE	Email support for collaborative writing	Email environment for collaborative writing
Baydere *et al.* (1993)	18	Collaborative writing	Case study	6	1 group	Academia	Direct observation	–	CAR	Multimedia conferencing can provide rich communication	Usage protocols are needed
Halasz (1988)	19	Hypermedia	System description and evaluation	–	–	–	Direct observation	–	NoteCards	Limitations of current hypermedia systems	Research issues for next generation hypermedia

3 Collaborative Authoring Dynamics

CHAOMEI CHEN and ROY RADA

INTRODUCTION

This chapter presents a theoretical framework and an illustrative research result to help the reader understand the rationale of research in collaborative authoring with a shared information space. The framework is developed on the basis of a review of related literature.

The framework addresses significant issues regarding computer-supported collaborative authoring, including the role of a shared information space, users' accessing strategies, the complexity of performing tasks, and the impact of activity of concurrent users on the use of this information space.

A recurring theme in the research of sociotechnological systems in general, and computer-supported collaborative work (CSCW) and computer-mediated communications (CMC) in particular, is that an interaction process is oriented to deal with either task-oriented problems or socio-emotional problems at a time (Lea, 1992). This theme appears in the work of many researchers in CMC. The division is influenced by Bales' work in interaction process analysis (Bales, 1951). This theme is particularly echoed by an emerging paradigm in the design of collaborative hypertext systems. This paradigm conceptualizes the closeness of concurrent users of computer systems as loosely and tightly coupled modes. In this chapter, research questions on collaborative authoring dynamics with hypertext are offered that accord with the theory of cognitive dissonance.

Designing and evaluating co-authoring systems raise further questions on the understanding of collaborative writing. There is still a lack of empirical fundations as to how the existing collaborative information systems have been used in reality and how the tools and users change each other (McCarthy, 1994). The usability of the existing models of collaborative work is still subject to systematic, longitudinal analyses of these systems being used by real people in real work settings.

GROUPWARE AND AUTHORING
ISBN 0-12-575005-6

TECHNOLOGY AND SOCIAL STRUCTURE

According to Kling (1980), there are two broad schools of theoretical perspectives particularly concerning the interrelationships between an organization and computer technologies used in the organization: *systems rationalism* and *segmented institutionalism.* Systems rationalism includes rational and structural perspectives. The philosophy of systems rationalists is that an organization has a consensus on the goals to be achieved and the use of computer systems is to help people achieve the goals more effectively and efficiently. The role of computer systems is simply a means to an end. The organizational impact of using computer systems is often overlooked.

The work of Bales (1951) has useful implications for an investigation of collaborative writing from a process-oriented point of view. Collaborative writing extends over a much longer period of time than a face-to-face meeting. Distributed computing imposes technical constraints over the interactivity and expressiveness of communication. According to Bales' model, communication is the most elementary-level task, which forms the basis for higher-level interactions. Asynchronous use of the system and geographically distributed collaborators are two factors that may significantly weaken the efficiencies of communication.

Activity theory is an evolving theoretical framework for user interface analysis and CSCW systems (Kuutti and Arvonen, 1992). Activity theory uses the concept of activity as the minimum meaningful context to interpret individual and interpersonal behaviour. An activity is usually mediated by various tools and artefacts, such as hammers, computer systems and languages. This conceptualization emphasizes the intermediatory role of the tools and artifacts in group interaction and collaborative construction of a common information space.

Each activity has an active subject, who understands the motive of the activity. This subject can be an individual, a group, or an organization. According to Kuutti and Arvonen (1992), there are three modalities in which a subject can be engaged in an activity:

- using an existing artifact in a prescribed manner,
- using an existing artifact in a dynamically formulated manner, and
- creating a new artifact.

A case study found that the second modality is closely related to the interests of CSCW research. Collaboration involves two types of sharing:

- Shared material refers to the sharing of access to the artifacts among people involved in the activity.
- Shared meaning refers to the relationship between individual actors and the social structure of the community.

The shared meanings are represented by rules and conventions, which form the culture of the social structure. Activity theory focuses on breakdowns and contradictions in the work which may affect the effectiveness of technologies.

Individuals are expected to experience a variety of types of change as a result of interactions among group members. First, individual perspectives are mutually adjusted and become more similar; individuals become aware of the growing similarity. This process is now known as the social construction of meanings. The culture of the group includes the perspectives and expectations that are shared by the group members. Second, interactions result in the differentiation of group members in terms of their roles in the group and how they see the group.

COLLABORATIVE WRITING

The nature of collaborative writing has been studied by researchers from many disciplines, including social psychology, education, philosophy and computer science (Ede and Lunsford, 1990). Collaborative writing presents a significant challenge to choosing or designing information technologies that support group work (Kraut *et al.*, 1992). Collaborative writing takes place in different situations. Creating a complex document collaboratively entails a considerable amount of social and intellectual complexity.

Why writing together

Surveys of collaborative writing have shown that there are various reasons for people to take part in collaborative writing activities (Ede and Lunsford, 1990). The most commonplace reasons for group writing are political, organizational, and practical. Ede and Lunsford analysed two mainstream perspectives of collaborative writing: neo-Romantic and neo-Classic. Neo-Romanticists believe that collaborative writing is essentially individual-based. Neo-Classicists emphasize the impact of social nature on collaborative writing and suggest that collaboration is significantly influenced by cultural and social factors.

Theories and models of collaborative writing are few. There is a lack of empirical studies which systematically address how people write together with modern information technologies (Sharples *et al.*, 1993). Many of the classroom studies consider collaborative writing as a pedagogical instrument which might help students to improve social skills such as negotiation and cooperation, and acquire subject domain knowledge and writing skills. Many computer systems for collaborative writing have been essentially based on individual writing models. For example, in these systems, collaborative writing is an individual process in which a single individual would draft the complete document, then the draft document would be reviewed within the group of participants. Finally, the document would be revised according to the feedback on previous drafts. The information flow in such processes is known as *peer-evaluation*, where coauthors serve as a general audience and take turns drafting (Ede and Lunsford, 1990; Fish *et al.*, 1988; Hahn *et al.*, 1991).

Morgan and Murray (1992) addressed motivating factors in collaborative writing on the basis of the theory of cognitive dissonance (Festinger, 1957). The theory was developed to explain behaviour of individuals who are under the conditions of cognitive dissonance. Cognitive dissonance is the stress experienced by people who find some incompatibility with their existing knowledge structure; it is a motivating factor in its own right. According to the theory, the existence of dissonance will motivate the person to reduce the dissonance and, by doing so, the person's knowledge structure may be reorganized as a result of the rationalization.

Dissonance has been regarded as one of the fundamental reasons for the search for social interactions in collaborative writing. Insights into a domain topic can be reached through a recursive process of identifying cognitive dissonance and achieving consensus at a more profound level (Morgan and Murray, 1988). Cognitive dissonance is more likely to occur in collaborative writing than in individual writing. Resolving cognitive dissonance may lead to more insights into the work. Morgan *et al.* (1987) gave an empirical example of relationships between cognitive dissonance and insights in collaborative writing.

The process of collaborative writing

The key issue of understanding any new technology is whether one can perceive the new phenomena beyond traditional notions that have been used for describing activity patterns without the technology (Jessup and Valacich, 1993). Behavioural and cognitive patterns of cooperating actors are characterized by the new technology. Leading researchers in collaborative writing have been investigating the extent to which the strategies and organizations of work should be formalized and incorporated in CSCW systems.

Haythornthwaite *et al.* (1994) explored the use of media and the organizational structure of work in a research group. They analysed the use of various communication media, including unscheduled and scheduled face-to-face contact, e-mail, telephone, fax and desktop videoconferencing. Unscheduled encounters, e-mail and scheduled meetings appeared to occur more frequently as people interacted in their social network. Twenty-four work relationships were grouped into six categories of interactive patterns:

- receiving work,
- giving work,
- collaborative writing,
- emotional support,
- sociability, and
- computer programming.

Kraut *et al.* (1992) studied the phase structure of collaborative writing projects of college students. They found that groups plan before they write and write before they revise. The phase structure of planning, drafting and revising is consistent with models of individual writing processes (Flower and Hayes, 1981b). The phases of planning, drafting and revising in collaborative writing only captured the macrostructure of collaborative writing. To understand the dynamics of collaborative writing, one needs to understand the structure of each phase and its relationships with collaboration processes.

In a survey of collaborative writing experiences (Beck, 1993), people who have experience in collaborative writing were asked whether they discussed the material and related issues before, after, or during the actual writing. The results of the survey indicated that discussions are likely to occur throughout the process. The findings of Beck's survey confirm the general expectation that co-authors need to keep interacting throughout the process to deal with situational issues and they need to modify their plan frequently.

Very little is known about the social aspects of long-term collaborative writing relationships. What is the extent to which a dynamic system can be captured by prescriptive models? Can small workgroups capitalize on the free access they have to a shared workspace without requiring a facilitator or an embedded work process in the software? Neuwirth *et al.* (1990) studied how the effectiveness of loosely coupled collaboration can be enhanced by CSCW systems. Neuwirth *et al.* suggested that merely providing users with a hypermedia tool with a sharable database is unlikely to be adequate for accommodating co-authoring and commenting.

Olson *et al.* (1993) compared 19 three-designer groups using a shared editor called ShrEdit with groups who worked with conventional whiteboard, paper and pencil. It appears that the ShrEdit tool helped the supported groups focus on key issues in the design and avoid spending more time on less important topics. They found that the groups working with ShrEdit generated fewer but better design ideas. The findings of Olson *et al.* suggest a promising alternative to role-based approaches. The provision of a shared workspace may help the convergence of collaboration in small groups. Neuwirth *et al.* (1990) and Olson *et al.* (1993) explored different aspects of collaborative writing, regarding the process, or discourse, and the role of a shared workspace. However, they did not focus particularly on the structure of work processes with these systems and how a process evolves.

Kraut *et al.* (1988) produced empirical evidence which shows that physical proximity fundamentally influences how scientific collaboration is initiated, advanced and maintained. The physical proximity influences the way that researchers meet each other, define problems, plan projects and discuss situation-specific issues. Informal communication between collaborators was predominant in terms of its frequency.

Irish and Trigg (1989) identified three levels of interaction among co-authors with a hypertext system: procedural, annotational and substantive.

Annotating is a major form of informal and asynchronous interactions among co-authors over a shared workspace.

Annotation is a very important type of collaborative task. Surveys on collaborative writing show that one of the most popular ways of writing collaboratively is that one person would be asked to draft the document, the draft is then circulated for inputs from other co-authors, and the feedback is incorporated into a revised version. This process may be repeated several times.

The use of spoken and written annotations in collaborative writing was analysed by Kraut *et al.* (1992). Spoken annotations paid more attention to interpersonal relations, the status and the success of collaborative writing, whereas written annotations mainly focused on technical problems such as spelling and grammar, and interpersonal relations seemed to be overlooked. Subjects making spoken annotations were more likely to use softer directives, avoid giving offence, and give a sense of equality, thereby strengthening the social tie between the speaker and the listener. For instance, the following phrases were frequently used 'I would change ...' and 'I think you should ... '. In contrast, subjects using the written modality rarely used these mitigating phrases. The written annotations sometimes included blunt and almost hostile phrases.

WORKING WITH CO-AUTHORING SYSTEMS

The emergence of CSCW is partially due to the dissatisfaction with the traditional usability-oriented approach to the development and evaluation of computer systems in human–computer interaction. CSCW studies emphasize the mutual impact between social, cultural and organizational contexts and computing technologies.

Reviews of existing CSCW studies show that the majority of these studies in recent years have been focusing on engineering issues of CSCW systems (Olson *et al.*, 1993; McCarthy, 1994). This technique-driven trend, however, does not necessarily lead to a deeper understanding of CSCW. Designers and engineers face a complex, open system. The design of a successful application calls for a deep understanding of the phenomena.

Researchers have adapted various theories and research methods in this field. Collaborative writing covers a broad range of tasks and many issues need to be investigated from different perspectives. Surveys of experiences in collaborative writing and anecdotal descriptions of issues related to computer support are frequently used. Qualitative and subjective methods have been used partially due to a lack of theories and empirical experiences of collaboratively writing with designated co-authoring systems in reality.

Co-authoring and argumentation systems are a general class of system which aim to support and represent the coordination and argumentation involved in group working. The collaborative authoring of documents represents the product of a process of coordination among co-authors. Some hypertext systems were designed to support collaborative writing, such as gIBIS, Context SEPIA, Intermedia, and Argument. Halasz (1988) addressed seven major problems to be solved for shared hypertext systems to support collaboration. For example, the disorientation is more likely to occur as the information space changes because of the activities of other authors. In collaborative use of NoteCards, the solution to this problem was to open a special area in the hypertext-based, shared information space for co-authors to communicate with each other and to use different fonts for text written by each author (Irish and Trigg, 1989).

Hypertext systems demonstrate some appealing features for collaborative writing. Hypertext systems have been used to facilitate early stages of collaboration such as brainstorming and planning (Conklin and Begeman, 1988). Some hypertext systems provide support to organize writing of individual co-authors and merge their contributions at later stages of collaborative writing (Delise and Schwartz, 1987). Some hypertext systems can respond quickly to provide appropriate communication support for collaboration in accordance to the positions of co-authors in activity spaces for all stages of writing (Streitz *et al.*, 1989; Haake and Wilsen, 1992).

Hypertext systems that aim to support collaborative writing activities can be identified by two generations according to the underlying theoretical basis used and implementations derived from the theory. In the first generation, hypertext systems do not deal explicitly with interactions arising in collaborative writing. These systems depend on established collaboration patterns to organize and coordinate the work of co-authors. There are some generic conditions which stem from practical reasons. For instance, in KMS it was assumed that the number of frames tends to be considerably greater than the number of collaborating authors so that co-authors are unlikely to encounter each other in the same frame during a session (Akscyn *et al.*, 1988). Turn-taking in NoteCards relies on established conventions among co-authors (Irish and Trigg, 1989). Users of NoteCards developed a convention to cope with coordination problems, i.e. users communicate through a special area in NoteCards.

The second generation, hypertext systems, are based on theories of collaborative writing and provide explicit support to some activities identified in corresponding models. For instance, the implementation of the Neptune system particularly includes mechanisms to resolve the clash of multiple perspectives in collaborative writing (Delise and Schwartz, 1987). Neptune uses the concept of *context*, a collection of nodes and links that have to be evolved consistently, to facilitate versioning transitions between the individual workspace and the shared workspace. Some basic mechanisms such as conflict detection in terms of versioning trees are provided to facilitate mutual intelligibility among co-authors.

MODELLING AND DESIGN

User-centred vision has resulted in the predominant ethnographical methodology in CSCW. Although ethnographical studies are widely accepted in the CSCW community, ethnographical results are not usually in a form which is readily accessible to the designers and implementers of sociotechnological systems. There is a lack of quantitative and longitudinal studies on the use of collaborative support systems. Improving users' social and historical awareness in an ongoing collaborative process with a shared information space has been of extensive research and engineering interest. It has been seen as one of the key issues to the success of a CSCW application (Dourish and Bellotti, 1992).

Groups may be quite flexible at changing their division of labour to cope with unexpected situations. The social structure of a group for collaborative writing is dynamic (Beck, 1993). Previous studies have recognized the important role of informal working practices and sharing of artifacts in coordinating work activities. The advance of technology can have dramatic effects on the social interactions and dynamics of the group. The question is how and whether it is possible to design systems that support change.

Interpretive evaluation is particularly appropriate for understanding the complex interactions that occur in natural environments and this is important if systems like CSCW systems are to be successful. Whiteside *et al.* (1988) have identified several key differences between a natural work environment and an experimental environment:

- *Work context*: Word processing benchmark tasks are 6 pages long, whereas most of the people in practice working with documents 30–50 pages long.
- *Time context*: Experiments generally have a prescribed time context, whereas in real work environments people tend to have some choice about the order in which they do tasks and how long they take.
- *Motivational context*: In the experimental context the experimenter controls the situation, whereas usually in the work context there is scope for some negotiation.
- *Social context*: In the work environment there is normally a social network of support which does not exist in the experimental context.

Approaches such as ethnographics, which emphasize studying actual users working in actual work environments, challenge the researchers and designers of computer systems with a series of fundamental questions. If the course of actions is determined by momentary changes in the situation, then a fundamental question is how one can meaningfully capture the situational characteristics and organize one's own course of actions.

Dynamic modelling of user behaviour

The process of working collaboratively with computer systems may consist of an independent working mode and various coordinating modes. In particular, the following three-modality model of collaboration with computers is popular in CSCW systems:

- independent mode,
- loosely-coupled mode, and
- tightly-coupled mode.

The IBIS method has proven to be effective in structuring exploratory thinking. Yakemovic and Conklin (1990) studied the use of a simple Issue-Based Information System (IBIS) over an extended period of time, regarding the process and the problems in capturing the design rationale of large and complex computer systems. IBIS systems mainly address how the rationale of design is to be incorporated into a database and how the rationale is to be retrieved effectively.

Much of the data presented by Yakemovic and Conklin (1990) is anecdotal. They observed the use of a simple IBIS system over a period of 18 months and found that the most frequently discussed topics are design, requirements and platform. The discussions on process were significantly less than the other three groups of topics. These findings indicate that the process of collaborative work focuses on task-oriented problems. In terms of Bales' model, IBIS systems should pay more attention to socio-emotional problems raised in collaboration.

Johansen (1988) summarized 17 approaches to team support technology. One might consider an IBIS containing design rationale as a type of shared memory for the project team. Although the information in this memory is generated in a serial manner (across time), the information needs to be well-organized and cross-linked in the memory.

Situated actions and awareness

Awareness indicates a state of knowing of the activities of collaborating members of a group. Markova (1987) gives a broad definition of human awareness in sociology:

1. People's ability to recognize their own existence and experience, and the existence and experience of others;
2. People's ability to monitor events in their own lives, and to make decisions about their own future on the basis of that knowledge;
3. People's ability to communicate their awareness of themselves and others to other human beings.

Dourish and Bellotti (1992) gave the following definition of what awareness is: Awareness is an understanding of the activities of others and it provides the context for one's own activity. Awareness mechanisms are necessary requirements for supporting collaboration.

A related research field is distributed artificial intelligence. There the beliefs, preferences and responsibilities of each agent are characterized in terms of *agent models*. Awareness mechanisms are designated to meet the needs for being aware of the activities that can affect the course of one's own actions in the subsequent interactions with the collaborative system and the human interactions mediated by the system.

The concept of *context* is used in a CSCW system such that collaborators can make sense of each other's activity regarding the goals and the workflow of collaboration. According to Dourish and Bellotti (1992), there are two kinds of awareness mechanisms in current CSCW systems – informational and role restrictive. Informational mechanisms explicitly update the information on the activities of users. Role-restrictive mechanisms define and support the function of roles in collaborative systems. A role specifies the relationships between an individual user and the shared working artifacts, and between the individual and other users involved. A role system has its limitations. It is difficult for a role system alone to handle the dynamics of a complex setting of collaboration. Dourish and Bellotti (1992) recommended passive awareness mechanisms for users to move smoothly between close and loose collaboration, as opposed to active awareness mechanisms.

Co-authors often need to communicate about the goals and constraints in order to adjust their views of the goals mutually and to generate integrated products. Explicitly defined social roles reduce the contingencies by specifying responsibilities of collaborators and patterns of interaction. Co-authoring systems which explicitly specify roles, for example, as in Quilt have been found inadequate due to the complex and dynamic nature in most informal collaborative writing (Fish *et al.*, 1988). One of the major disadvantages of a role-oriented approach is that the social structure defined in terms of roles gives little flexibility to respond to a process which is dynamic and complex in nature.

Transitions of modality

Interacting with non-linearly organized information in hypertext incurs considerable cognitive overhead (Wright, 1991). Such cognitive overhead tends to be higher with a changing, collaborative hypertext. Users need to rationalize the changes made by other co-authors and make sense of the changes regarding their own cognitive models associated with the common information space as a shared group memory.

The SEPIA system is one of the most comprehensive hypermedia systems for collaborative writing. SEPIA has several virtual activity spaces (Streitz *et al.*, 1989; Haake and Wilson, 1992). SEPIA emphasizes that planning, translating and reviewing may not appear in any prescribed order in collaborative writing. In fact, empirical evidence of other studies shows that they may considerably overlap and are related to specific situations (Kraut *et al.*, 1992; Beck, 1993). In SEPIA, collaborative writing processes are supported within a framework of four activity spaces: (a) planning space; (b) content space; (c) argumentation space; and (d) rhetorical space. The system helps monitoring and organizing interactions among co-authors. Two types, or modes, of interaction among co-authors are conceptualized in terms of co-authors' relative positions in corresponding activity spaces. The two types of interaction are loosely and tightly-coupled collaboration.

ILLUSTRATIVE EXPERIMENT

Interacting with a collaborative hypertext database is a dynamic process. Some recurring behavioural patterns of user–computer interaction can be expected to be captured with statistical analysis. A study is presented to illustrate how these recurring patterns are affected by changes in the contexts. Quantitative approaches are employed in contrast to the ethnomethodological approaches that have proven useful in recent CSCW studies. Quantitative approaches appear to have the following advantages to the field of CSCW: (a) easier to repeat in different settings so as to transform empirical findings easily from one field to another; (b) more readily accessible to designers and engineers of CSCW systems; and (c) more cost-effective to fit into the iterative development cycles of a large and complex CSCW system.

The MUCH system

This study is based on the use of a multi-user hypertext database system, Multiple Using Collaborative Hypertext (MUCH). The design rationale and details of the MUCH system can be found in Chapter 5 by Roy Rada. Social structures introduced by the MUCH system are built on the following actions, which shape the way that users interact with a collaborative hypertext database:

- *Unfold*: to expand the hierarchical view in a breadth-first manner;
- *Read*: to load and display the content of a node in the hierarchical view;
- *Lock*: to lock the content of the focal node from concurrent editing, but other users still can use Read on the node;
- *Info*: to display various information stored in an embedded object of each node;
- *Update*: to save changes since last Update or since the latest lock and to release the updated content to concurrent users.

Each node in the MUCH system contains a chunk of multimedia information. The system persistently stores evolutionary information of each node and attached links. The maintenance information is accessible via a function called INFO, which is available from each node in the hypertext network. A user can always check the history of the currently displayed node for information, such as who modified the node recently and how many times the node has been visited by users other than the original node creator. Figure 3.1 shows the dialogue box of the INFO function. The number 2 in the field of Selection Credits indicates that the node has been visited twice by users other than the creator, who has the username much and the content of this node has not been changed since 14 July 1994.

Patterns of using the INFO function and associated contexts are of particular interest in this study. Calling the INFO function on a node indicates an interest of the user in mutual intelligibility issues in collaborative work. Recurring behavioural patterns with the INFO function are expected to reveal some insights into the nature of using this function in asynchronous collaborative writing and help the designers of the system to capture the most salient dynamics in the context-behaviour relationship.

Method

Users of the MUCH system include a research group with more than 15 members and a class of 30 graduate students for a Master of Science degree course in information systems. Five databases in the MUCH system were used collaboratively throughout the three-month observation period.

Computer-logged transactions from the class correspond to two independent phases. In the first phase (three weeks), the students used an electronic

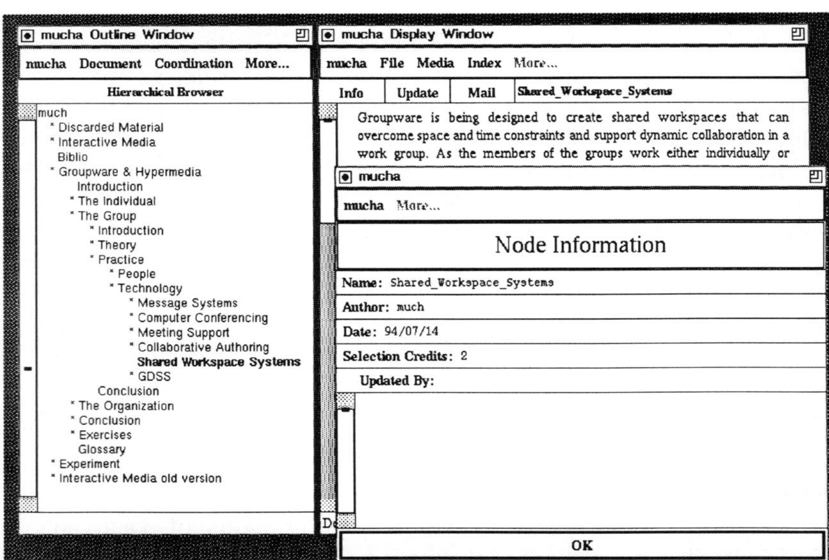

Figure 3.1 The Node Information dialogue box to the call of the INFO function.

textbook in the MUCH database in the classroom where all the users were present. In the second phase (three weeks), the students formed ten three-person groups to write a group essay into the MUCH system on one of the recommended topics on groupware. Students were allowed to use external communication tools along with the MUCH system. Each student was also requested to produce an individual report of the experience gained in the group writing phase.

The process of interacting with the shared database is denoted by a sequence of events. Each event denotes that an action is performed at the recorded time on a specific node. Every node in the database is associated with a set of organizational or evolutionary attributes, such as its hierarchical position in the presentation layer and a list of users who modified the node recently. Events other than INFO were removed from the sequence. The resultant sub-sequence was aggregated on a chosen attribute in each time interval. For instance, let n.attr denote the value of the attribute attr of the node n and the sequence of nodes $\{n_{i1}, n_{i2} \ldots n_{ik}\}$ correspond to the events in the ith interval in the sub-sequence, the aggregated attribute level entry in the ith time interval is given by

$$s_i(\text{level}) = \Sigma_{j=1,2,\ldots,k}\, n_{ij}.\text{level}.$$

The aggregated sequences of INFO events on all the node attributes are called the awareness-seeking paths of users interacting with the database. Explanatory variables such as *Zlevel*, *Zcredit*, and *Zword* are derived from the awareness-seeking paths. They are standard scores of corresponding path items. For instance,

$$Zlevel_i = s_i(\text{level}) \,/\, s.d,$$

where $s.d$ is the standard deviation of the sequence $\{s_i(\text{level})\}$. The *Zlevel*, is called the overall level of the path in the ith time interval. Other explanatory variables were similarly calculated.

A Kolmogorov–Smirnov (K–S) test on the probability distribution of the occurrences of the INFO event yielded an adequate goodness-of-fit statistic to a Poisson distribution. A Poisson regression model can be specified via a log-linear model in which the dependent variable follows a Poisson distribution. A procedure GENLOG (for general log-linear model analysis) in Statistical Package for the Social Sciences (SPSS) was used for the modelling. The occurrences of the INFO event are the cell values of the contingency table associated with the log-linear model. Let $Y(t)$ denote the occurrences of the INFO event in a one-hour time interval t, $X_s(t)$ the value of the ith explanatory variable with its coefficient β_i in the same time interval t. The specified model has the following form:

$$ln(Y(t)) = \text{constant} + \Sigma \beta_i X_i(t)$$

These one-hour time intervals are consecutive for 24 hours a day and 7 days a week. The explanatory variables were transformed to their standard scores. An adequately fitted Poisson regression model was subsequently selected to represent the context-behaviour relationship in further analysis.

Results

The nature of the situated action of the INFO event is studied via the relationship between the occurrences of the INFO event and several contextual, explanatory variables in the collaborative hypertext database. The occurrences of the INFO event are likely to indicate an increasing concern of some social and coordination issues of an ongoing collaborative process. The resultant model of the context-behaviour relationship is developed within the framework of the study so as to provide empirical evidence for the evaluation of existing models of collaborative work in CSCW studies.

The use of the five collaborative hypertext databases in the MUCH system resulted in thousands of transactions during the three-month longitudinal observation. The scale of use for each database varies. The class database was accessed by the largest group of users (User = 30) with the widest spectrum of functions from the presentation layer (Function = 25).

Table 3.1 summarizes the overall scale of use for each database, in terms of the total number of transactions observed, the total number of unique nodes involved, the size of the user pool, and the number of distinct functions required.

The average percentage usage of the INFO function is about 1% over the five databases. It is rather small in contrast to the percentage use of functions such as UNFOLD, READING and LOCK. The dispersed occurrences of the INFO event suggest that the INFO function is only required for some needs relating to higher degrees of coordination coupling in collaborative writing. The independent working mode is primarily supported by the MUCH system as the system is designed to facilitate asynchronous collaborative writing. Although it is difficult to define the range of tasks to be enclosed by the independent mode, it appears that tasks can be fulfilled via the INFO function go beyond this range.

Table 3.1 Usage of the five collaborative hypertext databases over three consecutive months.

Database	Transaction	Node	User	Function	Started	Ended
Groupware	12089	750	11	22	Tue Apr 19	Mon July 25
Class	9247	474	30	25	Wed Apr 20	Fri July 15
Management	7068	698	16	22	Wed Apr 20	Thu July 21
OSCAR	3148	315	7	18	Tue Apr 19	Mon July 25
General	1590	96	10	21	Tue Apr 19	Fri July 15

The occurrences of some rare event in the world are generated by Poisson processes. The probability distribution of the occurrences of the event associated with a Poisson process is called a Poisson distribution. The Kolmogorov–Smirnov (K–S) goodness-of-fit test of the null hypothesis, that the data are drawn from a population with a Poisson distribution, indicated that the occurrences of the INFO events follow a Poisson distribution with the mean = .0308 (K–S $Z = 0.7694$, $p = 0.5946$, two-tailed).

Table 3.2 shows the occurrences of the INFO event observed in one-hour time intervals. In the vast majority of the time intervals observed, INFO events did not occur at all. In 19 time intervals, the INFO event occurred once. The higher the count of the INFO event in an interval, the fewer number of such intervals can be found, except one case (Occurrences = 6). The highest count of the INFO event for the class database is 7.

Several Poisson regression models were fitted to the time series data of the occurrences of the INFO event and corresponding contextual characteristics of the awareness-seeking path of users in a given time interval. In particular, the model specified as follows resulted in an adequate goodness-of-fit statistic for the data:

$$ln(\text{count}) = \beta_0 + (\beta_1 \times Zcredit) + (\beta_2 \times Zlevel) + (\beta_3 \times Zlink) + (\beta_4 \times Zword) + (\beta_5 \times Zsize) + (\beta_6 \times hour)$$

The explanatory variables, or independent variables, were specified as the covariant variables in the model, except the hour variable, which is categorical. The GENLOG procedure in SPSS revealed that the model adequately represents the data set (Pearson $\chi^2 = 0.0960$, $DF = 1$, $P = 0.76$). The Poisson distribution of the count of the INFO event was specified in the model.

Table 3.3 shows the results of the estimates for the model and associated significance tests. For a given explanatory variable x, a positive sign of the estimate suggests the likelihood of the INFO event count increases with the level of x, with the other xs held constant. A negative sign suggests that the likelihood of the INFO event count decreases with the level of x. An insignificant test at a conventional α level such as 0.05 suggests that the effect of an x on the response variable is not statistically different from zero.

Three estimates in this model are statistically different from zero. Among these, *Zlevel* has a positive coefficient, whereas both *Zcredit* and *Zsize* have negative coefficients. For example, the estimate of $\beta_{\text{level}} = 19.28$ ($p < 0.05$) for *Zlevel* suggests that the occurrences of the INFO event in a given time interval are likely to increase as the *Zlevel* in the same interval increases.

Table 3.2 The occurrences of the INFO event in one-hour time intervals in using the class database.

Occurrences	0	1	2	3	4	5	6	7
Intervals	2269	19	6	2	1	1	3	1

Table 3.3 A Poisson regression model of the relationship between INFO events and contextual characters of the path activated in the same time intervals. (Source Database: Class; Observation: 20 April to 15 July 1994).

Parameter χ_k	Estimate β_k	SE	Z-value $^{*}p<0.05$	Marginal effect
Zlevel	19.2786	7.5654	2.55*	0.5938
Hour	0.2060	0.3023	0.68	0.0063
Zword	0.9397	9.7437	0.10	0.0289
Zlink	−0.6285	1.4958	−0.42	−0.0194
Zcredit	−11.2120	4.1423	−2.71*	−0.3453
Zsize	−15.2472	2.6603	−5.73*	−0.4696
Constant	1.4017	3.1006	0.45	0.0436

The Poisson regression model can also be interpreted in terms of the marginal effect of an x on the expected INFO count. The marginal effect of x_k on expected y is given by $\theta\beta_k$, where $\theta = 0.0308$ is the expected occurrences of the INFO event in a given time interval.

The marginal effect of *Zlevel* on the INFO count is $(0.0308)(19.2786) = 0.5938$. In other words, if the value of *Zlevel* increases by one, the expected INFO count will increase by 0.5938, other things being equal. In contrast, the marginal effect of *Zcredit* is $(0.0308)(-11.2120) = -0.3453$, suggesting that the expected INFO count will decrease by 0.3453 as the *Zcredit* increases by one standard deviation.

Preliminary analyses found the contextual variable *Zlevel* is negatively correlated with the frequency of UNFOLD and it is positively correlated with the frequency of LOCK (Pearson's $r = -0.529$, $p < 0.001$ and $r = 0.187$, $p = 0.001$, respectively).

Finally, if a dummy variable *Phase* is included in the model to specify the two phases of reading and authoring, the *Phase* variable would have the most predominant effect on expected occurrences of the INFO. The writing phase considerably increases the probability of a higher INFO count. The frequency of the INFO events was indeed increased when group essays were emerging in the MUCH system. Students were more interested in new nodes coming into the shared repository.

Discussion

The Poisson regression model suggests that the INFO function is more frequently needed on nodes involved in substantive work. The use of the INFO function tends to be triggered by specific problems in an independent working mode. A field study of the use of an IBIS system also found a similar tendency.

INFO events occurred rarely with all the five MUCH databases that have been studied. The occurrences of the event were found to follow a Poisson distribution. This finding in its own right may lead to some insights into the awareness-seeking behaviours in asynchronous collaborative authoring with the MUCH system. The knowledge of the probability distribution of the INFO event count of the INFO is necessary for applying appropriate tools and making sense of the empirical data observed.

The relationship between the INFO events and some contextual characteristics of the paths of users interacting with a shared hypertext database reveals some patterns related to the interaction between users and the database. These factors affect users' behaviours with INFO and they are likely to be important to users who may be motivated to change from one mode of collaboration to another. The total number of words involved in the awareness-seeking path was expected to correlate with the occurrences of the INFO event positively, but the estimate is not significantly different from zero. The overall linkage, the total number of parent → child links, involved in a given interval was expected to correlate with the INFO count negatively, but the significance test did not provide sufficient evidence for the proposition. On the other hand, the effects of the overall level, the overall credit, and the total number of concurrent users were all statistically significant from zero. These patterns help us to understand what information is important to users. The users may be motivated to seek further social interaction and move to a working mode with a higher degree of coupling or they may remain working in the current collaboration mode with updated views.

Experiences of students in group essay writing showed that the most coordination-demanding phase was the initial brainstorming. The initial brainstorming was followed by task allocations among the members of a group. The majority of the groups followed a process similar to the ones studied by Kraut *et al.* (1992). The detailed transactions show an increased frequency of the INFO events as the submission deadline was approaching. The regression models suggest that students needed more awareness assistance in the group writing phase than in the browsing phase. The regression model must be understood in a broader context of users, task and tools

CONCLUSION

This chapter reviews central issues regarding computer support for collaborative writing, the dynamics of human interaction and the intermediate roles of computer systems. Few theories and models have been developed to address the dynamics of collaborative writing with co-authoring systems. Empirical studies adapt different theories such as contingency theory, cognitive dissonance theory and saturation theory to address how the social network is shaped in a process of collaborative writing. The structure of the dynamic social network relies on the nature of tasks and the communication media (Kraut *et al.*, 1992), encounters between knowledge structures of individual participants, and mutual influences between technology and organization.

Empirical evidence and subjective views of users suggest that a process of collaborative writing consists of substructures such as planning, drafting and revising. More detailed understanding of collaborative writing with co-authoring systems is needed. For instance, how do people plan with co-authoring systems; what roles emerge implicitly or explicitly during the process?

Many co-authoring systems are based on conceptual models of collaborative writing, whereas the theoretical and empirical foundations of these models are subject to empirical validation in the real world. How do people approach each other's work in a shared workspace? What and how much are people interested in as they share the same infrastructure? Approaches to these questions should take into account that the results can be reliably generalized to closely related settings, and that the results can be transformed and incorporated into refined co-authoring systems, and finally that the refined co-authoring systems can be assessed by the same method.

ACKNOWLEDGEMENTS

The authors are grateful to Dr R. J. Bhansali, Department of Statistics and Computational Mathematics at the University of Liverpool, for his valuable advice on Poisson regression models and to Dr D. Diaper for his comments on an earlier draft of the chapter.

REFERENCES

Akscyn, R., McCracken, D. and Yoder, E. (1988) KMS: a distributed hypermedia system for managing knowledge in organisations. *Communications of the ACM*, **31** (7), 820–835.

Bales, R. (1951) *Interaction Process Analysis*. Addison-Wesley, Cambridge, MA.

Beck, E. and Bellotti, V. (1992) Informed opportunism as strategy: supporting coordination in distributed collaborative writing. *Proceedings of the Third European conference on Computer-Supported Cooperative Work, ECSCW'93*, Milan, Italy, 13–17 September, Kluwer Academic Publishers, pp. 233–248.

Beck, E. (1993) A survey of experience of collaborative writing. Mike Sharples (ed.) Computer supported collaborative writing, pp. 87–112. London: Springer-Verlag.

Conklin, J. and Begeman, M. (1988). gIBIS: a hypertext tool for exploratory policy discussion. *ACM Transactions on Office Information Systems* **6** (4), 303–331.

Delise, N. and Schwartz, M. (1987) Contexts – a partitioning concept for hypertext. *ACM Transactions on Office Information Systems*, **5** (2), 168–186.

Dourish, P. and Bellotti, V. (1992) Awareness and coordination in shared workspaces. *Proceedings of the ACM Conference, CSCW'92*, ACM Press, New York, pp. 107–114.

Ede, L. and Lunsford, A. (1990) *Singular Test*/Plural Authors: Perspectives on Collaborative Writing. Southern Illinois University Press, Carbondale and Edwardsville, II.

Engestrom, Y. (1990) *Learning, Working and Imaging: Twelve Studies in Activity Theory*. Orienta-Konsultit Oy, Helsinki.

Festinger, L. (1957) *A Theory of Cognitive Dissonance*. Stanford University Press.

Fish, R., Kraut, R., Leland, M. and Cohen, M. (1988) Quilt: a collaborative tool for cooperative writing. *Proceedings of COIS'88 Conference on Office Information Systems*, ACM SIGOIS, pp. 30–37.

Flower, L. S. and Hayes, J. R. (1981a) A cognitive process theory of writing. *College Composition and Communication*, **32** (4), 365–387.

Flower, L. and Hayes, J. (1981b) Plans that guide the composing process. Frederiksen, C. H. and Dominic J. F. (eds) *Writing: The Nature, Development and Teaching of Written Communication*, Vol. 2, New Jersey: Lawrence Erlbaum Associates.

Haake, J. and Wilson, B. (1992) Supporting collaborative writing of hyperdocuments in SEPIA. *Hypertext '92 Proceedings*, ACM Press, New York, pp. 138–146.

Hahn, U., Jarke, M., Eherer, S. and Kreplin, K. (1991) CoAUTHOR: a hypermedia group authoring environment. In Bowers, J. M. and Benford, S. D. (eds) *Studies in Computer Supported Cooperative Work: Theory, Practice and Design*, North-Holland, Amsterdam, pp. 79–100.

Halasz, F. (1988) Reflections on notecards: seven issues for the next generation of hypermedia systems, *Communications of the ACM*, **31** (7), 836–852.

Haythornthwaite, C., Wellman, B. and Mantei, M. (1994) Media use and work relationships in a research group, *Proceedings of the 27th Hawaii International Conference on System Sciences*, Vol. IV: Information Systems: Collaboration Technology Organizational and Technology (Cat. No. 94TH0607-2), IEEE Comput. Soc. Press, Los Alamitos, Ca, pp. 94–103.

Irish, P. and Trigg, R. (1989) Supporting collaboration in hypermedia: issues and experiences, *Journal of the American Society of Information Science*, **40** (3), 192–199.

Jessup, L. M. and Valacich, J. S. (eds) (1993) *Group Support Systems: New Perspectives*. Macmillan Publishing Company, New York.

Johansen, R. (1988) *Groupware: Computer Support for Business Teams*. Free Press, New York.

Kling, R. (1980) Social analyses of computing: theoretical perspectives in recent empirical research, *ACM Computing Surveys*, **12** (1), 61–110.

Kraut, R., Egido, C. and Galegher, J. (1988) Patterns of contact and communication in scientific research collaboration. *Proceedings of the ACM Conference on Computer-Supported Cooperative Work (CSCW'88)*, 1–12 September 1988.

Kraut, R., Galegher, J., Fish, R. and Chalfonte, B. (1992). Task requirements and media choice in collaborative writing. *Human–Computer Interaction*, **7**, 375–407.

Kuutti, K. and Arvonen, T. (1992) *Identifying Potential CSCW Applications by Means of Activity Theory Concepts: A Case Example*. Proceedings of ACM CSCW'92 Conference on Computer-Supported Cooperative Work, ACM Press, New York, pp. 233–240.

Lea, M. (ed.) (1992) *Contexts of Computer-Mediated Communication*. Harvester Wheatsheaf.

Markova, I. (1987) *Human Awareness: its Social Development*. Hutchinson, London.

McCarthy, J. (1994) The state-of-the-art of CSCW: CSCW systems, cooperative work and organization, *Journal of Information Technology*, **9**, 73–83.

Morgan, M. and Murphy, C. (1992) Insight and collaborative writing. In Lay, M. M. and Karis, W. M. (eds), *Collaborative Writing in Industry: Investigations in Theory and Practice*, Maywood, New York, pp. 64–82.

Morgan, M. and Murray, M. (1988) Insight and collaborative writing. Lay, M. M. and Karis, W. M. (eds) *Collaborative Writing in Industry: Investigations in Theory and Practice*, Baywood Publishing Company, Inc., New York, pp. 64–82.

Morgan, M., Allen, N., Moore, T., Atkinson, D. and Snow, C. (1987). Collaborative writing in classroom. *Bulletin of the Association for Business Communication*, **50** (3), 20–26.

Neuwirth, C., Kaufer, D., Chandhok, R., and Morris, J. (1990) Issues in the design of computer support for co-authoring and commenting. *Proceedings of CSCW'90* October 7–10, Los Angeles, CA, ACM Press, New York, pp. 183–194.

Olsen, J., Olson, G., Storrosten, M. and Carter, M. (1993) Groupwork close up: a comparison of the group design process with and without a simple group editor, *ACM Transactions on Information Systems*, **11** (4), 321–348.

Olson, J., Card, S., Landauer, T. and Olson, G. (1993) Computer-supported cooperative work: Research issues for the 90s, Special Issue: Human–computer interaction research agendas, *Behaviour and Information Technology*, **12** (2), 115–129.

Sharples, M., Goodlet, J. S., Beck, E. E., Wood, C. C., Easterbrook, S.M. and Plowman, L. (1993) Research issues in the study of computer supported collaborative writing. In Sharples, M. (ed.) *Computer Supported Collaborative Writing*. Springer-Verlag, London.

Streitz, N., Hannemann, J. and Thuring, M. (1989). From ideas and arguments to hyperdocuments: travelling through activity spaces. *Hypertext '89 Proceedings*, The ACM Press, New York, pp. 343–364.

Whiteside, J., Bennett, J. and Holtzblatt, K. (1988) Usability engineering: our experience and evolution. In Helander, M. (ed.), *Handbook of Human-Computer Interaction*, North-Holland, Amsterdam.

Wright, P. (1991) Cognitive overheads and prostheses: some issues in evaluating hypertext. *Proceedings of the ACM Conference on Hypertext, Hypertext '91*, pp. 1–12.

Yakemovic, K. C. B. and Conklin, E. J. (1990). Report on a development project use of an issue-based information system. *Proceedings of ACM Conference CSCW'90*, ACM Press, New York, pp. 105–118.

4 A Portrait of the Author as an Interacting Group

JO ANN ORAVEC

INTRODUCTION

Groups interacting face-to-face confront a number of problems (including those of motivation, coordination, and shared focus). Groups interacting via computer-supported writing tools face a number of additional kinds of hurdles: how can the various kinds of computer-mediated, video, and voice stimuli that group members receive and contribute be interpreted in ways that make sense and lead to productive interaction? How can meaningful and coherent accounts of system-based group interaction be generated, shared, stored, and reviewed (either by group members themselves, or by those considered 'outsiders' to the group)? How, in effect, can the 'group' as an entity be constructed in the vehicles these systems provide?

Integration of artifacts into prominent places in group activity is not new to computer-supported group writing vehicles. Varieties of kinds of group-rendered documents serve pivotal roles in construction of the group as a unit, both in its internal interactions and its relations with various outsiders. The familiar vehicle of the committee or task force report, for example, can serve such roles. Consider the following report of several groups associated with the effort to stimulate and coalesce the 'collaboratory' movement (National Academy of Sciences, 1993). In the preface, there is an account of the history of the report's generation as well as a set of statements about the NAS teams that cooperated to produce the report. Accounts and statements in the preface show a linear, organized development; there are few signals of discord, dissension, confusion, or backtracking. Whether or not the production of the report was as smooth as stated is not known to outsiders; a certain, sterilized image of these productive efforts is presented for outsiders' consumption.

With collaborative writing tools, a number of kinds of traces of group interaction becomes available to group members (and often can also be accessed by non-group members). Video and voice combine with various writing and outlining tools to produce environments for group interaction and production. The 'groups' that emerge in these environments are apparently not as organized and well coordinated as the reportedly well-mannered groups portrayed in the

GROUPWARE AND AUTHORING
ISBN 0-12-575005-6

NAS task force report just described. An assortment of traces of the groups' interaction is made available, and accounts constructed with these traces (either by group members or by outsiders) are often richer and more revealing.

One of the emerging themes of many current approaches in social science is that the individual uses narratives (stories and their linkages) to guide his or her attempts to 'account for human actions across time' and to construct reflexively a notion of self (Gergen and Gergen, 1986, p. 6). The narrative perspective can fruitfully be extended to consideration of how groups use narrative to create various accounts – as well as to construct narrative voices and characters that reflect the group itself and through which the group is constructed. Computer-based group support systems introduce new dimensions of issues concerning both individual and group narrative efforts.

The narrative perspective (or 'narrative paradigm' as labelled by Fisher, 1987) is not restricted in application to any particular genre or artifact. People create stories or accounts with diaries, in poetry, with songs, and with drawings. Construction of narratives by groups is often done with film, video, and photography (Oravec, 1995). The narrative perspective construes both audience and authors as 'storytellers' who evaluate stories on the basis of their cohesion and fidelity, regardless of the vehicles in which they are presented:

> Viewing human communication narratively stresses that people are full participants in the making of messages, whether they are agents (authors) or audience members (co-authors). (Fisher, 1987, p. 18)

Thus, one of the narrative perspective's major benefits for research and development of computer-supported cooperative work and other network-based computer systems is that it has relevance not only for written and printed communication, but also for oral, pictorial, and multimedia vehicles.

Many investigations of groups and their interactions focus on group members' own satisfaction with and perceptions of group proceedings, and downplay or ignore ways in which group members attempt to establish and shape images and styles of the group, group products, and group proceedings for others (including other group members). Groups have 'audiences': in the workplace, these audiences may include managers, competing and cooperating groups, as well as potential group members. Images of how a document is produced, and notions about who produces it, are often critically important elements in how it is received by these audiences. Levels of access to the narratives, and control over their construction, serve in part to determine degrees of group membership and position in the group.

GROUP HISTORIES, MEMORIES, AND VOICE

Group histories and memories provide shared focus and meaning for a group. They emerge over time in large groups and localities (as in the communities described in Middleton and Edwards, 1990) as well as in short-term, small groups (for example, the jazz ensembles portrayed in Eisenberg, 1990). Notions of 'group memories' and 'organizational memories' associated with computer-supported cooperative work systems have been explored in Conklin (1992) and Oravec (1996).

In several forms of group narrative, careful attention is paid to constructing an account of group activities most group members will likely accept (even if the account becomes fairly sparse and sketchy as a consequence). For example, minutes kept of a meeting and approved in ceremonial fashion at the beginning of the next meeting are generally a selective reconstruction of what transpired, and seldom provide a controversial account. One person is assigned the role of 'taking the minutes', but full participation of group members in construction of the account is obtained at least symbolically when the minutes are formally approved. Minutes provide a kind of memory for the group, a set of threads that links the group from session to session.

Many kinds of group narrative are characterized by overlapping or 'multi-phasic' accounts; the group memory comprised of such accounts is often not consistent or integrated (see Toolan, 1988). Toolan contends that a 'collective style of telling' is more frequently adopted where there is substantial individual and collective uncertainty about kinds and sequences of events; each member of the group helps to piece the stories together. In 'group testimony', common in the legal systems of certain cultures, accounts are constructed by more than one individual of the incident or situation in question. (In contrast, in our legal system, single individuals are interrogated in tandem on the witness stand.) In group testimony, the focus is on building a single account of what happened through a process of mutual validation, consensus, and agreement – although it is very apparent that the collective account (the congealed 'voice' of the group produced during the testimony's extraction) may miss some important information.

Group 'voice' is a construct that plays a role in a variety of group settings. It can be seen in some ways as akin to a 'group stream-of-consciousness', a reflection (often with considerable retrospective components) of ongoing group process. For example, a proposal outline produced in a group writing system may serve as such a retrospective voice, reflecting a consensus achieved via verbal communication among group members, but being rendered at a time later than when that consensus was reached. (The essentials for the outline may have taken some time to generate, or the group member best equipped to produce the outline could have been otherwise occupied when the consensus was indeed reached.) Many cognitive scientists and artificial intelligence researchers have raised serious questions about our commonsense notions of the 'consciousness' of individuals (Minsky, 1986). In comparable terms, the notion of a group stream-of-consciousness (the idea that coherent trails of discussion or interaction emerge from group interaction) may indeed be best regarded as a useful and hard-to-dissipate fiction that often attends our constructions of groups. A selection of distinct group voices may co-exist in systems in which there are several levels of group interaction (video and voice channels, for instance) or a number of subgroups.

CONSTRUCTING WRITTEN PRODUCTIONS AS COLLABORATIVE ACTIVITIES

Our current sets of vocabularies, images, and perspectives for discussing written production generally have an 'individualistic' quality, despite the many acknowledged collaborative efforts throughout history, contributions of editors, publishers, curators, and gallery owners, as well as interpretative roles of reader and critic. Individualistic constructions of the author are reinforced through what Danzinger (1990) labels the 'Robinson Crusoe' perspective, the idea that the individual can be considered as a solitary object of analysis (effectively removed from social and cultural influences).

The image of the act of 'writing' as a solitary and individual activity is deeply wired into much of Western culture. Few of the works that are considered 'great literature' and studied by literary critics and scholars are labelled as products of a group, and much of our current writing pedagogy is framed from an individualistic perspective. This view of writing can be unfortunate, given growing amounts of research data and speculation that show that 'for certain groups of people and for certain types of documents, collaborative writing supports the production of better documents than non-collaborative writing' (Rada *et al.*, 1989, p. 1106). Reither and Vipond (1989) declare that perspectives that construe writing (all kinds of writing) as 'collaboration' are more fruitful than those that construe it as an individual-centered activity.

Just as literature and artistic endeavor have spawned a number of distinguishable genres (such as novels, poetry, and watercolor), computer applications have been construed as falling into an enlarging set of interrelated genres. A variety of computer application genres has risen into prominence in the past several decades (including spreadsheets and word processing packages); the genre of computer-supported cooperative work (CSCW) systems (or 'groupware') has recently emerged, and has directed considerable academic and public attention toward the notions of group composition and production. The CSCW subgenre (or variety) of group writing support has been very influential in its impact on the CSCW genre – as reflected in popular and scholarly accounts of CSCW development (Seybold, 1987; Greenberg, 1991; Baecker, 1993; Oravec, 1996) and in interest on the part of the software product-buying public.

Increased concentration on group-level production, interaction, and composition inspired by CSCW systems has only made small changes in the individual-centered social and intellectual trends of the past decades, yet some interesting shifts in vocabulary, image, and perspective are becoming noticeable in many quarters (as reflected in the bulk of this chapter).

'ADEQUACY' AND 'AUDIENCE' IN NARRATIVE PRODUCTION

Attention to narrative as a perspective has cut across disciplinary boundaries, with each discipline contributing viewpoints on how narratives are constructed and how they relate to each other. Some administrative theorists have described 'organizational narratives' and 'stories' as playing important roles in organizational culture (Martin *et al.*, 1980). Self-proclaimed 'narratologists' (Genette, 1980; Todorov, 1990) have concentrated their efforts in building a science of narrative. From a philosophical and ethical perspective, MacIntyre (1984) declares that 'narrative history of a certain kind turns out to be the basic and essential genre for the characterization of human action' (p. 208).

Narratives often do not admit of strict truth and falsity evaluations, however much we would like to stretch our constructions of what is 'true' and 'false' to apply to them. Rather, as argued by Shotter, we generally judge the 'adequacy' of stories by asking questions such as the following: (a) is the story compatible with what we believe to be fundamental facts?; (b) does it lend intelligible order to our experience?; (c) is it revealing? (does it render intelligible processes that are otherwise invisible to us?); (d) does it destroy illusion and make clear to us ways in which we have deceived ourselves in the past? (e) is it practically productive in the sense that the paradigms and prototypes it represents can provide the roots for other practices, for example, research practices? (Shotter; 1986, p. 78). In addition to Shotter's dimensions of adequacy, narratives composed in real-time group contexts should have a certain level of compatibility with each other and coherence as a unit (since they are juxtaposed in a limited time-frame and relatively restricted context).

Considerations related to 'audience' are given pivotal roles in a number of formulations of the narrative perspective. In group narratives (such as group sagas, told around campfires or at various gatherings) possible distinctions between the story's authors and listeners become blurred, as do lines between 'fantasy' and 'objectivity'. Bennett (1983) describes the group saga as being told and retold more for purposes related to group cohesion and reminiscence than for the dissemination of information (although the latter is certainly a factor in the use of group sagas to convey information across generations). Polanyi (1989) relates that certain elements of fictionality and reinvention are not only tolerated but also appreciated in many group contexts. Images and accounts produced by a group about itself and its environment are seldom entirely reasonable and consistent (they may exaggerate group strengths and underestimate its weaknesses, for example) – yet they provide useful functions for the group in buffering it against sometimes-hostile environmental and interpersonal pressures.

The notion of a group's 'collective consciousness' or 'group mind' can be readily associated with forms of group narrative construction in which linkages are drawn among parts of the narrative through consensus (rather than strict applications of various formulas or logics). For example, Haynes provides a portrait of an 'ideal' group collaboration, one that (in his example) produces a piece of research. Consensus apparently plays a role in linking aspects of the narrative produced by the group:

> Consider the process of a task-oriented small group of students assigned to investigate and reach consensus on public policy concerning any controversial issue or exigency of the day. If their research is thorough, then the interests of everyone concerned with the exigency will be represented in the group's collective consciousness. The resulting narrative will include everyone's stories of the exigency in the cumulative fashion of orality. (Haynes, 1989, p. 115).

The episodic 'stitching together' of the students' accounts may certainly have a logic other than that of formal argumentation, and may also have a number of internal contradictions (whether or not these are openly recognized); the narrative is considered in terms of its 'adequacy' rather than logical form or completeness. The narrative the group produces is a mosaic of the topics it has covered in its interactions, along with some indication of how the topics were received by group members (how deeply and thoroughly they were discussed and whether some common understandings were reached).

COMPOSING OURSELVES: CONSTRUCTION OF SELF AND GROUP

Construction of 'self' intimately involves construction of narratives about the self and its interactions with the world. Gergen and Gergen (1986) label as 'self-narratives' the individual's linkages among self-relevant events across time. Familiar vehicles for self-narrative include autobiography, although video portraits, dance, and drama can also serve to convey a self-narration. A self-narrative can serve to demonstrate or convince others of something, to configure memories in a certain way, and to construct, reflect, and make obvious patterns and trends pertaining to that particular individual.

Group efforts in narrative construction have a variety of dissimilarities with those that are considered to be 'individual' efforts – but there are also a number of commonalities and couplings between the two. In collaborative writing activities, in group drawing projects, in group decision making, in discussion, and in conflict resolution, groups compose narratives that interrelate events and sequences relevant to the group (events and sequences that can have a number of common threads or be quite disparate in form or features). Collaborative writing efforts can involve construction of a single, unified voice (the 'we') as well as a mosaic (or cacophony) of individual voices.

In some group-narrative efforts, identities of participants are submerged and the individual has a certain level of anonymity. In the social psychology literature, the state of reduced focus on the individuals is labeled as 'deindividuation' (Mullen and Hu, 1986). Some apostles of anonymity in group interactions have been increasingly vocal in its support: for example, Fox (1989) declares that for certain kinds of group production, 'assured anonymity will produce more and better-quality input' (p. 146). Pseudonyms and individual-chosen characters can also be associated with individual group members and be used to shape the style of the group's interaction. Myers (1987) describes how contributors to a computer bulletin board developed and maintained elaborate and original identities in the context of their participation. Proliferation of the creation of such virtual identities in computer-mediated vehicles may be one of the most significant dimensions these tools bring to human interaction (Oravec, 1996).

Increases in kinds and styles of efforts to craft individual identities are only some of the many impacts of introduction of computing into writing activities. Barrett (1988) asserts that there is a 'natural affinity between writing and computers, almost a genetic relationship' (p. xvii), with both being mechanisms for knowledge representation. Extending Barrett's analogy, mutations and variations of this 'genetic relationship' have spawned new ways to construct the activities of reading and writing. Slater (1989) states that the problem of developing systems for support of the co-authoring of documents is 'as much a psychological research area as a technical one' (p. 109), and involves the restructuring of human relationships.

How computer-based support may affect relationships among individuals both within and outside the immediate context of written production is an active topic for analysis. Accounts produced in a group setting can be framed in ways that serve to establish or reinforce the positions of individuals within the group context as well as to establish participants' and/or the group's positions in relation to non-group members.

Self and group characters

Construction of readily identifiable 'characters' is a major aspect of narrative production and consumption. Toolan (1988) presents a perspective in which reader and writer, listener and teller participate in the construction of characters:

> Character is an illusion in which the reader is a creative accomplice: a variety of descriptions of some posited individual, together with descriptions – implicit or explicit – of that individual's actions and reactions, suffice to lead most readers to conceive of a person of whom these references and insights are just glimpses. (Toolan, 1988, p. 91)

Toolan employs an 'iceberg principle' to capture how readers 'read' a character: readers generally assume that much more lies 'beneath the surface' than is conveyed on the written page. Readers bring various assortments of expectations and stereotypes to their reading efforts. Fowler (1977) provides a set of character components often used to construct the characters that we have become so familiar with in novels, movies, and television tales (e.g. heroes or heroines, villains, and innocent bystanders).

Groups have 'characters' as well as individuals, and participants' and observers' expectations concerning these characters play substantial roles in their development and interpretation. Jazz performance is an example of group interaction in which group characters dramatically and quickly emerge (e.g. as the tempo changes or as different soloists are featured). A particular group may have a variety of characters, some being expressed simultaneously (by different sub-groups), others being expressed at various stages of group development. Kinds and qualities of group characters in work group contexts are expanding as more emphasis is being placed on the notion of 'teamwork' in organizations and as more people write, talk, and think in terms of groups. Stocks of readily-recognizable group images and labels are growing: 'skunkworks' and other renegade groups are being distinguished from other, more conforming, groups and quality circles have proliferated in some organizations (Peters, 1987).

As consciousness of group process increases in the advent of the proliferation and widespread use of CSCW systems, various character components associated with the systems are becoming distinguished:

1. *Character components associated with the facilitator/scribe-led group:* one group of people is construed as providing the 'creative' element, and often gets credit for the production, while others serve roles as scribes or recorders. A non-involved facilitator can also serve the role as scribe (as in the 'chauffeur-driven' CSCW systems described in Dickson *et al.*, 1989).
2. *Character components associated with the casual or spontaneous group*: some forms of writing and artistic development can be construed as kinds of casual, informal interaction. Group characters may emerge in which the theme of spontaneity plays considerable roles. Eisenberg (1990) describes the phenomenon of 'jamming' (unbridled creative activity) as emerging in a variety of group contexts. Such CSCW systems as CRUSIER (described in Root, 1988) are designed to support such informal interactions by affording opportunities for non-scheduled video-based meetings and discussions.
3. *Character components associated with the 'star-dominated' group*: one or two individuals serve as the focal point for group interaction and help to shape its identity.
4. *Character components associated with 'deindividuated' groups*: these are groups in which (at some level) individual participants remain anonymous. The deindividuated self as part of a group writing or drawing effort can be seen in contrast with the highly individuated writer or artist of some group efforts – for example, the individual who is distinguished in the group as composing a dissenting opinion or who is openly credited with an idea or motion.

A discussion of aspects that may play a role in group character construction is provided in a later section.

Questions of how best to reflect group processes in group products such as documents and drawings (rather than to decontextualize those products) are important ones for writing system developers to consider. In many of today's group-produced documents (such as task force reports, grant proposals, etc.) there are few direct clues as to group process. This is not surprising: Aldridge (1993) shows ways in which research reports produced by individuals lose many of their couplings with sources and origins of their production, and Smith (1990) explores how various public records and writings also become decontextualized. In comparable ways, group-produced writings and drawings eventually become decontextualized to some degree as traces of their production are removed, forgotten or lost.

Finished documents, designs and drawings that emerge from group deliberations can be seen as kinds of political and social compromises. There may be no direct effort to distort or disguise the kind or extent of these deliberations. However, the vehicle of the paper-rendered group report does not afford substantial means for their expression (although attempts to 'read between the lines' of the report may expose some of these deliberations). The purpose of the group is framed in terms of its final products rather than its own exploration and development. In many ways, such a notion of the 'group' is limiting and restrictive. The notion is tightly linked to the print-culture bias that assumes when a document is printed it is somehow 'finished', and the group's purpose (at least in regard to that particular document) effectively terminated. Group writing systems have the potential to alter this relatively static perspective toward the group by providing better means to produce and to access accounts of group interaction and on-going production efforts.

WHO'S GOT THE FLOOR? SOME CONTROL-RELATED ISSUES IN DESIGN AND APPLICATION OF GROUP WRITING SYSTEMS

Some of the central problems of control that attend the design and application of group writing systems (along with other systems in which shared resources and joint activities play substantial roles) include the following:

1. *The problem of shared access to resources (how to construct resources so as to be amenable to shared access)*: what access do group members have to various resources, and how are potential conflicts relating to access resolved? How are non-group members (individuals considered as 'outsiders') excluded from use of these resources (if at all)?
2. *The problem of identifying participants and their contributions*: this can be an especially difficult problem in large groups with shifting membership.
3. *The problem of affording some sort of shared focuses, involvements or narrations*: As the number and variety of resources and modes for their

development increase, how are mechanisms for direction of attention of group members provided? Who may utilize these mechanisms? The ability to say, in effect, 'look HERE' – and direct the group's efforts and attention toward a certain aspect of the document or drawing being worked on – is a considerable mechanism for shaping the group and its activities.

The image of the group as a whole as constructing a document or decision can have a powerful hold: we often say 'Congress came to a decision' or 'the committee produced a report'. Nevertheless, groups take action through the individuals that comprise them, and someone (or something, in the case of an intelligent agent or surrogate) must perform some activity. Collaborative writing tools, campfire circles, and corporate meeting rooms all have mechanisms through which individuals can take turns at constructing the group narrative, or through which they can work simultaneously or in conjunction.

The fact that an increasing number of group-based writing procedures are composed out of traces and through the utilization of resources that are widely scattered in space and time – and not largely constructed in a face-to-face meeting of the group as a whole – makes the narrative perspective even more useful. What makes a group history or narrative account that is pieced together over space and time (and which may include asynchronous interaction and review) a 'satisfying' account?

There have been a number of recent attempts to construct accounts of the processes involved in collaborative writing, processes that can serve to structure and make sense out of joint writing activities. Morrell (1988) outlines two models of writing collaboration: versioning and assembly-line (or 'segmentation') models. In versioning, a collaborator produces a draft, then another collaborator edits and otherwise modifies it. In the assembly-line model, collaborators divide up writing tasks and work in relatively independent modes, later combining their efforts into a single document.

Both of the models just described involve allocation of discrete roles and functions to members of the team. Depending on how these roles are allocated, the two models may produce significantly different kinds of documents. A document that is prepared in segments and then congealed into a whole may have several 'voices', each distinct in tone and perspective; the level of distinctiveness may relate to whether a skillful editing job is done on the final document in the effort to commingle the various voices. Versioning itself can serve to reduce the multi-voice problem (a problem that many groups may indeed not wish to reduce, e.g. if those separate voices are intentionally distinguished and labeled by discipline or by approach).

Landow (1990) describes another variation on collaborative writing process that does not involve allocation of separate roles and functions to co-authors:

> I have worked on an essay with a fellow scholar in this manner. One of us would type a sentence, at which point the other would approve, qualify, or rewrite it, and then we would proceed to the next sentence. (Landow, 1990, p. 408)

In the above model, a more fluid, consensus-dependent pattern replaces explicit allocation and implementation of discrete roles and functions.

Hypertext creation and use are often considered as yet another mode of collaborative writing production (Rada *et al.*, 1989), one that incorporates aspects of process (e.g. in the formation of links). Some real-time group hypertext systems (for instance, rIBIS) have 'tightly coupled' modes, in which all group members are afforded a simultaneous view of certain material (Rein and Ellis, 1991). 'Loosely coupled' modes of rIBIS (modes that can be construed as aspects of an alternate 'group character') allow individuals means of viewing and producing hypertext segments in an individually controlled manner.

The group characters associated with hypertext production are often linked with anti-authoritarianism, a coupling that has some historical underpinnings (see Nelson, 1987). For example, Landow makes a case for the 'democratic' or 'levelling' nature of the Intermedia system, stating that the system 'allows collaboration not only among those of equivalent academic rank or status, but also among those of widely-different rank or status' (1990, pp. 422–423).

Group characters associated with hypertext use and production also currently have strong associations with 'exploration' (Smith *et al.*, 1987) and an emphasis on idea expansion and connection (even to the point of losing track of the initial point of an investigation). Nelson (1987) declares that 'everything should be available to everyone. Any user should be able to follow origins and links of material across boundaries of documents, servers, and networks, and across boundaries of individual implementation' (p. v). Some hypertext developers have worked to control and constrain these associations, in part so that possibly more mundane applications of hypertext can be developed for organizational contexts that are oriented toward regularity and predictability.

CONTROLLING THE TRANSITIONS FROM 'INDIVIDUAL CONTRIBUTION' TO 'GROUP PRODUCT'

One of the major arenas of control in the group context is the kind and extent of identification of individual contributions. An individual's contribution to the group (e.g. the mark an individual writes on a surface, or the words uttered by an individual) often makes a transition from strong association with the individual him- or herself to identification as a product of the group as a whole. How the group navigates these transitions in identity of contributions is critical to its style and character (and affects strongly the quality-of-worklife for all members of the group). Is an idea or document produced with one's keystrokes going to be construed as 'one's own', or will it be more closely associated with the group one works with? The answer to this question may be related to the stage one's group is in (is the group just 'brainstorming', in the process of developing specific project proposals, or is there an impending deadline?).

Social stigmas attached to misinterpretation of individual–group boundaries and distinctions are substantial. We hold in great contempt those who plagiarize, but we also hold in contempt those who do not try to establish rightful possession of their contributions and ideas. There is a spectrum of positions between where an expression or image is tightly coupled to an individual group member and where it becomes fully 'in play' (and open to adoption, modification and adaptation by others). Clarity as to what 'character' is currently dominant in the group can often dispel confusion as to how linkages between individuals and their contributions are best interpreted and handled.

'Control' in the context of group interaction can often include placing the 'breaks' on the group (or pacing the group) in certain ways. These levels of control can be especially important in real-time system contexts, where major changes can occur at a dizzying pace. Considerations other than efficiency often play major roles in aspects of narrative production; some relatively common group writing conventions apparently relate to traditions in which groups are construed as needing to be slowed down – encouraged to be more methodical – rather than simply more efficient.

Much as the QUERTY keyboard was reportedly designed to slow typists down (so as not to allow the typewriter's keys to jam), many of our writing and group decision-making conventions may indeed have served over the years to make group narrative construction more deliberate and systematic. Turn taking, for instance, can often be dysfunctional to some groups in terms of productivity indices: the groups would fare better in measures of productivity by letting productive members head off in their preferred direction and pace. Concerted group efforts to outline premises, assumptions, or constraints prior to the writing of a paper are yet another mechanism for slowing groups down and making their activities more methodical. Affordances for these and comparable control mechanisms can be integrated in various ways in group writing systems.

GROUP WRITING SYSTEMS AS THE MIRROR OF THE GROUP

Turkle (1984) labels the personal computer as the first 'psychological machine', due to its apparent mirror-like ability to reflect and put in relief certain aspects of human intellectual skills. In comparable terms, various kinds of computer-supported vehicles for group support may be construed as 'socio-psychological machines' in their capacity to underscore and magnify certain aspects of group interaction (as well as de-emphasize others).

Just as mirrors can present distorted images to those reflected in them, group writing tools can provide an image of group process to their users that may indeed have elements of distortion. For example, the individual who actually puts fingers-to-keyboard to write a phrase in a group writing context (and who is linked with the phrase by the system) is often not the person who originally generated the idea associated with the phrase. Various social conventions for credit allocation have emerged over time in non-computer-mediated contexts. The fairness of many of these conventions has been questioned (for example, fairness of adding a laboratory head's name to the roster of authors of a paper to which he or she did not directly contribute). However, long-standing traditions associated with the conventions often serve to heal wounded egos.

Traditions for credit allocation have not had the opportunity to emerge in group writing systems (though it can be expected that such traditions will materialize). The non-participation of certain members that was previously concealed through kindness or in consideration of past contributions may be all-too-readily apparent. Glaring errors or omissions, sources of which were forgotten, may be easily re-attached to their sources through later analysis of system-generated records of group interaction (if such are available). Individuals may properly want and demand increased levels of control over their contributions to the system (see Oravec, 1993). Discussion and development of means for handling these issues – for making the 'mirror' of the group a useful tool for group expression rather than a vehicle for blame allocation and micro-management – should be a focal point of system design efforts along with the tools themselves.

GROUP CHARACTER AND VOICE CONSIDERATIONS IN DESIGN AND APPLICATION OF TOOLS FOR CSCW

Awareness of emerging varieties of group characters and voices, and notions of how they are constructed and modified, can add important dimensions to the design and utilization of writing systems. Such considerations may also help the 'consumers' of these tools select among various tools for particular occasions and purposes. For example, where expression of all participants is desired (and efficiency is not a major requirement), systems that afford the development of democratic and participatory characters may be favored; where deadlines are looming (and group participants apparently care little about who does what) another kind of choice may be made.

Some aspects of group writing systems that are intimately involved in construction of group character and voice include the following:

1. Granularity and level of detail of system-mediated accounts of group activity. Accounts can be produced in minute detail and may include a number of aspects of a working session – or they may be less finely grained, and capture only a few significant dimensions of group interaction (e.g. who entered or left the group and when, or what major events transpired in the group context).
2. Control of narrative production. Aspects of control over who participates and when, over how participants' contributions are exhibited to others, and

over other aspects of narrative production in network-based systems are essential to the overall pacing of the group and the kind and quality of the group's voice(s).

3. Perspectives on system-level activity. What kinds of information are group participants afforded as to who is included in the group (either as 'observer' or 'participant'), what subgroups are forming, and what other group-related activities are transpiring?
4. Time-frame considerations. The time frame in which system-produced accounts are placed is linked with how they are utilized (and expected to be utilized) in current and future group interaction. In real-time interaction, time-frame considerations may include the rapidity in which various kinds of feedback are given to group members. (For example, what clues are there as to how 'pauses' or 'silences' are to be constructed?)
5. Construction of group routine and ritual. Many procedural aspects of group narrative construction provide structure and sense-making to group interaction (for example, periodically polling the group for ideas or asking for a consensus before proceeding to another phase of group composition).
6. Roles of intelligent agents and surrogates. The extent to which agents and surrogates associated with group members (see Ellis *et al.*, 1991) play a role in real-time interaction may have a substantial effect on the character of the group: the 'presence' of some group members may be felt in the system's environment without their immediate participation. Agents may be associated with the group as a whole, as well as with individual group members (Oravec, 1996). Agents and their interactions with their principals (the extent of the roles the agents play, for example) may have a significant effect on the overall quality and character of group interaction.

SOME CONCLUSIONS AND REFLECTIONS

Many of the basic notions of group construction are apparently useful and applicable across the various vehicles and artifacts incorporated in group expression. These notions are now just emerging: for a number of decades, many social scientists, literary theorists, rhetoricians, and even human–computer interaction researchers considered the 'author' in an individualistic manner. Notions of 'group authorship' promise to add new dimensions to these analytic enterprises. In fact, a sort of combinatorial explosion can result as various kinds and levels of interactions among group members produce new planes for interpretation and exploration.

Why should we be interested in the character of the 'group' as a unit – why should we direct attention to it, as well as to the finished products associated with it? In the advent of such tools as hypertext, aspects of group 'process' have become tightly integrated in (if not inseparable from) the resulting 'product' of the group. Many kinds of written group products will be increasingly considered as 'products-in-transition', temporary focuses for group interaction (and vehicles for subsequent group expression and development) rather than polished and completed artifacts. Emerging group characters may also be important factors to consider when choosing leaders for a group. Effectiveness of various leadership styles may differ with group characters; for example, charisma may be critical in leading a spontaneous, real-time brainstorming session but other, less flamboyant styles may be more effective when detailed backstage planning and consensus building are required. Leadership styles may also have strong reflexive impacts on group character development and refinement.

The characters of the groups we are part of, we observe, and whose products we utilize play a role in the quality of our working and social lives. Designing systems that afford means to develop and sustain humane, involving, and creative group characters should be a major goal of system designers; user empowerment should be a major theme in this development (see Clement, 1993). Interesting and rich characters can help promote the user involvement in CSCW systems that Grudin (1989) has shown to be critical in their success. Many of these characters will emerge as the systems are utilized by individuals in real-life (rather than laboratory) settings, so designers should work closely with users in exploring the possibilities for such character development.

As more of our group-level interaction becomes computer-mediated, the narratives that groups construct will grow in importance; groups will need strong, sustaining, powerful stories to make sense out of the fragmentary and disjointed traces of group interaction they often receive. With the impending expansion of the number and kinds of computer- and non computer-supported groups we interact with, strong images and characters will help to keep the groups distinct for us and to make working life more manageable. The systems that groups utilize will play a role in shaping the narratives they construct and their voice or voices.

Many of the computer-based systems that enable group interaction (such as real-time writing tools) provide new forms of information about the group, both to group members and to outsiders. Outsiders (those constructed as 'readers' or 'audiences' for group-produced materials) can be afforded new dimensions as to group process, with their comprehension of the group's insights, creations, and discoveries enriched as a result. Rather than a limited and restricted set of stereotypical group characters, multidimensional group characters, voices, and narratives emerge – accounts that can serve to enhance our understanding of a group's products as well as the group itself.

REFERENCES

Aldridge, J. (1993) The textual disembodiment of knowledge about research account writing. *Sociology*, **27** (1), 53–66.

Baecker, R. (ed.) (1993) *Readings in Groupware and Computer-Supported Cooperative Work.* Morgan Kauffman, San Mateo, CA.

Barrett, E. (1988) Introduction: a new paradigm for writing with and for the computer. In Barrett, E. (ed.) *Text, ConText, and HyperText.* MIT Press, Cambridge, MA, pp. xiii–xxv.

Barrett, E. and Paradis, J. (1988) The on-line environment and in-house training. In Barrett, E. (ed.) *Text, ConText, and HyperText.* MIT Press, Cambridge, MA, pp. 227–250.

Bennett, G. (1983) 'Rocky the Police Dog' and other tales. *Lore and Language*, **3** (8), 1–19.

Clement, A. (1993) Cooperative support for computer work: a social perspective on the empowering of end users. In Baecker, R. (ed.), *Readings in Groupware and Computer-Supported Cooperative Work.* Morgan Kaufmann, San Mateo, CA, pp. 315–329.

Conklin, E. J. (1992) Capturing organizational memory. In Coleman, D. (ed.), *Proceedings of Groupware '92*, Morgan Kauffman, San Mateo, CA.

Danziger, K. (1990) *Constructing the Subject.* Cambridge University Press, New York.

Dickson, G. W., Lee, J. E., Robinson, L. and Heath, R (1989) Observations on GDSS interaction: chaffeured, facilitated, and user-driven systems. *Proceedings of the 22nd Annual Hawaii International Conference on System Sciences*, pp. 337–343.

Eisenberg, E. (1990) Jamming: transcendence through organizing. *Communication Research*, **17**, 139–164.

Ellis, C. A., Gibbs, S. J. and Rein, G. L. (1991) Groupware: some issues and experiences. *Communications of the ACM*, **34** (1), 39–58.

Fisher, W. R (1987) *Human communication as narration: toward a philosophy of reason, value and action.* University of South Carolina Press, Columbia, SC.

Fowler, R. (1977) *Linguistics and the Novel.* Methuen, London.

Fox, W. H. (1990) Anonymity and other keys to successful problem-solving meetings. *National Productivity Review*, **8** (2), 145–156.

Genette, G. (1980) *Narrative Discourse.* Cornell University Press, Ithaca, NY.

Gergen, K. J. and Gergen, M. M. (1986) Narrative form and the construction of psychological science. In Sarbin, T. R. (ed.) *Narrative Psychology: The Storied Nature of Human Conduct.* Praeger, New York.

Greenberg, S. (ed.) (1991) *Computer-Supported Cooperative Work and Groupware.* Harcourt Brace Jovanovich, San Diego, CA.

Grudin, J. (1989) Why groupware applications fail: problems in design and evaluation. *Office: Technology and People*, **4** (3), 245–264.

Landow, G. P. (1990) Hypertext and collaborative work. In Galegher, J., Kraut, R. E., and Egido, C. (eds) *Intellectual Teamwork.* Lawrence Erlbaum, Hillsdale, NJ, pp. 453–488.

MacIntyre, A. C. (1984) *After Virtue: A Study in Moral Theory* 2nd edition. University of Notre Dame Press, Notre Dame, IN.

Martin, J., Feldman, M. S., Hatch, M. J. and Sitkin, S. B. (1980) The uniqueness paradox in organizational stories. *Administrative Science Quarterly*, **28**, 438–453.

Middleton, D. and Edwards, D. (1990) *Collective Remembering*. Sage, London.
Minsky, M. (1986) *Society of Mind*. Simon and Schuster, New York.
Morrell, K. (1988) *Teaching with Hypercard*. Perseus Project Department of Classics, Working Paper 3. Harvard University, Cambridge, MA.
Mullen, B. and Hu, L. (1986) Group composition, the self, and religious experience. Cardiff, Wales, July: Paper presented to the British Psychological Society's *International Conference on Eastern Approaches to Self and Mind*.
Myers, D. (1987) Anonymity is part of the magic: individual manipulation of computer-mediated communication contexts. *Qualitative Sociology*, **10** (3), 251–226.
National Academy of Sciences (1993) *National Collaboratories: Applying Information Technology for Scientific Research*. National Academy Press, Washington, DC.
Nelson, T. (1987) All for one and one for all. *Hypertext 87*, pp. v–viii.
Neuwirth, C., Kaufer, D. S., Chandhok, R., and Morris, J. H. (1990) Issues in the design of computer support for co-authoring and commenting. In Baecker, R. (ed.) *Readings in Groupware and Computer-Supported Cooperative Work*. Morgan Kauffman, San Mateo, CA, pp. 537–549.
Oravec, J. (1993) Secret sharers: consensual and participatory surveillance in the context of network-based computer systems. *SIGOIS Bulletin*, **14** (1), 32–40.
Oravec, J. (1995) The camera never lies: construction of self and group in video, film, and photography. *Journal of Value Inquiry*, in press.
Oravec, J. (1996) *Virtual Individuals, Virtual Groups: Human Dimensions of Computer Networking*. Cambridge University Press, New York.
Peters, T. (1987) *Thriving on Chaos*. Alfred A. Knopf, New York.
Polanyi, L. (1985) *Telling the American Story*. Ablex Publishing Company, Norwood, NJ.
Rada, R, Keith, B., Burgoine, M., George, S. and Reid, D. (1989) Collaborative writing of text and hypertext. *Hypermedia*, **1** (2), 93–110.
Rein, G. L. and Ellis, C. A. (1991) rIBIS: A real-time group hypertext system. *International Journal of Human–Machine Studies*, **34** (3), 349–368.
Reither, J. A. and Vipond, D. (1989) Writing as collaboration. *College English*, **51** (8), 855–865.
Root, R. W. (1988) Design of a multi-media vehicle for social browsing. *Proceedings of CSCW-88*. ACM Press, New York, pp. 25–38.
Seybold, P. (1987) Collective force: tools for group productivity. *Computerworld*, **21** (48A), 35–48.
Shotter, J. (1986) Realism and relativism, rules and intentionality, theories and accounts: a response to Morse. *New Ideas in Psychology*, **4**, 71–84.
Slater, S. W. (1989) Computer support for the authoring of documents. *Information Media and Technology*, **23** (3), 109–111.
Smith, D. (1990) *The Conceptual Practices of Power*. Northeastern University Press, Boston, MA.
Smith, J. B., Weiss, D. F., and Ferguson, G. J. (1987) A hypertext writing environment and its cognitive basis. *Hypertext*, pp. 195–214.

Todorov, T. (1990) *Genres in Discourse.* Cambridge University Press, New York.

Toolan, M. J. (1988) *Narrative: A Critical Linguistic Introduction.* Routledge, London.

Turkle, S. (1984) *The Second Self.* Simon and Schuster, New York.

5 Coordination and Reuse

ROY RADA

INTRODUCTION

The history of life can be understood as an evolutionary process of copying with change and selection of the fit. More specifically, the history of culture can be seen as reuse of information and coordination of people. This viewpoint sees reuse as copying with change and selection of the fit as one aspect of coordination. New technology should be reusable and become effectively part of the coordinated work of people.

Reproduction with change and selection of the fit in uncertain environments only succeed when changes in the structure of entities corresponds in a clear and simple way to changes in function. Various levels of people plus technology system should somehow reflect a graceful structure–function relationship: the structure is readily changed to give new function. What is the structure of groupware such that variations in it map gracefully to various authoring functions?

This chapter describes with an evolutionary perspective some groupware systems developed by the author's research and development team. Only a few aspects of these groupware and authoring systems will be considered. The semantics of links in hypertext is addressed. Authors are allowed to write with various link types and to generate documents from the hypertext – do they benefit from a rich set of link types or not? Managerial questions about the authors in a university research team and a company are considered from the perspective of the management models that are stored in the information space and how people use them. Several systems, namely the Many Using and Creating Hypermedia system, the Open System for Collaborative Authoring and Reuse system, and the Reuse on the Web system, and experiences with them are presented.

EVOLUTIONARY FRAMEWORK

Authors create information for a purpose, and one such purpose is to disseminate information to others. On the basis of an evolution metaphor, a measure of success in disseminating information can be made precise. Success occurs

GROUPWARE AND AUTHORING
ISBN 0-12-575005-6

along two dimensions: the amount of information and the amount of time. Short-lived success occurs when information is widely disseminated but quickly disappears (see Figure 5.1). For example, the disk jockey who persuades a stadium full of people to dance may have a short-lived but large impact. A small, long-lived success occurs when information is seldom noticed but survives a long time. An illustration of this case might be the philosopher whose published work is referenced by one other person after many years but not noticed by other people. Successful messages are copied by others when they create their own messages (Garfield, 1979). For this reason, academicians may be evaluated by how frequently they are cited, or advertisers by how frequently customers use their product names.

What can be learned from biological evolution about criteria for successful information creation and dissemination? Successful evolutionary systems manifest gradualness. Gradualness means that a small change in structure results in a meaningful but small change in function. To illustrate the role of gradualness in evolution, imagine that an organism is described by a 1000-bit string. Furthermore, imagine that a marked improvement in fitness occurs when five particular bits are changed, but that no other set of bit changes improves fitness. When the probability of mutation in each bit is $10^{**}-3$, in the order of $10^{**}15$ trials are required to produce a new string of the desired fitness. On the other hand, if any of the five desired bit changes produces a string whose fitness is slightly greater than the fitness of the initial string, then only about $10^{**}3$ trials are required to obtain the significantly improved string (Rada, 1981).

The biological arguments are relevant to information technology. A software architectural description may have four different perspectives:

- *Functional*: what the system does, usually described in terms of a number of conceptually simple and distinct pieces of functionality.
- *Structural*: how the system is statically divided into a collection of interacting computational elements.

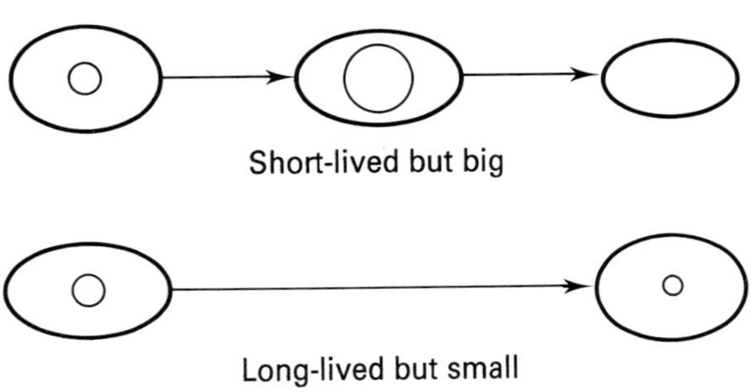

Figure 5.1 Growth in sets: the large ellipse is the World relative to which the analysis is being made. The circle is the local community whose success is being measured across time. In the top sequence the circle has grown quickly and then disappeared. In the bottom figure the circle has not changed in size over a long period of time.

- *Allocation*: how the pieces of functionality map onto the structure.
- *Coordination*: how computation evolves.

One sign of a mature domain is the emergence of a canonical functional partitioning. For example, in compiler design, the overall function of the system is broken into phases for lexical analysis, syntactic analysis, semantic analysis, and code generation. For groupware there is still the need to develop the canonical forms for each of the four different perspectives (Abowd, 1995). Studies in the evolution of software systems have shown the importance of certain structure–function relationships.

The Dexter Reference Model for hypertext (Halasz and Schwartz, 1990) has been extended to groupware (Gronbaek *et al.*, 1994) and to multimedia (Hardman *et al.*, 1994). These extended Dexter models could provide part of a description of a canonical structure and function for groupware authoring tools. These and many other architectural models of groupware systems leave much unspecified as regards coordinated authoring.

SEMANTICS OF LINKS

The principal groupware and authoring system that has been developed by this author's research team is called the Many Using and Creating Hypermedia (MUCH) system. The structure and function of the MUCH system relative to the semantics of its link types will be emphasized here.

Part of the MUCH system design is based on the Dexter model. A network of nodes and links is defined in a storage layer. A within-component layer contains the actual media content to which nodes point. The links and nodes form a semantic net.

A document can be generated by traversing the semantic net following a certain strategy (Min and Rada, 1994). The user can specify which type(s) of link the traversal program will follow. For example, one can generate a document with or without annotations by selecting or deselecting the annotation link types for the traversal program. The depth of the document can be specified, and the traversal program will not go deeper than this depth.

The first version of the MUCH system was built in 1985 on an IBM 4341 with SQL/DS. For a class in introductory information systems to graduate students at George Washington University, the draft textbook (Rada, 1989) was entered into the computer. The Table of Contents of the book was stored as a hierarchical semantic net and the text material between headings was stored in records in the database that were associated with the appropriate headings. Students were encouraged to edit the textbook. In particular they were asked to create new headings with new links, such as annotation links, and thus to create a kind of living text for the course as well as refine the book.

Students were asked to create hierarchical or non-hierarchical relations.

These relations were evaluated for their clarity and utility. Hierarchical relations proved more commonly used and more often of high quality. Others have done such exercises with other technology and other emphases. Collaborative augmentation of documents by students has been explored by various groups at Brown University with the Intermedia system (Landow, 1990). The semantics of the link types have not been carefully assessed elsewhere.

The 1988 version of the MUCH system worked on a network of Unix workstations. The system used Emacs utilities on a file store that was writeable and readable to all users; authors were expected to create a semantic net and to attach text to the links of the semantic net. A book was successfully authored on this version of the MUCH system (Rada, 1991). Authors, however, had difficulty distinguishing the semantics of the link types and dealing with the network structure. The system included utilities to generate documents by traversals of the network. Authors could work with paper generated in a consistent way from the hypertext version and gradually de-emphasized the role of link types for anything but rendering a hierarchical document structure (Rada, 1990).

Users wanted a semantic hierarchy that they could easily manipulate. In the 1990 version of the MUCH system, the information is presented on two separate windows with a fold-unfold outline in one window and the content of a selected node in another. When the user selects a node in the fold-unfold outline, the associated content appears in the content window. Although on the interface the logical network is presented as a tree, the data in the logical

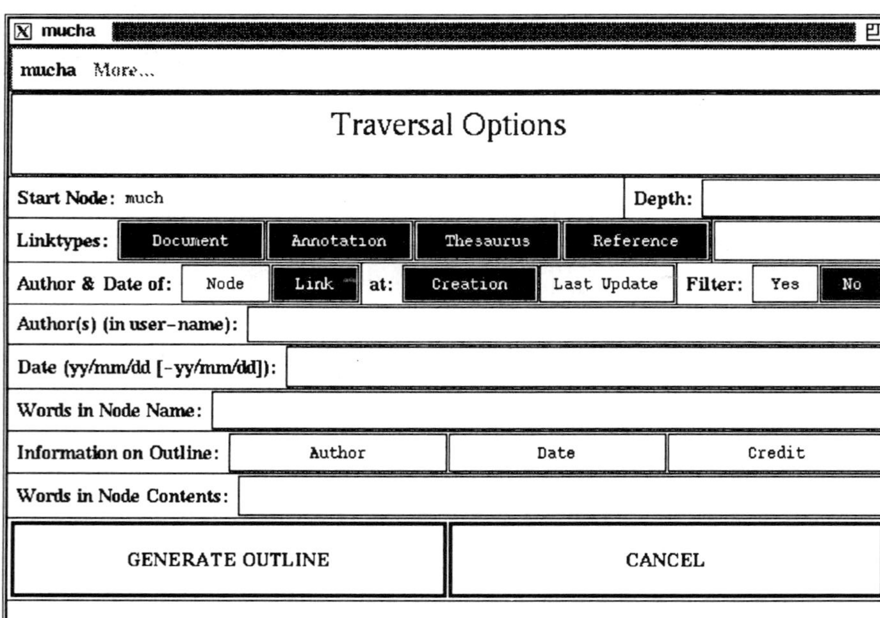

Figure 5.2 Traversal Dialog Box: with the traversal option dialog box the user specifies features of the traversal that the MUCH system will execute.

network is truly an unrestricted network rather than a tree. The outline on the hierarchical browser (outline window) is only a specific view of (a part of) the logical network. To enable users to follow the links that are not shown in the outline, a network browser is also provided. The traversal program is accessed from a dialog box (see Figure 5.2).

The semantic net access to the hypertext is powerful in some ways and weak in others. Thus, a function to exploit the structure within a node's content was added. A word index is automatically maintained as authoring occurs. The MUCH system provides a word index window on which all words in the database are listed; once a word is selected, the occurrences of the selected word are shown on the outline window as a number in front of the node including that word (see Figure 5.3). In fact, the occurrence number appears at not only the node including the selected word but also its ancestors in order that one can easily find the node of interest when it is folded under a high level node. However, the number shown at the ancestor node is the occurrences in the whole sub-tree. This fold-unfold view of word distribution has proven valuable in searching tasks (Egan *et al.*, 1989; Chen *et al.*, 1994).

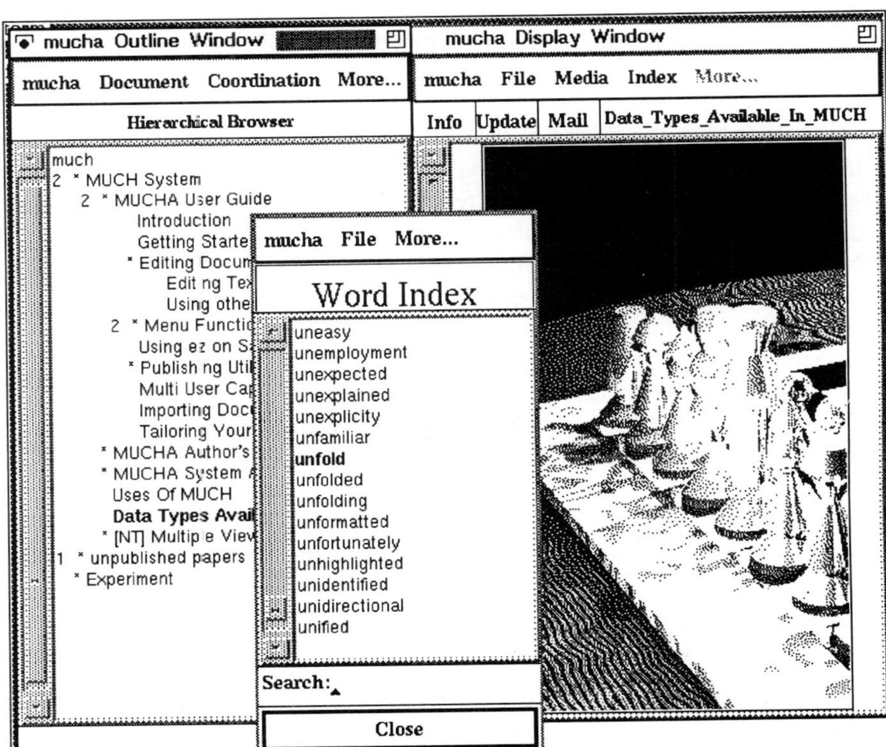

Figure 5.3 Word Index: word index utility in the MUCH system to help users find information. Once a word is selected, the occurrences of the selected word are shown on the outline window as a number in front of the node including that word.

The MUCH system has been used by over 300 people during a seven-year period. Applications have included the collaborative authoring of textbooks, collaborative learning in classrooms, and management of research publications. In the three-year period between 1991 and 1994 over 200 people used the system and created 11 151 links. Of these links, 10 806 were of the default hierarchical type, called 'document link', and 278 links were of the 'comment' type (Wang and Rada, 1995).

MANAGING PEOPLE

Large research projects within a university depend on external sources for funds (Iya and Akhilesh, 1992). The MUCH project was richly funded by external sources and grew from a group to an organization in a rather short time, by passing through several stages. An electronic planning document reflecting the visions, objectives, and activities was introduced into the MUCH system to support this growth (Deakin *et al.*, 1994).

The rapid growth of the project generated the need to induct and supervise new staff. The traditional communication modes (face-to-face meetings and email interaction) between the research professor and the research workers that had been used previously were no longer sufficient to cope with the number of people and range of activities. As the project grew to 30 people, a hierarchical administration was instituted.

In a research group that is aimed at producing quality journal papers, a researcher's performance is mainly reflected in the number of journal papers published. One of management's objectives is to raise the productivity of paper production. While the process of paper production consists of many stages, hypothesis formulation and paper revision are here treated as the key stages for the attention of research management.

The management information requirements for the hypothesis formulation and refinement stages include:

- knowledge of all hypotheses the group has worked on and is currently working on, and
- awareness of the background literature.

Management can enhance the revision process by coordinating the (often collaborative) authorship, selecting appropriate journals and internal reviewers, and allocating resources for the paper submission. The management information requirements for this stage include:

- awareness of the appropriate journals as well as of the special characteristics of each journal in each area,
- knowledge of successful author collaborations and reviewer collaborations,
- historical records of the submission and publication of the team in each journal, and
- the current progress on paper writing and revision.

The management information needs regarding paper production could not be fully met by manual information systems alone in view of the volume and changeability of the information (Deakin *et al.*, 1994). Accordingly, it was decided to explore the feasibility of meeting the information needs through the support of the MUCH System.

A 'Hypotheses & Paper' information subspace was created within the MUCH information space. A network browser displays the incoming and outgoing links to any node of interest. Navigation takes the place of query formulation, although specific queries can be additionally formulated by using the word search facility. As well as accessing information by reading a node, users may obtain different views of the information through folding/unfolding nodes, as follows (see Figure 5.4):

- *People's view*: the list of hypotheses and the list of papers related to each researcher.
- *Group view*: the list of hypotheses and the list of papers related to each group.
- *Area view*: hypotheses are classified into areas of research and the list of hypotheses by area can be obtained.
- *Journal view*: papers previously published in a journal or currently targeted for a journal can be listed by journal.
- *Status view*: papers have five statuses – published, rejected, accepted,

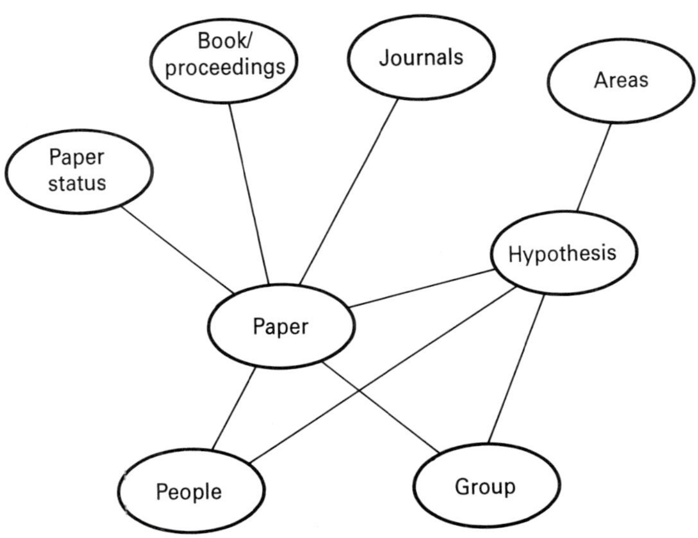

Figure 5.4 Hypotheses & Paper: the Outline Window shows the current unfolded logical structure of the system with 'in preparation' taken as the current node. Correspondingly, the Network Browser shows the nodes linked to the current node. One of these nodes has been visited. Its content, a 'Schedule Node' for the paper, is displayed in the Display Window.

submitted and in preparation. The list of papers in each status can be obtained.

After the database had been in use for three months, data were collected by questionnaire and through a facility in the MUCH system that records author credits.

The questionnaire was distributed to all members of the MUCH project; eleven replies were received. The response to the question as to whether members found the database closely related to their work resulted in two positive, three neutral, and six negative replies. When classified by member 'status', responses to this and other questions indicated that the project head and two of the middle managers found the information helpful in their managerial and paper production work.

Access data was analysed to compare access to the 'Hypotheses & Paper' information with access to other parts of the management information space. The access measurement is based on author credits. A credit is recorded under an author's name each time a node is accessed (by a member other than the author of the node). From the results of the questionnaire, the managers, rather than the ordinary (non-management) members, are the main readers of the Hypotheses & Paper information.

The Hypotheses and Paper information was expected to be useful to line staff when it was designed. However, the questionnaire responses indicated that ordinary members of the group did not feel the information was closely related to their work and they were not motivated to use it. One reason for the divergence seems to be that even though the information was expected to be helpful to researchers by providing a rich context for generating ideas and formulating hypotheses by reference to other hypotheses, communication through face-to-face discussion is perceived by researchers to be a more appropriate approach to paper production than, for example, accessing the information in the MUCH system.

REUSE AND AUTHORING MODELS

The MUCH system was successfully used to author and publish three books through the kind of management information support described for the journal article authoring. In the case of the book, large amounts of information from project internal reports was considered reusable and teams of temporary staff worked on initial drafts. Small teams of research staff writing journal papers may benefit from groupware but these people have a task in which email communication or face-to-face meeting is perhaps adequate. Large-scale authoring projects in which reuse of information is vital are more likely to lend themselves to being supported by tools for coordinated authoring. For such large applications, models of reuse and of human organizations are particularly germane.

Diverting resources, both human and financial, into building a base of reusable information has a number of organizational implications, including team structures and cost imputations. In addition to the typical project team structure of information organizations, a reuse library team is needed (Agresti, 1986). Minimally, the library team would be responsible for what gets added to the reuse library (Prieto-Diaz and Freeman, 1987). The librarians may work closely with the project teams that develop information as those project teams both use material from the library and contribute new material to the library.

One framework for reuse consists of dual, interconnected functions called *reuse management* and *reuse engineering* (see Figure 5.5). The framework is generic with respect to domains, organizations and technologies. Framework concepts should generally be applicable to reuse in any information-intensive context (Boeing Company, 1993). Reuse management focuses on people and describes a cyclical pattern of planning, enacting, and learning.

Reuse planning encompasses both strategic planning and tactical, project-oriented planning within a reuse program. Planning includes assessment, domain selection, and project planning. Assessment characterizes the current state of reuse practice within an organization, the readiness of the organization as a whole for practicing reuse, and the reuse technology and expertise available. A first step in domain selection is to identify and characterize promising candidate domains, based on the organization's business interests and key areas of expertise. The final stage of project planning is to plan the reuse project's resource needs, budgets and schedules in detail and then obtain the necessary commitment to implement the plans.

Reuse enactment addresses initiation, performance, and retirement of the various reuse-related plans. The goal of *reuse learning* is to enhance the per-

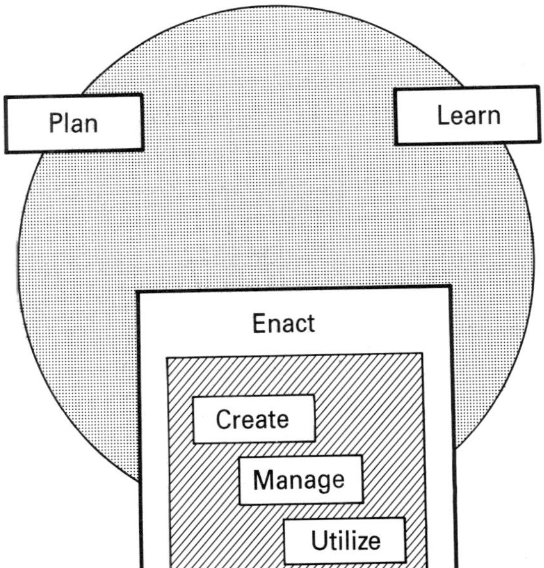

Figure 5.5 Reuse Management and Reuse Engineering: Plan, Enact, and Learn are in the Management idiom. Create, Manage and Utilize are in the Engineering idiom.

formance of a reuse program. The results of reuse learning are fed back to reuse planning in the form of recommendations for the next reuse program cycle.

Reuse engineering addresses the creation, management, and utilization of reusable assets. Asset creation can be viewed as consisting of domain modeling and asset implementation. The goal of *asset implementation* is to produce the assets in the asset base. This could be done by creating the assets from scratch with guidance from the domain models as to what kinds of components should be developed. Alternately, a company may require that its information developers provide whatever information they develop to the reuse librarians so that it can be considered for incorporation into the library. *Asset Management* includes acquiring, installing and evaluating individual assets in a library, and developing and operating libraries that house collections of assets, provide access to those assets, and support their utilization.

The goal of *asset utilization* is to construct new application products using previously developed assets. Asset utilization generally involves determining a set of criteria to use in selecting assets for reuse, identifying suitable candidate assets in the context of those criteria, selecting and tailoring assets to meet the criteria, and integrating the tailored assets with the target application.

For serious corporate work on authoring, reuse may be critical. To support the library and authoring functions of large-scale document production in organizations, a language for modeling organizations is useful (Smith *et al.*, 1989). Two categories of structures and functions with two categories within each are of value:

- Structures
  - workspaces
  - messages
- Functions
  - activities
  - roles

People are associated with roles. Roles define responsibilities that are taken by one or more people.

A workspace is a conceptual work area that contains resources associated with a particular role. Multiple role instances may be associated with a workspace. The workspace also contains message handling resources.

A company that makes interactive media for training purposes could benefit from information technology support in many aspects of its work. One phase of the development cycle is the *evaluation* phase. This evaluation is critical to improving the effectiveness of the product (Figure 5.6). Three messages are involved in this activity:

- storyboarding production forms,
- partially revised storyboarding production forms, and
- definitive revised storyboarding production forms.

The subject matter expert, the designer, the communication expert, and the

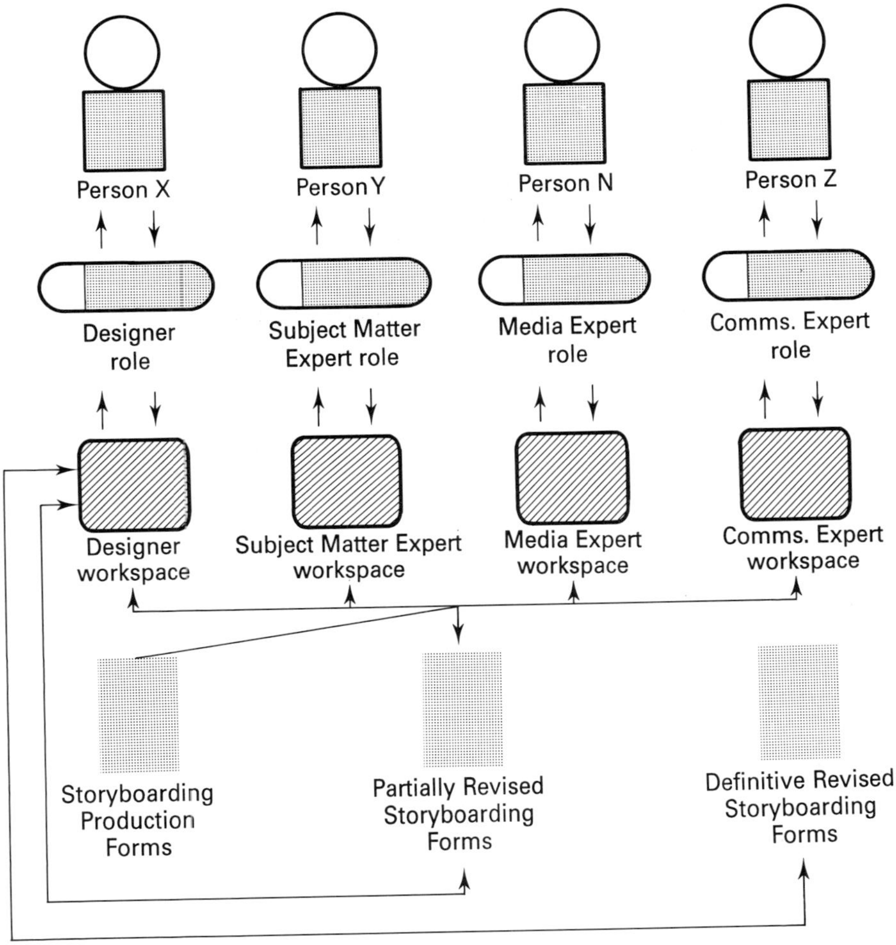

Figure 5.6 Evaluation: the story-board is evaluated by several roles.

media expert are the four roles which process the three messages as they conduct a quality review and do a pilot test.

OSCAR

A training division of a large, Italian, aerospace manufacturing company, called Augusta, has produced a particularly sophisticated prototype courseware reuse system. The system is called the Open System for Collaborative Authoring and Reuse of Courseware (OSCAR) (Chen and Rada, 1994). The OSCAR architecture above the operating system includes (Figure 5.7):

- *Communication space*: provides services supporting the distribution of the system and the network management.

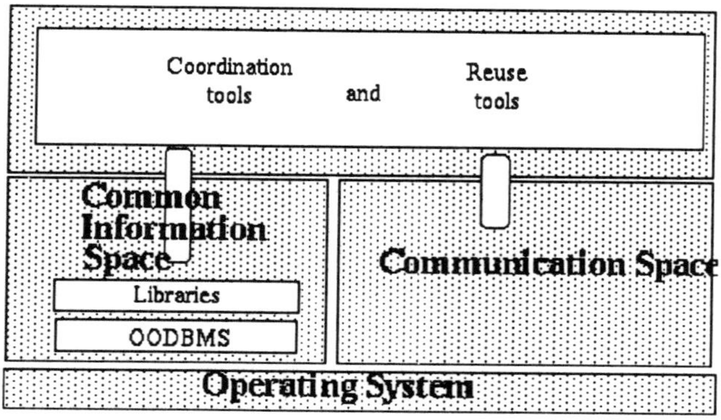

Figure 5.7 The OSCAR layers: the OSCAR Architecture above the operating system includes the Common Information Space, the Communication Space, and Coordination and Reuse tools. OODBMS means object-oriented database management system, and for OSCAR the OODBMS is Object Store from Object Design Incorporated.

- *Common information space*: supplies information management services relevant to the library and authoring functions and uses an object-oriented database management system.
- *Coordination and reuse tools*: these tools provide high-level services to support coordination and reuse.

The OSCAR Common Information Space (CIS) includes ‘instructional objects’ each of which has an ‘instructional component’ and a ‘presentational component’. The Instructional Component includes objects derived from a domain analysis and includes also pedagogical attributes, such as targeted student backgrounds and teaching techniques. The Presentational Component includes the presentation of the actual learning material to the user and addresses such features as screen layout (Persico *et al.*, 1992).

The reuse tools support both the retrievability and the customization of training material. Users can specify desired assets by selecting portions of a semantic network and the system will retrieve appropriate assets. Other functionalities offered by the reuse tools include conversion tools to reuse material originally available in a format different from the desired one.

The OSCAR system was implemented according to corporate requirements of library reuse and collaborative authoring. The cost of building the OSCAR system exceeded US $3 million. Staff at Augusta have developed a library of reusable components and experimented with the utility of the authoring facilities. The management at Augusta is convinced that a system such as OSCAR could be useful in streamlining courseware development. One of the developers of the OSCAR system, Tecnopolis Csata Novus Ortus in Bari, Italy, is actively using the system for team authoring of multimedia courseware.

The structure and function of the OSCAR system are reasonably well defined. Function is allocated to structure in a systematic way that facilitates coordination both of the software components and of the human users. The problem is that the OSCAR system is large and expensive and does not easily fit as part of the users' everyday work space. Extensive work with other systems has suggested that a new functionality (in this case coordination or reuse) should fit smoothly into the workflow of users in order to be accepted. A major study of reuse at IBM concluded that fingertip reuse was the key to success – people had to find that the reuse functionality could be found only a fingertip from where they needed to find the other functions that they routinely exercised on the computer (Wasmund, 1993).

For instance, a tool which was affiliated with Microsoft Word for Windows™ might be seen to fit easily into the workflow of people who already spend much of their day in front of Word for Windows. In this regard, the most popular tool today for something akin to groupware for authoring is the World Wide Web (WWW). While Lotus Notes™ is very successful in many ways it has not the degree of usage that the WWW has. In part this is because use of the WWW is free to people on the Internet.

REUSE ON THE WEB

An assignment gave a class of senior-level students the opportunity to work together as small companies. The end goal of each company was to link together about 600 megabytes of WWW information into a coherent theme for subsequent publication on CD-ROM. Electronic information was identified and collected by one group in the company and then adapted to be used 'locally' by another group in the same company. The hypothesis was that coordination of people and reuse of information could occur effectively through the WWW. From the class of 60 students, 4 companies of 15 people each were formed. The students spent 10 hours a week for 3 weeks on the project. Each company had three groups:

- management
- librarian
- authoring.

The company management needed to assign tasks and monitor progress so that the assignment was completed to schedule and specification. The final mark for each student was broken into three equal parts: individual report, peer–peer assessment, and final company product.

Although the students were given careful instruction in the use of the MUCH system and encouraged to use it for storing information that would help them coordinate their work, in reality students did not use the MUCH system for this assignment. Instead they found creative uses of the WWW to support coordination. As the librarians found items on the WWW, they needed to collect pointers to the relevant information and share these pointers with the other librarians and the authors. No instruction in how to do this was given to the students but most used the hotlist functions of Mosaic and Netscape and e-mailed those hotlists from person to person.

Each company made a WWW home page on which the overall structure of their information product was given. Without any guidance from the instructors, the drafts of these WWW home pages were also used by the students to store dynamic information about the progress of a company and to guide the work of the members of the company throughout the project (see Figure 5.8).

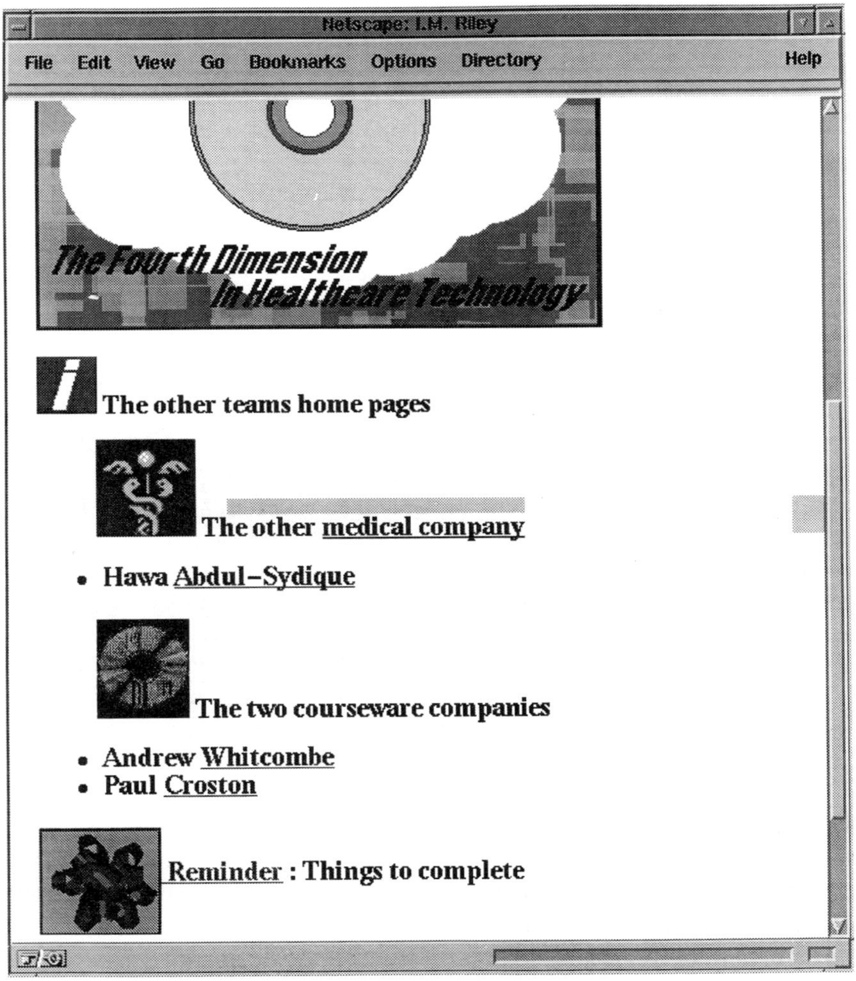

Figure 5.8 Things to complete: these two windows from the WWW information of the student company which called itself 'The Fourth Dimension of Health Care Technology' show on the left an icon for 'Reminder: Things to complete' and on the right the result of selecting this icon. The window on the right shows requests from the leader of the company for reports from company members.

Figure 5.8 *(continued)*

Each author tended to store the information he or she created for the WWW product in his or her own directory. Through e-mail and face-to-face communication, agreement was reached as to who should put a link in his or her file to another student's file. Eventually, the entire product was linked in this way. Many of the students reported that the experience was rewarding and fun.

The students taught themselves how to use the WWW and found it to be an effective information space for company communication. E-mail and face-to-face meetings remained very important, but the WWW was surprisingly flexible. Extensions of the classroom work have taken place and have led to results consistent with those of the classroom. The WWW is an attractive vehicle for coordination when augmented with other communication and decision-making media. Also, information on the WWW can be effectively reused.

CONCLUSION

Architectural issues for groupware for authoring typically include centralized databases versus distributed databases and synchronous versus asynchronous communication. This paper has looked instead at issues of structure and function as they relate to coordination and reuse. At the same time, a very specific history of some systems developed by the author's research team has been provided to illustrate a few structure and function relationships.

Groupware can provide a logical infrastructure to the documents that are being authored and that both the people and the machine can manipulate. The semantic net has limited computational features but can support traversals to generate different kinds of documents. The experiences related in this chapter suggest that the usage of unrestricted link types in these semantic nets does not facilitate collaborative authoring. Authors seemed particularly fond of hierarchical, document relations and not much else.

If the collaborative authoring system is viewed largely as a shared information space, then storing managerial information on it might facilitate collaborative authoring in a way that bulletin boards and local administrative libraries might. To this end, a 'hypothesis and papers' information network was placed in the MUCH system to support management of journal article authoring. The managers found the information useful but the line staff that were expected to maintain the information found it unhelpful. A suggestion for future work of this kind would be to have managerial support staff maintain the managerial information rather than expect line staff to do so.

Long experience with groupware to support collaborative authoring has suggested that for small projects, simple tools are enough. The challenge is largely one of human–human coordination with tools being provided to communicate and share information. For large-scale projects which may involve hundreds of people authoring and revising documents over years, sophisticated coordination and reuse tools are more likely to be valuable. The structure and function which such tools might usefully have is suggested by the results of the OSCAR project. In the OSCAR project the organizational model is based on careful requirements gained from the end-user corporation, and an object-oriented database management system is used to store both sophisticated product information and corporate information. With an artificial intelligence slant, one can want organizational manuals installed on the computer which will be so precise that not only can they capture what happens in the organization for human consumption, but the computer can occasionally play an active and intelligent role by performing some of the tasks otherwise entrusted to people.

To fit groupware into the workflow of an organization requires more than anything else a keenly focused and consistently managed human organization. To this end the author proposes that a particularly attractive direction for exploration of groupware and authoring is the use of the World Wide Web. The WWW is widely available and has many public domain tools that support various aspects of the authoring process.

REFERENCES

Abowd, G. (1995) Defining reference models and software architectural styles for cooperative systems. *SIGOIS Bulletin*, **15** (3), 4–5.

Agresti, W. (1986) Framework for a flexible development process in *New Paradigms for Software Development*, Agresti, W. (ed.), IEEE, New York, pp. 11–14.

Boeing Company, IBM Federal Systems Company, and Unisys Corporation (1993) *STARS Conceptual Framework for Reuse Processes (CFRP), Volume 1: Definition, Version 3.0*, United States Air Force, Hanscom Air Force Base, Massachusetts, October 25.

Chen, C., Rada, R. and Zeb, A. (1994) An extended fisheye view browser for collaborative writing. *International Journal of Human–Computer Studies*, **40**, 859–878.

Chen, C. and Rada, R. (1994) A conceptual model for supporting collaborative authoring and reuse. *Knowledge Organization*, **21** (2), 88–93.

Deakin, A. G., Gouma, P. I. and Rada, R. (1994) The plan-facilitator and the plan-document: a new aspect of computer supported management. *Intelligent Systems*, **4** (1–2), 83–111.

Egan, D. E., Remde, J. R., Gomez, L. M., Landauer, T. K., Eberhardt, J. and Lochbaum, C. C. (1989) Formative design-evaluation of 'SuperBook'. *ACM Transactions of Information Systems*, **7** 30–57.

Garfield, E. (1979) *Citation Indexing: Its Theory and Applications in Science, Technology, and Humanities*, John Wiley and Sons, New York.

Gronbaek, K., Hem, J. A., Madsen, O. L. and Sloth, L. (1994) Cooperative hypermedia systems: a Dexter-based architecture. *Communications of the ACM*, **37** (2), 65–74.

Halasz, F. and Schwartz, M. (1990) The Dexter hypertext reference model, *Proceedings of the Hypertext Standardization Workshop*, US Government Printing Office, Washington, DC, pp. 95–134.

Hardman, L., Bulterman, R. C. A. and van Rossum, G. (1994) The Amsterdam hypermedia model: adding time and context to the Dexter model. *Communications of the ACM*, **37** (2), 50–62.

Iya, S. and Akhilesh, K. B. (1992) Technology as perceived by R&D team leaders: an analysis. *R&D Management*, **22** (3), 265–276.

Landow, G. P. (1990) Hypertext and collaborative work: The example of Intermedia in *Intellectual Teamwork: Social Foundations of Cooperative Work*, Galegher, J., Kraut, R. E., Egido, C. (eds), Lawrence Erlbaum Associates, Hillsdale, New Jersey, pp. 407–428.

Min, Z. and Rada, R. (1994) MUCH electronic publishing environment – principles and practices. *Journal American Society Information Science*, **45** (5), 300–309.

Persico, D., Sarti, L. and Viarengo, V. (1992) Browsing a database of multimedia learning material. *Interactive Learning International*, **8**, 213–235.

Prieto-Diaz, R. and Freeman, P. (1987) Classifying Software for Reusability, *IEEE Software*, January 6–16.

Smith, H. T., Hannessy, P. A. and Lunt, G. A. (1989) The activity model environment: An object-oriented framework for describing organisation communication. *Proceedings of the 1st European Conference on Computer-Supported Cooperative Work*, Computer Sciences House, Slough, UK, pp. 160–172.

Rada, R. (1981) Evolution and Gradualness. *BioSystems*, No. 14, pp. 211–218.

Rada, R. (1989) Guidelines for multiple users creating hypertext: SQL and HyperCard experiments, in *Computers and Writing: Models and Tools*, Holt, P. and Williams, N. (eds), Blackwell/Ablex Publishing, pp. 61–89.

Rada, R. (1990) Hypertext writing and document reuse: the role of a semantic net. *J. Electronic Publishing*, **3** (3), 3–18.

Rada, R. (1991) *Hypertext: from Text to Expertext*, McGraw-Hill, London.

Wasmund, M. (1993) Implementing critical success factors in software reuse. *IBM Systems Journal*, **32** (4), 595–611.

Wang, W. and Rada, R. (1995) Experiences with semantic net based hypermedia. *International Journal of Human–Computer Studies*, **13**, 419–439.

Part 2

Studying Users

6 The Effectiveness of Simple Shared Electronic Workspaces

GARY M. OLSON and JUDITH S. OLSON

INTRODUCTION

We have been studying how shared electronic workspaces can support the synchronous work of small task-oriented groups. While we know that collaborative work involves many different kinds of work situations, we feel that the synchronous case is of sufficient practical importance and theoretical interest to warrant this focus. We have concentrated on the kinds of work done in meetings, including both traditional face-to-face meetings and distributed meetings made possible by computational and communication technology.

Our research strategy begins by understanding group work in the field (Olson and Olson, 1991; Olson *et al.*, 1992a) where we get a broad appreciation for the flow of activity in real meetings within the actual organizational setting. This field work allows us to note important baseline features of group work and gives us ideas about how various kinds of technology can help. We then move to the laboratory to study specific phenomena, such as how technologies change the flow of activities in meetings or affect the quality of the work. From these laboratory studies, we move back to the field, assessing the use of these new technologies in the full organizational context. This strategy has the benefit that we are informed by actual practice and can test ideas eventually in the field, but also puts the burden on us to construct laboratory situations that mirror the field in important ways. In this chapter we report on two aspects of our work, the design of a simple electronic workspace and an evaluation of its effectiveness for face-to-face groups.

BUILDING A SIMPLE SHARED WORKSPACE: SHREDIT

In our field studies of group work we noticed a number of difficulties that we thought might be helped by having a shared, editable workspace in which to record and organize their ideas. We saw that the individual notes that members of a group took during a meeting were often inconsistent; for example, different people concluded that they had decided to eliminate a different

GROUPWARE AND AUTHORING
ISBN 0-12-575005-6

architectural component, a misunderstanding that would be discovered eventually, but at some cost. We also noted occasions when discussion stopped because the whiteboard was full. In addition, typically, only one person ever wrote on the whiteboard, and lots of things were said that never got written down.

On the basis of these ideas we developed a shared editor called ShrEdit (see McGuffin and Olson, 1992, for specific details about ShrEdit; and Olson *et al.*, 1990; Olson and Olson, 1991; Dourish and Bellotti, 1992; and Olson *et al.*, 1993, for general discussions of the design space of such tools). ShrEdit is a shared text editor that runs on Macintoshes on a LAN. Although sketching and diagrams are often important to group work, we also knew the text alone could be useful. Since the tasks that we used in our evaluation – both the field groups that gave us baseline data and the laboratory group used for evaluation – asked for lists, paragraphs and outlines at best, we thought that a text-based system would be sufficient for an initial exploration into the design of groupware systems.

Figure 6.1 shows a screen dump from a typical ShrEdit session. ShrEdit has no theoretical limit on the number of users, but in reality it works best for

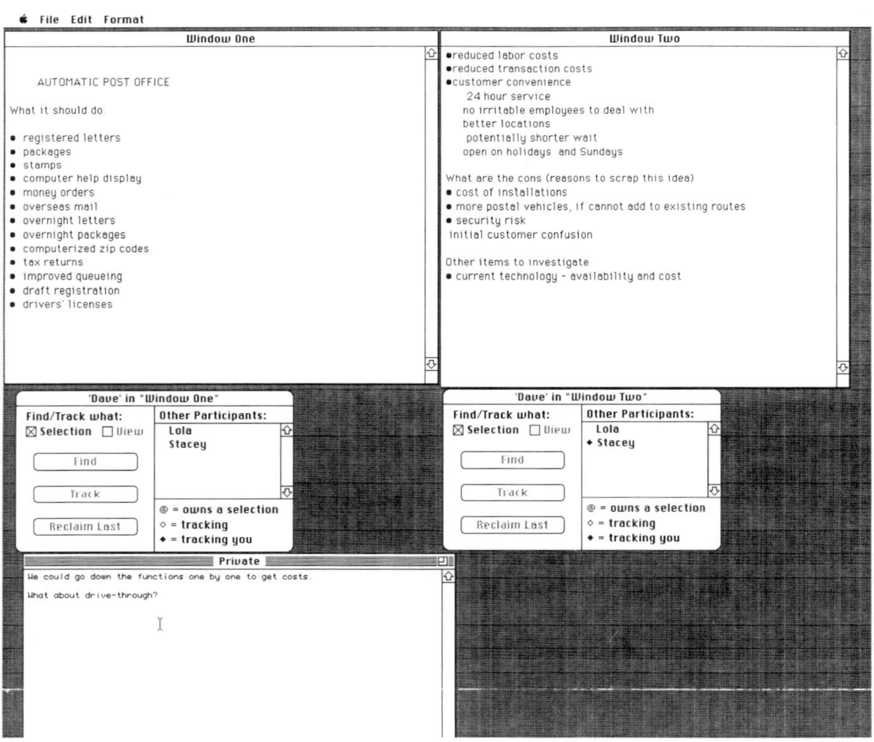

Figure 6.1 A ShrEdit screen dump.

groups up to about seven or eight. A number of shared windows can be opened to create separate but shared workspaces (although in practice performance degrades significantly when there are more than three shared windows). Each person can also have a private window. The editor is a vanilla Macintosh one, with only the most basic functions. In the shared window, anyone can type anywhere. Concurrency control is handled through selection locking. No one can edit within someone else's selection, though it is possible to copy from another selection. Although the individuals' views of the document are normally independent (each can scroll to a different part of the document or arrange the windows on the screen in a unique way), the views can also be locked together ('WYSIWIS', Stefik *et al.*, 1987) through the use of Find or Track.

The windows at the bottom in Figure 6.1, called 'status windows', are for coordination. Everyone else who is currently participating in the session is listed. The functions, Find and Track, allow users to locate where others are working, and there are indicators by each person's name as to whether they are working in that window and whether or not they are tracking someone. There is a status window for each shared window that is open.

ShrEdit was built with a client-server architecture to simplify its development and early use. The server runs on a different machine than any of the clients. People can join and leave a session whenever they like, as long as the server is running.

We assume that ShrEdit is always used in conjunction with other communication channels. ShrEdit provides no direct support for Chat or Talk style functions. (There was one occasion when by fluke the audio went out in one of our distributed trials and the group members merely continued their work by making one of the shared windows serve as a chat window. Though there was no explicit support for chat, the flexibility of the shared space made this function possible.)

Here we review groups working in face-to-face settings like that shown in Figure 6.2, where each person has access to the shared workspace in ShrEdit via their own computer built into special desks called ELMERs (Olson *et al.*, 1992b) and talk freely. But of course, this can also be used in a distributed setting, where the groups have voice or video communication (Olson *et al.*, 1995).

AN EMPIRICAL STUDY OF SIMPLE SHARED WORKSPACES

To evaluate how group work changes when people have a simple group editor like ShrEdit, we examined the meetings of 38 groups of people, half of whom were given ShrEdit, half conventional tools like paper and whiteboards. We analyzed their moment-by-moment talking and typing to study the *process* of group work. Since they were doing a standard task, we could compare the quality of the *outcome* of their work both across groups and across conditions. And through questionnaires we measured their *satisfaction* with their work

Figure 6.2 A group working in a Collaboration Technology Suite.

Method

Subjects

Thirty-eight existing groups of three professionals served as subjects. In all groups, the members had worked together before and all knew at least one Macintosh application.

Setting

The group members were seated in a meeting room called the Collaboration Technology Suite (CTS) shown in Figure 6.2 in which workstation units make up a conference table, with the monitors recessed in the table top so as not to interfere with normal eye contact. One wall of the room has two large panels of whiteboard, which all groups were allowed to use.

The task

We chose to study the task of group design, that of early requirements definition, because it is both important and interesting. The early or upstream stages of design are probably the most important in the development of useful, usable, maintainable software (Dunn, 1984; Curtis *et al.*, 1988). In terms of McGrath's (1984) task taxonomy, this activity is a blend of planning, creativity, decision-making and cognitive conflict. In terms of Steiner's categorization (Steiner, 1972), this is a unitary task, in that the contributions of group members must be combined; one person could probably accomplish the task but if others contribute, their input is blended with that of the rest, not just tacked on.

In this study, all groups were instructed to draft the initial requirements definition for an Automatic Post Office (APO), a collection of postal services offered through a stand-alone device similar to an ATM for which a prototype could be built by their fictitious company of 30 people in a year (adapted from Goel and Pirolli, 1989). They were instructed to determine the core services they would offer, how it would work, some of the required equipment, the rough cost/benefit analysis, and a list of things they would like to investigate before the next time they would (hypothetically) meet. They were given 1½ hours to complete the assignment, producing meeting notes that could be read by a (fictitious) additional group member who could not attend that day's meeting.

Procedure

The subjects came to the CTS for a single three-hour period, broken into two 1½ hour portions with a 15-minute break in-between. In the first half, the subjects filled out background questionnaires and permission forms, and solved two small problems. These tasks served both to allow the subjects to warm up to the task situation and, for those in the supported condition, to learn the software and adjust to the software's capability for simultaneous editing. Those taught the technology were instructed in a 20-minute period before the two small problems. The instructions demonstrated the system's capabilities and how to control them, but did not prescribe how to use these features to support work. Those in the control condition were encouraged to use paper and pencil or whiteboard as is natural for their group. Following a 15-minute break, the groups did the APO task in a single 1½-hour sitting. All groups filled out the questionnaire on satisfaction after the session. The unsupported groups were taught the software and given a 10-minute group task after the questionnaire. (Since all groups were recruited with the same 'pitch' about testing technology to support group work, we felt obliged to fulfil the promise, even for the unsupported groups. Since the unsupported group started the practice tasks and APO without taking time to learn ShrEdit, we filled in their time at the end of the three hours with ShrEdit training and a small brainstorming task.)

Study design

Groups were recruited en masse through various MBA classes, and encouraged to sign up at convenient times, either morning, afternoon, or evening sessions for three hours. The groups were assigned to conditions at random as they came in with the proviso that at the end of each week the conditions were balanced for time of day.

Measures

Our goal was to assess three things: the quality of the product, the participants' satisfaction with the process, and the process of design and coordination. Most studies of technology support of group work focus on the first two variables here; we are looking at both those and the process that underlies the outcome.

Outcome

We assessed how the technology affected the outcomes of the meetings, the quality of the written design as reflected in the final document of each group. In order to allow fair comparisons, the unsupported groups' written outputs were typed in the same style as the supported groups' output.

We developed a quality measure after extensive discussion with both designers and researchers of design. Three major aspects of the groups' output were scored: whether the output covered all the aspects of the assigned task, the ease of understanding of the ideas reported in the document, and the judged practicability and marketability of the post office design. This measure has a possible range of values from 0–80; our inter-rater reliability is 0.85, well above acceptable. One researcher coded the quality of all 38 meetings using the same instrument. The range of actual values was 25–78.

Satisfaction

To assess satisfaction, we constructed a post-session questionnaire that asked the participants to (a) rate their satisfaction with the process that they used (adapted from Gouran *et al.*, 1978; Green and Taber, 1980) as well as with the design result (Green and Taber, 1980); (b) assess the evenness of the participants' contributions (Green and Taber, 1980) and (c) identify a leader if one emerged.

Process

The transcripts of the meetings were coded for what kinds of activity were taking place at each moment, using the categories devised and tested in our study of field design meetings (Olson *et al.*, 1992a). The measures of group interaction focus on various key aspects of activity related to design itself (with origins in the Design Rationale literature; see Moran and Carroll, in press). In particular, we separated statements of the *issues* at hand, the *alternatives* or solutions raised, and the various *criteria* brought to bear on that idea. We also catalogued the time it took the group to organize themselves (activities we call *meeting management*, *project management*, *summary* and *walkthrough*), to *clarify* their ideas, or engage in side *digressions*.

One additional category was required to account for the work surrounding producing the output: time when the group would plan the organization and wording of the final document or dictate the words, called *plan and write*. In the supported groups, we required yet another two categories: time when they were confused about something having to do with the technology, and other comments about the placing their work into the windows on the screen. We called these *technology confusion* and *technology management*, respectively. The division of activity into the major clusters of task and process management was inspired by work in the literature by Putnam (1983) and Zigurs *et al.* (1988).

The reliability of the coding of these categories was, again, well over acceptable levels. Cohen's k was 63%, and the correlation between the two rater's summary statistics was 0.97.

We also analyzed the groups for the breadth and depth of their discussions. To do this, we noted in the transcripts which particular topic they were discussing at each moment. That is, we constructed a design rationale diagram, which connects the topic or issue, the alternative solutions to the question posed, and the evaluative comments (criteria) raised both for and against each proposed solution. All of these are noted without regard for when each event occurred, nor how many times the same alternative was mentioned. The notation is similar to that developed by researchers who advocate the use of a notation scheme to capture the aspects of design while it is happening (Moran and Carroll, in press). We use it instead to code the development of natural design activity. An example of part of a connected issue, alternative set, and associated criterial comments are shown in Figure 6.3. By coding the topics in this way, we can count the number of issues that are raised in the meeting, the number of ideas or alternatives generated per issue, and the evaluative criteria brought to bear on the alternatives. Thus, we have a detailed look at the design discussions.

Results

The results are organized by the major classes of measures as described above: outcome, satisfaction, and process.

Outcome differences

Two key measures of the output of the session are shown in Table 6.1: the quality, as described above, and the length of the document. The average judged quality of the designs produced by groups supported by ShrEdit was significantly higher than that for conventional groups ($t(36) = 2.32$, $p < 0.03$). Interestingly, the distribution of quality scores for the unsupported groups was far wider than the supported groups ($F(18,18) = 2.83$, $p < 0.05$). Something about the technology not only added to the average quality, but significantly raised the lower tail of the distribution.

On average, the groups using ShrEdit produced final documents that were twice as long ($t(36) = 2.78$, $p < 0.01$). There was, however, no correlation between length of document and quality overall ($r = 0.29$, $p > 0.05$), nor within each of the conditions (unsupported $r = 0.12$, $p > 0.05$, supported $r = 0.27$, $p > 0.05$). For the people with ShrEdit, the text explanation of their ideas was either in sentence form or more fully fleshed out, whereas the output from unsupported meetings consisted mainly of bullet lists.

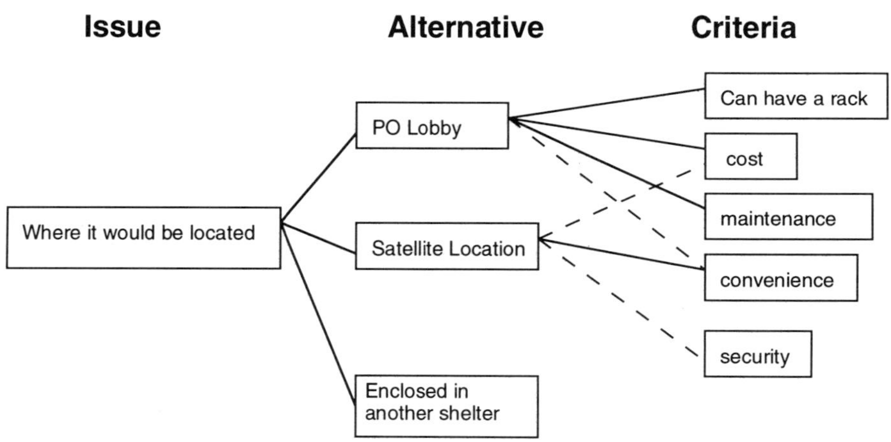

Figure 6.3 Design rationale.

Table 6.1 Analysis of features of groups' output.

	Quality	Length
Supported groups	64.0*	692* words
std dev	*7.9*	*468*
Unsupported groups	55.5	391 words
std dev	*13.3**	*196.2***

Significance at $p < 0.05$ is indicated by *, $p < 0.01$ by **.

Satisfaction

Analysis of the questionnaires on satisfaction revealed very few differences between the two groups. In general, both kinds of groups were satisfied with the process they used in generating, discussing and deciding on their design, and they liked their final post office design. However, the unsupported groups were slightly but significantly more satisfied with the discussion quality ($t = 2.74$, $p < 0.01$) and they rated the problem solving process to be more even and fair ($t = 2.24$, $p < 0.03$). However, both kinds of groups rated their groups equally when indicating whether one individual influenced the outcome more than others.

Table 6.2 Comparison of the Percentage of Time in Various Task Categories. Lines that are Starred and in Italic are significantly different at $p < 0.01$.

Category	Unsupported groups	Sum	Supported groups	Sum
Issue	2.9		2.0	
Clar Issue	0.4		0.3	
Alternative	*22.4*		*14.9**	
Clar Alt	*4.6*		*2.1**	
Criteria	*21.1*		*12.6**	
Clar Criteria	*1.5*		*0.3**	
		53.0		*32.2**
General Clar	0.8		0.7	
Artifact Clar	0.1		0.2	
Summary	*3.1*		*0.9**	
Clar Summary	0.0		0.0	
Walkthrough	*1.5*		*0.7**	
Clar Walk	0.0		0.0	
Goal	1.9		1.2	
Clar Goal	0.0		0.0	
Project Management	0.0		0.9	
Clar Proj Mgmt	0.0		0.0	
Meeting Mgmt	4.5		4.4	
Clar Meeting Mgmt	0.1		0.0	
Digression	12.0		10.6	
Clar Digression	0.1		0.0	
Plan and Write	8.7		11.5	
Manage Technol	*0.1*		*2.5**	
Technology Conf	*0.0*		*6.7**	
Other	0.6		0.3	
Clar Other	0.0		0.0	
		33.5		40.6
Pause	*13.2*	*13.2*	*27.9**	*27.9**

Process differences

What is it that produced the differences in quality? How did the groups spend their time, how did they move among activities in the course of design, and what was the breadth and depth of their discussions?

Table 6.2 shows the amount of time spent in each of the categories of activity. Most categories of activity are very similar. Of interest, about the same amount of time (4%) is spent in managing the flow of meetings in both conditions, and they plan the writing for about the same amount of time (11% and 9% for supported and unsupported, respectively). The ShrEdit groups spend 7% of their time asking each other questions about the technology because they are unsure or confused.

Groups in these two conditions, however, differ in several striking ways. There is a clear tradeoff between the amount of time spent in discussing the design itself (the alternatives and their evaluative criteria) and the amount of time dictating and writing. (There was more writing than indicated here. This is the writing that is done when no one is speaking. It does not include time when someone wrote while other talking was going on. This is particularly important in interpreting the category 'Digression', which often occurred between two people while a third wrote, especially in the unsupported condition where the non-writers could not see the text being written.)

People supported with ShrEdit spend less time than the unsupported groups in direct discussion of issues, alternatives, and criteria (32% vs 53% for supported vs unsupported, respectively). They spend much more time writing down their design than the unsupported groups do (28% vs 13%).

The groups supported by ShrEdit also differ in the flow of activities that produce the actual design. Figure 6.4 shows a side-by-side view of the flow of activities. Each category of activity is represented by a circle, the area of which represents the total time the group spent in that activity, aggregated over the whole meeting. White portions of the circle represent the direct discussion of that topic, while the black wedges represent the time spent clarifying that topic. The arrows indicate the transitions between the topics, with the width of the arrow reflecting the frequency with which that transition is made. (To make this diagram readable we eliminated the very low frequency transitions. There are a few transitions that never happen, but there are many that occur only once or twice. We include here only those transitions that occurred at least 1% of the time).

Of note here is the heavy amount of transition to writing for the groups using ShrEdit. In fact there are four times as many writing episodes in the supported groups compared to unsupported. In the groups using ShrEdit, the writing of the ideas raised in the meetings is much more interspersed than in the unsupported groups, and the average time spent writing is shorter for the supported groups (5 seconds (s) per episode on average vs 10 s for supported vs unsupported). Unsupported meetings concentrate their discussion of

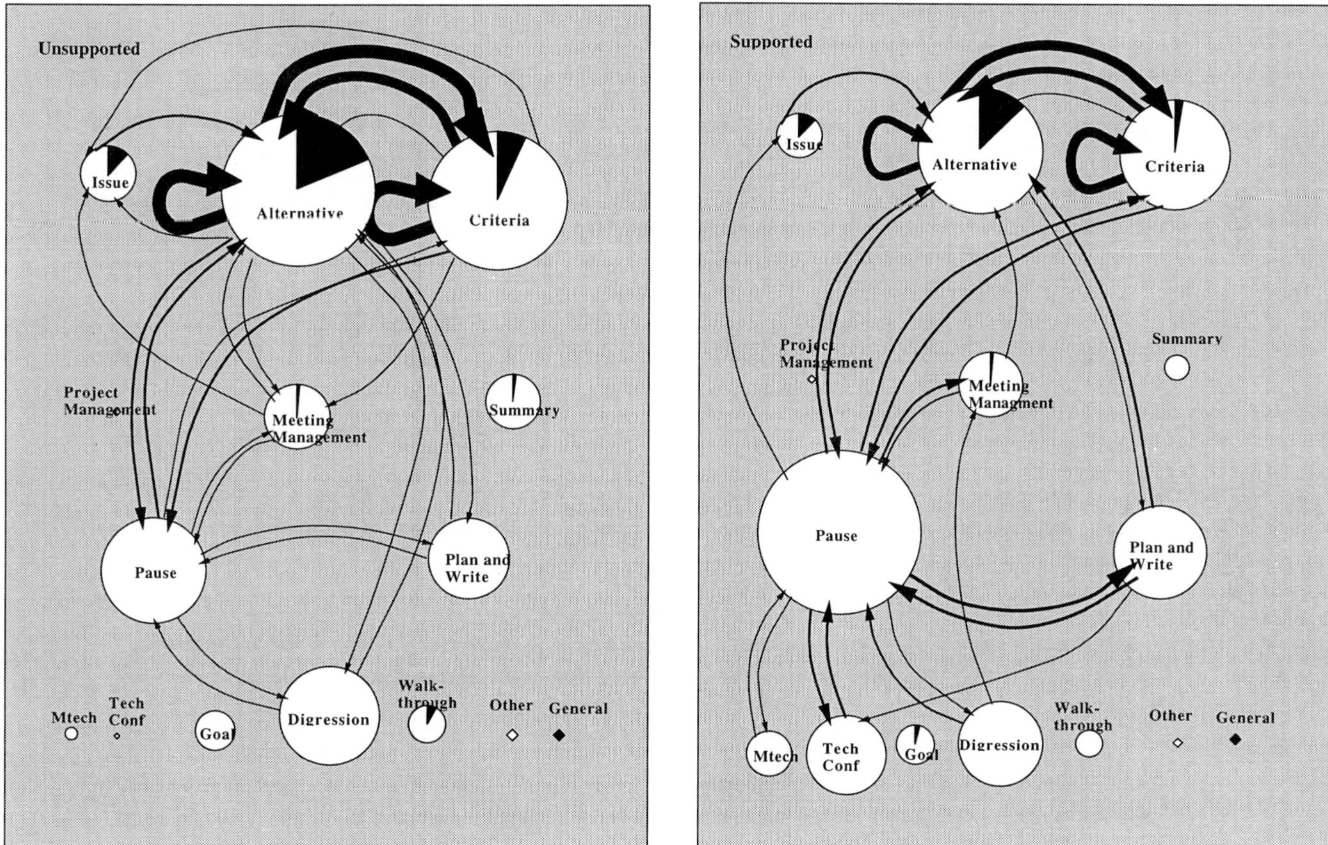

Figure 6.4 Flow of activities. *Left*: unsupported groups; *right*: supported groups.

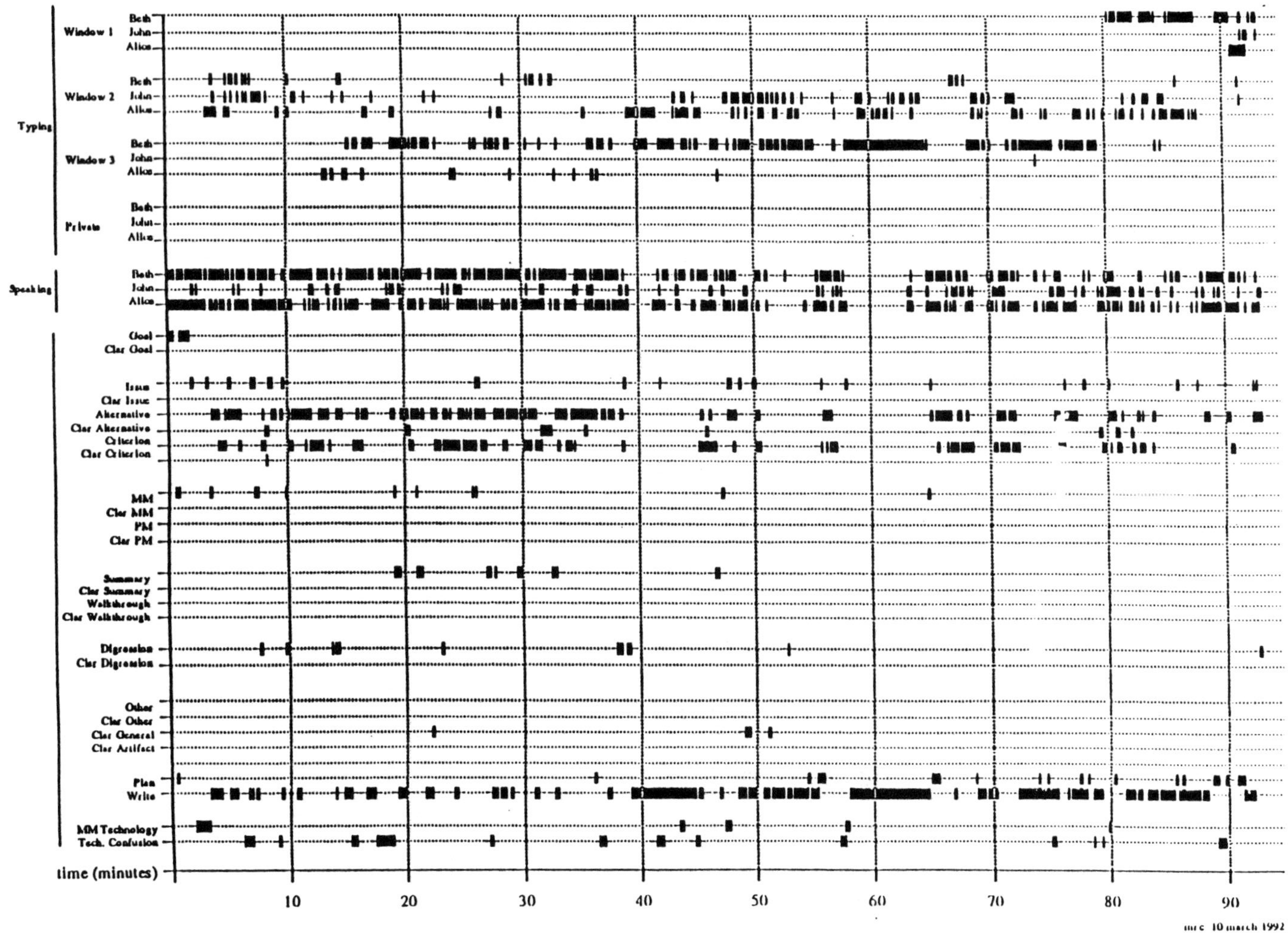
Typing
Window 1
Beth
John
Alice
Window 2
Beth
John
Alice
Window 3
Beth
John
Alice
Private
Beth
John
Alice
Speaking
Beth
John
Alice
Goal
Clar Goal
Issue
Clar Issue
Alternative
Clar Alternative
Criterion
Clar Criterion
MM
Clar MM
PM
Clar PM
Summary
Clar Summary
Walkthrough
Clar Walkthrough
Digression
Clar Digression
Other
Clar Other
Clar General
Clar Artifact
Plan
Write
MM Technology
Tech. Confusion
time (minutes)
10
20
30
40
50
60
70
80
90
mrc 10 march 1992

alternatives with some note-taking on the board while they talk and then write their final reports on paper.

Figure 6.5 shows a more detailed plot of the flow of activity across one group's meeting. In this diagram, time flows left to right, and the lines represent different classes of activity, with tick marks representing each event. The top 12 lines picture the group members' activity in aggregate typing, each three lines representing activity in the same window. The fourth set of three lines represent typing in the private window. The remainder of the plot shows the talking about issues, alternatives, criteria, meeting management, etc. In the meeting shown, the top portion shows that everyone typed; they used two windows initially then finished up in a third 'final' window. This group typed throughout, sometimes while others were talking, sometimes in silence. An hour into the meeting, they typed silently in parallel, a good example of the 'divide and conquer' strategy we describe later.

Next, we analyzed the groups for the breadth and depth of their discussions. Table 6.3 shows the distribution of issues, alternatives, and criteria raised. Some striking differences appear. Contrary to expectations from the brainstorming literature, where parallel input allows more ideas to be generated, leading to higher scores, the unsupported groups generated more issues, and raised more alternatives than the supported groups did ($t(36) = 3.11$, $p < 0.004$; $t(36) = 2.24$, $p < 0.03$). The unsupported groups differed widely among themselves in the number of issues covered, the variance being significantly higher than that for the supported groups ($F(18,18) = 3.42$, $p < 0.01$).

In our informal observations, we noted that unsupported groups in some cases raised many more ancillary issues (unique to each meeting). We then counted the number of 'core' issues that were covered in each meeting, those that explicitly were cued in the problem statement and others that would naturally follow (e.g. location), separately from the number of 'ancillary' issues. For example, several unsupported groups spent a large amount of time on discussing an appropriate name for the facility and the company; others discussed at great length how to automate the internal operations of the post office. Neither of these topics contributes strongly to the overall quality of the design and are therefore considered 'ancillary'. Table 6.4 shows the tallies.

Table 6.3 Details of the depth and breadth of design discussion.

	Average numbers of		
	Issues	Alternatives	Criteria
Supported	13.3	120.8	128.5
std dev	*3.02*	*26.73*	*79.96*
Unsupported	17.9**	144.6*	169.5
std dev	*5.59***	*37.75*	*58.32*

Table 6.4 Details of the depth and breadth of design discussion for core and ancillary topics.

	Average numbers of					
	Core ancillary issues		Core ancillary alternatives		Core ancillary criteria	
Supported	9.1	4.2	108.6	12.2	115.4	13.1
std dev	*1.06*	*2.55*	*22.54*	*9.19*	*74.4*	*13.15*
Unsupported	9.4	8.5**	120.0	24.6**	147.2	22.4
std dev	*1.01*	*5.54***	*30.03*	*19.26***	*60.0*	*16.56*

It turns out that although the two kinds of groups raised the same number of core issues, the unsupported groups raised and discussed twice as many ancillary issues ($t(36) = 3.08$, $p < 0.005$), and twice as many ancillary alternatives ($t(36) = 2.51$, $p < 0.02$). Not only were the means different, the variances were higher for the unsupported groups for both the number of issues raised and the alternatives considered ($F(18,18)$ 4.72, $p < 0.01$ for issues; $F(18,18) = 4.39$, $p < 0.01$ for alternatives).

Each of these ancillary issues was discussed narrowly; each had an average of three alternatives and only one evaluative statement. In contrast, core topics in both conditions had on average 12 or 13 raised.

What correlates with quality?

Since all groups in this study were solving the same problem, we had a chance not only to look at the aggregate differences between the two support conditions and quality, but also to look within conditions for relationships among our process measures and quality. We examined whether quality was related to the time spent on writing, on raising alternatives, or on evaluating with various criteria, as well the number of issues and alternatives raised, and the number of criteria generated and items in the final document.

For supported groups none of the variables were significantly correlated with quality, likely because the variance among the quality scores was relatively small (from 49 to 78 on an 80-point scale, with a large number clustered very near the mean of 65). For the unsupported groups, which had a wider variance, an interesting pattern emerged, fitting with the major pattern of differences between groups. The more alternatives that appeared in the final document (discussed later), the better the quality ($r(18) = 0.58$, $p < 0.01$). Interestingly, the less time spent on design (issues, alternatives, criteria and their clarifications), the higher the quality; the more time on writing (which includes 'pauses' and 'digressions' which cover occasions when one person is writing and the others are having a side conversation), the higher the quality ($r(18) = -0.44$, $p < 0.06$ for design; $r(18) = +0.58$, $p < 0.01$ for writing). Unsupported groups were better when they spent less time per alternative ($r(18) = -0.43$ $p < 0.07$). Quality was better when core issues had more alternatives explored ($r(18) = 0.58$, $p < 0.02$). Nearly all of these correlations suggest that the more the unsupported groups spent their time like the supported groups, the higher the quality of their designs.

The Use of ShrEdit

How much of the time is the technology being used? Do people ever type simultaneously? What do they do when typing simultaneously? Note that in teaching the groups ShrEdit we introduced them to the features, but we did not tell them how to use them to support various aspects of the meeting's work.

To answer these questions, we catalogued the timing of the keystrokes for each person individually and noted overlap. Since a keystroke is an instantaneous event, we assumed that a person's attention was paid to typing both a second before each keystroke and a second after. Using this technique (analyzing 11 supported groups), we found that, on average, simultaneous typing occurs 10% of the time. Figures 6.6a, b, and c show the patterns of this activity. In these figures, the meeting time is divided into 10-minute intervals. The ordinate shows the proportion of each ten-minute period in which either one or more than one person is typing. Figure 6.6a shows the aggregate over the 11 groups. Here the pattern looks fairly regular, with growing simultaneous use over the session.

This aggregate view, however, hides the more striking individual group patterns, shown in Figures 6.6b and c. Of note in both of these are the bursts of activity where more than one person is typing. For the group in Figure 6.6b, there are two such bursts, one near the beginning and another near the end. In the group in Figure 6.6c, there is only one such burst, in the second half of the meeting.

Looking at the transcript for these episodes, we note two types of activity in these bursts. In the earlier bursts, the group is typically brainstorming for features the post office should have. The second burst is typically what we call 'divide and conquer', where group members take various sections of their emerging document and flesh it out. In several groups, for example, one wrote the introduction, while others expanded on the costs and benefits of this particular design.

In contrast, the unsupported groups use the white board to capture ideas as they occur, one at a time. They then stop their discussion early to begin the slow job of getting the ideas down on paper. This is typically done by one person who 'dictates' the ideas out loud for the others to confirm and/or question. Only one unsupported group organized themselves into a 'divide and

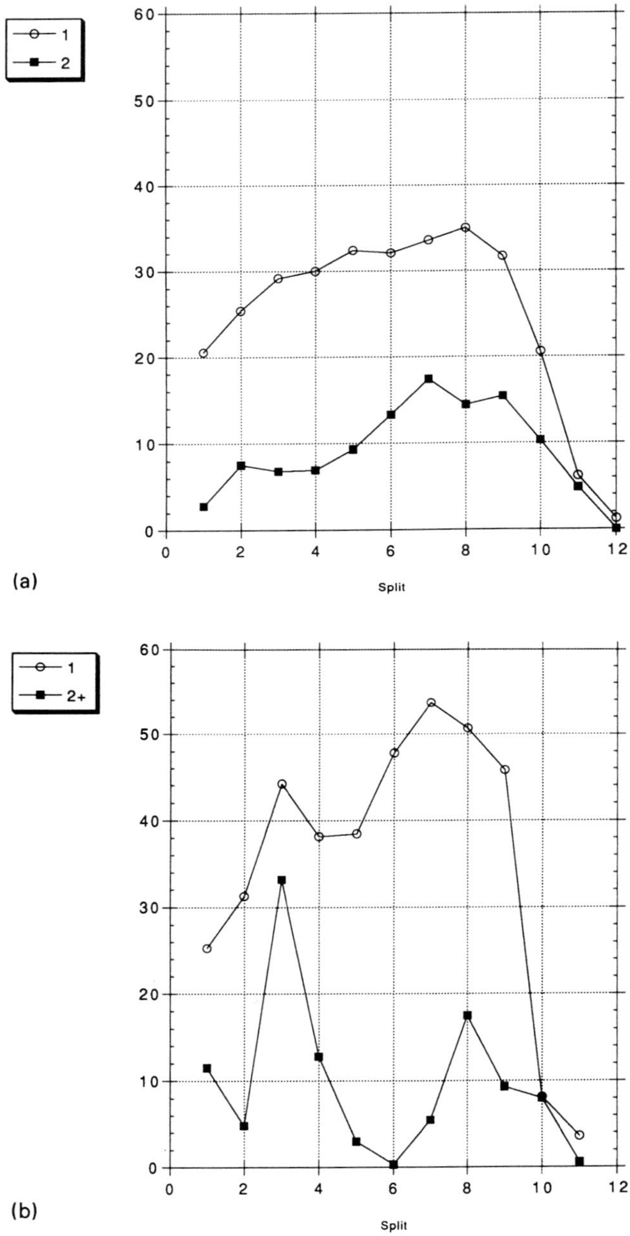

Figure 6.6 Patterns of typing activity: (a) aggregate for 11 groups; (b) and (c) individual group patterns.

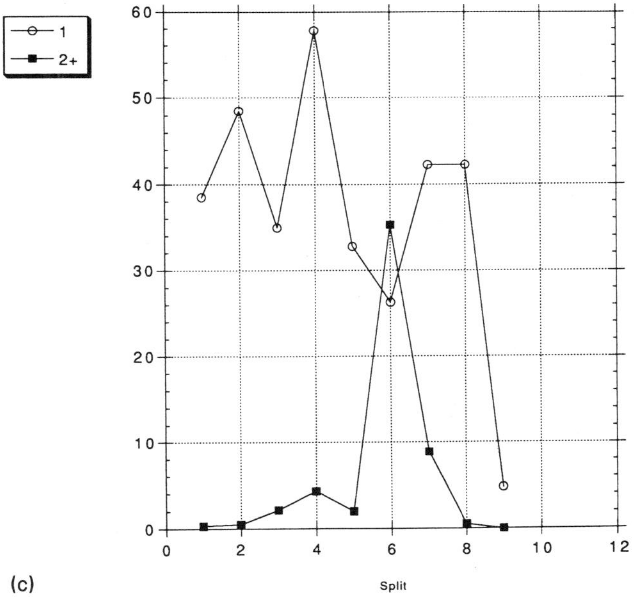

(c)

Figure 6.6 *(continued)*

conquer' mode, where they each took a topic and a separate sheet of paper and wrote simultaneously, asking for occasional confirmation of the others, but not doing as much 'writing out loud' as the serial groups did.

Looking more closely at the content of the writing, Table 6.5 shows some of the comparisons between what appears in the final document and what is spoken for the groups in the two conditions.

Several things are of interest here. First, many more ideas are raised, totally, in the unsupported groups than in the supported groups. But by the time the final document is crafted, the tide shifts: More ideas tend to appear in the supported groups' documents than in the unsupported. (Recall that the t-test of this was not significant, though the number of ideas in the final document was correlated with quality, and the Supported group on the whole had higher quality.) As one might expect with more access to the documents in ShrEdit, fewer items were lost, spoken but never written. Of those, a larger portion are retained in the final document in the ShrEdit condition than in the unsupported condition. Said alternatively, fewer items were lost between being written originally and then appearing in the final document. This is understandable since in the unsupported condition things must be transferred from the group-space, the whiteboard, to the final document space, the handwritten on sheets of paper.

With ShrEdit, the items are either cut and pasted from rough document windows to the final document or merely remain in the working/final document untouched after initial entry.

Table 6.5 The history of alternatives raised, captured, and appearing in the final document for the supported and unsupported groups.

	Supported	Unsupported	sig
Total items	121.3	145.1	
$p < 0.01$			
Items spoken	99.4	129.1	
$p < 0.01$			
Items written at any time	59.9	63.0	n.s.
Items in the final document	56.9	51.8	n.s.
Items written in the final doc but not spoken, 'extra'	20.0	15.6	n.s.
Items spoken but never written	61.0	81.0	$p < 0.03$
Items written at some time but not in final document	2.0	11.0	$p < 0.01$

But also of interest are the numbers of 'extra' ideas written in both conditions. There are some ideas that appear on the final document that were never discussed. Both groups add these extra ideas, and in equal numbers. It appears that the one who 'holds the pen' has some license. In the supported groups, however, all held the pen, and all could see the extra items if they chose. Except for one unsupported group where they passed the paper version of their output around to the other group members for checking, none of the unsupported groups' members saw the final output except its author.

DISCUSSION

We gave subjects who were doing an interesting problem solving task (i.e. design) a simple collaborative tool to assist them in their face-to-face work. The tool provided no particular process support or made them structure their work in any particular way. They were free to organize their activities as they wished. By the time they did our target design task they had had about an hour's practice in using the new electronic workspace tool.

Yet this simple tool and this limited experience had a profound effect on their work. The designs they produced were of higher quality than those of the control groups who worked in a more traditional fashion. They liked the process a little less, perhaps not surprising given the use of a new technology. But most surprising of all was the way in which they worked. They actually did a less extensive exploration of the design space than the traditional, unsupported groups. Our expectation had been just the opposite. So instead of encouraging a more exhaustive look at design ideas, something about the technology led them to a more selective examination of what turned out to be better ideas. They seemed to focus more on the core issues. They captured and examined by reading what they were thinking while they worked, rather than in two stages – once on the whiteboard and once on paper while those other than the scribe talked about other things. In the two-stage process, ideas were lost.

A lot of things likely produced the effect: shared access to an easily editable workspace that permitted parallel work when appropriate; an easier blending of the activities of idea generation, idea selection, and report generation; early capture of good ideas that led to a quicker consensus about a sensible design; a mixed mode of participation (talking and typing) that favored consensus development as opposed to unfettered exploration of fringe design ideas.

A striking feature of this result is that the tool, though without an embedded procedure for structuring a meeting, encouraged focus and deliberation. The more the unsupported groups looked like the supported groups in behavior (keeping to the core issues, writing as they went), the higher their quality output. The technology made the groups more homogeneous, in particular helping the less functional groups. Small groups in particular can capitalize on the power of the shared editor without needing facilitation, either human or software-embedded. For these kinds of fast-moving, intense design sessions, simplicity is good. This simplicity also allowed groups to adapt the technology to their own style of working.

The technology had other direct effects on the behavior of the Supported groups. They spent a large amount of their time (7%) trying to figure out the technology itself. On average they spent 10% of their time doing parallel work, though as we showed, in general this tended to be concentrated at specific stages of their work. They used the technology to capture ideas that they never felt compelled to talk about, since everyone could see the ideas as they emerged and comment if they disagreed.

We designed ShrEdit deliberately to provide its users with a tool that has as few constraints as possible (Olson and Olson, 1991; McGuffin and Olson, 1992). We did this because we wanted to provide groups with some basic functionality – a shared electronic workspace with as few constraints on its use by individual members as possible – and let them develop their own strategies for working with it. If you look at common collaborative tools like whiteboards or paper and pencil, the tools provide few constraints and groups invent (or are sometimes taught) techniques for making effective use of them in their work. We have watched our groups invent simple techniques for voting and for highlighting and directing attention. We have seen them create tables or parallel lists by using several side-by-side skinny windows. We have watched them organize their work and transition from individual parallel work to a group focus via cutting and pasting of information within and between windows. These were all low-overhead, socially created ways of using the possibilities offered by the tool to organize their work in an effective way.

Dourish and Bellotti (1992) have used the data we collected on distributed groups using ShrEdit to analyze the way in which these people used the flexibility of ShrEdit to carry out their work. (See Olson, Olson and Meader (1995) for a more formal report on the use of ShrEdit by distributed groups.) They noticed in particular that the shared workspace provided an effective though passive form of awareness information about what others were doing. This allowed the groups to move back and forth easily between close and loose collaboration. Furthermore, they could easily assign and coordinate tasks and roles on the fly. They contrasted this with systems that provide active mechanisms for coordination support. In these systems awareness information was provided and controlled separate from or instead of a shared workspace. They claim that these kinds of systems are much more difficult for groups to use, because often the groups' needs or goals are at odds with what the system allows them to do. In contrast, with passive awareness support of the sort provided through a shared workspace like ShrEdit the group can easily adapt the workspace features to their own style of coordination.

If we compare the present study and its results to those reviewed (Hollingshead and McGrath, in press; McLeod, 1992), several things stand out. First, we found, as did McLeod (1992), that our subjects using the technology were less satisfied. As we noted earlier, this is not surprising since our subjects were working in a very new way for the first time. Second, in contrast to almost all of the studies they reviewed, we used a software tool that did not structure the group's activities. We none the less found an improvement in the quality of the group's work. Since we fixed the time available for all groups, this improvement in quality did not come at the cost of greater time doing the task. Third, through our extensive analyses of group processes, we were able to learn much more about how our groups worked, what effect the technology had on this, and how this related to the differences in outcome. This focus on process details is a substantial advance over the earlier studies.

Our overall impression is that the simple group editor we gave these subjects was a functional and useful tool. This was true despite its shortcomings of functionality and interface that were revealed by the subjects' use and comments. On the basis of relatively little experience the subjects were able to organize their work with the aid of this tool. In the final analysis, both the significant and non-significant results are interesting. Some confirm our notions of what makes a good meeting; some tell us that prescriptions we hold about good meetings (e.g. that discussing more alternatives is better) may not be widely true.

ACKNOWLEDGEMENTS

This work has been supported by the National Science Foundation (Grant No. IRI-8902930), by the Center for Strategic Technology Research (CSTaR) at Andersen Consulting, by Arthur Andersen & Co., by Apple Computer, and by Steelcase, Inc. Others involved in the building and testing of ShrEdit include

Lola McGuffin, Martin Sonntag, Dan O'Leary, and Brian Holtz. Many people have participated in the collection and analysis of the data reported here, including Stacey Donahue, Alex Eulenberg, Barb Gamm, Jim Herbsleb, Robin Lampert, Mary Jane T. Lu, Brenda Montgomery, Max Rahder, Meredith Reitman, Adrienne Royce, Henry Rueter, Sue Schuon, Michael Walker, Rodney Walker, Garrick Wang, and Corinne Weirich.

REFERENCES

Curtis, B., Krasner, H. and Iscoe, N. (1988) A field study of the software design process for large systems. *Communications of the ACM*, **31**, 1268–1287.

Dourish, P. and Bellotti, V. (1992) Awareness and coordination in shared workspaces. *Proceedings of the Conference on Computer Supported Cooperative Work.*

Dunn, R. (1984) *Software defect removal.* McGraw-Hill, New York.

Goel, V. and Pirolli, P. (1989) Motivating the notion of generic design within information processing theory: the design problem space. *AI Magazine*, (2), 18–36.

Gouran, D. S., Brown, C. and Henry, D. R. (1978) Behavioral correlates of perceptions of quality in decision-making discussions. *Communication Monographs.* **45** (1), March, 51–63.

Green, S. G., and Taber, T. D. (1980) The effects of three social decision schemes on decision group process. *Organizational Behavior and Human Performance.* **25**, 97–106.

Hollingshead, A. B. and McGrath, J. E. (1995) The whole is less than the sum of its parts: A critical review of research on computer-assisted groups. In Guzzo, R. (ed.) *Team Decision Making in Organization.* Jossey-Bass, San Francisco.

McGrath, J. E. (1984) *Groups: Interaction and Performance.* Prentice-Hall, Englewood Cliffs, NJ.

McGuffin, L. and Olson, G. M. (1992) *ShrEdit: A shared electronic workspace.* CSMIL Technical Report, The University of Michigan.

McLeod, P. L. (1992) An assessment of the experimental literature on electronic support of group work. *Human–Computer Interaction.*

Moran, T. and Carroll, J. (eds) (1995) *Design Rationale.* Lawrence Erlbaum Associates, Hillsdale, NJ.

Olson, G. M., McGuffin, L. S., Kuwana, E. and Olson, J. S. (1993) Designing software for a group's needs: A functional analysis of synchronous groupware. In Bass, L. and Dewan, P. (eds) *User Interface Software.* Wiley, New York, pp. 129–148.

Olson, G. M. and Olson, J. S. (1991) User-centered design of collaboration technology. *Journal of Organizational Computing*, **1**, 61–83.

Olson, G. M., Olson, J. S., Carter, M. and Storrøsten, M. (1992a) Small group design meetings: An analysis of collaboration. *Human–Computer Interaction.*

Olson, G. M., Olson, J. S., Killey, L., Mack, L. A., Cornell, P. and Luchetti, R. (1992b) Flexible facilities for electronic meetings In Bostrom, R. P., Watson, R. T. and Kinney, S. T. (eds), *Computer Augmented Teamwork: A Guided Tour*. Van Nostrand Reinhold, New York, pp. 183–196.

Olson, J. S., Olson, G. M., Mack, L. A. and Wellner, P. (1990) Concurrent editing: The group's interface. In Diaper, D. *et al.* (eds), *Human–computer Interaction INTERACT'90*, Elsevier, North-Holland.

Olson, J. S., Olson, G. M. and Meader, D. K. (1995) What mix of video and audio is useful for remote real-time work? *Proceedings of CHI'95*, ACM SIGGCHI, 362–368.

Olson, J. S., Olson, G. M., Storrøsten, M. and Carter, M. (1993) Groupwork close up: A comparison of the group design process with and without a simple group editor. *ACM Transactions on Information Systems*, **11**, 321–348.

Putnam, L. L. (1983) Small group work climates: a lag-sequential analysis of group interaction. *Small Group Behavior*, **14** (4), 463–494.

Stefik, M., Bobrow, D. G., Foster, G., Lanning, S. and Tatar, D. (1987) WYSIWIS revised: Early experiences with multiuser interfaces. *ACM Transactions on Office Information Systems*, **5**, 147–167.

Steiner, I. D. (1972) *Group process and productivity*. Academic Press, New York.

Zigurs, I., Poole, M. S. and DeSanctis, G. L. (1988) A study of influence in computer-mediated group decision making. *MISQ*, **12**, 645–665.

7 Computer-mediated Communication for Intellectual Teamwork: An Experiment in Group Writing

JOLENE GALEGHER and ROBERT E. KRAUT

INTRODUCTION

In most kinds of work success depends on matching talents, tools and procedures to the demands of specific tasks and projects. The development of new information technologies designed to aid communication and task performance has raised new questions about fit, and stimulated new research programs intended to assess the appropriateness of these technologies for tasks of many different kinds. In the investigation reported here, we assess the effects of a particular information technology – computer-mediated communication – on the experiences of people involved in a complex collaborative writing project. The purpose of this investigation is to determine how well the opportunities and constraints provided by computer-mediated communication fit the demands of this kind of work, when compared to face-to-face communication.

In a project of this sort, success is ordinarily viewed as multidimensional, involving not only instrumental achievements, but also individual satisfaction and the maintenance of the group as a performing unit (Hackman, 1983; McGrath, 1990). This distinction between the dimensions of small group effectiveness suggests that a comprehensive assessment of the impact of computer-mediated communication should also be multidimensional. Thus, our analysis focuses on multiple outcomes, including the task activities of group members as they carry out their work, the resulting performance, and the attachment of group members to each other.

Our interest in the effects of computer-mediated communication is both theoretical and practical. Communicating by computer has the potential to alter ordinary patterns of communication and task performance in many ways. Identifying those effects would enable us to expand and update existing theoretical descriptions of the relationship between patterns of coordination and communication and workgroup outcomes. On the more practical side,

GROUPWARE AND AUTHORING
ISBN 0-12-575005-6

computer-mediated communication could reduce or eliminate the expense and inconvenience associated with distributed work. But, although research about its effects has grown rapidly in the recent past, there are still few studies that have examined sustained, project-oriented teamwork of the sort that is important in most real-world organizations. Furthermore, studies that do look at longer-lived project groups typically involve too little control to identify the variables of interest (Hiltz, 1984). Thus, a rigorous analysis of the effects of computer-mediated communication in a sustained project seems warranted.

To make possible such an analysis, we have chosen to study groups engaged in collaborative writing projects. By this, we mean projects in which the group must formulate a response to a problem and create a document that communicates that response. The rationale for this choice is, again, partly theoretical and partly practical. On the theoretical side, there are significant group process problems involved in completing the project. These include negotiating the meaning of the facts with which the group is presented, establishing consensus as to an appropriate solution, dividing tasks among group members, coordinating the execution of work, and confronting questions of authority within the group as it attempts to insure both on-time completion and product quality.

The practical importance of research involving projects of this sort stems from their frequency in the world of work. Although definitions of collaboration differ, research by Couture and Rymer (1989), Ede and Lunsford (1990), and Faigley and Miller (1982) has demonstrated that collaborative writing in business and other professional contexts is frequent, and that it plays an important role in organizational activity. Recognizing the importance of collaborative writing and the potential to enhance this process technologically, some investigators (Forman 1991; Horton *et al.*, 1991) have begun to examine the use of computer support for these activities. The present study differs from the Forman study in that it is experimental, rather than observational, and from the Horton *et al.* study in that it involves a more complex project carried out over a longer period of time; this project also differs from these earlier investigations in the specific nature of the computer support provided. In the following sections we review the theoretical foundations for our investigation.

THE INTERRELATIONSHIPS OF COMMUNICATION MODALITY, TASK TYPE AND GROUP PERFORMANCE

Assessing the effects of information technology on the execution and outcome of particular tasks requires a conceptual model that identifies important task dimensions and the theoretically relevant features of particular information technologies. Several such models have been proposed. Although they differ in emphasis and in the terminology they employ, they have in common the idea that work on open-ended problems requires interactive, expressive communication. Interactive communication involves the ability to exchange information rapidly, adjusting messages in response to signals of understanding or misunderstanding, questions or interruptions from one's communication partners. Expressive communication involves the ability to convey ideas fully, presenting not only their semantic content, but also using intonation and gestures to reveal intensity and physical artifacts to clarify or amplify meaning (Kraut *et al.*, 1992).

One example of a model that embodies this linkage between task type, a technique or medium for managing the task, and task outcome is structural contingency theory (Lawrence and Lorsch, 1967). According to this formulation the critical task variable is uncertainty and the task management process is a coordination practice of some kind. Van de Ven and his colleagues (Van de Ven *et al.*, 1976), as well as other researchers working in quite different settings (Tushman, 1978, 1979) have found that when task uncertainty is high, people engage in higher levels of informal communication to coordinate their work than when task uncertainty is low. This finding has been interpreted as evidence that coping with uncertainty requires a level of mutual adjustment within and between work groups that is unattainable when individuals are relying on formal policies and procedures or other less flexible means of coordinating their work.

The conclusion that expressiveness and interactivity are required for communication about complex problems can also be derived from the results of research that explicitly examines the effects of variations in communications media (Short *et al.*, 1976). In this research, the crucial task variable is the extent to which the task requires negotiation over meaning or resources, and rather than coordination mechanism, the variable linking task type to task outcome is the social presence of the communication medium. Social presence is the extent to which a communication medium elicits the same psychological experience as unmediated, face-to-face communication. In our terms, media that provide social presence do so because they permit interactivity and expressiveness. To test their version of the contingency hypothesis, Short *et al.* (1976) manipulated communication modality and task type, and observed the effects of these variations on task outcomes. Although complex, the results of these experiments were congruent with the correlational findings of Van de Ven *et al.* (1976). When tasks involved straightforward information transmission or problem-solving on cooperative tasks, the outcomes were unaffected by variations in communication modality. But when the task involved conflicts over resources or point of view, variations in communication modality had significant effects. In particular, carrying out tasks involving conflict via communications media that were low in social presence produced negative outcomes.

These observations anticipate a more recent analysis of the contingencies between task characteristics, ways of managing work, and performance. In the model proposed by Daft and his colleagues (Daft and Lengel, 1986; Trevino *et al.*, 1990), equivocality is the task variable, and media choice is the 'task management' variable linking task type to task outcome. According to this analysis, richer communications media permit communicators to modify their messages in response to cues from their partners, to amplify their messages using nonverbal and paralinguistic channels, to speak naturally and colloquially and to direct their messages to a particular individual or group. For our purposes, these attributes can be summarized in terms of interactivity and expressiveness. Examinations of the relationship between media richness and media choice have shown that more equivocal tasks are typically associated with high levels of direct, informal, face-to-face, i.e. interactive and expressive, communication (Daft and Macintosh, 1981; Daft *et al.*, 1987). According to Daft and Lengel (1986), people understand media differences in carrying capacity and, when allowed to choose, select a communication modality that maximizes the fit between the richness of the information they seek to convey and the richness of the information that particular communication modalities can carry.

Recall, now, that we have described collaborative writing as involving negotiation about the meaning of facts, a demand for consensus as to an appropriate solution, division of labor based on concerns for fairness and quality of work, coordination of individual contributions, and resolution of questions about authority within the group. Whether labelled uncertain, conflictful or equivocal, such an enterprise clearly involves considerable cognitive and interpersonal complexity. Further, comparative ratings of various communications media have shown that computer-mediated communication is generally perceived as low in terms of its ability to support interactive, expressive communication (Zmud *et al.*, 1990). Thus, taken together, the conceptual analyses and previous research described here predict that using computer-mediated communication for collaborative intellectual work will be quite difficult. This prediction stems from the mismatch between the properties of the medium and the nature of the tasks involved, a mismatch that may manifest itself in several ways.

First, the lack of interactivity associated with asynchronous computer-mediated communication may reduce the efficiency of the sequential communication needed to clarify complex ideas. Because communicators cannot immediately assess their partners' understanding, they cannot easily tailor their utterances to insure comprehension. The absence of interactivity may also lead to uncertainties about the activities of others. To keep the flow of information moving, individuals must check their computer accounts regularly and must also signal receipt of new messages to the sender because the sender cannot observe directly whether the message was received or acted upon. Second, computer-mediated communication reduces expressiveness, not only in the familiar sense of expressiveness as the communication of nuances of feeling, but also in the sense of expressiveness as the full expression of an idea, including perhaps, its representation in text, drawings, diagrams or marginal comments. Because most commercially available computer-mediated communication systems do not permit users to view and manipulate a shared document or other artifact, or to coordinate their conversation with attention to specific parts of the object, their ability to express their ideas fully is limited.

It is important to remember, however, that an extended project is likely to involve a number of tasks, and that these tasks may differ in the extent to which they require interactive, expressive communication. Thus, the impact of computer-mediated communication may depend on the specific task the group is working on at a given time. Typically, long-term projects involve several loosely bounded phases (Kraut *et al.*, 1987–1988; Kraut *et al.*, 1990; McGrath, 1990). At the outset, the participants may have only the vaguest ideas of what they should be trying to achieve and how to go about it. Thus, project initiation – setting on a shared interpretation of the problem, defining goals and planning work – is likely to require intensive communication. Once the group members begin to execute their plans, communication between group members is likely to shift from lengthy, highly interactive sessions to brief conversations in which group members exchange progress reports or otherwise coordinate their separate activities. Finally, as the project moves toward completion, the participants enter an integration phase during which they may again require extensive interaction to weave together the results of their individual work.

This model of the temporal sequence of communication between project members implies a differential impact of computer-mediated communication across time. Specifically, we would expect that the negative effect of computer-mediated communication on task performance will be most dramatic during the most communicatively intense phases of the project. Applied to the example of collaborative writing, this means the deleterious effect of computer-mediated communication should be greatest for planning – during which group members are establishing a sense of direction, defining goals, and agreeing on procedures for carrying out their work – and for revision, when group members are refining and integrating independently created drafts. Thus, in addition to our prediction that computer-mediated communication will adversely affect work on these projects, we expect that the strength of that effect will vary with the communication requirements of project components, with the most negative impact occurring when group members are planning and revising their work. Finally, because the group's achievements depend on its ability to carry out its tasks, we expect the documents produced by groups whose communication is restricted to be inferior to those created by groups that are able to communicate face-to-face.

COMMUNICATION MODALITY AND THE SOCIAL EXPERIENCES OF WORKGROUP

As noted above, the outcomes of collaborative work include not only the group's performance and the efficiency of the processes by which that performance is achieved, but also the affective experiences of the group members. Although not necessarily correlated with performance in the short run, these affective experiences can be important determinants of the group's longevity and long-term productivity (Hackman, 1983). Thus, both for the sake of creating or maintaining a benign work environment, and for the sake of preventing any detrimental effects of negative social experiences on work performance, it is important to consider how the reduction in interactivity and expressiveness imposed by computer-mediated communication might affect the social experience of group members.

In the Short *et al.* (1976) studies comparing interactions carried out face-to-face with those carried out over a video channel and an audio-only channel, participants in the more restricted communication conditions typically rated their interaction partners more negatively. In addition, assessments of subjects' metaperceptions – their sense that their communication partners understood them and that they understood their partners revealed a greater sense of uncertainty about the quality of their interactions. One interpretation of these results is that the reduction of behavioral cues and the resulting difficulty of assessing a communication partner's reactions preclude the development of smooth social interactions. Although these studies do not involve computer-mediated communication, they suggest that the social effects of using electronic communication for group work may be problematic.

Because computer-mediated communication is even leaner, even lower in social presence than the audio and video modes examined by Short *et al.* (1976), we should expect to observe similar, or perhaps even greater, disruptions in patterns of social interaction. A recent summary of research on the effects of using computers to communicate (Sproull and Kiesler, 1991) suggests that such disruptions do, in fact, occur with some frequency. While acknowledging the advantages of computer networks for establishing connections across time and space, and for reducing isolation and compartmentalization within organizations, these authors point out that computer-mediated communication none the less involves a substantial reduction in the social cues that regulate and facilitate communication. This reduction leads to more socially inappropriate behavior and to a greater focus on the task at the expense of focus on the audience, the target of the communication.

Based on these observations, then, we anticipate that using computer-mediated communication for a task such as collaborative writing will interfere with the development of positive social relationships between group members. Because communicating by computer makes it more difficult to share jokes, to soften the presentation of critical feedback, and to interject irrelevant, but entertaining, comments, the members of these groups are likely to be less attached to each other than are members of groups who work without these impediments. Unlike in the task domain, however, we do not expect these differences to vary with the task structure of the project. Although there may be variations in the social 'work' that group members need to do over time (e.g. getting acquainted versus smoothing out conflicts), we have no *a priori* grounds for predicting a particular pattern of social experiences over the course of the project. Thus, we expect that the social experiences of group members will be negatively affected by restrictions in communication modality, but do not expect specific time- or task-related variations in these experiences.

THE EXPERIMENT: OVERVIEW AND HYPOTHESES

In the previous section, we have argued that two important, socially relevant properties of communication modalities are interactivity and expressiveness. To examine the effect of communication modalities that differ with regard to these characteristics, we designed the experiment reported here. In this experiment, we compare the effects of Face-to-Face, Computer + Phone, and Computer Only communication conditions on the work processes, performance and affective experiences of small groups engaged in collaborative writing projects. The Face-to-Face condition embodies traditional communication modalities, and thus provides a baseline according to which the effects of restricted interactivity and expressiveness can be assessed. The Computer Only condition is intended to provide a sort of lower bound, an extreme, but theoretically relevant, test of the effects of limited interactivity and expressiveness. The Computer + Phone condition, which simulates the communication possibilities that might be available to the members of a distributed work group, occupies an intermediate position. Adding the telephone means that groups in that condition have better mechanisms for interactive and expressive communication than do those in the Computer Only condition, but this condition none the less embodies some qualities that might be expected to be particularly problematic for collaborative writing. In particular, telephone conversations are typically pairwise, and thus may not be as effective as face-to-face meetings for achieving consensus or establishing a state of mutual knowledge among all the members of a work group. In addition, the absence of a shared visual channel may make communication about interim drafts quite difficult.

In this experiment we expect to find that these restrictions on face-to-face communication impede work on the collaborative writing project, and that these negative effects will be most problematic early and late in the project when group members are planning their work and integrating their individual contributions. As a result of these problems, we expect that group performance will be adversely affected. Further, we expect that limiting opportunities for face-to-face interaction will undermine normal patterns of social interaction, resulting in lower levels of attachment to the group on the part of individual group members.

METHOD

Design

All 117 first-year MBA students (68 men and 49 women) enrolled in a managerial communication course conducted by the first author participated in this experiment. The students were randomly assigned to three-person groups, which were, in turn, randomly assigned to experimental conditions. Each student participated in two groups, one for each of two projects.[1] For each project, there were three communication conditions (Face-to-Face, Computer Only, and Computer + Phone). For the first project, half of the groups were assigned to the Face-to-Face condition and the rest were evenly divided between the Computer Only and Computer + Phone conditions. For the second project, new groups were formed with the restriction that work groups were made up of different individuals than in the first project. Students who had previously been in Face-to-Face groups were assigned to one of the two Computer-mediated groups, and students who had previously been in Computer-mediated groups were assigned to Face-to-Face groups.[2]

Procedure

Students were required to carry out two projects, each of which involved responding to the dilemmas presented in a business case. For the first case, drawn from Micheli *et al.* (1984), students were to announce and explain a large-scale corporate layoff to the employees who were to be terminated, to the remaining employees, to the company's stockholders and to the community in

[1] Originally, these two projects were intended to vary in divisibility. That is, one project was intended to embody characteristics that made it possible to divide the work between group members, and the other was intended to require a higher level of communication in order to integrate the contributions of individual members. However, the manipulation of project type was ineffective. Although there were clear variations in amount of communication over time *within* projects, there were no differences *between* projects in the extent to which people communicated to carry out their work. In retrospect, it appears that both projects required a great deal or integrative planning. The failure of this manipulation is reflected in our outcome measures; none of the dependent variables was affected by project type. Thus. we have eliminated discussion of this variable in presenting our rationale for this research, and have collapsed across it in our data analyses.

[2] Because this project was carried out within a university class, it was necessary to assign students to conditions in a way that would insure a sense of fairness among the participants. This meant making sure that each student participated in one Face-to-Face group and one Computer-mediated group. Thus, for each project, half of the groups were assigned to the Face-to-Face condition and one quarter of the groups to each of the two Computer-mediated conditions, resulting in unequal numbers of groups across communication conditions. Conducting the experiment in a class setting also precluded counterbalancing the order of projects: that is, it was impossible to have half of the class working on one project and the other half working on the other project at the same time. However, as noted above, this confounding of order and project turned out to be inconsequential because there was no effect of project.

which it operated. The second case, drawn from Schuler and Youngblood (1986) described an organization facing a number of complex personnel problems. The students were to analyze these problems and recommend solutions in a report to management.

Each case was discussed during a regular class session. Following the discussion, students were given a set of guidelines that defined the substantive goals they were to try to achieve and a two-week deadline for completing the project. In that interval, they were free to work on the project in any way that did not violate the terms of their experimental conditions. Packets containing blank copies of daily work reports were handed out, and students were instructed to complete one form on each day of the project. Post-project questionnaires were completed during class sessions.

Students assigned to the Computer-mediated conditions communicated via a system called ICoSy, a program that supports both electronic mail and computer conferences. Using the e-mail function, individuals could send private messages to other individuals or to several people at a time. Using the conference function, an individual could post entries, much as one would post notices on a bulletin board. These entries could be of any length or type (e.g. personal messages, outlines, draft versions of documents, or comments on entries submitted by other group members). The system also contains a reference function which enables users to follow a sequence of entries (i.e. comments on a draft document and revised versions can be linked to the entry containing the draft). In addition, mail messages could become conference entries and vice versa by copying the relevant message to a 'scratchpad', and forwarding it to the appropriate destination. Finally, the system supports uploading and downloading, making it possible for individuals to create and manipulate documents in their own word processors and transmit ASCII versions of those documents to the conference space.

To complete their work, students in the Computer-mediated conditions could use either their own computers or computers in a university lab open only to MBA students. Eighty-four percent owned their own computers; modems and communications software (either KERMIT or ProComm) were provided for any student who needed them. The students were reasonably experienced computer users; on a 3-point scale of previous experience with word processing (with 3 high) the class mean was 2.41,[3] and 37% reported some previous experience with electronic mail. Many, however, were new to computer-mediated communication, and most were new users of ICoSy. Thus, a training session was held to demonstrate the use of the computer conference, and participants were given specially created documentation to guide them as they acquired the necessary computer skills. In addition,

[3]Note that these data were collected on the first day of the semester, but the project described here began about four weeks after the beginning of the class. By that time, all subjects had had to complete several assignments using word processors; thus, this value would likely have been somewhat higher when the experiment began.

students could obtain follow-up advice about the use of the computer conference on-line in the open conference or through mail messages, by telephone, or in person, from the experimenter, from university computer consultants or from their classmates. For practice using the conferencing system prior to beginning work on their projects, all students joined an open conference. For project work, however, each group had its own computer conference. Thus, each individual was a member of two conferences – an open conference that remained accessible throughout the course as a vehicle for communication among students and between students and the professor, and a closed conference accessible only to the student and the other members of his or her work group.

Participation in this research was voluntary, and all students signed consent forms indicating their willingness to participate. Executing the experiment within a regular class meant that students were aware of the variations in communication conditions. To minimize their concerns about the potential effect of these variations on their performance (and the biases that such concerns might introduce into the research findings), the instructions pointed out that any advantages or disadvantages associated with communication condition would be evenly distributed because each individual would participate in one Face-to-Face group and one Computer-mediated group. In addition, students were told that the instructor would eliminate any effects of the experimental manipulations in determining grades. To preserve the students' privacy, they were also told that none of their responses would be examined until after the end of the course.

Manipulation of communication modality

In the Computer Only condition, students were required to conduct all project-related interactions, including both substantive and procedural discussions of their work and the exchange and review of interim documents, through the ICoSy system. As noted above, each work group had its own conference, and any member of the group could read any message posted in its conference.[4] In the Computer + Phone condition, students were allowed to use the ICoSy program and the telephone. In the Face-to-Face condition, the participants

[4] Previous observations of behavior in computer conferences have focused on conferences as a vehicle for communication between individuals in 'communities' of some sort, e.g. residents of a particular town, scientists in a particular field of study, or employees in a particular organization. This research has been concerned with variables such as the extent of participation by the members of these communities and how participation rates might be affected by various incentives (Hiltz, 1984; Markus, 1990; Connolly and Thorn, 1990). In the current study, however, the computer conferences were strictly a vehicle for communication among the members of each work group. Thus, considerations such as whether the proportion of the group participating was sufficient to create a 'critical mass' of interested users do not apply in this instance. In every work group, 100% of the relevant 'community' participated in the conference.

could meet, conduct telephone conversations, and exchange documents, but were not allowed to use ICoSy.

Dependent variables

Time series data

The time series data were derived from the students' daily work reports. On these reports, students used a checklist to record the type of work they had done each day. They also reported how many 'communication occasions' they had had with other group members that day, and provided detailed information (time of day, type of contact, duration, identity of individuals present, topics discussed, and assessments of enjoyableness and productivity) about a selected communication occasion.[5] In addition, the students provided daily evaluations of several aspects of their experience including the difficulty of coordinating work, the fairness of the division of labor, the quality of their communication procedures, and their attachment to other group members. These evaluations, as well as the evaluations of the enjoyableness and productivity of the focal communication occasion, were reported on 7-point Likert scales.

To create scales for the analyses, we first grouped these items in conceptually relevant categories. For instance, activities were classified as planning (e.g. planned how to complete the assignment; planned who would do what), drafting (e.g. did new writing on project documents), revising (e.g. evaluated initial drafts; revised another's writing), or social (e.g. discussing other school work; discussing social activities). The internal consistency of each scale was then assessed using the Spearman-Brown measure of reliability. The items that make up each scale and the results of these reliability analyses are shown in Table 7.1.

Retrospective data

After each of the two projects, students completed questionnaires containing items about the group's work procedures and performance, their own experiences during the course of the project, and the interpersonal dynamics of the group. After completing both projects, students compared face-to-face

[5] As was noted previously. participation in this experiment, including completion of these daily questionnaires was voluntary. There was no possibility of assessing the honesty or accuracy of these work reports, nor was there a specific reward or incentive for accuracy and honesty or any threat of punishment for failing to follow instructions. Thus, our faith in the validity of these reports must depend on the students' willingness to acknowledge violations of their assigned conditions (See Table 2). and on the reasonableness of the patterns in the data. It seems implausible, for instance, that students could have acted either individually or in concert to produce patterns of results such as those shown in Figure 1.

Table 7.1 Scale items and Spearman-Brown reliabilities

	Measure	Reliability
Planning Activities		0.84
Outlined major elements of the project	Communication about dividing the work	
Planned how to complete the assignment	Communication about scheduling the work	
Planned who would do what	Communication about scheduling meetings	
Discussed alternative ways of completing the assignment	Communication about planning document contents	
Drafting Activities		NA
Did new writing on project documents		
Revising Activities		0.78
Revised another's writing	Revised my own writing	
Exchanged initial drafts	Communication about writing	
Evaluated initial drafts	Communication about evaluating or revising drafts	
Social Activities		0.71
Discussing social activities	Discussing other school work	
Coordination Difficulty		0.84
I am not satisfied with the progress we are making in completing our project.		
We have difficulty coordinating our work.		
I am dissatisfied with the procedures that our team uses to communicate.		
Perceived Fairness		0.72
We are all contributing fairly to this project.		
Other members of our project team have worked very hard on this project.		
I am doing more than my share of the work for our team.		
The other members of the group don't seem to respect my contributions.		
Satisfaction with Workgroup		0.87
I have enjoyed working with members of my project team.		
I really feel that I am a part of this project team.		
I have learned a lot from the other members of this group.		
I'd like to work with this group again.		
Meeting Quality		0.77
How productive was the session?		
How enjoyable was the session?		
Total Communication		NA
Number of communication occasions on a day × duration of the focal communication occasion.		
Perceived Project Quality		NA
The work we've produced so far is exceptionally good.		

communication and other modalities used in the experiment in terms of their usefulness for work and social activities.

Performance data

Each group's project was scored by three people, the first author and two individuals who were employed as graders for the course. These individuals were blind to experimental condition. Their evaluation of the completed projects followed the usual practices in the course. That is, after the projects had been turned in, the first author scanned the submitted papers and selected a small number of examples (without regard to experimental condition) to illustrate successful and unsuccessful responses to the assignment; these were then discussed in a meeting with the graders. Subsequently, each rater worked independently, assigning holistic scores to each paper. The effective reliability (Rosenthal, 1973) was 0.77. and the mean of the scores assigned by the three raters was used as the measure of performance.

Analysis

Both our experimental method and the theoretical analysis on which it is based treat groups as the unit of analysis. That is, we are interested in group-level phenomena such as coordination difficulties and performance on a jointly created product. Thus, the research participants were assigned to the experimental conditions as groups, rather than as individuals. Some dependent variables, such as group performance, are naturally group-level outcomes. Others, such as time spent on various tasks, were measured at the level of the individual. To create the group-level measures needed, it was necessary to calculate group means for these dependent variables. First, however, we assessed the statistical (as opposed to conceptual) appropriateness of treating groups as the unit of analysis by computing the effects of group membership on individual scores for five dependent variables (coordination difficulty, attachment to the group, perceived fairness, perceived quality of the focal communication occasion and duration of the focal communication occasion). These analyses indicate that group membership accounted for between 43% and 64% of the variance in these dependent variables, a powerful demonstration of the effect of the circumstances the group shared on the individual experience of its members. Thus, where appropriate, the analyses that follow are based on group means.

The goal of this research was to assess the effects of computer-mediated communication on a group's ability to perform sustained intellectual teamwork and on the interaction between group members as the work is carried out. In addition, we wanted to determine whether any such effects depend on project phase. As we have discussed, the consequences of variations in communication condition are expected to vary depending on the communication requirements of the specific tasks being performed at a particular point in the life of the project. For instance, if computer-mediated communication interferes with the interactive communication required to carry out communication-intensive tasks such as planning and revision, we would expect to see the largest differences between the Face-to-Face and Computer-mediated conditions early and late in the life of the project. Thus, the data analysis focuses on the effects of Communication Modality, and on the interaction of this variable with time.

The time series measures described in the previous section were created by finding the mean values within each group for each day of the project. These values were analyzed using a 3 (Communication Modality) × 15 (Days) analysis of variance, with days as a within-group factor. As noted above, Communication Modality × Time interactions are taken as evidence that the effects of computer-mediated communication depend on the phase of the project. Significant interactions indicate that behavior (e.g. planning) and subjective experience (e.g. perceived difficulty in coordinating work) depend on communication modality and project phase. For most analyses, the Computer Only and Computer + Phone groups are combined, and then contrasted with the Face-to-Face condition. In this study, as will be shown below, a significant Communication Modality × Linear Time interaction typically reveals that a difference between the Computer-mediated and Face-to-Face groups increases over time. Similarly, the Communication Modality × Quadratic Time interaction typically shows that such differences are greatest during the middle of the project, when groups are most actively working, and a Communication Modality × Cubic. Time interaction suggests that these differences are greatest both early and late in the projects, when groups are planning and revising.[6] In general, these effects reflect interactions between the characteristics of particular communication modalities and time-based task variation.

RESULTS

Effects of communication modality and within-project task variations

Table 7.2 shows that the Communication Modality manipulation affected participants' use of communication channels appropriately. Students in Face-to-Face groups communicated primarily in scheduled meetings, although a substantial minority of their communication occurred via impromptu meetings and phone calls. Communication in the Computer + Phone condition was approximately evenly divided between the two electronic modalities.

The small proportion of face-to-face meetings in the Computer Only and Computer + Phone conditions indicates that, some students violated the terms of their experimental conditions. Interestingly, however, almost no one in the Face-to-Face condition cheated by using computer communication. Also, the number of violations is small. Thus, even if we assume some under-reporting, the Communication Modality manipulation appears to have been successful. Moreover, violations should reduce the difference between communication conditions. Therefore, the analyses that follow constitute a conservative test of the hypothesis that communication modality makes a difference in intellectual teamwork.

[6] Below, we call these effects the Face-to-Face vs. Computer × Linear interactions, the Face-to-Face vs Computer × Quadratic interaction, and the Face-to-Face vs Computer × Cubic interaction, respectively.

Table 7.2 Use of each communication channel within each communication condition

Communication modality used	Communication modality condition		
	Face-to-Face	Computer + Phone	Computer Only
Schedule face-to-face	64.7%	2.3%	1.1%
Unscheduled face-to-face meetings	23.1%	2.3%	1.1%
Phone calls	12.1%	40.6%	0.0%
Computer messages	0.1%	54.3%	97.9%
Total	1650	875	763

Note: Entries are column percentages (i.e. 100 × number or focal communications using a medium/ column total). Column totals are the number of focal communications per condition (i.e. number of projects × number of days per project). Recall that approximately twice as many respondents were assigned to the Face-to-Face condition as to either of the two Computer-mediated conditions.

In addition to the variations in communication patterns associated with the Computer Modality manipulation, we anticipated within-condition variation in communications as a consequence of the differences in the component tasks required to complete each project. Based on prior research (Kraut *et at.*, 1987–1988), we assumed that planning and revising were more integrative than drafting, and therefore would require more intricate or intensive communication. To assess the validity of this assumption, we computed, for each group, the Pearson correlations between the proportion of the group involved in planning, drafting, and revising and two measures of communication – time spent communicating and proportion of the group involved in the focal communication occasion – for each day of the project. These correlations, then, reveal the relationship between the type of work the group was doing and its communication patterns. After averaging these correlations across groups (using the Fisher Z transform), we used a standard t-test to compare the strength of the relationships between the two communication measures and work on the three tasks. As shown in Table 7.3, the proportion

Table 7.3 Association of proportion of group working on specific tasks with amount of time spent communicating and with proportion of group involved in focal communication occasion.

	Plan	Draft	Revise
Time spent communicating	0.42^{**a}	$0.27^{**a,b}$	0.52^{**b}
Proportion of group involved in communication	0.17^{**}	0.09^{*c}	0.29^{**c}

Note: Asterisks are used as indicated below to indicate the probability that each of the average correlations in the table differs from zero. Correlations sharing a common superscript are significantly different from each other.

$^{**}p < 0.001$

$^{*}p < 0.05$.

of the group performing any activity is significantly correlated with the amount of time spent communicating, and with the proportion of the group involved in communication. The more the group worked, the more time they spent communicating and the higher the proportion of the group involved in particular communication occasions; this was true for all three of the component tasks.

Recall, however, that our question concerned not only whether work on a particular task was correlated with communication intensity, but whether the strength of those correlations differed across tasks. To assess the relative demand for intensive communication, we compared drafting, the less integrative task, to planning and revising, the more integrative tasks, in terms of the amount of communication associated with each task, and in terms of the proportion of group members involved in communicating about each task. Three of these four comparisons (Table 7.3) reveal significant differences in the strength of the relationship between communication intensity and the level of involvement in the various tasks. Specifically, the correlations of time spent communicating with planning and with revising were significantly higher than the correlation of time spent communicating with drafting (for planning vs. drafting, $r = 0.42$ vs. 0.27, $t = 2.51$, $df = 75$, $p < 0.02$; for revising vs. drafting ($r = 0.52$ vs. 0.27, $t = 5.21$, $df = 75$, $p < 0.0001$). Among the correlations with proportion of the group involved in communication, the correlation with planning ($r = 0.17$) was not significantly different from the correlation with proportion drafting ($r = 0.09$), but the correlation with proportion revising ($r = 0.29$) was significantly higher than the correlation with proportion drafting ($r = 0.09$, $t = 4.52$, $df = 75$, $p < 0.0001$). Thus, the results of these comparisons generally support the idea that planning and revising demanded more intensive communication than drafting.

In sum, the Communication Modality manipulation produced the intended variations in communication patterns, and, although higher levels of work of any kind were associated with higher levels of communication, the positive relationship between working and communicating was, in general, stronger for planning and revising than for drafting. This last result provides partial confirmation of our conception of planning and revising as more integrative tasks, tasks that demand more intricate communication.

Phases of the project

The phase structure of work on the project is revealed in the daily time-use measures. As shown in Figure 7.1, the average proportion of group members who reported that they spent time planning, drafting, and revising varied systematically over the two-week life span of the projects.

Collapsing across communication conditions, we see, first, that most groups did very little on the first few days of the project. Between Day 4 and Day 6

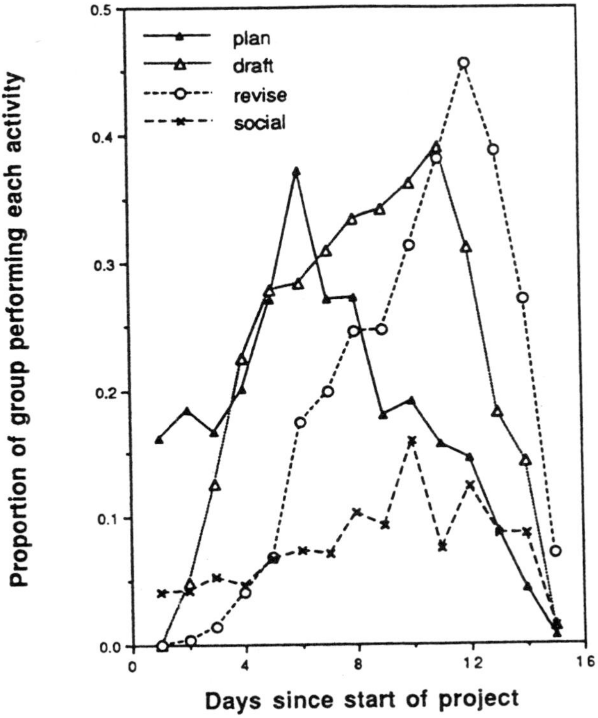

Figure 7.1 Proportion of group performing each activity on each project day, across communication conditions.

planning rose quickly, then peaked sharply on Day 6 and fell to its starting level by Day 8. Original drafting rose gradually from Day 5 to a peak on Day 11 and then sharply declined. Revising peaked on Day 12, three days before the project was due. In addition, these data reveal a relatively curvilinear pattern of social activities, suggesting that social activity is linked to the overall level of task activity, but does not vary in relation to the execution of particular tasks.

Further analyses indicated that the pattern of task activities shown in Figure 7.1 unfolded at different rates across communication conditions. With planning, for instance, the overall amount was about the same across communication conditions, but students in the Face-to-Face groups were apparently more efficient than students in the Computer-mediated conditions. The level of planning peaked earlier in the Face-to-Face groups than in the Computer-mediated groups, indicating, we believe, that face-to-face communication made it possible to move through this phase of the work more rapidly. Moreover. students in the Face-to-Face groups were apparently more effective in their initial planning, because, subsequent to the peak planning period, these groups were less likely to report additional planning than groups in the Computer-mediated conditions. That is, students in the Face-to-Face condition were apparently more able than those in the Computer-mediated conditions to proceed without having to revisit questions about what they were doing and how they should do it. This pattern is revealed in Figure 7.2a. The earlier peak in the line representing the Face-to-Face group is evidence of the greater efficiency of these groups, and the sharper decline is evidence of the greater effectiveness of their initial planning ($F(1, 74) = 12.0$, $p < 0.001$ for the linear component of the Communication Modality × Time interaction and $F(1, 74) = 7.2$, $p < 0.01$ for the quadratic component of the interaction). The contrast between the Computer Only and Computer + Phone conditions was not significant.

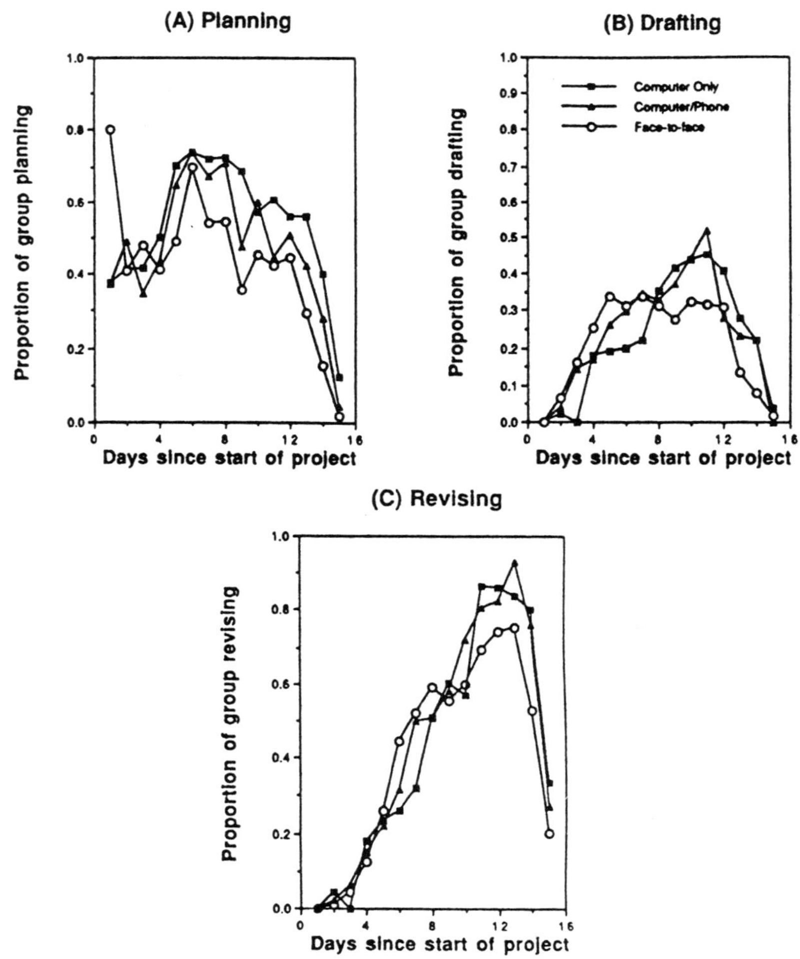

Figure 7.2 Proportion of group planning, drafting and revising in each communication condition on each project day.

Similar patterns of results (an earlier peak, followed by a more rapid decline of activity) were obtained for both drafting ($F(1, 74) = 10.0$, $p = 0.002$ for the linear component of the Communication Modality × Time interaction and ($F(1, 74) = 5.7$, $p = 0.02$ for the cubic component of the interaction) and revising (F(1, 74) = 9.3, p = 0.003 for the linear component of the Communication Modality × Time interaction and $F(1, 74) = 4.8$, $p < 0.05$ for the quadratic component of the interaction). The proportion of group members reporting these activities peaked earlier in the Face-to-Face groups than in those where communication was restricted. These results are shown in Figures 2b and 2c.

The interpretation of these patterns of task activity as an indication of the difficulty of communicating by computer is confirmed by the students' reports of how they did their work. These measures indicate that, as shown in Figure 7.3, students in the two Computer-mediated conditions reported working on more days over the course of the project than did students in the Face-to-Face condition ($F(1, 74) = 8.38$, $p < 0.01$). This gap in the proportion of students working increased over time and was especially apparent during the second week of the project when the students were revising their work (for the Face-to-Face vs. Computer × Linear Time interaction $F(1, 74) = 7.44$. $p < 0.01$).

A second measure of how students did their work is the amount of time spent communicating. In this analysis, the dependent variable is the product of number of communication occasions reported for a day and the length of the focal conversation, averaged over group members. Our results show that students who could use only the computer to discuss their work spent more

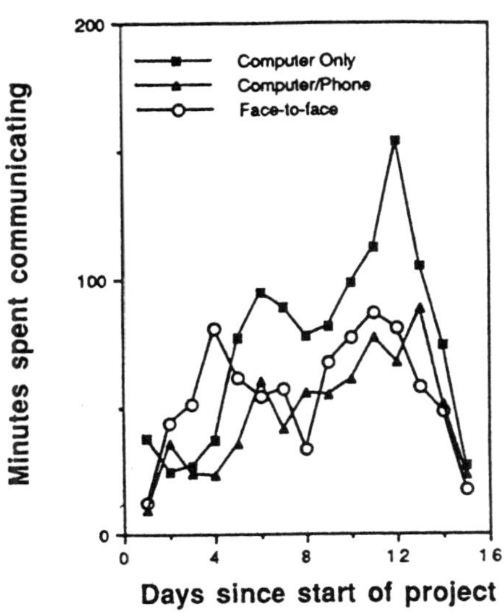

Figure 7.3 Minutes spent communicating in each communication condition on each project day.

time communicating than did students who could talk to each other either face-to-face or by phone (for the contrast comparing the two voice conditions to the Computer Only condition, $F(1, 74) = 10.0$, $p < 0.01$). In the second week of the project, students in the Computer Only condition were spending almost twice as much time per day communicating (107 minutes), as did students in the two voice conditions (Face-to-Face = 55 minutes and Computer + Phone = 61 minutes).

The relationship between Communication Modality and time spent communicating depended on the phase of the project. As shown in Figure 7.4, the difference in communication time between those in the Face-to-Face condition and those in the Computer-mediated groups increased over the course of the project and was especially intense during the revision phase (for the Face-to-Face vs Computer × Linear Time interaction, $F(1, 74) = 5.3$, $p < 0.01$). The two Computer-mediated conditions did not differ from each other in their changes over time.

Evaluations of work process

Although this difference in effort could reflect differences in commitment or greater enjoyment of the process, the data suggest that students in the computer-based groups worked longer because their task was more difficult. For instance, they reported more difficulty in coordinating their work than did students in the Face-to-Face condition (for the Face-to-Face vs Computer

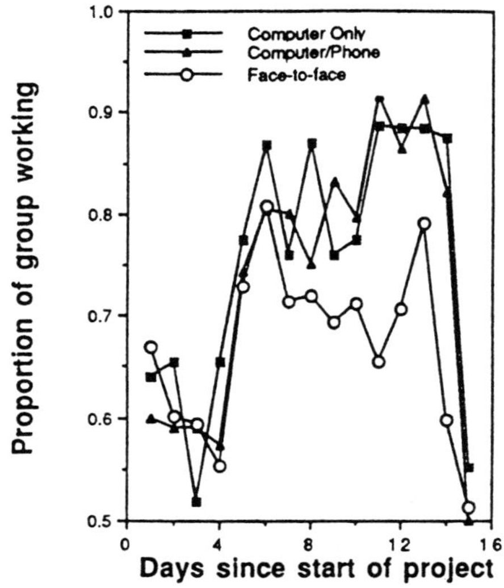

Figure 7.4 Proportion of group working in each communication condition on each project day.

contrast, $F(1, 74) = 81.44$, $p < 0.001$). Within the Computer-mediated conditions, students who could use the telephone had an easier time coordinating than did those who could use only the computer ($F(1, 74) = 3.8$, $p < 0.06$).

However, as is shown in Figure 7.5, the difficulty of coordinating work also varied with project phase. In the Face-to-Face groups, coordination difficulties dropped off early and continued to decline throughout the life of the project. In contrast, students in the Computer-mediated groups reported that difficulties in coordinating their work increased as they became more deeply involved in the project, and did not diminish until they were nearly finished (for the Face-to-Face vs Computer × Linear Time interaction $F(1, 74) = 7.8$, $p < 0.01$: for the quadratic component of the interaction $F(1, 74) = 14.8$. $p < 0.01$).

Association of evaluations and work activities

The preceding time-based analyses are based on the assumption that the phases of a project proceed uniformly and linearly for most groups (i.e. groups first plan, then draft and then revise, and that the steps in this sequence occur at the same time across communication conditions). But the hypothesis that computer-mediated communication is especially difficult when planning and revising a document can be tested more directly. Such an analysis would involve assessing the strength of the association between the activities a group is performing and the group's difficulty in coordinating their work across days, and determining whether those associations were affected by communication

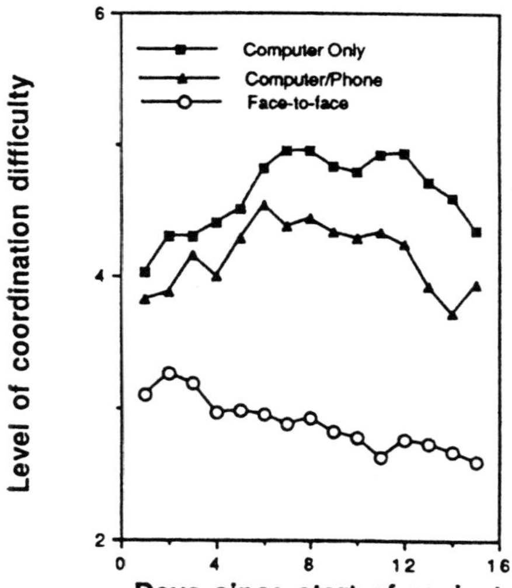

Figure 7.5 Level of reported coordination difficulty in each communication condition on each project day.

condition. Although our data do not include measures that directly link reported coordination difficulties with specific tasks, it is possible to create proxy measures that enable us to carry out this analysis.

First for each group, we computed the regression of coordination difficulty on planning, drafting, and revising (i.e. Coordination = Constant + β^*Planning + β^*Drafting + β^*Revising), with an N of 15 days.[7] The beta weights from this analysis indicate the extent to which each task was associated with coordination difficulties for each group, controlling for the performance of the other tasks. The mean beta weights are shown in Table 7.4.

Across all communication conditions, we observe a significant positive association between coordination difficulty and planning (Mean$\beta_{\text{Planning}} = 0.15$), but no relationship between coordination difficulties and drafting or revising (Mean$\beta_{\text{Drafting}} = 0.01$; Mean$\beta_{\text{Revising}} = -0.01$). That is, groups had more coordination difficulties on days in which they planned than on days they did not plan.

We then contrasted the Face-to-Face condition with the two Computer-mediated conditions using as dependent variables these standardized beta weights, which again, reflect the relationship between coordination difficulty and performance of each of the three component tasks.[8] This analysis reveals that the

Table 7.4 Association of proportion of group working on specific tasks with coordination difficulty in face-to-face and computer-mediated groups

	Plan	Draft	Revise
Face-to-Face			
Mean beta	0.09	−0.06	−0.13
Standard error	0.04	0.05	0.07
Number of groups	38	38	38
Computer-mediated			
Mean beta	0.22	0.07	0.10
Standard error	0.05	0.05	0.07
Number of groups	39	39	39

Note: Mean betas were obtained by regressing difficulties in coordination on planning, writing and revising for each group, with an N of 15 days (i.e. Coordination = Constant + $\beta_1 \times$ Planning + $\beta_2 \times$ Drafting + $\beta_3 \times$ Revising), and averaging the resulting beta weights over groups.

[a7] Note that a test for multicollinearity confirmed that the correlations between levels of planning, drafting and revising were low enough to permit estimates of the independent effect of each task. The correlation between planning and drafting was 0.20, between planning and revising 0.04, and between drafting and revising 0.39.

[8] The regression equation for this analysis is $\beta_{\text{Planning}} + \beta_{\text{Drafting}} + \beta_{\text{Revising}} = \text{Constant} + \beta \times$ Face-to-Face vs. Computer: that is, the relationship between coordination difficulty and work on all tasks, as a function of Communication modality. For a single task (e.g. planning), the equation is $\beta_{\text{Planning}} = \text{Constant} + \beta \times$ Face-to-Face vs. Computer: that is the relationship between coordination difficulty and planning, as a function of Communication Modality.

relationship between planning, drafting and revising with coordination problems was greater for Computer-mediated groups than for Face-to-Face groups ($F(1, 75) = 19.6$, $p < 0.001$). On average, the more students in Computer-mediated groups planned, drafted, or revised, the more coordination problems they had, but, in the Face-to-Face groups, no such association between increased activity and increased coordination difficulty was observed. On an individual task basis, the interaction was significant for revision ($F(1, 74) = 5.99$, $p < 0.02$), and marginally significant for drafting ($F(1, 74) = 2.81$, $p = 0.10$) and for planning ($F(1, 74) = 2.28$, $p < 0.11$). Finally, and contrary to our expectations, the difficulties that students in the Computer-mediated groups experienced relative to students in the Face-to-Face groups did not differ across tasks (Fs comparing drafting to planning and drafting to revision <1). That is, students in the Computer-mediated conditions were as likely to report coordination problems when they were drafting as when they were planning or revising.

Evaluations of communication quality

The difficulties students were experiencing were also reflected in other aspects of the questionnaire data. For example, on a measure of the quality of meetings that combined the students' reports on the productivity and enjoyment of focal communication occasions, face-to-face communication was superior to computer-mediated communication ($F(1, 74) = 8.9$, $p < 0.005$). The Computer-mediated conditions did not differ from each other in terms of meeting quality. On the retrospective questionnaire, students in the Face-to-Face conditions rated their circumstances more favorably than did students in the Computer-mediated conditions on three separate measures: ease of reaching agreement about how to proceed ($F(1, 74) = 4.15$, $p < 0.05$); ease of completing the project ($F(1, 74) = 69.024$, $p < 0.0001$); and overall satisfaction with communication conditions ($F(1, 74) = 261.72$, $p < 0.0001$). On the retrospective questionnaire, however, we did observe differences in the ratings of students in the Computer Only and Computer + Phone conditions, with the more favorable ratings occurring in the Computer Only condition: For ease of reaching agreement about how to proceed ($F(1, 74) = 15.94$, $p < 0.0001$), for ease of completing the project ($F(1, 74) = 5.54$, $p < 0.05$), and for overall satisfaction with communication conditions ($F(1, 74) = 8.42$, $p = 0.005$). These differences may be a result of adding the problems of orchestrating pairwise telephone conversations to the problems of using an asynchronous, noninteractive, text-based medium.

Project performance

Despite the difficulties that students in the Computer-mediated conditions experienced, their performance was not affected by communication condition

($F(1, 75) = 0.175$, $p = 0.647$). The average scores on the reports they produced were not significantly different than the scores of students who were able to meet face-to-face. Apparently, the greater costs they endured (greater investment of time in communication and in work on the project) paid off in product quality. But the students' own views of their work were more negative than the views of the raters. They perceived the quality of their work less favorably in the Computer-mediated conditions than in the Face-to-Face condition ($F(1, 74) = 6.7$, $p < 0.05$). Presumably, the problems encountered by students in the Computer-mediated conditions diminished their satisfaction with the work itself.

Social effects

Additional negative consequences of restricted communication appear in the social domain. In response to questions (on the daily questionnaire) about whether they had talked to other group members about other school work or about other topics, students in the Face-to-Face groups reported more social communications than did students in the Computer-mediated groups ($F(1, 75) = 23.7$, $p < 0.001$), and this difference persisted over the course of the two-week project. Adding a more interactive medium did not seem to increase the level of social interaction between students, those in the Computer + Phone groups didn't have significantly more social conversations than those in the Computer Only groups ($F(1, 74) = 2.2$, $p = 0.14$).

Students' affective reactions to their groups also showed main effects of communication modality. The scale measuring satisfaction with the work group (see Table 7.1) revealed that students in Computer-mediated groups were less positive toward the other members of their group than those in Face-to-Face groups ($F(1, 74) = 10.6$, $p < 0.01$). Again, this difference remained constant throughout the project. The two Computer-mediated groups did not differ from each other.

A scale measuring student perceptions that they and other members of their group were contributing fairly to the joint project showed that students in the Face-to-Face group rated the work process as more fair than did those in the two Computer-mediated groups ($F(1, 74) = 9.7$, $p < 0.01$). Moreover, this difference was largest in the middle of the project, presumably because, compared to other phases, individual work during the drafting phase was less visible and this problem was heightened by computer-based communication (for the Face-to-Face vs Computer × Quadratic interaction, $F(1, 74) = 14.8$, $p < 0.001$).

Taken together, this evidence – lower levels of social interaction, lower levels of reported liking for other group members, and a lower level of perceived fairness in the distribution of labor – suggests that social relationships surrounding the project were strained by channeling all communication through the Computer Only or Computer + Phone combination. (See Kiesler *et al.*, 1984, for a discussion of the social effects of computer-mediated communication.)

These effects, however, seem to be specifically associated with work on the project. Other evidence indicates that the computer conference supported social interaction on a broadly distributed, albeit less intense scale. Throughout the class in which this experiment was conducted, students used the computer conference extensively for social purposes. Class members exchanged hundreds of personal and social e-mail messages with other students outside their project teams, and, during the 10 weeks of the term, the 117 members of the class posted more than 2500 messages devoted to such topics as sports, outdoor recreation, politics, and school gossip in the open computer conference. Although the computer conference did not seem to provide an appropriate vehicle for the flashes of humor and goodwill that can help to alleviate strain on difficult projects, its utility as a community forum was confirmed in post-project evaluation, in which students reported that the computer system was superior to telephone and face-to-face communication in keeping up with school gossip.

DISCUSSION

Based on previous conceptualizations of the communicative demands associated with collaborative intellectual work, we hypothesized that using computer-mediated communication to carry out a project of this type would affect both task and social outcomes. With regard to the work process, we hypothesized: (1a) that computer-mediated communication would impede work on the project; (1b) that the impact of computer-mediated communication would vary over time; and (1c) that its negative impact would be most severe when the demand for interactive, expressive communication was believed to be highest. With regard to group performance, we hypothesized (2) that the performance of students in computer-mediated groups would be inferior to that of students who could communicate face-to-face. With regard to social experience, we hypothesized (3a) that computer-mediated communication would undermine relations among group members, but (3b) because social relations have a less well-defined temporal structure, this degradation would be unrelated to time-based task variation. Our results reveal substantial congruence with these hypotheses, but some discrepancies as well. Below, we discuss the fit of the data to the hypotheses.

Effects of communication modality on task execution

The most general hypothesis – that computer-mediated communication would impede project work – was confirmed. Computer-mediated groups required more time to complete each stage of their work, and also spent more total time working and more time communicating with each other than did the students in the face-to-face groups. But, despite this investment, they still reported greater difficulty in coordinating their work. We also obtained clear evidence that the impact of the communication modality manipulation varied over the course of the project. In particular, the quadratic and cubic components of the Time × Communication Modality interaction suggest that the negative impact of computer-mediated communication is a function of the communicative requirements of particular tasks.

The more specific assertion that computer-mediated communication was especially poor at supporting more integrative tasks was, however, only partially supported. The idea that the significant quadratic and cubic components of the Time × Communication Modality interaction reflect the detrimental effect of restricting communication at periods of maximum interdependence is supported by the pattern of task activities shown in Figure 7.1. None the less, in the time series analyses, the link between task activities and reported experiences can only be established by inference. And, contrary to the contingency hypothesis, more direct analyses revealed no differential impact of communication modality on coordination difficulty across tasks. The correlations between reported task activities, the proportion of the group working and the proportion involved in communication indicate that tasks defined as requiring more intensive interaction do, in fact, evoke that interaction. But these measures of involvement in specific tasks were not associated with differential levels of coordination difficulty for groups in different communication conditions. Self-reports of the extent to which groups were working were associated with the negative effects of computer-mediated communication, but the predictions were not stronger for the more integrative tasks (planning and revising) than for the more individualistic task (drafting).

It seems unlikely, however, that task characteristics are irrelevant to judgments about the utility of particular communications media. More likely, the absence of task-specific effects of communication modality is a function of imperfections in the link between the theoretical concepts on which our hypotheses are based and the concrete properties of collaborative writing. In particular, the framework used here breaks collaborative writing into phases thought to reflect the variations in the need for detailed coordination of individual activity described by the contingency theorists cited earlier (i.e. Van de Ven *et al.* 1976; Short *et al.*, 1976; Daft *et al.*, 1987). But analysts of individual writing projects have shown that planning, drafting and revising are likely to comingle and to be recursive (Flower and Hayes, 1978). In group work, the necessity for joint planning and allocation of tasks to individuals might impose a more linear process than has been observed with individuals (note, for instance, the orderly sequence of peak activity levels in planning, drafting and revising portrayed in Figure 7.1), but a close-up view would likely reveal that this process encompasses considerable task-cycling. For instance, groups might plan, draft, and revise an outline, but within the outline, they might plan, draft, and revise the introductory argument, the body of the document, and their conclusions. This task-cycling may dampen the effects of high-level differences in the components that make up a long-term project.

This line of argument suggests the need for more controlled research with better measures of the components of intellectual teamwork. If group members are rapidly shifting from planning to drafting, from drafting to revision and back again, activity measures that only permit respondents to characterize their work at a general level may be too gross or insensitive to portray the sequence of group work accurately. Thus, rather than seeking contingencies between communication requirements and projects, work groups or organizational level (Daft and Lengel, 1986; Rice *et al.*, 1989; Tushman, 1978, 1979), researchers should be encouraged to look for contingencies at a more molecular level of analysis. Intellectual progress is likely to depend on matching detailed features of tasks with detailed attributes of the communication modalities (cf Zmud *et al.*, 1990).

The idea of task-cycling should not, however, be seen as merely a rationalization for failure to confirm our hypothesis. Rather, the idea that collaborative writing, as well as other forms of intellectual teamwork, involves intricately interwoven task variations may help to explain not only the absence of task-based effects of communication modality, but also the presence of the substantial negative effects of communication modality that we observed. To the extent that such rapid task-cycling exists, group members are likely to need a highly flexible communications medium. Indeed, the advantage of face-to-face communication might not be that it makes possible specific forms of communication that no other medium can provide, but that it makes possible all, or most, of the forms of communication that other media can provide. In face-to-face groups, members can move easily from individual thoughts to group discussion, to initial sketches of their plans, back to discussion and modification of those plans, all within the space of a single meeting. When opportunities for interactive and expressive communications are constrained, movement between these activities becomes much more difficult. Group members are likely to endure delay in obtaining responses to their ideas, to have difficulty establishing that a goal has been reached and a new activity can be initiated, and to feel constrained by reductions in bandwidth that prevent the full expression of ideas.

Effects of communication modality on project performance

As noted above, despite the many frustrations they endured, the students in the computer-mediated communication conditions produced documents that were similar in overall quality to those produced by the students who were able to meet face-to-face. Although the process data make it clear that this achievement was hard-won, the absence of an effect of communication modality on project performance reveals the limitations of contingency theory. In particular, contingency theory holds that particular tasks demand particular ways of communicating, and that the inability to communicate in the theoretically prescribed fashion should undermine performance. But this proposition ignores the possibility that, faced with an inappropriate task/technology match, people can nevertheless carry out their work by adjusting their behavior to meet their goals. The equifinality of results observed here implies that the greater amounts of time that the students in the restrided communication conditions spent working and communicating about the project can be seen, not merely as liabilities, but as adaptations to a difficult set of circumstances. This interpretation suggests that rather than focusing solely on questions about performance and user satisfaction, future research about human uses of technology should also focus on questions about patterns of adaptation (Orlikowski and Robey, 1991; Yates and Orlikowski, 1992).

Effects of communication modality on social experience

As we anticipated. restricting communication not only interfered with the students' ability to do their work efficiently, but also undermined their ability to establish amicable relationships. However, in contrast to the temporal variation observed in the task domain, our measures of social experience reveal a simple main effect of communication modality. Many studies have shown that ease in communication among individuals increases the likelihood of friendship formation and contributes to group cohesiveness. Thus, the most likely explanation for the detrimental effect of computer-mediated communication on social relations is simply that it interferes with the smooth flow of conversation, making it more difficult for individuals to come to know and appreciate each other.

Methodological considerations

One might argue that the results reported here – especially the effects on work processes – are artifactual, resulting from differential levels of experience with face-to-face and computer-mediated communication rather than from the constraints imposed by the technology. However, the structure of the experiment makes it unlikely that lack of experience with computer-mediated communication per se can account for our findings. The two class projects involved in this experiment were several weeks apart. Doing this interval, many students used the computer conference regularly to exchange e-mail messages and to post notices meant to entertain the professor and other members of the class. If the results were entirely an artifact of experience with the medium, this extended opportunity to practice should surely have led to some difference in the pattern of results obtained on the two projects. As noted earlier, however, the results showed no changes in the effects of technology over time between projects; rather, there were variations in the effects of communication conditions over time within projects. These within-project temporal variations make it unlikely that the results are solely, or even mainly, a result of limited expertise or dislike for computer-mediated communication.

A somewhat more serious criticism of this experiment is that, rather than reducing obstacles to communication as it might in a distributed work situation, computer-mediated communication interfered with familiar and reasonably effective ways of working. Students' reactions to the computer-mediated communication technology might have been more positive if, as in authentic distributed work, they had been unable to communicate about their work without it. Even in this more artificial situation, however, computer-mediated communication could potentially have served student needs. The projects they were working on were, for them, their real work, not a task designed for and limited to the experimental context. The effort they invested in completing their work makes it clear that they believed performance mattered. Furthermore, despite common membership in the MBA community, arranging out-of-class face-to-face meetings was often problematic. In this class as well as others, students frequently complained about the difficulty of squeezing group meetings into schedules that were already crowded with coursework, part- or full-time jobs and, quite often, family responsibilities as well. In sum, their motivation to perform well, the scheduling problems associated with group work and the enthusiasm students showed in using the computer conference for less demanding communication tasks suggest that computer-mediated communication would have been viewed more favorably if it had provided an effective mechanism for communicating about project work.

Still, both the concern about lack of experience and lack of real benefit of electronic communication are, almost certainly, valid to some extent. The projects in this study were much longer and more complex than the tasks used in many experimental studies of computer-mediated communication, but they are still, when compared to many 'real world' forms of intellectual teamwork (cf. Kraut *et al.*, 1987–1988), short-term projects. In longer projects, and in situations where computer-mediated communication becomes an integral, taken-for-granted aspect of organizational life, people undoubtedly become more skilled in using it. Thus, we applaud efforts such as those in which McGrath and his colleagues (1993) are examining the effects of computer-mediated communication over longer time periods and across a broad range of tasks. Projects such as this will help to identify which of the effects of computer-mediated communication we have observed here endure over time, and which dissipate as this way of communicating becomes more familiar. They will also help to distinguish tasks that seem to require the interactivity and expressiveness of face-to-face communication from those which distributed workers can perform easily and efficiently using leaner media.

Our own analyses of communication among collaborating scientists hint at what such clarifying research may reveal. For instance, we have found that, despite access to and experience with computer-mediated communication, the researchers we have interviewed typically discuss their work face-to-face, and are especially likely to choose this medium during the early stages of a project. In more than 100 interviews with researchers in several disciplines, only one has reported initiating a new project and carrying out the primary planning electronically. Moreover, many have reported that, despite a history of successful joint work and, often, strong personal relationships, they find it difficult to begin new projects when once co-located colleagues move to new institutions. In our view, these difficulties are not a matter of lack of experience; rather, they reflect fundamental difficulties in conducting the complex conversations required to launch a new project when interactivity and expressiveness are reduced (Galegher and Kraut, 1992). Recent observations of distributed teams in a multinational corporation have produced similar findings; computer-mediated communication plays an important role in helping members of these teams coordinate their activities, but discussions of complicated problems, especially during the early stages of project work appear to demand face-to-face communication. In addition, the participants claimed that their experience had taught them that, despite the great differences between them and the considerable expense of travel, the project tended to go 'off track' without face-to-face meetings at regular intervals (Johnson, 1992). We believe that these two examples illustrate both the extended connectivity that computer-mediated communication makes possible, and its limitations as a medium for approaching new problems.

Summary

The essence of contingency theory is its claim about the importance of the task/technology fit. Our results provide partial confirmation of this basic premise; when constrained to using technologies inadequate for their tasks, group members experienced substantial difficulties. But, as McGrath (1990) and others have argued, understanding behavior in groups and the impact of technology on that behavior requires both observations over time and attention to multiple outcomes. When the full range of outcomes, and their temporal patterns, is considered, the results are much more complicated than could be predicted solely on the basis of contingency theory. In particular, this experiment revealed an interesting combination of interrelatedness and independence in the relationship between various measures of group performance. The quality of group performance was apparently unrelated to the process that generated it, and although the negative effects of computer-mediated communication on the work process were also reflected in group members' social experiences, the temporal pattern of results differed substantially across the two domains. These results suggest that theoretical statements that postulate simple relationships between tasks and technologies are almost certain to be wrong, at least with regard to some aspect of group effectiveness. Clearly, alternative theoretical formulations based on more sophisticated understandings of tasks, technologies and human behavior are required. In our current work, we are attempting to develop such formulations.

Practically, the results of this study suggest some of the limits of computer-mediated communication systems. As recent news reports show (Kolata, 1990), these systems permit speedy collaboration across barriers of time and distance. And, as we have noted, students in the computer-mediated groups in this experiment were able, despite considerable difficulty, to complete their work and to produce reports similar in quality to those produced in more traditional ways. The computer conference also allowed students to keep in touch with a wide network of information and gossip, and they acknowledged that computer-mediated communication could be satisfactory as a means of handing off independently completed interim products. But the results of this study indicate that electronic groups have a more difficult time carrying out their work and form weaker bonds for member support than do face-to-face groups. As a result, at least until more satisfactory technologies become available, complex, long-term collaborative work is likely to involve a recurring need for face-to-face interaction.

ACKNOWLEDGEMENTS

An earlier version of this manuscript was presented at the Conference on Computer-Supported Cooperative Work, Los Angeles, California, October, 1990. We are grateful to the CSCW reviewers, and to the anonymous reviewers who commented on earlier versions submitted to this journal. The data described in this report were collected while the first author was on the faculty at the University of Arizona, and this research was partially supported by a grant from the Office of the Vice-President for Research at that university. Similarly, Robert Kraut was employed by Bellcore when these data were collected, and his work was supported by that organization.

REFERENCES

Connolly, T. and Thorn, B. K. (1990) Discretionary databases: theory, data and implications. In Fulk, J. and Steinfeld, C. (eds), *Organizations and Communication Technology*, Sage Publications, Newbury Park, CA, pp. 219–233.

Couture, B. and Rymer, J. (1989) Interactive writing on the job: definitions and implications of collaboration. Kogen, M. (ed.). *Writing in the Business Professions*, NCTE and ABC, Urbana, IL. pp. 73–89.

Daft, R. L. and Lengel, R. (1986) Organizational information requirements, media richness and structural design. *Management Science*, **32**, 554–571.

Daft, R. L., Lengel, R. and Trevino, L. (1987) Message equivocality, media selection and manager performance: implications for information systems. *MIS Quarterly*, **11**, 355–366.

Daft, R. L. and Macintosh, N. B. (1981) A tentative exploration into the amount and equivocality of information processing in organizational work units. *Administrative Science Quarterly*, **26**, 207–224.

Ede, L. and Lunsford, A. (1990) *Singular Texts/Plural Authors: Perspectives on Collaborative Writing*. Southern Illinois University Press, Carbondale, IL.

Faigley, L. and Miller, T. P. (1982) What we learn from writing on the job. *College English*, **44**, 557–569.

Finholt, T., Sproull, L. and Kiesler, S. (1990) Communication and performance in ad hoc task groups. Galegher, J., Kraut, R. E. and Egido, C. (eds), *Intellectual Teamwork: The Social and Technological Bases of Cooperative Work*, Lawrence Erlbaum, Inc., Hillsdale, NJ, pp. 291–325.

Flower, L. and Hayes, J. R. (1978) A cognitive process theory of writing. *College Composition and Communication*, **32**, 365–387.

Forman, J. (1991) Novices work on group reports: problems in group writing and in computer-supported group writing. *J. Business and Technical Communication*, **5**, 48–75.

Galegher, J. and Kraut, R. E. (1992) Computer-mediated communication and collaborative writing: media influence and adaptation to communication constraints. *Proceedings of the Conference on Computer-Supported Cooperative Work*, ACM Press, Baltimore, MD, pp. 155–162.

Hackman, J. R. (1987) The design of work teams. Lorsch, J. W. (ed.), *Handbook of Organization Psychology*, Prentice-Hall, Englewood Cliffs, NJ, pp. 315–342.

Horton, M., Rogers, P. R., Austin, L., Brimm, D. and McCormick, M. (1991) The impact of face-to-face collaborative technology on group writing. *Proceedings of the Hawaii International Conference on Systems Sciences*.

Hiltz, S. R. (1984) *On-line Communities: A Case Study of the Office of the Future*. Ablex, Norwood, NJ.

Johnson, P. (1992) *Managing Global Teams*. Presented at MIT Center for Coordination Science, Boston, MA, March.

Kiesler, S., Siegel, J. and McGuire, T. (1984) Social psychological aspects of computer-mediated communication. *American Psychologists*, **39**, 1123–1134.

Kolata, G. (1990) In a frenzy, math enters age of electronic mail. *New York Times*, June 26, C1.

Kraut, R. E., Fish, R., Root, R. and Chalfonte, B. (1990) Informal communication in organizations: form, function and technology. Oskamp, S. and Spacapan, S. (eds), *Human Reactions to Technology: The Claremont Symposium on Applied Social Psychology*, Sage Publications Inc., Beverely Hills, CA, pp. 145–199.

Kraut, R. E., Galegher, J. and Egidox, C. (1987–1988) Relationships and tasks in scientific collaboration. *Human–Computer Interaction*, **3**, 31–58.

Kraut, R. E. and Galegher, J. (1994) *Informal Communication and Scientific Work*, Unpublished manuscript.

Kraut, R. E., Galegher, J., Fish, R. and Chalfonte, B. (1992) Task requirements and media choice in collaborative writing. *Human–Computer Interaction*, **7**, 375–407.

Lawrence, P. R. and Lorsch, J. W. (1967) *Organization and Environment*. Irwin, Homewood, IL.

Markus, M. L. (1990) Toward a critical mass theory of interactive media. In Fulk, J. and Steinfeld (eds), *Organizations and Communication Technology*. Sage Publications, Newbury Park, CA, pp. 194–218.

McGarth, J. E. (1990) Time matters in groups. In Galegher, J., Kraut, R. E. and Egido, C. (eds), *Intellectual Teamwork: The Social and Technological Bases of Cooperative Work*, Lawrence Erlbaum, Inc., Hilldale, NJ, pp. 23–61.

McGarth, J. E. (1993) Special Issue, *Small Groups Research*, **24**.

Micheli, L. M., Cespedes, F. V., Byker, D. and Raymond, T. J. C. (1984) *Mangerial Communications*, Scott Foresman and Company, Glenview, IL.

Orikowski, W. J. and Robey, D. (1991) Information technology and the structuring of organization. *Information Systems Research*, **2**, 143–169.

Rice, R. E., Hughes, D. and Love, G. (1989) Usage and outcomes of electronic messaging at an R&D organization: Situational constraints, job level and media awareness. *Office: Technology and People*, **5**, 141–161.

Rosenthal, R. (1973) Estimating effective reliabilities in studies that employ judges' ratings. *J. Clinical Psychology*, **29**, 342–345.

Schuler, R. S. and Youngblood, S. A. (1986) *Case Problems in Personnel and Human Resource Management*. West Publishing Company, St. Paul, MN.

Short, J., Williams, E. and Christie, B. (1976) *The Social Psychology of Telecommunications*, Wiley, New York.

Sproull, L. and Kiesler, S. (1991) *Connections: New Ways of Working in the Networked Organization*, MIT Press, Cambridge, MA.

Trevino, L. K., Daft, R. L. and Lengel, R. H. (1990) Understanding managers' media choices: a symbolic interactionist perspective. Fulk, J. and Steinfeld, C. W. (eds), *Organizations and Communication Technology*, Sage, Newbury Park, CA.

Tushman, M. L. (1978) Technical communication in R&D laboratories: the impact of project work characteristics. *Academy of Management J.*, **21**, 624–645.

Tushman, M. L. (1979) Work characteristics and subunit communication structure: a contingency analysis, *Administrative Science Quarterly*, **24**, 82–97.

Van de Ven, A., Delbecq, A. and Koenig, R. (1976) Determinants of coordination modes within organizations. *American Sociological Review*, **41**, 322–338.

Yates, J. and Orlikowski, W. J. (1992) Genres of organizational communication: a structurational approach to studying communication and media. *Academy of Management Review*, **17**, 299–326.

Zmud, R., Lind, M. and Young, F. (1990) An attribute space for organizational communication channels. *Information Systems Research*, **1**, 440–457.

8 Learning to Write Together[1]

ILONA POSNER, ALEX MITCHELL and
RONALD BAECKER

INTRODUCTION

Writing together, while often necessary, is never easy. We have seen this repeatedly in our research into the ways in which people write together, how people learn to write together, and how computer-based tools can help with the learning and writing processes (Baecker *et al.*, 1993; Mawby, 1991; Nastos, 1992; Posner, 1991). Other investigators have studied collaborative writing among mature writers (Beck, 1993; Ede and Lunsford, 1990; Kraut *et al.*, 1990; Posner and Baecker, 1992). A number of theories of collaborative writing have been developed (Ede and Lunsford, 1990; Posner and Baecker, 1992; Sharples *et al.*, 1993) to characterize the writing process. There have also been a number of tools designed to support collaborative writing (Baecker *et al.*, 1993; Ellis *et al.*, 1991; Leland *et al.*, 1988; Neuwirth *et al.*, 1992; Olson, Olson, Mack and Wellner, 1990).

We learned that experienced writers have biases towards groupware based on the way they write using conventional non-groupware tools, and they often resist the new paradigms introduced by groupware technology. In order to learn more about the process of collaborative writing, we decided to focus this study on novice writers learning to use groupware to write collaboratively. We chose to observe extended usage of groupware technology in the realistic setting of a classroom in order to observe the effects of groupware tools on the collaborative writing process and to learn how to design better software.

In our study, two groups of grade six students worked together for twelve weeks to produce a magazine on prejudice (see Figure 8.1). The students learned how to use Aspects (developed by Group Logic Inc., formerly Group Technologies Inc.), a commercial synchronous collaborative editor, and developed the skills necessary to work as a group and to successfully write together. Although collaborative writing is a common practice among mature writers, our experience with the SASSE (Baecker *et al.*, 1993) group editor suggests that novice writers are uncertain as to how to proceed, and often have

[1] Some of this material appeared previously in Mitchell *et al.* (1995)

GROUPWARE AND AUTHORING
ISBN 0-12-575005-6

Figure 8.1 Magazine cover, created by Ryan Field, age 12.

difficulty even understanding what is meant by collaborative writing. Other researchers have dealt with group writing in the classroom (DiPardo and Freedman, 1987), identifying the difficulties facing novice writers in collaborative situations, without the added complexity of using groupware tools. Our early trials using naive collaborative writers highlighted the importance of demonstrating to novices a variety of approaches to group writing. Because of this, we began our study by providing the students with training in collaborative writing, and concluded by observing their attempts to write together using groupware.

This paper presents the results of this study. We begin with an overview of the study itself, and describe the methods used to observe the sessions and analyze the collected data. We then discuss the process of learning to write together by describing the writing approaches and activities employed by the students, and the ways in which these approaches and activities developed over the twelve hours of the study. We continue with a brief look at the effects of these writing approaches and activities on the resulting documents. We also discuss the impact of the project on the participants. A detailed section examines the effects of the technology on the process of learning to write together; it describes the students' experiences and how our observations can inform the design of future collaborative writing tools. We conclude the paper with implications for future studies.

THE PREJUDICE PROJECT

The Prejudice Project took place at the Huron Street Public School in Toronto between February and May 1994. The goal of this project was for grade 6 students to learn about prejudice while collaboratively writing and producing a magazine on that topic.

We conducted an ethnographic study of two groups of four grade six students preparing the written material for this magazine. Eight students were selected, with the assistance of their teachers, from 14 volunteers out of two grade 5/6 classes. The students were familiar with the Computer-Supported Intentional Learning Environment (CSILE), a shared knowledge building system (Scardamalia *et al.*, 1989) but had never used synchronous collaborative software.

Through the course of the study the students learned to write together using Aspects on networked Macintosh computers. Aspects is a synchronous text editor, which allows multiple users to work concurrently on a document, entering text at the same time in different paragraphs, with changes immediately visible on all users' screens. Aspects also provides telepointers, individual cursors which can be made visible on all users' screens.

The study

Each group met once a week for one hour after school over a period of 12 weeks. The students worked in one classroom, sitting at four adjacent Macintosh computers (see Figure 8.2). The computers were connected by a local area network, and all ran Aspects, allowing the sharing of documents among different machines. Seating arrangements were rotated weekly to reduce the likelihood of subgroup formation and to assign the preferred seats equally among the students. During the study they were given training in the use of Aspects, introduced to collaborative writing techniques, and given the freedom to use their new skills.

The first five weeks were highly structured in order to allow us to cover a variety of topics related to prejudice and to introduce a number of collaborative writing techniques. Students were shown the mechanisms provided by Aspects which were required to perform the assigned writing tasks. These tasks included working as a group to write a poem and a story. The tasks were designed to expose the students to a variety of writing approaches (Posner, 1991; Posner and Baecker, 1992), which were introduced by the instructor to show them the various different ways of writing together.

The following schedule outlines the breakdown of the first five weeks of the study:

1. *Introduction to the project*: Goals, rules, responsibilities
   Exercise – Differences: Interview a partner, getting to know each other better and tell the group.

Figure 8.2 Physical setup of the study.

Exercise – Similarities: As a group find what makes you all happy and sad.
Exercise – Perception: Look at a picture, write down three things you find most interesting.
Goal of exercises: Get students talking, expressing their opinions, more comfortable with each other. See that they are all unique and have different opinions but that they agree about other things.
Technical goals: Start writing on-line using CSILE. Writing approaches: independent and scribe.

2. *Exercise – Perception*: Advantages and disadvantages of differences in perception
   Goal of exercise: To show that people have different perceptions of the same things, people, events.
   Technical goals: Introduction to groupware and group writing exercise, introduce concept of revising their work. Writing approaches: scribe, parallel, joint.
3. *Exercise – Minority poem*: When I'm in the minority I feel ...
   Goal of exercise: To introduce concept of minority and how it might feel to be a member of a minority.
   Technical goals: Introduction to groupware. Use both CSILE and Aspects, learn how to Cut/Paste between two applications. Writing approach: parallel and joint.
   Exercise – Develop orientation plan: How to welcome a new student to your class.
   Technical goals: More practice with software and collaborative writing. Writing approach: joint/parallel.

4 *Exercise – Generalization*: Need to qualify what we say, 'Basketball players are tall' better 'most ...
Exercise – Stereotypes: Discussion how stereotypes are created and group writing exercise.
Goal of exercises: To introduce concept of generalization, stereotype, and prejudice. Make them aware that all generalizations, particularly those about people, need to be qualified.
Technical goals: More practice using software and doing collaborative writing. Writing approach: parallel.

5. *Exercise – Prejudice*: Define concepts, read a sample story, group writing exercise (story).
Technical goals: More practice in collaborative writing. Writing approaches: scribe and joint.

In the remaining weeks the students were free to choose what they wanted to work on and how they would work together. The students' work during the second half of the study included doing research, writing articles, creating artwork, and editing materials created in the first five weeks which they had chosen to include in the magazine. After the initial training in the uses of technology and the group writing approaches, we minimized our guidance so that we could observe the choices the students would make.

Data collection and analysis

During each weekly session all of the groups' interactions were videotaped (see Figure 8.3). Two cameras covered the students working on the computers, and two cameras captured screen images. In addition, time-indexed notes were made using the Timelines (Harrison *et al.*, 1994) sequential data analysis and video annotation software while the sessions were in progress. Exploratory analysis was conducted on the video records of the sessions by two people

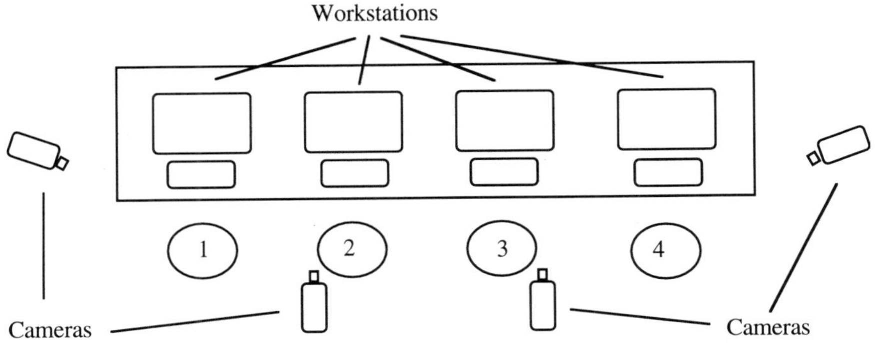

Figure 8.3 Data collection.

using Timelines. This analysis focused on identifying common problems, incidents and trends in the data.

A number of other measures were used to provide a rich view of the sessions. The students' teachers were asked to evaluate the students' writing skills and ability to work together. Each individual's writing skills were rated using a seven-point scale according to vocabulary, spelling, grammar, ideas and creativity, and writing style. The teachers also provided blind evaluations of a selection of work, both individual and group, using these categories. These scores were then averaged for each individual, and across each group, to give an indication of general writing level. Each student's ability to work in a group was also rated according to interpersonal skills, communication skills, leadership skills, maturity, and task focus.

We also conducted two questionnaires, one at the halfway point and one at the end of the project, and a final individual interview with each student. A few weeks after the end of the project, we came back and conducted a group discussion about the project, which gave additional insight into the students' experiences.

THE PROCESS OF LEARNING TO WRITE TOGETHER

By *writing together* or *collaborative writing* we mean the creation of documents with the participation of several individuals. There may be numerous stages in the creation process, including brainstorming, planning, choosing a writing approach, assigning activities, combining ideas, resolving conflicting ideas, entering text, editing, and reaching consensus about the final text.

Given this complexity, it was not surprising that when the students were asked to write together early in the project they did not understand what this meant. They gradually developed an understanding of group writing as they were coached about different writing approaches, experimented with different writing activities, and gained experience over the 12-week period.

We now look at the different writing approaches and activities used by the students, examining how these approaches and activities changed over the course of the study. We focus specifically on three texts: a poem written during the third week, a story written during the fifth week, and the introduction to the magazine written during the eleventh week. These documents were selected from among the documents that the students chose for inclusion in their magazine. The writing of these documents spanned the duration of the project and involved the use of a variety of writing approaches.

Writing approaches

When a group project is assigned during their everyday classroom work, the students generally use the *independent* writing approach – dividing the task into distinct components and working on those sections individually, with minimal feedback between group members. We started by using this approach to minimize the transition from the students' everyday writing, since they already had to contend with many changes due to the physical setup of our study. This early writing also provided us with samples of individual work that we could evaluate and compare to the students' individual in-class writing and to their group work.

Since all of our students enjoyed typing on the computers, they found the synchronous access provided by Aspects to be fun. However, introducing a shared workspace did not spontaneously lead to close collaborative work. The students tended to use the *parallel* writing approach, working on different parts of one document, and seldom examined each others' entries. This approach was used by both groups when writing the poem. When segments were written in parallel by different individuals, information was often duplicated. The students also noticed that this parallel writing approach often resulted in a fragmented writing style. Here Sue (names of the students have been changed, but their gender preserved) discusses how to improve the poem that the group had written in parallel:

Sue: I think we should write the whole thing over because it sounds like three poems stuck together.
Hope: Yeah, I think one person has to rewrite it.
Liz: Yeah.

The *scribe* writing approach, where one person enters the text at the keyboard while the rest of the group suggest ideas, was also familiar to the students. This approach is often used by individuals working simultaneously on one document using traditional writing software. By making the group document available to different writers on several different computers, Aspects subtly alters the dynamics of the scribe approach. Even though a document was accessible on several computers, in the early stages of the project the group would still gather around one machine with the scribe controlling the document and making all the final decisions. This is the way the scribe approach is normally used with a single-user word processor.

However, Aspects makes the shared document visible on all users' computers, letting all the participants have an equal opportunity to view the text. After a few weeks, when the students had become used to the idea of a shared document, they would follow the text being typed by the scribe on their own computers, suggest changes to the scribe, and use telepointers to indicate where the changes should be made. Despite the fact that the scribe still had control of the document, other group members provided input that led to very fine grain changes in the text, including spelling, wording, and grammar.

Later in the project, individuals were seen correcting the text which was just typed by the scribe as soon as it was accessible to them[1]; we call this the *joint*

[1] During the project we set Aspects' locking at the paragraph level, so paragraphs could be controlled by only one individual at a time.

writing approach. Joint writing involves all participants taking an active role in the actual manipulation of the emerging document, a role not possible in traditional single-user word processors.

These approaches should be viewed as four points in the space of collaborative writing possibilities. Real collaborations may include a combination of several approaches. For example, while writing the story, both groups used primarily the scribe writing approach, but there were some instances of joint writing; we shall call this *scribe/joint* writing.

As they gained experience with the technology and the group writing approaches, the students in the first group expanded their repertoire, using a *parallel/joint* writing approach. While writing the magazine's introduction on the eleventh day, each member of the group worked inside the shared document, writing quietly and making changes to his/her entries based on each others contributions but without much discussion. At times students would glance at other parts of the document or discuss ideas, assuming that everyone was aware of the entire document's contents.

As they became more experienced with collaborative writing, the students also became more selective in their use of writing approaches, to the point of switching strategies in the middle of composing a document. For example, when working on the magazine's introduction, the second group shifted between scribe/joint and parallel writing to solve a consensus problem. During the scribe/joint writing component, the group could not agree on the best wording for one section of the document. To solve this, three members worked in parallel to enter their own ideas. Once the ideas had been entered, they all read these entries and combined them into a single paragraph. The group then shifted back to scribe/joint writing to complete the document.

By the end of the study, both groups had progressed from the simple use of an independent writing approach to an understanding and use of a variety of collaborative writing approaches. They were able to select an approach appropriate to a given task, and to adapt their writing approach to suit the demands of each stage of writing. After 12 hours of training and practice, they had clearly developed significant proficiency and sophistication in collaborative writing.

Writing activities

Among writing activities (Posner and Baecker, 1992) we include planning, typing, dictating, correcting mistakes and editing, where editing implies clarifying the language, ideas, spelling, vocabulary, and grammar. The notion of different writing activities was familiar to the students. Each student participated in various activities throughout the project. We now discuss how the students perceived these activities and how the activities were assigned to individuals in the groups.

In the final questionnaire the students were asked to rate the importance of the various activities that are involved in group writing. At the same time they were asked to rate each activity according to how much they enjoyed it. The students felt that correcting mistakes was the most important activity, followed by planning and making changes. However, the most enjoyed activity was typing the words, followed by planning and dictating. All the students were willing to perform activities they did not necessarily enjoy since they recognized their importance.

The students used a variety of methods to assign activities to individuals. The easiest method was to have someone volunteer for an activity and have their suggestion remain unchallenged by the rest of the group. Another method was to have someone assign an activity to a willing individual. The remaining assignment methods involved negotiation, compromises, and at times even power struggles to attain a desired activity.

The most preferred and contested activity was typing. Both groups witnessed lengthy and intense debates over who should type the story, which was to be jointly written by the group:

Hope: I'll type
Liz: I'll type
Sue: I'm the fastest
Dan: I'm typing
Sue: We can all type
Liz: It's not fair
Instructor: Wait wait wait! The point here is not the typing. The point here is the story!
Dan: They always get to do everything! They're being sexist[2] and it's not fair! [punches table]
Liz: [typing already]
Hope: [also typing]
Dan: Okay I'm starting

The group went along with this, everyone dictating while Dan typed. Ideas were passed around and negotiated, but the final decisions were made by Dan.

The assignment of activities was often informal, and people frequently shifted between activities during the writing process. Which activity an individual chose was guided by the activity's perceived enjoyment as well as the individual's skill at each activity. Rob typed the group's story, but delegated the corrections to other group members after admitting that he is a bad speller. The ideas for the story originated mostly with the other group members. Carol fixed the grammar, which is her strength, and Kim corrected

[2] The groups consisted of three girls and one boy. This imbalance led to some subgroup formations and some disputes where gender differences became an issue. Dan complained that 'Group writing was very stressful ... they all ganged up on me, every time, because I'm a boy.' He did, however, obtain control of the group's document at critical moments.

the spelling. Thus, unlike individual work, where one person performs all writing related activities, participants on group projects are able to pick and choose among activities based on their strengths and their preferences.

Which activities to perform and in what sequence these are to occur are decisions that must be made explicit in group work. The resulting patterns evolve out of the writing habits of the individual participants. Rob tried to guide the second group into following his favorite writing scheme, of first producing a rough draft of the text then later going back to make changes. Some of his collaborators were not as comfortable with this scheme, and preferred to correct the spelling and grammar mistakes as soon as these occurred. While writing the story, the group compromised and corrected some mistakes right away, with minimal interruption to the creative process, and made a separate pass correcting the remaining mistakes. During the various passes, different people took control of the document performing different activities: Rob typed the text; Carol fixed the grammar, and Kim corrected the spelling. Throughout the entire writing process, the group remained extremely goal oriented and task focused with only a few distractions. This had a positive impact on the final product.

IMPACT OF GROUP WORK ON THE PRODUCT

There is some disagreement in the literature about whether group work has a positive or negative effect on the quality of the product (DiPardo and Freedman, 1987; Freedman, 1987). We will now examine how, in this study, the quality of the group document relates to the writing ability of the individual writers and to the quality of their individual work, and how the writing process seems to affect the product quality.

As mentioned earlier, the two teachers were asked to evaluate the students' writing created while working on our project. Each teacher also produced a score to estimate his students' *in-class writing average*; we used this score as a baseline measure of the students' writing ability. During this project, each group produced eleven writing samples including both individual and group work. We will focus our discussion on the students' independent work done during the project (*on-project average*) and on three jointly written documents (*poem, story, and introduction*). Table 8.1 summarizes our results.

When examining the students' individual work, we note that their in-class writing is rated higher than their on-project writing. Some of this difference may be due to the fact that the on-project work was evaluated blind – the teachers did not know the identity of the writer. We found that, in all but one case, the teachers' rating of students' in-class work was higher than their blind evaluations of the same person's on-project work. Another possible explanation is that the individual on-project writing was done in the early weeks while the students were getting used to the distractions of the foreign surroundings and the project setup.

Table 8.1 Teachers rating of students' individual and group work. The *average scores* are evaluated on a 7-point scale and each value averages ratings in these categories: vocabulary, spelling, grammar, ideas, and writing style. The first initials of the *writing approaches* are used as follows: I independent, P parallel, J joint, S scribe, Sj scribe/joint, Pj parallel/joint.

	Writing samples	Average score	Week no.	No. of no.	Writing approach: Plan	Write	Edit
GROUP 1							
Individual	In-class avg.	6				I	
Work	On-proj avg.	4.4	2,4			I	
Group	Poem	5.1	3	35	–	p[5 mins]	J[7]
Work	Story	6.1	5	26	J[6]	Sj[19]	Sj[10]
	Introduction	4.5	11	11	J[1]	Pj*[23]	while writing
GROUP 2							
Individual	In-class avg.	4				I	
Work	On-proj avg.	3.2	2,4			I	
Group	Poem	3.4	3	18	–	P[7]	Pj[9], J[6]
Work	Story	4.1	5	18	J[5]	Sj[20]	J[11], I[2], J[3]
	Introduction	4.7	11	7	J[3]	Sj[11], P[3], Sj*[11]	while writing

Note: Time estimates in minutes are displayed in [], for each writing approach.
* indicates that students were very distracted while working.

Next, we note that the students' group work shows an improvement over their individual on-project work. Since the individual work was done mostly earlier than the group writing, perhaps the students' performance was hindered by the fact that they were still becoming accustomed to our setup and to the new software. Another possible explanation for this improvement is that during group work each document is available for scrutiny to all the group members, thus increasing the number of potential criticisms and new ideas which, combined, produce an improved final product.

Let us now examine the group work segments of the table. In both groups the story is rated higher than the poem. First, the story is written two weeks later than the poem and the groups' writing may be improving with experience. Second, both poems were written using the parallel writing approach – segments were written separately by the students in different documents, and later combined into one document, with minimal feedback between participants. The stories were written using the scribe/joint writing approach – the scribe typed the document produced by the group working together from conception and initial ideas through the final editing changes. If we consider these two writing approaches it becomes clear that in scribe/joint writing there is significantly more task-related interaction among group members; the products are scrutinized by the whole group at every stage of the writing process. In addition, the poems were written with no planning prior to writing, whereas before writing the stories each group spent at least five minutes discussing their tasks away from the computers.[3] Note also that the story is rated slightly higher than even the baseline in-class individual writing.

The reader will have noticed that group one has higher overall ratings than group two. This occurred because we unintentionally formed two groups whose abilities differed in both writing skills and group work skills. However, despite this, the introduction written by group two is rated slightly higher than that of group one. Both groups spent minimal time (less than 3 minutes) planning prior to writing and spent a long time working on this relatively short document. The main difference lies in the writing approaches they used. Group one wrote using the parallel/joint writing approach, each member of the group worked inside the shared document, making changes to his/her entries based on each others contributions but without much discussion related to their task; this group was very distracted during this task. Group two, on the other hand, remained more focused, using the scribe/joint approach with everyone contributing ideas and comments to the scribe throughout the writing. At one point they switched to parallel writing for three minutes but later returned to their original approach. By increasing the scrutiny of the document during the writing process, scribe/joint writing enabled all participants to apply their talents, to the benefit of the final product.

IMPACT OF TECHNOLOGY ON LEARNING AND WRITING

In addition to learning about the task of writing together, the students had to learn to use the tools provided. The students had no problem working with the computers. All had extensive experience with computers both in the classroom and at home. In fact, the students were so comfortable with the computers that they took a cruel pleasure in causing the software to crash.

Collaborative writing is a very difficult task. To support it successfully, the tools provided must not add to that complexity. Experienced writers often get distracted from the content of their writing when composing on a computer (Haas, 1989). The vast number of fonts and styles available tend to encourage a focus on format and layout. This is especially true for novice writers. The students found it hard enough to stay on task without technological distractions. Tools such as chat boxes and cute telepointer shapes were often more distracting than useful. An interface that supports gradual disclosure of features would allow users to be comfortable with the system at all stages of learning (a).[4]

[3] The students found the computers extremely enticing; given the opportunity they usually wanted to explore or play with telepointers and chat boxes. On several occasions we had to resort to 'hands on the heads' and 'turn the machines off' techniques, in order to reduce chaos and regain the groups' focus.

[4] Throughout our discussion of the study we will use letters such as (a) to link our observations to the list of design recommendations appearing near the end of this chapter.

The feedback provided by the system was often obscure and confusing, leading the students to ignore it. When the messages were critical, such as when document consistency was lost, this led to later problems (b). The fact that documents are shared, yet replicated, caused continuous confusion to both the students and the experimenters. A number of documents were lost and had to be reentered because the various contributors all assumed that someone else had saved the document. The location of the document was not at all obvious from the interface (c).

However, as the students became more familiar with the concept of shared access to a common document, they developed working patterns that took advantage of the technology. As discussed below, the students came to realize how the technology could be used in different situations.

Having described the process through which the students learned to use Aspects to write together, we now focus on the various aspects of the collaborative writing experience, discuss how the tools provided influenced this experience, and suggest how these observations can inform the design of future collaborative writing tools.

Collaboration and awareness

The first major difference encountered by any user when moving from single-user to multi-user software is the notion of a shared space in which other people are working. The importance of collaborator awareness mechanisms has been well recognized (Baecker *et al.*, 1993; Dourish and Bellotti, 1992; Nastos, 1992). When dealing with novice writers, this is especially important.

Self-awareness

Even after becoming familiar with the notion of a shared workspace and having worked on the system for six weeks, the students still had difficulty determining where they were and what they were doing.

Where am I? There are several things that the students were asking when they asked 'Where am I?' The simplest is location in the shared document. However, it is also important to provide some feedback as to whether the user is in a conference or working alone, and whether the current document is private or shared with others (d).

It was common for people to become confused as to whether their work would be seen by others or not, and whether they would be able to see others' work. This was especially true when someone stopped working closely with the group, and then later returned. In one case, it turned out that the students who had been working together to edit a document had in fact been working in separate copies of the document (e).

Sue: [moving her mouse and looking at Hope's screen] Why doesn't it [her pointer] show up?
Instructor: Why don't I have a copy of that?
Dan: [moves mouse, looks at Sue's]

This situation wasn't discovered until Sue happened to glance at Hope's screen and notice that her telepointer was not showing up.

What am I doing? Similarly, in a multi-user conference with multiple documents it isn't always obvious what you are doing at a given moment. This can range from confusion as to whether you are telepointing or not, a simple interface problem, to more subtle concerns, such as whether you are interfering with someone else's attempts to edit text. The system needs to make the information about your relative location and influence on others readily available (e).

Collaborator awareness

Collaborator awareness is always important, but even more than usual when dealing with users who are learning to work together. Awareness not only includes awareness of where people are within a document, but who is present for collaboration and who is potentially present.

Where are you? Lack of any reminder of where others are makes it easy to forget that there is a shared workspace (f):

Group: [they start to divide the task up by questions – each group member tells the others what they wrote as if the others can't see it]
Instructor: Everyone can see the same thing [goes over and scrolls Sally's to show them]

What are you doing? When working individually, it is easy to lose track of what others are doing. This problem is often overcome by resorting to physical pointing and glancing at each other's screens (g):

Sally: I'm getting confused. Rob, what are we changing here?
Rob: [makes changes, points to screen to indicate what he is doing]
Carol: [watches what Rob is doing]
Sally: [doesn't notice Rob's gesture] Rob what are we doing here?
Rob: It's gonna look like a poem.
Sally: [sees gesture and looks over] Okay

Who did that? With synchronous shared access to the document, it is possible to enter text or to delete someone else's text without that person's knowledge. This can lead to confusion:

Dan: [deleting something]
Liz: No no don't erase it DON'T! who erased that?

Hope: Not me I just got in.
Liz: [looks over at Sue] Sue?!?
Dan: [looks around, says nothing]

Tracking of where other people are and what they are doing can come in many forms. Aspects provides bars along the side of the document indicating that someone has control of a region of text. This tells you that someone is there, but not who it is.

Pointing and gesturing

Users may also want explicitly to provide information to others about their actions. Aspects provides a simple telepointing mechanism, allowing each user to gesture with a remote cursor of a user-selected shape. However, the students often found it easier to use physical pointing and gestures:

Sally: Rob, can you show me what you're trying to do?
Rob: Take a look here. [points to her screen]

Telepointers were too limiting because they were both unable to draw collaborators' attention and lacked information about the person who was pointing. All this information is available in a simple hand gesture (g).

The telepointers also tended to be rather distracting; the students often ended up chasing each others' pointers around the screen. However, one group did learn to use them effectively when proofreading and editing:

Liz: Meant is spelled M-E-A-N-T [points at her screen]
Dan: Where is it?
Liz: Its, I'll mark it, there I've marked it. See? That's where it is [uses telepointer] where my little annoying thingy is.

Having discovered this function, Liz explains it to the others:

Liz: Say he spelt birth wrong [points with finger, Sue looks] you go to that [moves telepointer there] and go like that. [wiggles it]
Sue: OHHH.

The shared workspace encourages this type of consulting and collaborative learning.

Effect of physical placement

The students tended to take advantage of the physical placement of the computers to aid in their awareness of group activities. The computers were placed in a row, allowing each student to glance around at the other students and at their screens. From the start, they tended to glance around a lot, anxious to stay aware of what the rest of the group is doing. This ability to look at each other's computers also led to shifts between working independently or together on separate computers and working huddled around one machine.

The physical placement of the machines also allowed people to notice when someone is looking at their work; this is useful for encouraging and facilitating collaboration and consultation:

Group: [they start entering comments]
Liz: [glances at Hope's screen for confirmation she's doing it right]
Hope: [notices, gives her advice]

However, the physical placement can also lead to formation of subgroups and exclusion of peripheral group members. To minimize this, we rearranged seating patterns each session.

Document ownership

The perception of who has a claim to ownership of a section of text, or over the entire document, was independent of how ownership was represented by the technology. Aspects does not provide any explicit indication of who wrote a section of text. However, the students would often assume, especially in the early parts of the study, that the person who typed a section was the only person who could change it.

Similarly, there was a connection between who typed in a section of text and who got credit for the ideas contained in the text. We observed that the scribe usually provided fewer ideas than the rest of the group. Despite this, the scribe occasionally took credit for the content of the document. For example, in the first group, the person who typed a story claimed the next day that it was his story:

Dan: I wrote the story.
Sue: No I did.
Liz: I did.
Hope: We all did.
Dan: The one about the ...
Hope: I made up Tiger Lily.
Instructor: I thought everybody wrote it.
Dan: I wrote it most 'cause I typed everything.

Although the system did not provide explicit ownership information, the students tended to continue to identify text with the person who typed it. This showed up most clearly when the second group was editing one of the documents. In this case, the sections of the document were all written in parallel, with each section easily identifiable as belonging to a different person.

Two of the group members were suggesting changes, but refused to make the final alterations until the entire group gave permission.

However, when the group was working together on a document that had already been edited, the group members had no reservations about arbitrarily deleting someone else's text without telling them (h). This suggests that at this point the group members had come to regard the text as shared, rather than just owned by the person who typed it.

Document control

The system's assumptions about control over the document, both in terms of the ability of group members to edit sections of text and to access documents, had several effects on the collaborative writing process.

The students in the study used Aspects in paragraph locking mode. This allows each user to gain control of a paragraph of text and make changes within that paragraph. As long as the user doesn't move the selection point out of the paragraph, other users are locked out. This granularity of locking led to some interesting behaviour.

When working with physical documents, the students were able to gain control over a paper by grabbing it if necessary. In Aspects there was no way to force a shift in control. One student understood the technology to the extent that he deliberately kept an entire document as one paragraph to keep control of the changes being made to the text, even when encouraged to add paragraph breaks:

Instructor: Can I suggest you put some more returns in there? [gets up and puts returns in so Dan isn't locking the whole document]
Liz: [starts typing like mad as Instructor puts in spaces]
Sue: [starts typing like mad as Instructor puts in spaces]
Dan: I didn't want to or else they'll start doing funny things with it.

However, the group soon learned to overcome the limitations of the locking mechanism by simply using the other person's computer rather than trying to get control of the document from within the system.

Dan: [takes Sue's mouse when she's not looking, moves her out of a paragraph]
Sue: [looks back, sees Dan]
Dan: One sec ... stop, let me work on this part.

Control over the text also had an effect on the roles taken on by the group members. When deciding who would be the scribe, the group would either take a vote or argue until someone managed to get control of the text. For example, when the first group was composing a story, Dan ended up gaining control of the text. The group went along with this, everyone dictating while he types; ideas were passed around, negotiated, and the final decision was made by the scribe.

Although the system gave the scribe explicit control of the document, the other members of the group were still able to make significant contributions and provide feedback which affected the contents of the document. In the above example, where Dan had control of the document, there were several occasions where other students tried to make changes. Kim would attempt to alter a sentence, and failing that would ask Dan to make the change, using the telepointer to indicate the change. So, in spite of the control mechanisms provided by the technology, the entire group was able to influence the document (i).

Synchronous access and collaboration

The fact that everyone could access the workspace influenced the style of collaboration. Initially, everyone wanted to type just because they could. However, as they gained experience with the technology and with group writing, the students became more selective in their choice of writing style. For example, when working on the last day on the magazine's introduction, the second group shifted between scribe and independent parallel writing to solve a consensus problem. Sally was acting as scribe, but the group couldn't decide on the wording of one section of the document. To solve this, they all entered their own ideas, then all read them and selected the best. They then shifted back to scribe mode, and continued (h).

Working synchronously but on separate sections of the document worked well in a task that lends itself to division. On the tenth day, the two members of the first group were preparing the questions for an interview – they discussed the content, then split the task up, but talked back and forth while entering the text. Then, after the interview, they worked in a scribe fashion, one student dictating the answers while the other typed.

However, it was not always clear who had been given the role of scribe. In fact, the assignment of roles tended to change dynamically, since the technology lets anyone take control as long as the previous scribe is willing to relinquish control. In general the groups were able to adapt to this shifting of control. If someone's ideas were not being accepted or they were being ignored, that person would sometimes go off and start entering the ideas independently in a different section of the document.

The students were able to adapt their use of the system to suit their working patterns, and to take in to consideration the social and group interactions taking place as they worked. It was possible because the system did not attempt to impose strict roles and patterns of usage on the students (j).

Design recommendations

The above observations stress the importance of maintaining an awareness of both the shared space in which you are working, and the fact that there are other people working in that shared space. Dourish and Bellotti (1992) indicate that the use of shared feedback, the notion of providing implicit, peripheral information about everyone in a shared space, is a promising approach. Examples of this approach can be seen in ShrEdit (McLaughlin Hymes and Olson, 1992) and SASSE (Mawby, 1991; Nastos, 1992). ShrEdit allows you to request that the system find and track movements of others; SASSE provides peripheral information in the form of colour-coded, shared scrollbars, audio cues, a document overview (or gestalt), and a tracking mode.

Another important problem introduced by collaborative tools is the need to keep track of changes in a shared document. One way to provide the necessary information about changes in the document is through the display of differences in the document, often called 'diffs', either as change bars (Neuwirth *et al.*, 1992), through the use of annotations (Nastos, 1992), or through more active notification (Minör and Magnusson, 1993).

Ownership of and access to the shared workspace are also important considerations. As we have seen, the way in which both of these are handled by the system have an influence on the behaviour of the group. While some systems such as Grove (Ellis *et al.*, 1991) and PREP (Neuwirth *et al.*, 1990) assign roles to collaborators, most systems leave this up to the group. This, along with flexible access and floor control mechanisms, allows social interactions, not the system, to determine working patterns and group behaviour.

The above discussion suggests a number of design recommendations, which we will summarize below:

(a) Provide tools appropriate to the users' level of expertise; avoid distracting tools; use gradual disclosures.
(b) Make sure the system's feedback is simple and concise.
(c) Provide a clear and accurate mental model of the system.
(d) Provide self-awareness in terms of location in the shared workspace, and potential actions in that location.
(e) Provide awareness of the user's effects on others.
(f) Provide awareness of the presence of others in the shared workspace to encourage discussion and negotiation.
(g) Provide collaborator awareness in terms of shared feedback and explicit information such as gestures.
(h) Provide flexibility in terms of the representation of ownership information to allow for changes over time.
(i) Allow flexibility in terms of document control to allow for shifting roles at different stages of the writing process.
(j) Avoid imposing patterns on natural social interactions.

IMPACT OF THE PROJECT ON PARTICIPANTS

After a total of 12 hours of working on this project, the students felt that they had learned a lot about the topic of prejudice. They quickly became extremely conscious and sensitive about these topics in their everyday lives. They even enjoyed the learning process:

> *Liz*: I liked learning everything ... like prejudice, minorities, stereotypes, perception

Aside from the structured exercises, the students learned many important things from the extra projects that some of them elected to do. Sue and Liz conducted a survey around the school; they collected 37 responses, and compiled and tabulated the results. After the survey Sue discussed one surprising discovery:

> *Sue*: I didn't think that it would have happened so much, people getting insulted racially. I didn't know that there were actually so many people, that did and remembered.

In the group discussion, conducted several weeks following the project, the students expressed some insightful opinions that demonstrated a deep and mature understanding of these complex issues.

The product of their work, the magazine *Prejudice in the 90s*, was well received by their classmates and teachers. The students had differing ideas about the possible impact of their magazine, and about who would benefit the most from reading it. Sue felt that the people who wrote the magazine would benefit the most; others disagreed about its impact:

> *Carol*: Bad people [prejudiced people] will understand what they are doing is bad and they will become friends [with their victims].
>
> *Kim*: People who discriminate against people for their difference, they may learn how a person might feel and won't do that.
>
> *Dan*: Someone who doesn't understand about racism [will benefit from the magazine] ... I don't think that a racist person would benefit very much, cause they are ignorant and they'd ignore the magazine.

By working so closely together on this project, the students learned many things from each other. They learned new words and the correct spelling of other words. They also learned new concepts from group discussions. Rob described the most important thing that he learned from this whole project:

> *Rob*: Everybody is different period. I didn't know it that much. We looked at the topic a lot and learned how and why. I knew that people were different but not by how much.

Aside from these topics, the students learned about working and writing together. Rob reflected on the learning process:

Rob: When I first came I didn't think it would work out, but the computer helped, talking to the group helped, planning helped. I've never did this [collaborative writing] before.

With time, the students also began to appreciate the complexity of collaborative writing. Carol expressed what she learned about group writing:

Carol: It's important to hear other people's opinions. Important to talk before we write. [The result is] sometimes worse [than individual writing] because there are so many different opinions the story comes out messed up.

The groups experienced the frustrations and stress that accompany conflict resolution and consensus forming. The girls in particular felt that the worst part of their experience was arguing with their collaborators. The boys felt outnumbered and excluded (each group consisted of three girls and one boy), one boy complaining that 'they did not listen to me!' We have already seen that, despite these complaints, the boys were able to gain control of the group document at key moments during the writing.

In the final questionnaire all the students agreed that they enjoyed writing in a group. Several students stated that they felt more comfortable now about working in a group, writing in a group, and about writing in general. In these few weeks the group developed a sense of identity. In the eyes of their peers they became known as 'the after school group' and were viewed with some respect and envy, since they got to work on computers and be surrounded with a lot of special video equipment. The groups even developed a common language; group two coined a phrase 'prejudice matters' which then became transformed into 'minority matters' and other such expressions. The gender differences were put aside when the two groups joined together to produce a single magazine and do a presentation in front of two classes of their peers.

The students' feeling of ownership of the magazine increased towards the end of the project. In the early weeks, they would continuously ask the instructor for feedback about their ideas and writing. When this happened, they were instructed to consult with their group and sometimes minimal feedback was provided. In the later weeks of the project they requested much less feedback. In the final week, when Sally went to ask for help, Rob interrupted her saying 'No! Don't ask. This is our magazine!'

All the participants expressed a sense of pride about the finished product. From the final questionnaire we discovered that every student was happy to have their name on the magazine because 'it shows that I contributed' and because 'it is a good magazine and I like my name being on something my friends and I worked on!' This pride was also expressed in their decision to make a class presentation, explaining what they learned, and recounting their experiences from this project.

Despite never having previously worked with synchronous collaborative writing software, both groups managed to produce coherent documents which they felt reflected the work of the entire group. They testified to having written a magazine 'together', something that they did not even know the meaning of at the start of the study. Perhaps this in itself is the best definition of group writing – the perception that the results of your work are the results of the group's work, rather than the work of the individual members of the group.

SUMMARY AND CONCLUSIONS

The observations we have made of the students working together using Aspects are very encouraging. Over the 12 hours they were working with Aspects, they developed distinct, mature strategies for working together. Between them the two groups successfully produced a 32-page magazine which will be on display starting in early 1996 as part of an exhibit at the Ontario Science Centre. This achievement validates the concept of a synchronous shared text editor, and provides promise for the use of such technology in education, and for writing in general.

The group jointly learned about an important topic, prejudice. As one student said in the final group discussion:

> *Liz*: Everyone is different, we all have different beliefs, and we should respect that; this is what we learned.

They had become comfortable with the idea of writing together, and confident with the technology. From not knowing what it means to write together, they had progressed to feeling that they were able to succeed at, and enjoy, group writing. During the final group discussion, one student volunteered the following:

> *Rob*: The best thing was learning how to work with everybody, we weren't too good at that before.

By observing this learning process, we have been able to gain an insight into the nature of group writing, and identify some of the effects of the use of collaborative writing tools on this process.

We have seen that the technology has a distinct effect on the way in which novice writers approach the collaborative writing task. However, at the same time we have seen that writers, as they become familiar with both the task and the technology, are able to exploit the features of the system and use it to their advantage in creative ways. The observations we have made of the problems students have learning to write together are very similar to those seen among adult writers. From these observations we have drawn a series of recommendations for future design.

To summarize, we would like to briefly present a number of important insights.

- Groups of novice collaborators can learn to write together relatively quickly. The new skills required include flexibility in choosing the writing approach appropriate to the situation and task, and the ability to divide up writing activities to take advantage of each individual's strengths.
- Novice collaborators require some instruction. We helped the students learn to write together by guiding them through different writing approaches and activities. Many of these activities were already familiar to the students, but needed to be made explicit and become part of the groups' experience before the students felt comfortable using them in group writing.
- Groupware technology can be both a powerful tool and a compelling distraction. We had to carefully balance the students' need to experiment with the technology against their desire to play with the computers and forget about their tasks.
- The task had to be selected with great care in order to encourage interest and debate and thus lead the group towards a motivating and rewarding experience.
- When forming groups one must consider the following variables: gender, different ages, different writing levels, different maturity levels, and whether the group members were friends or just acquaintances.

During the project we observed fluctuations in the groups' power structures, changes in their attitudes towards the task, and changes in their utilization of the technology. This highlights the importance of studying real groups, in real situations, performing real tasks, over extended periods of time to observe interactions that typically cannot be seen in artificially constructed scenarios, experiments, and usability laboratories. This allows usage patterns to develop naturally, and provides the time needed for the participants to learn about the task and the technology. Although this type of ethnographic study is harder to run and much more time-consuming to analyze than a traditional lab study, the type of real usage that we have observed could never be seen in a usability laboratory.

ACKNOWLEDGEMENTS

The authors would like to thank the teachers and students at the Huron Street Public School for their time and enthusiasm, and the researchers at OISE for their help with the project. Ben Smith-Lea and Russell Owen provided valuable technical support. Hiroshi Ishii, Sara Bly and our reviewers provided valuable comments. We would also like to thank those who provide funding for our research, especially the Natural Science and Engineering Research Council of Canada.

REFERENCES

Baecker, R. M., Nastos, D., Posner, I.R. and Mawby, K. L. (1993) The user-centred iterative design of collaborative writing software. *Proceedings of InterCHI'93*, ACM, pp. 399–405, 541.

Baecker, R. M. (1993) *Readings in Groupware and Computer-Supported Cooperative Work: Facilitating Human–Human Collaboration*, Morgan Kaufman.

Beck, E. (1993) A survey of experiences of collaborative writing. In Sharples, M. (ed.), *Computer Supported Collaborative Writing*, Springer-Verlag.

DiPardo, A. and Freedman, S. W. (1978) *Historical Overview: Groups in the Writing Classroom*. Technical Report No. 4, Center for the Study of Writing, University of California, Berkeley.

Dourish, P. and Bellotti, V. (1992) Awareness and coordination in shared workspaces. *Proceedings of CSCW'92*, ACM, pp. 107–114.

Ede, L. and Lunsford, A. (1990) *Singular Texts/Plural Authors: Perspectives on Collaborative Writing*. Southern Illinois University Press.

Ellis, C. A., Gibbs, S. J. and Rein, G. L. (1991) Groupware: some issues and experiences. *Communication of the ACM*, **34** (1), 38–58. Reprinted in Baecker, 1993.

Freedman, S.W. (1978) *Peer Response Groups in Two Ninth-Grade Classrooms*. Technical Report no. 12, Centre for the Study of Writing, University of California, Berkeley.

Harrison, B., Owen, R. and Baecker, R. M. (1994) Timelines: an interactive system for the collection and visualization of temporal data. *Proceedings of Graphical Interface '94*, Morgan Kaufmann.

Hass, C. (1989) Does the medium make a difference? Two studies of writing with pen and paper and with computers. *Human–Computer Interaction*, **4**, 149–169.

Kraut, R. E., Egido, C. and Galegher, J. (1990) Patterns of contact and communication in scientific research collaborations. In Galegher, J., Kraut, R. E. and Egido, C. (eds), *Intellectual Teamwork: Social and Technological Foundations of Cooperative Work*, Erlbaum, pp. 149–171.

Leland, M. D. P., Fish, R. S. and Kraut, R. E. (1988) Collaborative document production using quilt. *Proceedings of CSCW'88*, ACM, pp. 206–215.

Mawby, K. (1991) *Designing Collaborative Writing Tools*. MSc Thesis, Department of Computer Science, University of Toronto.

McLaughlin Hymes, C. and Olson, G. M. (1992) Unblocking brainstorming through the use of a simple group editor. *Proceedings of CSCW'92*, ACM, pp. 99–106.

Minör, S. and Magnusson, B. (1993) A model for semi-(a)synchronous collaborative editing. *Proceedings of ECSCW'93*, pp. 219–231.

Mitchell, A., Posner, I. R. and Baecker, R. M. (1995) Learning to write together using groupware. *Proceedings of CHI'95*, ACM, pp. 288–295.

Nastos, D. (1992) *A Structured Environment for Collaborative Writing*. MSc Thesis, Department of Computer Science, University of Toronto.

Neuwirth, C. M., Chandhok, R., Kaufer, D. S., Erion, P., Morris, J. and Miller, D. (1992) Flexible DIFF-ing in a collaborative writing system. *Proceedings of CSCW'92*, ACM, 147–154.

Neuwirth, C. M., Kaufer, D. S., Chandhok, R. and Morris, J. H. (1990) Issues in the design of computer support for co-authoring and commenting. *Proceedings of CSCW 90*, ACM, pp. 183–195. Reprinted in Baecker, 1993.

Olson, J. S., Olson, G. M., Mack, L. A. and Wellner, P. (1990) Concurrent editing: the group's interface. *Proceedings of Interact '90* pp. 835–840.

Olson, J. S., Olson, G. M., Storrøsten, M. and Carter, M. (1992) How a group-editor changes the character of a design meeting as well as its outcome. *Proceedings of CSCW '92, ACM*, pp. 91–98.

Posner, I. R. (1991) *A Study of Collaborative Writing*. MSc Thesis, Department of Computer Science, University of Toronto.

Posner, I. R. and Baecker, R. M. (1992) How people write together. *Proceedings of the 25th Annual Hawaii International Conference on System Sciences*, pp. 127–138. Reprinted in Baecker, 1993.

Scardamalia, M., Bereiter, C., McLean, R., Swallow, J. and Woodruff, E. (1989) Computer supported intentional learning environments. *Journal of Educational Computing Research*, **5** (1), 51–68.

Sharples, M., Goodlet, J. S., Beck, E. E., Wood, C. C., Easterbrook, S. M. and Plowman, L. (1993) Research issues in the study of computer supported collaborative writing. In Sharples, M. (ed.), *Computer Supported Collaborative Writing*, Springer-Verlag, pp. 9–28.

Part 3

New Tools and Users

9 Flexible Diff-ing in a Collaborative Writing System

CHRISTINE M. NEUWIRTH, RAVINDER CHANDHOK, DAVID S. KAUFER, PAUL ERION, JAMES MORRIS and DALE MILLER

INTRODUCTION

In the course of a collaboration, co-authors often make changes to each other's documents. A principal difficulty co-authors face is coping with those changes, especially understanding why the other person made them. For example, in a study of eight writers' production of an insurance company's two-page annual report, Cross (1990, p. 193) observed that each writer 'omitted, added, highlighted or modified' the text to agree with his or her preconceptions, with unexplained changes causing 'considerable frustration' for other writers.

This chapter describes an approach to communicating about changes to documents. At the heart of the approach is a flexible text differencing system, *flexible diff*, that allows collaborative writers to tailor difference reports to their various social and cognitive needs. The program is imbedded in the PREP Editor (Cavalier *et al.*, 1991; Neuwirth *et al.*, 1990, 1994), a writing environment being developed to study and support collaborative writing processes. The PREP Editor allows difference reports to be annotated with such things as explanations of changes.

ISSUES IN THE DESIGN OF A FLEXIBLE DIFF-ING SYSTEM

The technical question in the design of a difference finding program is how to take an original text and a revision, and to produce – in a time- and space-efficient way – an edit script (or difference report) that describes changes between the two versions. From a time/space efficiency standpoint, the 'optimal' difference report is in the form of a list that describes the minimal number of editing changes required to transform the original text into the revision. This technical question has received considerable research attention (Hunt and McIlroy, 1975; Miller and Myers, 1985; Myers, 1986) and is not the

GROUPWARE AND AUTHORING
ISBN 0-12-575005-6

focus here. The focus in this paper is on the following human interface design questions and our approach to answering them:

- What changes should be reported?
- How should changes that are reported be pinpointed?
- What should the user interface to the change report be like?

In the course of answering these questions, we argue that, from a human factors standpoint, an optimal time/space difference report is not necessarily optimal.

What changes should be reported?

The most fundamental design question we addressed was 'What changes should be reported?' One might think that the answer is obvious: 'All of them.' This answer, however, is not unconditionally correct. Nachbar (1988) argues compellingly that reporting all changes is inappropriate for some tasks, such as comparing the output of floating point calculations (where roundoff errors result in spurious differences) and comparing program source code (where differences in white space and comments have no effect on the operation of compiled code). In response to these task demands, Nachbar's *spiff* (spiffy diff) provides a flexible diff-ing interface; for example, a user can instruct *spiff* to ignore differences between floating point numbers that are below a user-settable threshold, a feature that allows users to compare the outputs of a statistical package running on two different machines approximately 200 times faster than when using *diff* (Hunt and McIlroy, 1975) to generate the report.

We identified three aspects of collaborative writing tasks that require developing a flexible difference finding algorithm:

- different roles within a writing group;
- changes in the needs of collaborative writing groups over time;
- different types of collaborative writing groups.

Different roles within a writing group

A writing group is usually composed of different people fulfilling several different social roles. While a co-author may not be interested in seeing every change that a trusted co-author made, he or she may want to check every change from a less trustworthy editor. For example, Cross (1990) observed that a secretary acting as editor changed 'crises that could not be overcome' to 'crises', because of a belief that crises, by definition, could not be overcome.

Changes in the needs of collaborative writing groups over time

A writing group's needs for detecting changes may be different at different times during the lifetime of a project. At the beginning of a project, co-authors may be changing a draft so radically that it would not be useful to see changes at a detailed level. In those cases, it is less likely that a co-author would want to detect what was inserted, but he or she may want to answer the question, 'Where did my "good bit" go?' At later stages of the project, for example, when responding to reviewers' comments, it may be useful to look at each change a co-author made.

Different types of collaborative writing groups

Different groups often need very different ways to detect changes. For some tasks, writers want to see every last change that was made from the previous version – for example, lawyers doing contract work. If, for example, the reader is a lawyer whose task it is to find all the changes that may have legal implications, then it certainly makes sense to report all of them. To illustrate, Figure 9.1a depicts the original of a legal document; Figure 9.1b, a revision version, and Figure 9.1c, a change report with all changes shown.[1]

But in another type of writing group, writers might actually be distracted by seeing every last change because the task might be quite different. If the reader is a co-author, for example, the tasks might be to read the new draft for meaning and, at the same time, to build a representation of the problems that remain in the paper. Such a reader may not be interested in all the changes, many of which draw attention to problems in the previous draft that are no longer of interest because they have been solved.

Instead, the reader may prefer to see only some changes – for example, sentences or paragraphs that have been deleted, on the grounds that destruction of 'hard won' sentences or paragraphs is an interesting event (see Figure 9.2c). Indeed, a difference report of all the changes to the document might induce such a reader to focus on task-irrelevant information at the expense of building meaning and a representation of problems remaining (Figure 9.2b).

To understand how a change report might interfere with the tasks of building meaning and a representation of remaining problems, it is useful to look at what role attention plays in the process of reading. Most reading models assume that attention is required in order to derive meaning from texts and that the amount of attention available is limited, so attention must be allocated (Samuels and Kamil, 1984). When two or more tasks exceed attentional capacity, the tasks cannot be performed simultaneously and readers engage in 'attention switching', first allocating attention to one task, then the other. For

[1] Strike-through corresponds to deleted material; underline corresponds to inserted material.

a. Original

The Pennsylvania law also establishes a time limit within which injuries or occupational diseases must be reported to an employer. Under this provision, compensation will be paid based on the date of the injury only if the injury is reported to your employer within 21 days of its occurrence. After 21 days, compensation will begin based on when the report is made. The law bars compensation for any injury or disease reported more than 120 days after the occurrence.

b. Revised

The Pennsylvania law establishes a time limit within which injuries or work-related illnesses must be reported to an employer. In order to receive full compensation, that is, compensation based on the date of the injury or the onset of illness, you must report it to your employer within 21 days of its occurrence. If you report it between the 22nd and 120th day, you will receive partial compensation, that is, compensation based on the date you file the claim. If you report it more than 120 days after the injury or onset of illness, you will receive no compensation.

c. All changes reported

The Pennsylvania law ~~also~~ establishes a time limit within which injuries or ~~occupational diseases~~ work-related illnesses must be reported to an employer. ~~Under this provision,~~ In order to receive full compensation, that is, compensation ~~will be paid~~ based on the date of the injury ~~only if the injury is reported to~~ or the onset of illness, you must report it to your employer within 21 days of its occurrence. ~~After 21 days, compensation will begin based on when the report is made. The law bars compensation for any injury or disease reported~~ If you report it between the 22nd and 120th day, you will receive partial compensation, that is, compensation based on the date you file the claim. If you report it more than 120 days after the ~~occurrence~~. injury or onset of illness, you will receive no compensation.

Figure 9.1 An example revision and difference report.

example, beginning readers have difficulty decoding words and building meaning simultaneously, and must often switch attention from one task to the other; however, attention switching comes at a cost: it is time consuming, puts a heavy demand on short-term memory and tends to interfere with recall (Kahnemann, 1973).

Based on our experience with difference reports,[2] it is our hypothesis that reading for meaning, building a representation of remaining problems and

[2] Users have been members of the PREP Editor project group, their collaborators, and first-year students in a selected section of a college writing course.

a. Original	Finally, and somewhat speculatively, we wondered if more experienced teachers would use electronic communication modes differently than less experienced teachers. New computer technologies do not, in and of themselves, create educational improvements; instead, they create opportunities for improvements.
b. All changes reported	Finally, and somewhat speculatively, we ~~wondered if more~~ hypothesized the following about individual teachers: More experienced teachers ~~would~~ and their students will use electronic communication modes ~~differently~~ more than less experienced teachers. ~~New computer technologies do not, in and of themselves, create educational improvements; instead, they create opportunities for improvements.~~
c. Sentence level changes reported	Finally, and somewhat speculatively, we hypothesized the following about individual teachers: More experienced teachers and their students will use electronic communication modes more than less experienced teachers. ~~New computer technologies do not, in and of themselves, create educational improvements; instead, they create opportunities for improvements.~~

Figure 9.2 All changes reported vs sentence level changes.

detecting differences are tasks that require attention-switching for many readers. Indeed, the report of a change seems to invite the reader to focus on the change.[3] But an 'invitation' can distract the reader from more appropriate tasks. Lesser and Erman (1980) define 'distraction' as the degree to which an agent's focus can be shifted. Positive distraction shifts an agent to tasks that are more useful; negative distraction shifts the agent to tasks that are redundant or diversionary. The distraction in a difference report might be negative, leading the reader to switch tasks and focus on the changes to the detriment of constructing the gist of the new material. Moreover, a reader with limited metacognitive capacity may fail to detect distraction or may recover from the problem only after considerable misspent time.[4]

[3] This observation is consistent with the work of Gibson who observes that events – such as the notification of a change – have 'affordances', that is, they demand or invite certain behaviors.

[4] With time and practice, frequent readers of change reports may become skilled at 'decoding' them and be able to process them at the same time as reading for meaning and representing remaining problems; however, such a development is not inevitable. For example, it is generally not possible for proofreaders to become so skilled at finding errors that they are able to build meaning at the same time as they proofread (*cf.* Haber and Schindler, 1981).

This framework allows us to give a general answer to the question, 'What changes should be reported?' In general, only those changes should be reported that will reduce negative distraction and increase positive distraction. Since this depends, as we have argued, on the reader and the task, a differencing program for collaborative writing needs to be flexible, to allow readers to specify what changes to ignore.

Like *spiff* (Nachbar, 1988), *flexible diff* achieves flexibility by allowing users to specify whether to ignore changes in whitespace (spaces, tabs, and newlines) or to treat it as any other non-alphanumeric character (i.e. to parse each whitespace character into its own token). In both systems the goal is to avoid the introduction of spurious and semantically meaningless entries in the difference report. For numerical values, *spiff* goes one step further and allows numerical differences within a threshold 'epsilon' to be ignored. For text values, however, there is a question of how to measure differences. To address this issue, we have extended the *spiff* paradigm to text by introducing a heuristic for measuring differences. The user can instruct the program to ignore differences that are smaller than a specified grain size, with the choices for grain size being word, phrase, sentence, or paragraph. Differences are measured by the following heuristic: differences between two units are ignored if some percentage of their parts are equal. Setting the value to anything except 100% places the burden of difference detection on the reader.[5] For example, a co-author interested in not losing any 'hard won' sentences might specify a grain size of a sentence, and a 70% change threshold (Figure 9.2c). While we have not had any experience with lawyers using *flexible diff*, the appropriate setting for examining revisions of contracts might be 100% (Figure 9.1c). To complement our notion of 'change threshold', we are experimenting with notations for showing relative amounts of differences in the interface. In other words, if some of the actual differences are suppressed from the report via the change threshold, the interface might still (through change bars, color or shading) indicate that there are changes to be explored. Paramount to the effectiveness of such a visual notation is its unobtrusiveness – it must not draw undue attention to the suppressed changes, or it will subvert the purpose of the change threshold completely.

Another aspect of the question 'What changes should be reported?' concerns the type of events that should be reported. In particular, a 'move' can be defined as a deletion followed by an insertion of the same material elsewhere. Our initial experience with difference reports, however, suggests that readers appreciate a move being signalled explicitly, because it reduces their search task. We developed a simple technique that searches for insertions and deletions of identical text and remaps them to a move operation. The user can control a parameter, 'minimum length for a move', in units of the current grain

[5] It is important to note that this is not to say that a co-author might not notice a change below the sentence level; simply that the change report would not point it out.

size, that controls the minimum length of an insertion/deletion before it is interpreted as a move, on the grounds that multiple occurrences of short strings such as 'the' and so forth should not be interpreted as moves. Based on our initial experience, it appears to be useful to allow larger units of text, such as sentences and phrases, to be treated as moves even though they have some changes within them, but this is not yet implemented.

How should changes that are reported be pinpointed?

Our experience with differencing tools for texts suggests that several factors – the number, density and complexity of changes – should condition how changes in a text are pinpointed. Above a certain threshold of change intensity, writers seem to prefer a report that shows the entire region of text as changed rather than one that pinpoints each change piecemeal. To illustrate, Figure 9.3a depicts an original text and Figure 9.3b, a revision. Figure 9.3c is a change report with the changes pinpointed at the word level; Figure 9.3d pinpoints the changes by concatenating replacements that are closer together than a user-controlled number of words away. Notice that the change report in Figure 9.3d is no longer strictly accurate: The word 'brown' is reported as having been deleted and inserted, even though it was constant across the two versions. Yet many readers prefer the second version, reporting that it increases the readability.

In response to this observation, *flexible diff* defines several parameters that allow users to control how changes are pinpointed. The first parameter is 'coarseness' of pinpointing: character, word, phrase, sentence, or paragraph.

a. Original text:	**It was cold. The quick brown fox jumps over the lazy dog. Her bowl is over there, by the car.**
b. Revised text:	**It was morning. It was cold. The slow brown dog jumps over the lazy cat. Her bowl is over there, by the truck.**
c. Fine pinpointing:	**It was morning. It was cold. The ~~quick~~ slow brown ~~fox~~ dog jumps over the lazy ~~dog~~ cat. Her bowl is over there, by the ~~car~~ truck.**
d. Medium pinpointing	**It was morning. It was cold. The ~~quick brown fox~~ slow brown dog jumps over the lazy ~~dog~~ cat. Her bowl is over there, by the ~~car~~ truck.**
e. Coarse pinpointing:	**It was morning. It was cold. ~~The quick brown fox jumps over the lazy dog.~~ The slow brown dog jumps over the lazy cat. Her bowl is over there, by the ~~car~~ truck.**

Figure 9.3 Pinpointing changes.

For example, if the user sets the coarseness parameter for how the change should be pinpointed to the sentence level (and the grain size parameter for what changes are to be reported to the word level), then an insertion of a word in a sentence will be reported, but it will be reported as the whole sentence having been deleted and inserted.

In addition to grain size, the user can control how precisely replacements (insertion/deletion pairs) are pinpointed. Three parameters are defined: 'maximum distance to look for commonalities', 'maximum percent of differences', and 'maximum distance to concatenate'. The first two parameters control the recursive top-down application of the differencing process which is applied, for example, at the phrase level before it is applied at the word level: If two phrases are very different in length ('maximum distance to look for commonalities') and have a great many differences ('maximum percent of differences'),[6] a replacement is reported at the phrase level on the grounds that it is less worthwhile to examine them for commonalities, many of which may be cryptic and fortuitous (e.g. they may contain function words in common such as 'the', 'of', etc.); otherwise the differencing algorithm is continued and the replacements are pinpointed more exactly. Figure 9.3e depicts a change report that results when the parameters are set so that the algorithm does not recurse to the word level for the phrases 'The quick brown fox jumps over the lazy dog' and 'The slow brown dog jumps over the lazy cat'.

The third parameter, 'maximum distance to concatenate', controls a bottom-up concatenation process. As the list of differences (or edit script) is being built by the differencing process, it is examined for replacements that occur within the range of 'maximum distance to concatenate' on the grounds that concatenating replacements that are adjacent or relatively close together increases the readability of the report. Figure 9.3d depicts a change report that results when the 'maximum distance to concatenate' parameter is set so that '~~quick~~ slow brown ~~fox~~ dog' (*cf.* Figure 9.3c) is concatenated to '~~quick brown fox~~ slow brown dog'. Depending on how the user sets the parameters controlling the top-down and bottom-up processes, they will produce identical or different results for any given example.

Incidentally, the parameters described in this section allow users to trade-off accuracy of pinpointing changes and execution speed because the speed of the differencing algorithm is proportional to the number of input tokens and to the number of differences between the two versions. Thus, users have an additional motivation to select parameters that are appropriate to their cognitive and social needs. In particular, users are motivated to initially generate an initial coarse description of changes (which is faster) and then to look

[6] The number of differences is computed by the first phase of the differencing algorithm. Our experiences are that the first phase of the algorithm (which yields the number of changes but not their exact values) generally executes in less than one-half the time required for a complete comparison.

selectively at the details of particular changes (which is more accurate). Our implementation actually uses heuristics like this to improve overall performance.

What should the user interface to the change report be like?

We have implemented an interface for flexible diff in the PREP Editor, a writing environment that supports side-by-side columns of text, with horizontal alignment that enables 'at-a-glance' viewing of large numbers of annotations and related texts. The comparison interface produces its report in a new column, with the differences linked to the original column for easy, side-by-side evaluation. To illustrate, Figure 9.4 depicts four columns: an original draft, its revision, the comparison report and an evaluation column. The evaluation column in Figure 9.4 consists of annotations to the comparison report that a co-author produced in order to explain some of the changes or to solicit advice about them.

This interface has two important features. The first is horizontal alignment of the changes to the point of difference in the text. There is evidence that readers accustomed to horizontal writing read faster in the horizontal direction than in the vertical (*cf.* Taylor and Taylor, 1993, p. 137). Thus, side-by-side,

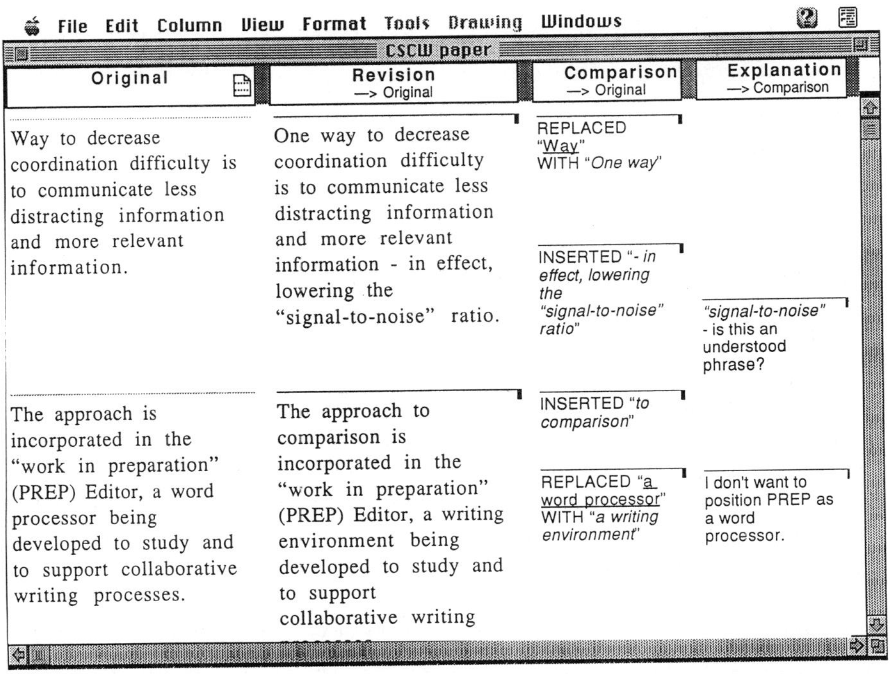

Figure 9.4 Actual PREP Editor column interface showing *flexible diff*.

horizontal alignment of the changes to original and revised documents is consonant with what we know about the cognitive processing demands of the task of seeing what changed. The following excerpt from a 'think-aloud' protocol of a reviewer looking at an author's original text, the reviewer's comments on that text, the author's revised text, and a change report is typical of those we have observed when changes are aligned horizontally and illustrates that users are able to understand changes quickly:

> ... *the object-oriented developers encountered fewer of the classic and costly surprises.* So he didn't actually change anything really here. Well all right – he changed a little, but it wasn't exactly what I wanted him to do.[7]

Because the comparison exactly links the changes to the source text, we have also provided a mechanism to accept or reject each change easily (as in InterNote (Catlin *et al.*, 1989)).

The second important feature of the interface is the ability of users to annotate changes with explanations of the change or questions to co-authors. Our group's experience with this feature suggests that reviewers will annotate changes selectively in order to draw their co-authors' attention to changes they want to discuss or explain. Likewise, a co-author can ask a reviewer to explain a change. Our hypothesis is that the ability to annotate changes will greatly alleviate writers' frustrations with unexplained changes that Cross (1990) observed.

The column layout just described requires a significant amount of screen real estate. In order to be usable with smaller screens, PREP provides flexibility in the comparison interface by allowing the user to display the text with the changes interspersed between the unchanged text (a common format used in commercial differencing tools). In this format, users can also annotate the changes.

Besides the interface to the change report, there is an interface to the parameters (described above) that control how the differencing process operates. While the parameters we have described allow enormous flexibility in our comparison tool, we also recognize that most users will not care to change the defaults. We chose the default values after testing the algorithm against widely varying input texts, including texts jointly written among ourselves in PREP (this chapter was co-authored in PREP). It is essential to note that we do not claim to have discovered the mappings between our heuristics, the parameter settings and output that is optimal for a reader trying to make sense of a report of differences across versions of text. We only claim to have created a tool where these settings and their effect on interpretability can be systematically explored. How the heuristics should be applied (and perhaps the proper defaults based on different task scenarios) is something we regard as important future research.

[7] In a 'think-aloud' protocol, subjects are asked to think-aloud – to say whatever it is they are thinking – and are video-taped or audio-taped. In the transcription italics indicate that the subject is reading, each '–' indicates a pause of 1 second duration. The author and reviewer, who were subjects in an experiment evaluating aspects of the PREP Editor, were working on an actual paper intended for publication.

In the networked version of the PREP Editor (Neuwirth *et al.*, 1994), we are experimenting with heuristics for automatically generating comparison reports, depending on role relationships among writers. The networked version of PREP allows authors and reviewers to send each other versions of drafts. We have defined parameters of interaction along two dimensions: sharing partial results and managing the task. Sharing partial results involves issues of what to share, when to share it, and how quickly to share it. Managing the task involves issues of negotiating about who to communicate with and under what conditions. Each user can set these parameters to define his or her own pattern of data exchange. Using these parameters, an author can instruct the PREP Editor about how he or she would like to see the version displayed when it arrives: for example, if the annotated draft is from a co-author, then display changes only upon request; if from a reviewer, then display all changes automatically. Apart from generating the comparison before returning the revision (which we, as co-authors, currently sometimes do), the revision's author has little control over how the comparison might be done. As this information might lead to a more productive exchange, we plan to experiment with adding 'comparison settings' information to revisions that would serve as hints from the co-author to anyone who would generate a difference report. For example, as a teacher, I might wish to hide/suppress character level changes (e.g., spelling corrections) so that my student's attention would be directed towards the more meaningful, higher-level changes.

OPERATION

Initially, *flexible diff* does a lexical analysis of the input streams based on the settings the user has specified. During this tokenizing process, any white space is distinguished and usually ignored. The resultant streams are then fed into the differencing process for generation of the edit script. Note that even this simple abstraction of separating the actual characters of the input stream from the sequence comparison gives the engine considerable flexibility in terms of generating reports based on different grain sizes.[8]

The differencing process

The differencing algorithm is modelled after the Myers (1986) O(ND) longest common subsequence/shortest edit script algorithm.

In *flexible diff*, the basic Myers algorithm is applied with a hierarchical decomposition strategy that exploits the grain size (character, word, phrase, sentence, paragraph) of comparison reports. For the sake of illustration, assume that the user has set the grain size to the word level (the default

[8] In our implementation, a tokenizer is a subclass of a generic 'tokenizer' C++ class, so adding different tokenizers is an easy task – ones for sound and graphics would be possible.

setting). The hierarchical application of the Myers algorithm can be described by the following psuedo-code:

1. Compare text-A and text-B at the phrase level.
2. For all string replacements in the edit script Do:
   If the original has little in common with its replacement
   Then report the whole string as changed
   Else compute and report diffs for the two strings at the word level.

After building a list of differences at a higher level (Step 1), several factors are examined to determine whether to diff recursively the corresponding strings at the next level (Step 2). The decision as to whether strings have 'a lot' or 'a little' in common are controlled by the parameters 'maximum distance to look for commonalities' and 'maximum percent of differences' described above.

Finally, concatenations of the edit script, controlled by the parameter 'maximum distance to concatenate', are done as the edit script is produced. This concatenation reduces co-located edit operations to one larger operation.

Performance

The Myers algorithm performs especially well when differences are small (i.e. sequences are similar) and is consequently fast in an application in which users adjust grain size to fit the stage in the writing process.

RELATED RESEARCH

Several researchers have argued recently that computer-support for cooperative work requires flexibility, that is, the ability to tailor the behavior of collaborative systems both to differences between groups and to differences among group members (Beck and Belotti, 1993; Dewan and Choudhary, 1991; Greenberg, 1991). We are especially indebted to Dewan and Choudhary's (1991) work on flexible coupling. Their thoughts about the collaborative negotiation that might occur and parameters for such negotiation have influenced our entire approach.

The technical problem of efficient and optimal change detection has been explored in detail by other researchers, most notably UNIX™; Hunt and McIlroy (1975), Miller and Myers (1985) and Myers (1986). We have not tried to improve on the efficiency and compactness of differencing algorithms themselves, but instead on the readability of the report. Our implementation based on their techniques is able to process realistically sized texts, from 10 to 40 pages and up to 15 000 words, in a user-perceived 'reasonable' amount of time.

The notion of flexible diff-ing in *spiff* (Nachbar, 1988) is closest to our research in its application of domain knowledge to reduce spurious difference reporting. Our work extends this idea by defining parameters we argue are appropriate to the domain of collaborative writing. Some of the settings for the parameters allow users to trade accuracy for efficiency. Others allow for tradeoffs between correctness of the difference report versus cognitive distraction due to unimportant information.

Surprisingly, little work has been done on how best to display difference reports to user. Existing tools pay little attention to the presentation of the comparison information. In the case of *diff*, the output is simply a list of the changed lines with an indication of whether the particular line was replaced, inserted, or deleted (Figure 9.5b). Likewise, editors that include 'change bars' indicate which lines have changed and do not report the actual site of the revisions (Figure 9.5a). Note that while *diff* gives information such as which lines were inserted, deleted or changed, the change bar interface does not show that detail. With change bars, the location of the change is less precisely pinpointed and the type of change is not specified. Commercial word processors and comparison tools produce output based on word-level differences, such as shown in Figure 9.3c. None of these interfaces support commenting on change reports in order to explain changes.

Minör and Magnusson (1993) present an interesting system to support an integration of writers' asynchronous and synchronous work strategies. Their model is similar to the approach taken in the networked version of PREP, in that it is based on working with copies of a document rather than actually sharing a document. It differs in that, when a user opens a version of a document that is currently being edited by another user, the system attempts to make users aware

It was morning. It was cold. The slow brown dog jumps over the lazy cat, her bowl is over there, by the truck.	*** 1,6 **** It was cold. !The quick brown !fox jumps over the !lazy dog, her bowl is over there, by !the car. --- 1,7 ---- +It was morning. It was cold. !The slow brown dog !jumps over the !lazy cat, her bowl is over three, by !the truck
a. Change bars	**b. "diff" output** *! Indicates a changed line* *+ Indicates an inserted line*

Figure 9.5 Typical difference reports in existing systems.

of each other's activities by showing the differences between two versions of the document using *active diffs* (i.e. differences based on the actual edit operations being performed). Other parameters of interaction (what to share, when to share it, etc.) are not defined. The underlying model relies on system knowledge of the hierarchical nature of documents (sections, subsections, etc.). In contrast, the PREP model requires minimal interpretation of the document structure *per se* (import/export algorithms that support reading documents produced in other word processors interpret paragraph breaks as chunks).

FUTURE WORK AND CONCLUSIONS

The notion of flexible differencing is clearly related to versioning and concurrency control. As techniques for dealing with inconsistencies improve, there may be less need for strict concurrency control, since users could resolve conflicts that have arisen more easily. We are exploring the application of *flexible diff* in this context (Neuwirth *et al.*, 1994).

Our approach can be improved in many ways. It will probably be useful to exploit semantic information such as a knowledge of function words (e.g. 'and', 'the', 'of', etc.). Likewise, it might be useful to exploit the semantic and pragmatic knowledge of users themselves. For example, a facility might be useful that would allow a co-author to select a region of text to draw to his or her co-author's attention in a change report, regardless of grain size or change threshold. Also, full support of collaborative writing groups may require supporting difference finding and reporting for objects other than text. Our observations of a group of physicists working collaboratively on a paper suggest that we may need to explore diff-ing pictures.

While we have designed *flexible diff* specifically for PREP and the context of collaborative writing, many aspects of it apply to any collaboration system.

In collaborative writing systems of the future, users will want to automatically recover changes that they made themselves at an earlier time or that are the result of work by another writer. In such a world, good comparison reports of versions will be essential. We have argued that a good comparison report depends not only on a tool's efficiency in detecting change, but also on the tool's ability to be tailored to different contextual assumptions of change and to a user's cognitive capacity to process information about change in various social contexts. In this paper, we have reported some progress toward the development of such a tool that, we have argued, will support a wide variety of tasks and texts. It remains to be seen which parameters make the biggest difference to which editing contexts. That determination awaits future empirical work. Such a tool, however, allows for a systematic study that varies number, density and complexity of change and could help us discover more about how each factor affects the task definition processes and goals of collaborative writers.

ACKNOWLEDGEMENTS

The work reported here has been supported by the National Science Foundation (grant number IRI-8902891) and by a grant from External Research at Apple Computer, Inc. Special acknowledgement is due to Paul Erion who was chiefly responsible for our implementation of the diff-ing. Thanks to David Banks for consultation on parameters for string similarity measures and to Davida Charney for comments on an earlier draft of this paper.

REFERENCES

Beck, E. E. and Belotti, V. (1993) Informed opportunism as strategy: Supporting coordination in distributed collaborative writing. In *Proceedings of the 3rd European Conference on Computer-Supported Cooperative Work* Sept 13–17, Milan, Italy, pp. 233–248.

Catlin, T., Bush, P. and Yankelovich, N. (1989) InterNote: Extending a hypermedia framework to support annotative collaboration. In *Hypertext '89 Proceedings*, Pittsburgh, PA, November 5–9, ACM, NY, pp. 365–378.

Cavalier, T., Chandhok, R., Morris, J., Kaufer, D. and Neuwirth, C. M. (1991) A visual design for collaborative work: Columns for commenting and annotation. In *Proceedings of the 24th Hawaii International Conference on System Sciences (HICSS-24)*, Kalua Kona, Hawaii, January 8–11, Nunamaker, Jr. J. F. (ed.) IEEE Press, Washington, DC, pp. 729–738.

Cross, G. A. (1990) A Bakhtinian exploration of factors affecting the collaborative writing of an executive letter of an annual report. *Research in the Teaching of English* **24**, (2) 173–203.

Dewan, P. and Choudhary, R. (1991) Flexible user interface coupling in a collaborative system. In *Proceedings of the CHI'91 Conference*, New Orleans, April 27–May 2, ACM, NY, pp. 41–49.

Greenberg, S. (1991) Personalizable groupware: Accommodating individual roles and group differences. In *Proceedings of the Second European Conference on Computer-Supported Cooperative Work*, Amsterdam, The Netherlands, September 25–27, Bannon, L., Robinson, M. and Schmidt, K. (eds) Computer Sciences Company, Slough, UK, pp. 17–31.

Haber, R. N. and Schindler, R. M. (1981) Error in proofreading: Evidence of syntactic control of letter processing? *Journal of Experimental Psychology: Human Perception and Performance* **7**, 573–579.

Hunt, J. W. and McIlroy, M. D. (1975) *An Algorithm for Differential File Comparison.* Bell Laboratories, NJ, Computing Science Technical Report No. 41.

Kahneman, D. (1973) *Attention and Effort.* Prentice-Hall, Englewood Cliffs, NJ.

Lesser, V. R. and Elman, L. D. (1980) Distributed interpretation: A model and experiment. *IEEE Transactions on Computers C-29*, **12** (December) 1144–1163.

Miller, W. and Myers, E. W. (1985) A file comparison program. *Software–Practice and Experience* **15**, (11), 1025–1040.

Minör, S. and Magnusson, B. (1993). A model for semi-(a)synchronous collaborative editing. In *Proceedings of the 3rd European Conference on Computer-Supported Cooperative Work* September 13–17, Milan, Italy, pp. 219–231.

Myers, E. W. (1986) An O(ND) difference algorithm and its variations. *Algorithmica* **1**, 251–266.

Nachbar, D. (1988) Spiff – a program for making controlled approximate comparisons of files. In *Proceedings of the Summer 1988 USENIX Conference*, San Francisco, CA, June 21–24, USENIX Association, Berkeley, CA, pp. 73–84.

Neuwirth, C. M. and Kauffer, D. S. (1989) The role of external representations in the writing process: Implications for the design of hypertext-based writing tools. In *Hypertext '89 Proceedings*, Pittsburgh, PA, November 5–8, ACM, NY, pp. 319–342.

Neuwirth, C. M., Kaufer, D. S., Chandhok, R. and Morris, J. H. (1990) Issues in the design of computer support for co-authoring and commenting. In *Proceedings of CSCW'90 Conference on Collaborative Work*, Los Angeles, CA, October 7–10, ACM, NY, pp. 183–195.

Neuwirth, C. M., Kaufer, D. S., Chandhok, R. and Morris, J.H. (1994). Computer support for distributed collaborative writing: Defining parameters of interaction. In *Proceedings of the Conference on Computer-Supported Cooperative Work (CSCW'94)* October 22–26, Chapel Hill, NC, ACM, pp. 145–152.

Samuels, S. J. and Kamil, M. L. (1984) Models of the reading process. In *Handbook of Reading Research*, Pearson, D. P. (ed.) Longman Inc., NY, pp. 185–224.

Taylor, I. and Taylor, M. M. (1983) *The Psychology of Reading*. Academic Press, NY.

10 Collaborative Writing with Synchronous and Asynchronous Support Environments

MARTINA ANGELA SASSE and MARK JAMES HANDLEY

INTRODUCTION

Collaboration between geographically dispersed groups has become increasingly common. In Europe, there are a number of programmes, such as ESPRIT, RACE and DELTA, to promote research collaboration on an international scale. Most of the projects funded in such programmes require the joint authoring of comprehensive reviews, reports or large-scale technical documentation. With many companies operating on a global scale, a similar requirement has emerged in the business sector.

The stages of the authoring process are often described as planning, execution, integration, review and revision. In addition, the collaborative authoring of a document requires functioning communication, coordination and social relationships between authors (Galegher and Kraut, 1990), and many authoring teams seek to provide these through holding meetings. Being involved in many such projects, there was a growing awareness in our research group that these meetings were costly in terms of time and travel funds, and, whilst they might provide opportunity for communication, collaboration and social relationships, they were sometimes not effective and efficient as far as the main task (producing a document) was concerned.

The first type of collaboration support which we investigated in our attempt to reduce the number of meetings related to joint authoring activities was multimedia conferencing. This was an obvious choice to us, since (a) we were involved in building such systems and therefore aware of its potential for synchronous collaboration support; and (b) it provided authors with an environment which is very similar to face-to-face meetings. Insights gained in a case study, which are described in the next section, led the development of an e-mail-based collaboration environment, which is described in the following section. The concluding section assesses the effectiveness and efficiency of synchronous and asynchronous support tools for collaborative authoring, and

GROUPWARE AND AUTHORING
ISBN 0-12-575005-6

gives some recommendations on how both approaches can be used for maximum benefit.

SUPPORTING COLLABORATIVE AUTHORING THROUGH MULTIMEDIA CONFERENCING

Multimedia conferencing integrates a user's existing software environment with the audio and video communication traditionally provided by videoconferencing systems, and allows users to exchange multimedia information in real time. During a typical conference, users will communicate through the audio and video facilities with each other in a way similar to a face-to-face meeting. In addition, users can share software applications, such as editors, drawing tools and CAD packages, and data with other users. This allows the conference participants to work interactively, each from their own workstation. The multimedia conferencing system used in the case study was developed under the RACE CAR project to support desktop conferencing between designs in the automotive industry (for a detailed description of the CAR system, see Handley and Wilbur, 1992).

Previous work by Chalfonte *et al.* (1990) has shown that ease and success of a collaborative writing project depends partly on the communication tools group members use. The authors concluded that, whilst communicating via a relatively static medium such as text (e.g. electronic mail) may be sufficient for the purposes of exchanging information, the complex interactions involved in performing intellectual teamwork normally require high levels of direct, informal, face-to-face communication.

Indeed, Galegher and Kraut (1990) found that collaborative writing is virtually impossible without face-to-face meetings. In a later study, the same authors found that, given a choice, authoring teams always seem to prefer face-to-face communication to computer-mediated sessions (Galegher and Kraut, 1992).

It is, therefore, reasonable to assume that, in circumstances where authoring teams cannot easily meet face-to-face (which the subjects in the Galegher and Kraut studies could, since they were students on the same course), collaborative writing could be improved if electronic means could be provided to support activities which normally take place in face-to-face meetings. Indeed, the ISO JTC 1 Special Working Group on Procedures has been instructed to investigate the procedural implications of conducting meetings via teleconferencing and electronic messaging, and a draft document for consideration by this group has been submitted (ISO, 1991). An interesting aspect of this approach is that support can be provided through a general-purpose tool such as a multimedia conferencing system, and does not necessarily require the development of specific authoring tools (such as MILO; Jones (1993)).

The case study

Together with four of our colleagues we conducted a case study in which we used the multimedia conferencing system to collaboratively write a book chapter. All interaction regarding the paper took place via the multimedia conferencing system and electronic mail only, to simulate the working between geographically distributed authors as closely as possible. Since we only had three workstations available in separate locations, in most sessions two authors had to share a workstation. In addition to electronic mail, the team used a shared filestore in which the log of e-mail messages, conference agenda, minutes and the partitions of the document were kept, and a revision control system to provide a concurrency control system and allow recall of any previous version of a document. (For a detailed description of the case study, see Baydere *et al.*, 1993.)

The main aim of this case study was to determine if multimedia conferencing could provide the rich channels of communication which collaborative writing allegedly requires (Chalfonte *et al.*, 1990), and whether if can provide an electronic equivalent of the face-to-face interaction which most authors seem to prefer (Galegher and Kraut 1992, 1990). The factors which distinguish rich channels of communication are interactivity and expressiveness (Chalfonte *et al.*, 1990). As far as interactivity was concerned, the speed of feedback provided by synchronous conferencing facilities could hardly be improved. The feedback provided through both audio and video channels was also found to be appropriate. The expressiveness of communication in multimedia conferencing does not reach the same level as it does in a face-to-face meeting: there is no eye contact between participants, and, the impact of facial expressions, gestures and body language is reduced (as described by Heath and Luff, 1990). The participants in the study were, however, able to adapt their style of communication accordingly, and did not rate reduced expressiveness as a major problem.

Conclusions

The study confirmed that multimedia conferencing can act as a support tool in the collaborative writing process, replacing face-to-face meetings. However, the study also revealed that synchronous interaction is no panacea for collaborative writing: the benefits of synchronous interaction were greatest in the planning and task allocation phases of the process (when authors decided what should go into the document, and who should take responsibility for which section), and when major decisions had to be made (e.g. to change the structure of the document). In the light of previous studies which emphasized the great importance of synchronous interaction (Galegher and Kraut, 1992,

1990; Chalfonte *et al.*, 1990), we were somewhat surprised to find that electronic mail was heavily used during the other phases of the project. Authors felt writing-by-committee during conferencing sessions was not very efficient: when it comes to writing text, authors seems to be most productive when working by themselves, at a time of their choosing. Many stages of collaborative authoring can be characterized as a distributed, asynchronous activity.

The second surprising finding was how much authors appreciated the support provided through the shared filestore and the version control tool to manage the document. Both tools helped greatly to keep track of a document's evolution (who had changed what, and when) and preserve its integrity (ensure that all authors are referring to the current version of the document). We found that these, the more mundane document management aspects of collaborative authoring had not received much attention in previous studies, which tended to focus on the more glamorous creative aspects of authoring. We were also very much aware that multimedia conferencing technology is too expensive to be widely available to authoring teams at this point in time. The combination of factors led us to rethink our approach to support environments.

SUPPORTING COLLABORATIVE AUTHORING THROUGH ELECTRONIC MAIL: THE MESSIE ENVIRONMENT

The second approach was to aim for a simple, low-cost collaboration environment, which should be easy to use. As Grudin (1990) points out, many sophisticated CSCW systems have been rejected by their intended users, because designers did not understand the nature of the collaborative task sufficiently well. We therefore chose to start with a small set of commands, offering core functionality, which would be extended in response to users' requests for additional tools.

During the previous case study, we had come to the conclusion that many phases of collaborative document authoring can be effectively supported through asynchronous communication, e.g. via e-mail. Messie's design concept fits into the Active Mail framework for implementing CSCW systems (Goldberg *et al.*, 1992): it piggybacks on ordinary e-mail, retaining all the features that have made e-mail successful. We also realized that the use of a shared filestore (in this case NFS) and a version control mechanism, which we employed in the case study, offered many benefits over simple e-mail for the management of a collaboratively written document.

The sum of these experiences and observations helped us to formulate a set of requirements and design objectives for a system to support collaborative authoring.

Requirements and design objectives

We identified two different sets of requirements for the environment: requirements of individual authors and requirements of the administrator, a role assumed by one member in every joint authoring team using the environment.

The author requirements which we identified for asynchronous collaborative writing support were to:

1. *Provide a mechanism that makes drafts available to all authors as soon as possible*
   To ensure misunderstandings are discovered as early as possible, and to ensure that the document grows in a uniform way, it is important that drafts of sections are made available early in the writing process.
2. *Preserve the integrity of the document*
   In order to preserve the integrity of the document, or its various parts, all authors should have access to the latest version of any file. Authors should have the facility to work on a single master copy of each part of the document. A simple way of providing integrity is to lock the master copy of a document section while one author is editing it. An important facility is the creation of an audit trail (the ability to trace who did what, and when) – even though this might be rarely used in practice, it greatly increases users' confidence in the system.
3. *Avoid duplication of effort*
   In order to avoid duplication of effort, all comments and additions to a document should be entered into the document itself, so that authors can see comments and additions which have been made by other authors.
4. *Distribute editing and formatting work*
   In order to distribute the effort involved in final editing and formatting of document, a prime requirement was to allow authors to exchange revisable text as quickly as possible. Imposing any single document exchange format for authoring teams would preclude this. Whilst it is not possible to support word processing (WP) and desktop publishing (DTP) applications which produce non-revisable formats, the environment should support handling of a variety of revisable text formats in addition to ASCII. In order to deal with diagrams, the system should handle PostScript, which, even though it is non-revisable, is so ubiquitous that most authors can view or print such files locally. There is also a requirement for tools which facilitate compilation of reference lists and glossaries.
5. *Avoid large learning overhead*
   The system should be simple to use and require users only to learn and remember a small number of commands. It should allow users to use familiar tools for familiar activities.

6. *Access without direct login*
   Not all authors have the facility to directly access remote machines today. In addition, it is important to consider that not all sites that might wish to install such an environment would want to allow remote logins and give direct access to a shared filestore facility.
7. *Deal with heterogeneity*
   Although there are several synchronous authoring tools available, the required system must provide access from a wide range of remote systems. No existing tool would run on all the available remote systems, and the overhead in developing any software to run on all such systems would be too great. Thus the system should only involve new software at one site.
8. *Policy-free collaboration*
   The system should be as policy-free as possible. It should provide the basic collaboration environment, but the users should decide the details of how that environment should be applied to their collaborative task.

The requirements of the authoring team's administrator can be summarized as follows:

1. The system should be simple to install, maintain and port.
2. Storage overhead for the documents should be kept to a minimum.
3. It should be possible to manage documents remotely as well as locally.

We decided that these requirements could be met by integrating and developing the functionality provided by existing tools – shared filestore, electronic mail, and a version control tool – into a support environment which would provide authors with a basic set of facilities to submit, read, edit, delete and list files. The environment allows authors to submit text at various stages of gestation (e.g. list of topics, first draft) to the shared filestore via e-mail. All authors collaborating on a document can request files submitted by the other authors, and add suggestions, comments and additional material directly to the document.

It should be stressed that we felt that these are the minimal requirements for such a system. Many features and tools could be envisaged, but we decided that additional, meaningful functionality is best defined and created in response to requests from groups of authors who have explored, and understand, the functionality of a basic system. This should help to avoid the fate of the CSCW systems described by Grudin (1990).

Messie design and implementation

All parts of a collaboratively authored document supported by the environment are held in a shared filestore, which is administered by one of the authors. The document can be created and accessed by sending files and requests by electronic mail to a Messie e-mail account. Messie accepts e-mail messages containing Messie commands and new text performs the actions specified by the command (subject to access control), and returns the final status and results. This is shown in Figure 10.1.

Messie places no specific requirements on the end-user environment. An author composes a message using their favourite mail interface program – on a PC, workstation, mini or mainframe, running their respective operating systems. The message is then submitted to Messie as a command file. There is no restriction on the type of mail system authors can use, as long as the message can be gatewayed intact to the Messie address. When a message addressed to Messie arrives in the Messie mailbox, Messie is activated. A status message will always be returned to the user to provide an overview of the outcome of the command submission. Optionally, if the command generates outputs for the user, these outputs will also be returned to the author in message separate from the status message (see the section on user view of Messie, below).

Messie has been implemented using a number of simple C programs (approximately 100 lines of code), and shell/sed/awk/perl scripts; it contains very little system specific code. Since it adopts a modular design approach, any part found to be operating-system dependent can be easily rewritten. It also makes it easy to extend existing functionality. For a detailed description of the implementation, see Sasse *et al.* (1993).

Other systems

Several existing systems could be thought of as satisfying some of the above requirements. Such systems as AFS (the Andrew File System) provide a transparent distributed file system, and it is easy to add the required version control mechanisms. But like NFS (Network File System) which we used for our early trials, there is the problem of heterogeneity of end systems – we cannot dictate what software remote sites will use, or even that they have direct internet connectivity.

The same problem affects all systems, synchronous or asychronous, that

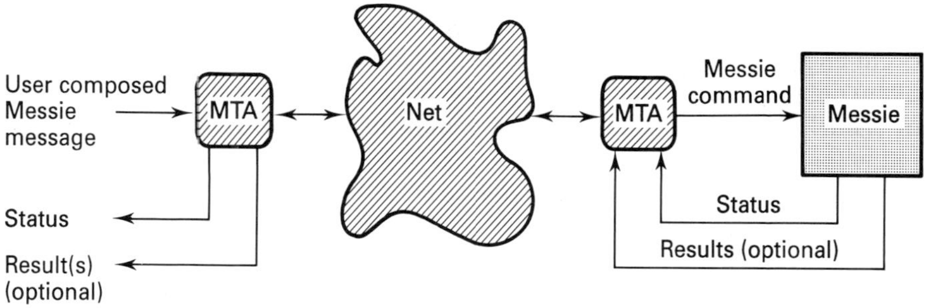

Figure 10.1 User interaction with the MESSIE system.

exchange data in any non-standard format – they require software to be written for all possible types of end system.

There are a number of infoservers (archives accessed through e-mail) available, but they were not really designed to be used in an interactive manner, and to our knowledge, none of them provide remote storage facilities with version control – a definite requirement for such a loosely coupled environment.

It would have been possible to have written Messie as a MIME User Agent (Borenstein and Freed, 1992) extending an MH automatic mailbox to cater for Messie-specific transactions expressed as MIME Content-type Values. However, at least for the time being, MIME User Agents are not as ubiquitous as we would desire being restricted to the rather technical end of the User Agent design spectrum.

Messie addresses some of the same issues as Computational Mail (Borenstein, 1992), but does so in a less generic way. One of the main problems with automatically executed e-mail is that of security – Borenstein's ATOMICMAIL closes the security loophole by providing a generic (LISP based) language, but with restricted system I/O functionality. We require less restricted I/O (read/write access to a part of the filesystem), as the incoming messages are parsed automatically without user intervention. We also do not require the richness of the ATOMICMAIL language, and so can close the security loophole by simply providing a restricted and rigid command set.

User view of Messie

This section describes how authors interact with the environment, and other authors, to produce a joint document.

All parts of a collaboratively authored document supported by the environment are held in a shared filestore, which is administered by one of the authors. (During the implementation and evaluation period, all those documents were are held in a filestore at UCL, which was administered by the authors.) The document can be created and accessed by sending files and requests by electronic mail to a Messie e-mail account (see Figure 10.2 for an example message).

Messie understands a set of commands contained in the body of an e-mail message sent to the e-mail account. All commands have to be placed at the beginning of a line, starting with the instruction #COMMAND, and consisting of a command name and directory/file name (see Figure 10.2 for an example of the READ command). The basic command set is fairly small, covering the following basic activities:

- submitting a new file;
- reading an existing file;
- editing an existing file;
- deleting an existing file;
- obtaining a listing of a directory.

```
From: a.sasse@uk.ac.ucl.cs
To: messie@uk.ac.ucl.cs
Subject:
------------------------------------------------------------
#COMMAND read Race_deliverable/chapter2
```

Figure 10.2 Example of an e-mail message to Messie (requesting a read-only copy of a file).

Regardless of the status of the request (i.e. whether it was successful or not), Messie will always send a request status report back to the sender (see Figure 10.3 for a successful request, Figure 10.4 for a failed one).

For requests that generate a return message (e.g. the READ command) this return message will always be sent in a separate e-mail message (see Figure 10.5). The message subject field in both return messages and status reports will indicate in response to which request the message is sent.

Messie can handle multiple commands in one request – it is possible to request more than one file in a single e-mail message. Each file will be returned as separate e-mail message.

In addition to return messages and status reports, Messie sends a variety of notifications to authors when requested files are locked, when checkout periods expire, and when changes have been made to a file.

Tools and functionality

Integrated into the e-mail are the shared filestore facility and the version control. Each authoring team keeps its document in a shared filestore, a

```
To: a.sasse@uk.ac.ucl.cs
Subject: Request reply read Race_deliverable/chapter2
From: The UCL-CS Messie Service <messie@uk.ac.ucl.cs>
-----------------------------------------------------
read Race_deliverable/chapter2: Valid command
Read done
```

Figure 10.3 Example of request status report (successful).

```
To: a.sasse@uk.ac.ucl.cs
Subject: Request reply read Race_deliverable/chapter2
From: The UCL-CS Messie Service <messie@uk.ac.ucl.cs>
-----------------------------------------------------
read Race_deliverable/chapter2: Valid command.
edit error: Race_deliverable/chapter2 does not exist;
   please choose another name
```

Figure 10.4 Example of request status report (unsuccessful).

```
To: a.sasse@uk.ac.ucl.cs
Subject: Request reply: read Race_deliverable/chapter2
From:  The UCL-CS Messie Service <messie@uk.ac.ucl.cs>
---------------------------------------------------
WARNING: This is a read-only copy

Chapter 2: The need for remote collaborative authoring support

The need for an environment to support collaborative authoring
of large-scale technical documents, such as Esprit, Race and
Delta deliverables, has been established in Chapter 1.  In this..
```

Figure 10.5 Example of return message.

tree-based structure of directories and files similar to UNIX and MS-DOS filestores. (Messie understands both UNIX- and MS-DOS-style file naming conventions.) To find out what files are available in the directory containing the document, authors can request a listing of the directory contents. Messie will return a list of all existing files and their current status along with additional information authors have supplied (see Document History). All files submitted to Messie will have one owner – the author who first submitted a particular file become its owner. The owner is notified of any changes made to the file, and only the owner can delete an existing file.

Once a file has been checked out for editing, Messie will lock its copy of the file – nobody else can change the document until it is returned. This locking mechanism is necessary to preserve the integrity of the individual files in the document. Read-only copies can still be obtained while a file is locked, and are automatically sent when a request for editing a locked file is received. If a file which has been checked out for editing is not returned within 48 hours (or the time specified at check-out), Messie will assume that the checked-out copy of the file has been 'lost' and unlock the last version. This timeout function prevents files from remaining inaccessible if an author requests an edit and then forgets to return the file. All changes made to a file are registered, and so all versions of a document can be accessed if authors wish to do so. Furthermore, Messie will notify the owner of a file when changes have been made by sending an e-mail message containing the name of the person who has made the changes and a list of the changes.

Diagrams, figures and drawings are stored as PostScript files. Read-only versions of PostScript files will be sent in response to requests for these files. Authors can print copies of these on their home printers. Each new version of a picture will be a new file with its own filename (e.g. pic1, pic2). Each diagram file has an associated text file, into which comments can be entered.

One of the biggest problems associated with collaborative authoring of larger documents tend to be the time and effort involved in compiling a glossary and references as a deadline approaches. The environment provided by Messie allows authors to collect such information throughout in a joint file for the glossary, and a joint file for references. Authors request a current version of these files, and, if the glossary entry or reference does not exist, send a message which appends the glossary entry or reference to the file.

User trials of Messie

To date, Messie has been used by three distributed research projects to produce major documents: RACE project CAR, DELTA project ACT and ESPRIT project MICE. The MICE project (Handley *et al.*, 1993; Kirstein *et al.*, 1995), with ten partners in six European countries, has used the system as its general document repository from the beginning of the project in December 1992. The system has not only been used for collaborative authoring of deliverables, but also to distribute the production of minutes (both of face-to-face meetings and the weekly audio- and videoconferences), task allocation (to-do lists), equipment lists, demonstration schedules, etc. It is also used by the (geographically very much distributed) Executive Committee of the British HCI Group (A Specialist Group of the British Computer Society) as a document store and organizational memory: committee members submit and request PostScript and RTF files for printing letterheaded paper and mailing labels, templates for forms and letters, etc., as well as use it for collaborative production and editing of minutes and policy documents.

The general response of those users to the system has been very positive indeed. The features the main advantages all users mentioned were:

- Small learning overhead: Users could continue to use their own e-mail and text editing facilities, and only had to learn a small number of additional commands in order to use the system effectively. Most authors felt that the environment provided very useful support for very little investment on their behalf.
- Small administrative overhead: Authors were able to produce their contributions, and read others, using the hardware and software that they were familiar with: IBM PCs, Apple Macs, Sun workstations, and IBM and DEC mainframes. Messie needs to be installed at only one (usually the group administrator's) site for each authoring team, and all other group members interact with it simply by sending messages.

On the basis of the logs of the system use, and authors' comments, we compiled a list of changes to prevent errors frequently made by authors, and additional functionality (a detailed description of both is given in Sasse *et al.*, 1993). These have been incorporated into the current version of Messie.

CONCLUSIONS

On the basis of the two studies, and further observations gained from our own use of both synchronous and asynchronous tools, we have come to the conclusion that both types of tools can offer valuable support for collaborative writing. As with most computer-based systems, appropriate support should be chosen with consideration of user and task characteristics. Whilst more strictly controlled studies will be required to devise tenable guidelines, we feel confident in making the following recommendations:

1. Synchronous support, such as multimedia conferencing, seems to be most effective
   (a) during the planning and task allocation stages of the project;
   (b) whenever negotiation and decision-making is required.
   Very few lines of text are actually written in meetings. Most authors also reported that – subjectively – attempts to produce text during a meeting ('writing-by-committee') proved to be a tedious and unnerving experience. Similarly, detailed reviewing of text seems to be an exercise most authors prefer to conduct on their own, in their own time.
2. Synchronous sessions are much more efficient when they are structured and documented. Authors were most satisfied with conference sessions in which a specific agenda was visible to all participants, and where significant points and decisions were minuted for all to see. Recent additions to audio and video in conferencing environments, from shared workspace tools for minuting and editing to facilities recording and replaying sessions (Kirstein *et al.*, 1995), should therefore improve synchronous sessions.
3. The support provided by the asynchronous tool in terms of document management was rated very highly by all authors, who compared it to previous experiences where documents and comments had been simply distributed to all authors by e-mail. Most groups, however, find that additional rules, or *human protocols* are required to coordinate activities effectively and communicate efficiently. We have observed this requirement, and gradual emergence of these human protocols, with all CSCW systems in which we have been involved (Sasse *et al.*, 1994). In the case of collaborative writing, authors particularly need to set rules regarding editing of and commenting on other authors' contributions (Baydere *et al.*, 1993).
4. In addition to human protocols, asynchronous authoring becomes more efficient when reference documents, such as glossaries and style guides, are provided early on. They help to achieve convergence between different authors' contributions, and reduce editing work.
5. Both types of support seem to be more effective with groups of authors who have actually met face-to-face. This seems to counteract the problem of reduced expressiveness and disembodied conduct, which is, naturally, greater with an e-mail-based tool than with a conferencing one.

ACKNOWLEDGEMENTS

UCL's work on computer-based collaborative authoring tools has been conducted with support from research projects funded by the Commission of the European Communities (CEC), in particular RACE project CAR. DELTA project ACT and ESPRIT project MICE. Messie was designed and implemented together with Shaw Chuang (Computer Lab, University of Cambridge).

REFERENCES

Baydere, S., Casey, T., Chuang, S., Handley, M., Ismail, N. and Sasse, A. (1993) Multimedia conferencing for collaborative writing: a case study. In Sharples, M. (ed.) *Computer Supported Collaborative Writing*, Springer, Berlin, pp. 113–134.

Borenstein, N. S. (1992) Computational mail as network infrastructure for computer-supported cooperative work. In Turner, J. and Kraut, R. (eds) *Proceedings of the Conference on Computer-Supported Cooperative Work (CSCW'92)* Oct. 31–Nov. 4 (Toronto, Canada), ACM, New York, pp. 67–74.

Borenstein, N. S. and Freed, N. (1992) *Request for Comments: 1341; MIME (Multipurpose Internet Mail Extensions): Mechanisms for Specifying and Describing the Format of Internet Message Bodies*, Network Working Group.

Chalfonte, B. L., Fish, R. S. and Kraut, B. (1990) Expressive richness: a comparison for speech and text as media for revision. In *Proceedings of CHI 1990* (Seattle, Washington, April 1–5), ACM, New York, pp. 21–26.

Galegher, J. and Kraut, R. E. (1992) Computer-mediated communication and collaborative writing: Media influence and adaptation to communication constraints. In Turner, J. and Kraut, R. (eds) *Proceedings of the Conference on Computer-Supported Cooperative Work (CSCW'92)*, Oct. 31–Nov. 4 (Toronto, Canada), ACM, New York, pp. 155–162.

Galegher, J. and Kraut, R. E. (1990) Computer-mediated communication for intellectual teamwork: a field experiment in group writing, *Proceedings of the Conference on Computer-Supported Cooperative Work (CSCW'90)* (Los Angeles, CA, October 7–10), ACM, New York, pp. 65–78.

Goldberg, Y., Safran, M. and Shapiro, E. (1992) Active mail – a framework for implementing groupware. In Turner, J. and Kraut, R. (eds) *Proceedings of the Conference on Computer-Supported Cooperative Work (CSCW'92)*, Oct. 31–Nov. 4 (Toronto, Canada), ACM, New York, pp. 74–83.

Grudin, J. (1990) Groupware and collaboratives work: problems and prospects. In Laurel, B. (ed.) *The Art of Human–Computer Interface Design*, Addison-Wesley, Reading, MA.

Handley, M., Kirstein, P. and Sasse, A. (1993) Multimedia integrated conferencing for European researchers (MICE): piloting activities and the conference management and multiplexing centre. *Computer Networks and ISDN System*, **26** (3), 275–290.

Handley, M. J. and Wilbur, S. R. (1992) Multimedia conferencing: from prototype to national pilot. In Ishida, H. (ed.) *Proceedings of the International Networking Conference (INET'92)*, (Kobe, Japan, 15–18 June), pp. 483–490.

Heath, C. and Luff, P. (1990) Disembodied conduct: communication through video in a multimedia office environment. *Proceedings of CHI, 1990* (Seattle, Washington, April 1–5), ACM, New York, pp. 99–103.

ISO (1991) *US Contribution to the JTC 1/SWG on Procedures Regarding Teleconferencing and Electronic Messaging*. ISO/IEC JTC 1, N1557, **19**, September.

Jones, S. (1993) MILO: A computer-based tool for (co)authoring structured documents. In Sharples, M. (ed.) *Computer Supported Collaborative Writing*, Springer, Berlin, pp. 185–202.

Kirstein, P., Handley, M., Sasse, M. A. and Clayman, S. (1995) Recent developments on the MICE project. *Proceedings of the International Networking Conference (INET'95)* (Hawaii, June 27–30).

Neuwirth, C. M., Chandhok, R., Kaufer, D. S., Erion, P., Morris, J. and Miller, D. (1992) Flexible diff-ing in a collaborative writing system. In Turner, J. and Kraut, R. (eds) *Proceedings of the Conference on Computer-Supported Cooperative Work (CSCW'92)*, Oct. 31–Nov. 4 (Toronto, Canada), ACM, New York, pp. 147–154.

Sasse, M. A., Handley, M. J. and Chuang, S. C. (1993) Support for collaborative authoring via email: the MESSIE environment. In De Michelis, G., Schmidt, K. and Simone, C. (eds) *Proceedings of the Third European Conference on Computer Supported Cooperative Work (ECSCW'93)* (Milano, Italy), Kluwer, Amsterdam.

Sasse, M. A., Handley, M. J. and Ismail, N. (1994) Coping with complexity and interference: design issues in multimedia conference in systems. In Rosenberg, D. and Hutchison, C. S. (eds) *Design Issues in CSCW*, Springer-Verlag, Berlin, pp. 179–195.

Part 4

New Tools

11 Using Multimedia to Support Cooperative Editing

A. SANTOS and B. TRITSCH

INTRODUCTION

For both computer-supported cooperative Work (CSCW) and for multimedia applications, success will be determined if and when they are accepted by industry. Most of the CSCW applications are communication critical – they demand communication technology (machine–machine), interaction concepts (human–computer communication) and know-how about social processes (human–human). In the same way, multimedia has also been around for quite a while and needs to be applied to serious and demanding applications in industry. We think that a mutually advantageous symbiosis can be achieved since the weak and strong points of the two disciplines are complementary: communication demanding vs communication powerful, latent industrial application vs enabling technology, human expressiveness required vs media expressiveness.

As an example, a significant portion of time within organizations is spent working or trying to work in groups (see Table 11.1 below). The estimates range from 60% to 70% for managers and 70% for office workers. A recent German study determined that managers spend 40% of their 59-hour work week on communication. A large proportion of time is spent in information production either individually or within a group: 18% (preparing documents, outgoing mail) of the time relates directly to document production; and 26% (classic informal and official meetings) directly to group work and indirectly to document production. The majority of the communication time is used for coordination–coordination of people working together towards goals they would not achieve alone. Thus the time spent in group work makes effectiveness (for example, through computer-supported cooperation) a key issue.

People often work alone, without computers, or use different tools in different computers. They move back and forth in the 'often' heterogeneous 'work spaces'. To succeed, new tools must provide continuity to existing and successful solutions. This key fact leads us to consider heterogeneous platforms (Sun and SGI workstations, PCs) as a significant issue to be addressed. Moreover, we did not intend to make a 'publishing system' for any of the media that we integrated. We aimed at building a prototype system that

GROUPWARE AND AUTHORING
ISBN 0-12-575005-6

Table 11.1 Time spent working in groups.

Work activity type	Time (%)	Work activity type	Time (%)
Classic informal meetings	19	Classical official meetings	8
Telephone	13	Incoming mail	8
Reading documents	11	Outgoing mail	7
Preparing documents	11	Other activities	23

Figure 11.1 A traditional editing session. Group members are either participating actively, working in private, pointing to something, simply listening to others, and so on. These are examples of activities we are trying to support with this work – but for group meetings spanning over distance and time.

would enable people to collaborate and process multimedia information and, if necessary, format or print it later using specialized tools.

This chapter approaches a solution to the problems mentioned above for three reasons: the quality of communication within the group can be maintained when using multimedia computer support – an integrated use of several communication media such as video, audio, text, and brainstorming graphics; the richness of the information processed can be enhanced through the use of multimedia information – text, graphics, video and audio; the adequate support for cooperation during the editing.

We first explain background ideas and key concepts of our work: multimedia editing, multimedia communication, and support for cooperation. We then refer to future work and draw our conclusions.

KEY CONCEPTS OF THE WORK

Cooperative editing systems are supposed to create a shared workspace which supports collaboration over time and distance. To be of collective benefit the tool must be accepted by the majority of the group members (Ishii and Kobayashi, 1992). Years ago Johansen presented a matrix classifying CSCW applications (see Figure 11.2). CoMEdiA extends for more than a quarter of the matrix because it is not confined to any of them in particular. It can easily have subsets that provide (although not as powerful as other specialised tools) for tele-conferencing, meeting support, multimedia-mail and collaborative writing (italic font).

CoMEdiA (Cooperative hyperMedia Editing Architecture – see Santos (1993) for description and comparison with other systems) is an architecture intended to support and encourage cooperation among several authors, multimedia communication, multimedia editing, and functionalities for the non-sequential organization of information. CoMEdiA is designed to support small groups of one to six co-authors working in possibly different locations (connected over a LAN) who wish to collaborate (but not compete) in order to produce a final document. We assume that each co-author works towards a goal of common interest, supports the other co-authors and promotes the progress of the group. Examples of documents to be produced this way are multimedia documents, which involve people with different backgrounds: scientific reports, newspaper articles, project proposals, source code production, design of rendering sciences for publicity, animation scripts or several kinds of object modeling (Santos and Marcos, 1993). In Figure 11.1 we showed example of a traditional editing session. Several member activities are shown, as examples

Place \ **Time**	Same	Different
Same	Meeting Environments	Team Work Work Shifts
Different	Tele-, Video-, Desktop- Conferencing	Electronic Mail Computer Conferences Collaborative Writing Workflow Management

Figure 11.2 The Johansen Time/Place (T/P) matrix where the location of CoMEdiA is overlayed. The areas where it is supposed to work better are ST/DP and DT/DP. It can be used as a Meeting Environment tool although with weak points. To support tasks on the area DT/SP it is not appropriate.

of activities supported by CoMEdiA – see the environments shown in Figure 11.4 – when the group meeting spans distance and time. In the design of this prototype system we adopted a problem-oriented rather than task-oriented approach. We built a flexible array of features which are 'open' and can be used and combined, according to the characteristics of the problem to be solved or the goal to be achieved. We did not conduct a task study to make clear prescriptions of a 'best way' of using them since we felt that too many task studies and too few systems were available; we felt that what is required are tools to investigate and test these theoretical concepts.

Multimedia is defined as the combination of three or more of text, graphics, animation, music, speech, images and video, according to the taxonomy (Hornung *et al.*, 1993; Hornung and Santos, 1993). The increasing use of multimedia brings with it a dramatic change in today's computer usage. The hitherto strong distinction between computing and communication is becoming blurred due to the integration of communication media with convenient access to multimedia information systems.

By video communication we mean human communication by means of a continuous sequence of digital video images captured, transmitted and then displayed in order to support an adequate communication channel between co-authors. Digital video as a communication medium is a combination of several related software and hardware technologies for video capture, on-line video compression and decompression (CoDec), video transmission over a network and video display in a workstation window.

Video CoDec is one of the areas of technology currently receiving a great amount of attention. MPEG (Motion Pictures Expert Group) is a standard for full motion video intraframe CoDec. Using a CoDec ratio of up to 100 this technique provides a high quality sequence of images, but is costly to encode and does not provide easy access to individual images of the sequence. JPEG (Joint Photographic Experts Group) is an industry standard for still picture CoDec that achieves a CoDec ratio of up to 30. It is still costly, although less than MPEG, but it can be implemented in software giving acceptable performances. If the JPEG standard is used for sequences of images it is called M-JPEG (Motion-JPEG). We decided to use M-JPEG for reasons explained in the section on video communication later in this chapter.

Perhaps one of the most important components of any system for human-to-human communication is audio. In fact, most user complaints about tele-conferencing are related to audio quality. Our research showed that more than half the information transmitted during a teleconference is verbal and therefore people notice when such an important information source is degraded. A major issue of the audio component is the sensitivity of the human ear with regards to timing errors. Here, the ear is significantly more sensitive than the eye. Delays and jitter within a certain time range ($\approx$50 to 200 milliseconds) that can be easily accepted with video sequences are unacceptable with audio sequences (Kraut and Fish, 1992). Therefore, the audio channel plays a key role in a prototype system such as CoMEdiA which aims at supporting co-authors' communication capacities. Also, we are taking the first steps in the important problem of synchronization of audio and video streams.

In non-computer-supported meetings, participants frequently make comments on what the others say or write, as well as private notes of ideas to be raised afterwards. To support these two important activities the co-authors can create and manipulate public comments and private annotations.

A known fact of collaboration theory and practice is that only rarely is a group composed of equally qualified people, people with equal rights inside the group, or even people who know each other. One way of dealing with this is to enforce the definition of a hierarchy of co-authors, defining the different levels' rights and duties. Another solution is to enable the group to define the granularity of the hierarchy, the rights and duties and so on. Although more flexible, the second method is more complex to use properly and to understand. We adopted the first method by defining a set of social roles. This reduces the coordination problems by specifying proper behaviours (responsibilities, permissible actions, restrictions, patterns of interaction) of the group members.

Multi-cursors are used for gesturing support[1] and tele-presence awareness. Hand gestures play a prominent role in all face-to-face activities (35% of all actions according to Hayne *et al.* (1993)) and it would be a major oversight to disable them when people use computer support to meet.

WYSIWIS (What-You-See-Is-What-I-See) is regarded, as a standard concept by most of the CSCW community. Since Stefik presented this technique (Stefik *et al.*, 1988) several papers, systems and studies have proved its usefulness (Olson *et al.*, 1992; Galegher and Kraut, 1992; Roseman and Greenberg, 1992). The main forms of WYSIWIS are called Strict-WYSIWIS and Relaxed-WYSIWIS, although there are a range of modalities in-between these extremes.

There are two different kinds of access techniques (lock mechanisms) generally referred to in the literature (Olson *et al.*, 1992); *Chunk Lock* and *Position Lock*. Using the Chunk Lock, the co-author requests chunks of the document for their own use. This way, there are operation cycles over chunks – Select-Ask-Edit-Free, which can be cumbersome because they require extra actions. Using the Position Lock, the co-author locks only the text position, pixel or 2D-graphic primitive they are currently editing, which is done automatically by the system.

MULTIMEDIA EDITING

When using CoMEdiA the co-authors are located in remote places (two different rooms of our institute) using heterogeneous platforms connected over

[1] (a) the use of body motions as a means of expression; (b) a movement of a body expresses or emphasizes an idea, sentiment, or attitude. Tele-pointing, multi-cursors and WYSIWIS are examples of mechanisms that support gesturing.

a standard Ethernet LAN. They have additional video and audio hardware for multimedia communication and a video communication channel (in the upper right-hand corner of the screens). The displays show an example of a cooperative editing system of CoMEdiA in which the multimedia document (MMDoc) being processed by the group has four chapters (one with text, one with 2D-graphics, and two with raster images). The organization of the MMDoc is shown (upper left corner) as well as the multimedia library and the multimedia document windows. From the multimedia library the the co-authors can select a medium (text, raster-images (statis pixel), 2D-graphics (object oriented), audio, or video) for another chapter of the MMDoc that they want to create. After selecting the medium they place the new chapter in the MMDoc window and make the connections that relate (connect) this new chapter to the rest of the MMDoc. After this, one more chapter of the document exists (although empty) and for editing purposes it must be activated/opened. Therefore, we can see that an MMDoc in CoMEdiA is not a sequential bundle of media pieces but rather an hyper-structured composite of chapters (each containing a single medium).

For each medium in the multimedia library we enable editing by providing an appropriate editor. We have implemented the editors for each of the media, and not relied upon others already in the market (MicroEmacs, FrameMaker, xfig, etc.), because of the cross-platform and heterogeneous nature of our work. In Figure 11.3 we present the text editor. The functionalities available are the

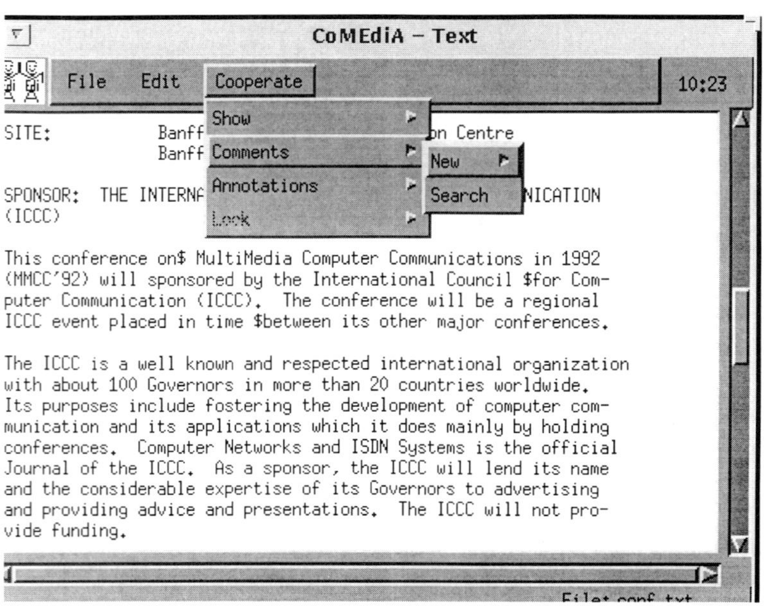

Figure 11.3 An example of how a text chapter might look.

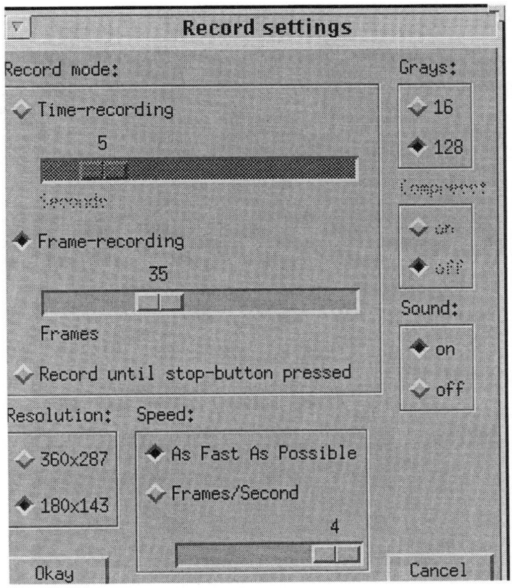

Figure 11.4 The chapter containing video information (windows to record and play a video sequence).

customary set common to most editors (emacs-like and MacPaint-like). The raster images chapter may have a previously scanned picture as its background, thus enabling the continued work on ideas that may have been originated outside CoMEdiA. The 2D-graphics medium has the editing functionalities of the raster images medium, plus others that are specific to object-oriented graphics (such as ROTATE, TRANSLATE, SCALE, (UN) GROUP and so on).

In Figure 11.4 we present the video editor. We decided to initially implement audio only as human voice; later we will implement music, noises, and so on. The functionalities supported are to load create and edit an arbitrary audio sequence. We use the WAVE format (see the section on audio communication below) and we aimed at implementing a tool that would enable co-authors to express ideas as quickly as possible – simplicity of use was preferred to completeness of features.

The video editor includes functionalities to record, preview, edit and play video sequences. We use the IFAV format (see below) and, as for audio, we aimed at implementing a simple and quick-to-use editor to compose video sequences.

MULTIMEDIA COMMUNICATION

Video communication has been technically possible for years (Gale, 1992), but at such great cost that it was not a realistic possibility for anyone but large organizations with especially designed network facilities for video-conferencing (Bellcore, NTT, Xerox). The use of standards and improvements in workstation technology have led to much smaller systems with lower costs. These developments have made multimedia communication affordable to a wider range of smaller organizations.

Video communication

The video we are used to seeing on our televisions and VCRs is an analogue signal. In order to capture the video signal and transmit it over a computer network the video data must first be digitized. Digitization requires special-purpose hardware to produce a digital image. Capturing and transmitting a continuous video sequence requires up to 216 Mbit/sec, which exceeds most system buses, LANs or WANs. This peak data rate is equivalent to the digitized PAL video signal following the CCIR 601 specification (PAL norm:

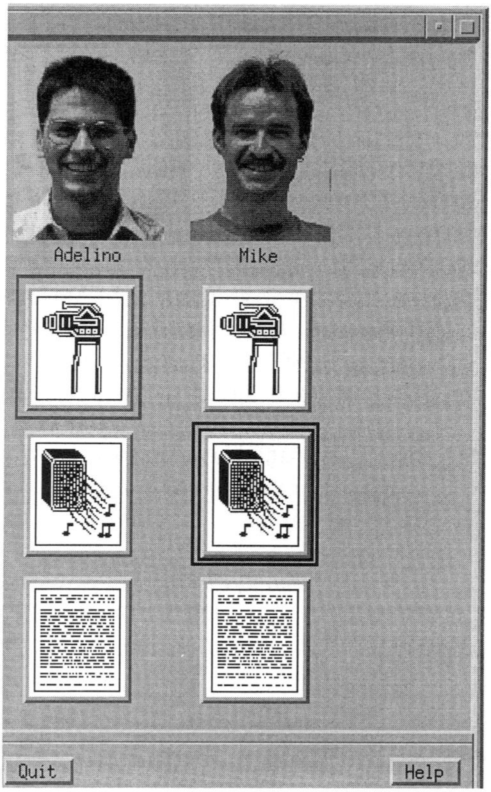

Figure 11.5 The window used to establish a communication channel (visual, spoken or written). This co-author is connected to 'Mike' by a voice channel and to 'Marcos' by a video channel.

625 × 833, 25 frames/sec, 2 Bytes colour/pixel). Therefore, on-line video capture will generally also include on-line video CoDec to reduce the bandwidth required. In CoMEdiA, we use VideoPix capture hardware on Sun workstations, IndigoVideo on SGI workstations, and MISTER COOL capture hardware on PCs. MISTER COOL (Multimedia ISDN Terminal for cooperation over long distances) is a PC-based low-cost hardware system that comprises a frame grabber and CoDec unit for transmitting video images over low-bandwidth networks (Jäger and Tritsch, 1992). The original resolution of our individual digital video images is given by the PAL video standard. These images are then reduced to 176 × 144 pixels with 16 grey scales per pixel, following the H.261 (P × 64) specification. Other operation models supported by our prototype use 360 × 288 pixels (the resolution of the Common Intermediate Format – CIF) or 176 × 144 pixels (the resolution of the Quarter Common Intermediate Format – QCIF) with 16 or 128 grey scales, or 160 colours (see next section and Kraut and Fish, 1992).

Video compression

With M-JPEG for a given CoDec ratio, the quality of images is not as high as with MPEG, but the computation costs are much lower. Additionally, each image is compressed individually, without regard to the previous or succeeding images. Therefore, each image is easily accessible. For CoMEdiA we needed a fast CoDec algorithm that could also be performed in real-time on low-end hardware or in software and which provided easy access to individual images. Therefore we decided to implement video communication following the M-JPEG specifications (see Figure 11.6) with several simplifications to improve the performance.

As a first step, we equipped a PC with MISTER COOL hardware, performing the video CoDec as described above. The resolution of the transmitted video is 176 × 144 pixels with 16 grey scales per pixel and a frame rate of 10 frames/sec (Jäger and Tritsch, 1992). The CoDec algorithm is optimized to achieve precisely the same data rate as one ISDN channel, 64 Kbit/sec. A reason for this optimization is that in the near future we want to use, besides Ethernet, ISDN lines for CoMEdiA networking purposes.

As a second step, the video communication system was implemented on UNIX workstations (Sun Sparc 2, Sun Sparc 10, SGI Indigo) under X11/Motif. With the software-only CoDec solution on Sun Sparc 2 workstations, the frame rate is approximately 4 to 5 frames/sec (see Figures 11.7 and 11.8). Most of the time, the receiving workstation is busy decompressing the video data, which makes it necessary to reduce the rate of transmitted frames. Therefore in order to increase the frame rate on the workstation, additional frames are interpolated from existing video frames using the intermediate image interpolation algorithm (Titsch and Hornung, 1992). As a result the frame rate is doubled at reasonable

Figure 11.6 The video communication: the original image seen locally (top), and the transmitted image applying the CoDec algorithm (bottom), in which there are losses due to the M-JPEG algorithm.

computing cost without additional network usage. However, the interpolated frames are sometimes blurred due to transversal object movements. Because of this we decided to enable the authors to switch the I^3 functionality on or off, as well as selecting the frame rate and image quality.

Video transmission and time rates

On Ethernet LAN, at a resolution of 176×144 and 16 grey scales per uncompressed image, we measured a peak video transmission rate of approximately 80

Minimum and maximum compression speed in images per second for:

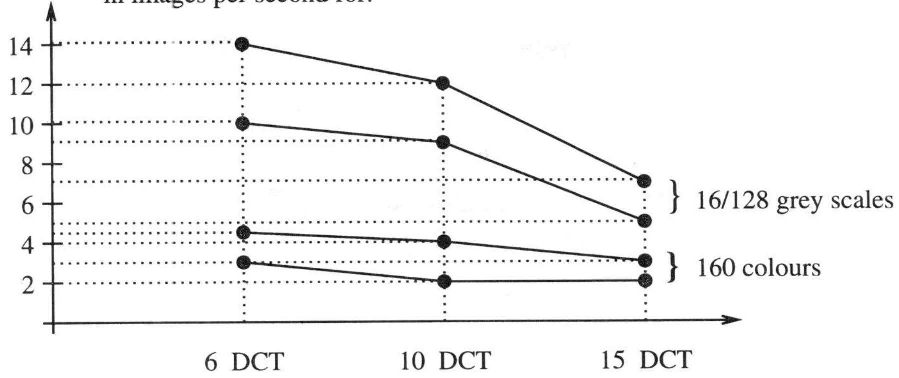

Figure 11.7 CoDec speed in relation to image quality. Increasing quality results in lower CoDec speeds.

Minimum and maximum compression rate for:

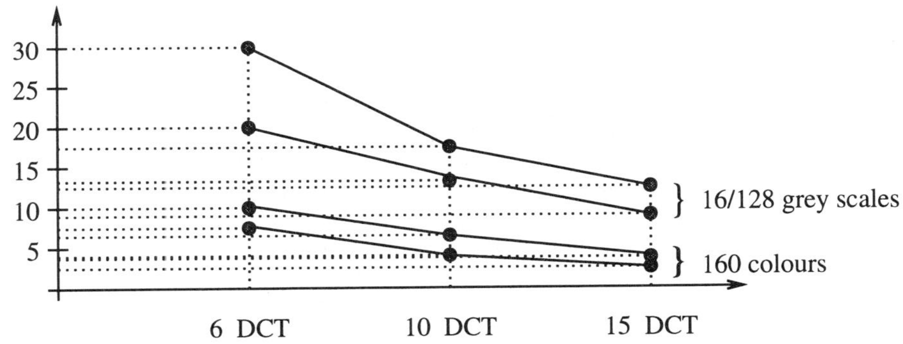

Figure 11.8 CoDec rates in relation to image quality. A CoDec rate of 1:30 means that the original image data (≈25 KB) is reduced by a factor of 30 (≈850 B).

images per second. Each individual uncompressed image is ≈12 KB (16 grey scales) or ≈25 KB (128 grey scales) which results in a peak transmission rate of about 1 MBsec. Applying the CoDec algorithms, the image data size is dependent upon the quality required. The CoDec rate of 20 to 30 (6 DCT – Discrete Cosine Transformation – coefficients) is the fastest (10 to 14 images/sec) but gives the lowest image quality. A medium CoDec rate of 13 to 17 (10 DCT coefficients) gives 9 to 12 images/sec with medium quality. The CoDec rate of 9 to 12 (15 DCT coefficients) is the slowest (5 to 7 images/sec), but gives the highest quality. This applies for both resolutions, 16 and 128 grey scales. Therefore, using a CoDec rate of 9 (≈2200 Byte/image) it would be possible to transmit about 500 images/sec using the same peak transmission rate. This shows that, with compressed images, the LAN is not the limiting factor but the CoDec algorithms.

We also measured performances using 160 colours' images of the same size. The CoDec rate of 7 to 10 (6 DCT coefficients) is the fastest (3 to 5 images/sec) but gives the lowest image quality. A medium CoDec rate of 4 to 6 (10 DCT coefficients) gives 2 to 4 images/sec with medium quality. The CoDec rate of 3 to 4 (15 DCT coefficients) is the slowest (2 to 3 images/sec), but gives the highest quality.

In the CoMEdiA prototype system, the current most significant limiting factor is access time to the frame grabber hardware. With the VideoPix hardware, it takes about three times longer to grab the video data than to compress them. Therefore, within the current prototype system, the video performance is no higher than 4 to 5 images/sec. In conclusion we state that by using fast frame grabber hardware and new-generation workstations, reasonable video frame rates of 10/sec could be achieved with the MISTER COOL algorithm. This is true for both sending and receiving video images simultaneously because the CoDec algorithm is symmetrical.

Audio communication

Different multimedia platforms provide different types of audio devices and services. Nevertheless, all of them offer a common set of functionalities, such as record, store and playback. In CoMEdiA, we realized on-line speech communication using these basic functionalities. In order to provide cross-platform usability, we defined a common, intermediate exchange format and realized a number of on-line bi-directional converters supporting different audio formats:

Sun workstations	SGI workstations	Multimedia PCs
U-LAW	AIFF	WAVE

Our intermediate exchange format used for all platforms is a subset of the WAVE format. The reason for the choice of the WAVE format was its simplicity and the superior processing speed of converters on Sun and SGI workstations in comparison to converters on the PC. On workstations, the converters produce delays of only approximately 20 milliseconds each. The multimedia PC accepts the intermediate WAVE format without any conversion which results in reduced computation costs. The WAVE format as used for CoMEdiA is based on the pulse code modulated (PCM) data format of 8-bit mono at a sample rate of 8 kHz. It can reproduce a limited dynamic range of the human voice. The audio transfer rate is 64 Kbit/sec, which is precisely the data rate of one ISDN channel.

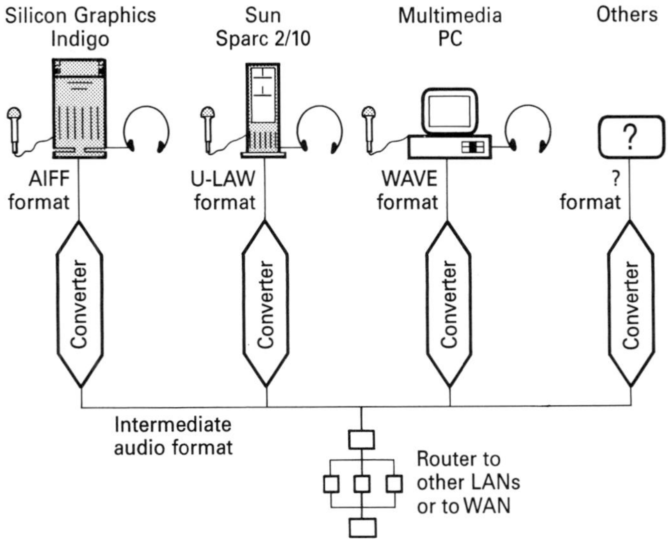

Figure 11.9 Architecture for audio communication using a heterogeneous environment. The data, in several formats, coming from/to the several devices is converted to/from a subset of the WAVE format.

Audio compression

Sometimes it might be useful to record audio data during a teleconferencing session for later playback or for editing. But even voice-quality audio is data intensive; one minute of voice-quality audio takes almost 0.5 MByte of storage space. Therefore, on-line CoDec algorithms to minimize storage space and network bandwidth are needed, covering both the raw data and precise timing information such as sampling rate, recording time and synchronization markers. We realized the ADPCM (Adaptive Differential Pulse Code Modulation) algorithm which enables a CoDec ratio of 2 to 3.

Audio transmission

In order to avoid overloading the network we introduced a noise gate. Only voice above a certain volume level is transmitted, but not the background noise during the time spans when no one is speaking, or when the microphone is switched off. As with the on-line converter, the noise gate is realized in software on the workstations. The delay produced by the noise gate during the audio data transmission is less than 7.5 milliseconds on Sun or SGI workstations, depending on the processing load. The on-line converters consume less than 12.5 milliseconds each. This produces a worst case delay of approximately 30 milliseconds for the entire conversion, not taking into account the delays due to the physical network.

Combining audio and video

Currently, we are working on combined audio/video mechanisms in order to reach media synchronization to maximize human comprehension. We have been defining an Integrated Format for Audio and Video (IFAV) that provides audio and video data in AV frames (audio/video frames). Each AV frame includes one or more video frames, the audio data belonging to those video frames and exact timing information in order to allow both synchronity and isochronity of the IFAV data stream. The IFAV mechanisms developed can be used as a basis for the implementation of the Audio Video Interleaf (AVI) or Quick Time standards. The IFAV mechanisms are supposed to reduce the number of transmitted or displayed video images in situations where the video bandwidth is decreased, without affecting the audio data stream or the synchronity between audio and video. The primary goal is to realize smart audio/video communication mechanisms that are self-adaptable to changing system capabilities.

A first prototype is already in the testing phase, providing experience with our synchronization mechanisms and IFAV format. We can record and play video sequences allowing isochronity. For example, the recording of sound corresponding to the video sequence is made by a parallel process. In the end of the recording they come together to merge and save the information recorded.

Written communication

Written communication allows non-ephemeral and safe communication concerning the editing task (discussing document plans or concepts or methods of drawing) or about the document (discussing ideas or formats) as well as matters outside the editing context.

SUPPORT FOR COOPERATION

- *Multimedia 'Post-it'*: Public comments and private annotations can contain textual, graphical and voice information. They are information fragments that refer to a certain area of the document and express an idea about this area. Their function is based on the traditional hypermedia paradigm – they can be accessed by following a link when clicking on the area (see Figure 11.10). Public comments are immediately distributed after their creation to

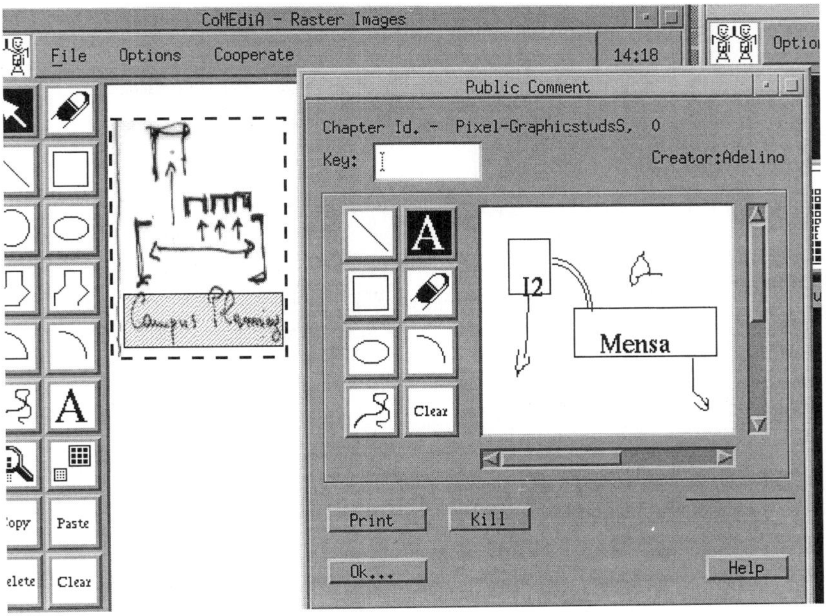

Figure 11.10 A public comment containing graphical information made on a spot of a raster image. The private annotations have a very similar user interface.

all co-authors. They are then common knowledge to the group and can be further edited by anyone (with a suitable social role). Annotations are appropriate to privately generated ideas connected to the ones expressed in a chapter, and may subsequently be communicated to the group (via a 'Make Public' option).

- *Multi-cursors*: During login, each co-author chooses a unique cursor symbol (see Figure 11.12) that will clearly identify them during the session. The selected cursor is then shown continuously to the others, during the editing process, so that gesturing information can be conveyed (see Figure 11.11). Cursors appear continuously without delay so that they remain synchronized with verbal communication. Only cursors which occur in the same screen are drawn, i.e. the ones that are visible for that co-author, which leads to relaxed-WYSIWIS (see below). Cursors are prominent enough to attract the attention of the co-authors. The cursors always maintain their absolute position on every display surface so that they retain a constant relation to the surface objects (the co-authors can then refer to them).
- *WYSIWIS*: In strict-WYSIWIS also known as 'synchronized views', all co-authors see exactly the same working area. Two main advantages are that the co-authors are always aware (without any further effort) of what the others are doing and that it realizes the metaphor of a piece of paper being worked upon by a group of people in a meeting. In relaxed-WYSIWIS the

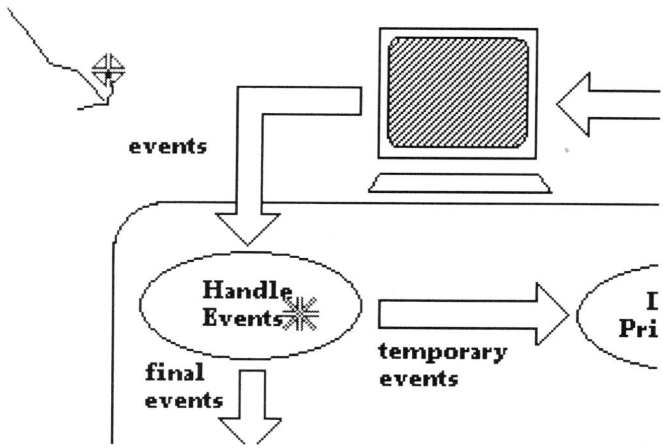

Figure 11.11 A raster image being edited by three co-authors. The cursors of two of them can be seen: drawing a pointer to the word events ('Diamond' form) and writing the word Handle ('Star' form).

co-authors can see the same working area if they want to or if they are working in the same region. By default CoMEdiA offers relaxed-WYSIWIS, although the co-authors have the option to toggle to strict-WYSIWIS (the 'Follow Co-Author' feature enforces the rule that two authors are in strict-WYSIWIS).

- *Access techniques*: The advantage of working with Chunk Lock is that it is guaranteed that no one will disturb a co-author while working on a chunk. It can be made more user-friendly if the Select Chunk and Ask Chunk operations are put together in the same action. It is much more prone to access conflicts and has common disadvantages with the distributed file systems that do file locking mechanisms. Using Position Lock, the co-authors have more editing freedom but the system has to work more in order to maintain coherency, mutual exclusion, and so on. It is much more user-friendly and, as long as the co-authors can see where the others are located in the document, it is easy to use.
- *Co-author information*: Each co-author has the option to ask for individual information about other co-author and global information about the editing session (see Figure 11.12). In this way individual and group identification is provided which enhances group cohesion and coordination.
- *Social roles*: The social roles in CoMEdiA (see Figure 11.12) are *Chairperson* – chairs an editing session; *Author* – one of the participants in the meeting who actively contributes to the production of documents; *Commenter* – only has rights to comment on the authors' writings; and *Reader* – only has rights to read. The social role of each of the participants in a meeting is defined during login and any co-author can also have her social role changed during the editing session by the Chairperson.

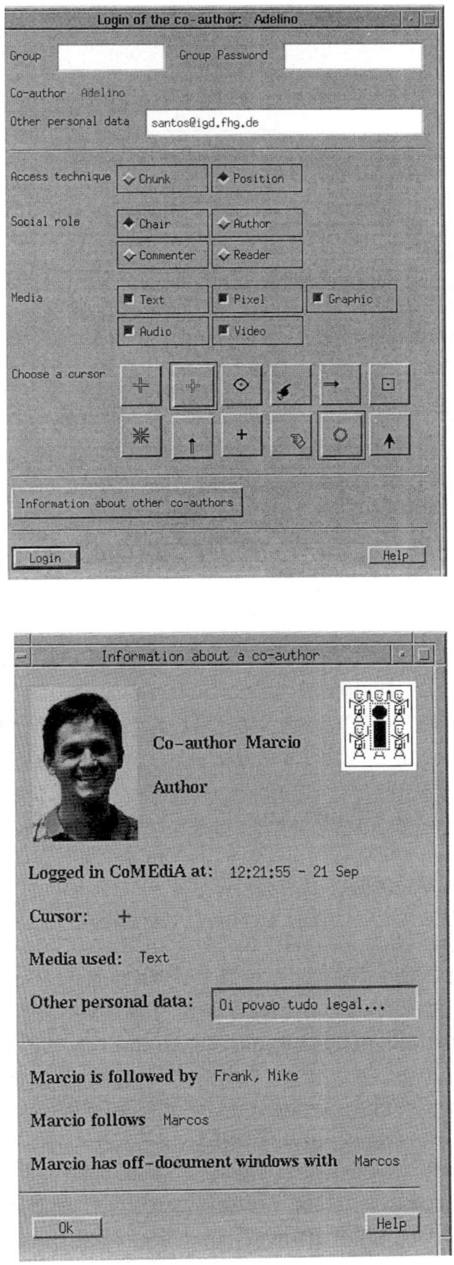

Figure 11.12 On the top the login window to enter the group identification, the access type, the social role, cursor, and so on. On the bottom the information window about a co-author.

- *Others*: CoMEdiA has further mechanisms to support cooperation. Examples include Tele-pointing, a Brainstorming zone, flexible registration protocol, non-fixed social roles, notion of group with enable/disable of participants, 'Follow' other co-author, and switch gesturing on/off.

Table 11.2.

Social role	Action
Chairperson	Manipulate MMDocs Enable or disable the login of co-authors in an editing session Change parameters of the editing process (e.g. Position Lock size) Control the workstation audio capacities (e.g. quality, volume) Control the workstation video capacities (e.g. quality, speed) Change the Social Role of other co-authors Choose a sequential path in the MMDoc (to print or mail) Lock a part or a version of a chapter from further editing
Author	Edit inside the several single-medium chapters Obtain individual and global information (Session Visualizer) Manipulate the hyper-connection in the MMDoc Use the Brainstorming tool
Commenter	Manipulate public comments Manipulate private annotations
Reader	Use the communication channels (video, audio, text) Modify private parameters (e.g. sound on/off, cursor colours) Use the 'Follow co-author' functionality (strict WYSIWIS)

FUTURE WORK

We intend to extend the audio medium to non-voice sounds – such as music and noises and use real-time voice compression and decompression by applying the ADPCM standard. We will also investigate the combination of audio and video streams until we achieve satisfactory results.

We are planning to use the prototype as the basis of several other tools. Examples are an editor for multimedia presentations, a 'Timing tool' that will record all the relevant actions during a meeting and then provide services to support version management, protocols and minutes, group undo, action search, support for persistency, and so on.

The CoMEdiA prototype system will be tested and evaluated both in real settings (a company) and in laboratory settings. We are working on an applicability study in which we parameterize the experience (type of group, task, environments, background, etc.), record it, prepare questionnaires and then analyse the results to produce a set of guidelines and recommendation for further developments. This will give the necessary feedback and expertise to improve the prototype system, develop other types of cooperative multimedia tools with extended real-time communication features, and will also influence standardization work.

CONCLUSIONS

We believe that groupware should not impose a barrier between 'individual' and 'group' ways of working. Systems should provide group members with access to individual spaces, to work privately and facilitate the import of the individual's knowledge to the group. Systems should not impose the cooperative mode of working but rather offer the authors freedom to choose their own working style. Appropriate communication channels (namely audio and video) should also be readily available.

In this chapter we have described the communication problems that often occur when people meet to work in a group. We described other motivations that lead us to the idea of using the communication power and expressiveness of multimedia to support cooperative editing processes. We built a prototype system – CoMEdiA – which supports group editing meetings that span distance and time using a range of multimedia techniques. We justified and described the function of the features realized, as well as describing the implementation itself.

ACKNOWLEDGEMENTS

We thank Prof. Dr. J. Encarnação, Dr. Ch. Hornung, M. Jäger, A. Marcos, S. Vieira, the students O. Eichhorn, R. Worsch, L. Zhu, S. Zolfaghari and CO-TECH's WG3, especially H. Lubich, J. Peiro, J. Rugeln, J. van der Velden, and S. Wilbur. This work is funded by ABB, DEC, the DELTA project DEDICATED, and a CIENCIA scholarship (BD/1736/91-IA).

REFERENCES

Gale, S. (1992) Desktop video conferencing: technical advances and evaluation issues. *Computer Communications*, **15** (8), 512–526.

Galegher, J. and Kraut, R. (1992) Computer-mediated communication and collaborative writing: media influence and adaptation to communication constraints. *Proceedings of CSCW'92*.

Hayne, S., Pendergast, M. and Greenberg, S. (1993) Gesturing through cursors: Implementing multiple pointers in group support systems. *Proc. Hawaii International Conference on System Sciences* (HICSS'93).

Hornung, C. and Santos, A. (1993) CSCW and groupware: cooperative user-interfaces and networks for collaboration. Tutorial notes, *Eurographics'93*.

Hornung, C., Jäger, M., Santos, A. and Tritsch, B. (1993) Cooperative hypermedia: an enabling paradigm for cooperative work. *The Visual Computer: an International Journal of Computer Graphics*, special edition on Techniques and Applications of Computer Graphics in the Context of telecommunications, **9** (6).

Ishii, H. and Kobaysshi, M. (1992) Integration of inter-personal space and shared workspace: ClearBoard design and experiments. *Proceedings of CSCW'92*.

Jäger, M. and Tritsch, B. (1992) Multimedia in a tele-cooperative environment – performing video communication on an ISDN-PC, *2nd Eurographics Multimedia Workshop*.

Jäger, M. and Osterfeld, U. (1994) Introducing video communication and presentation to desktop computers. *High-speed Networking and Multimedia Computing*, SPIE – The International Society for Optical Engineering, February, 350–361.

Kraut, R. and Fish, R. (1992) Audio/video networks for collaboration. Tutorial notes. *CSCW'92*.

Marcos, A. (1994) A distributed environment to support cooperative software development. *Proceedings of the 5th IFIP Conference on High-Performance Networking*, June.

Olson, J., Olson, G., Mack, L. and Wellner, P. (1992) Concurrent editing: the group's interface. *Proceedings of IFIP'90*.

Peters, R. and Neuss, C. (1995) CrystalWeb – a distributed authoring environment for the World Wide Web. In *Computer Networks and ISDN Systems*, Elsevier Science BV, pp. 861–870.

Roseman, M. and Greenberg, S. (1992) GroupKit: a groupware toolkit for building real-time conferencing applications. *Proceedings of CSCW'92*.

Santos, A. (1993) Cooperative hypermedia editing with CoMEdiA, *Journal of Computer Science and Technology*, **8** (2).

Santos, A. (1994) Evaluating multimedia availability for groupware. *Proc. IEEE International Conference on Multimedia Computing Systems*, Boston, May.

Santos, A. and Marcos, A. (1993) An algorithm and architecture to support cooperative multimedia editing, in *Proceedings of the 4th IEEE Workshop on Future Trends of Distributed Computing Systems*, September, Lisbon.

Santos, A. and Tritsch, B. (1994) Cooperative multimedia editing tool for enhanced group communication. *Computer Communications*, **17** (4).

Stefik, M., Foster, G., Bobrow, D., Kahn, K., Lanning, S. and Suchman, L. (1988) Beyond the chalkboard: computer support for collaboration and problem solving in meeting. *Proceedings of CSCW'88*.

Tritsch, B. and Hornung, C. (1992) Cooperative multimedia on heterogeneous platforms. *Proc. Dagstuhl Workshop on Multimedia System Architectures and Applications*.

12 SEPIA: A Cooperative Hypermedia Authoring Environment

NORBERT STREITZ, JÖRG HAAKE, JÖRG HANNEMANN, ANDREAS LEMKE, WOLFGANG SCHULER, HELGE SCHÜTT and MANFRED THÜRING

INTRODUCTION

This chapter addresses two main areas: (1) research on computer-based support for authoring and cooperation of groups of authors and (2) research on cooperative hypermedia systems. The first part presents a cognitive framework viewing authoring as design problem solving followed by requirements for authoring systems derived on the basis of this framework. The second part describes the system architecture and the implementation of SEPIA, a cooperative hypermedia system, meeting most of these requirements. SEPIA is a realization of our approach that hypermedia is not only the content or the subject matter but also a medium for computer-supported cooperative work in general (Streitz, 1994a), but especially for cooperative authoring.

In his 'Seven Issues: Revisited', Halasz (1991) mentions a 'broader vision of what constitutes the world of hypermedia'. He proposes a five-level system architecture and distinguishes: data storage substrate, data models, navigational facilities, applications, issues of situated use. Most of these aspects are treated in the context of the design, development, and implementation of the SEPIA cooperative hypermedia authoring environment. In this chapter, we will report about this ongoing research resulting in a hypermedia system which addresses four of these five levels. It provides results on persistent and shared data storage, hypermedia data model with composites, dedicated and comprehensive authoring functionality at the application level, support for a new rhetoric and for cooperative work at the situated use level.

The idea of SEPIA (Structured Elicitation and Processing of Ideas for Authoring) and its basic design principles were first described in Streitz *et al.*

Updated and revised version, previously published in *Proceedings of ACM Conference on Hypertext (ECHT'92)* (pp. 11–22). New York: ACM Press.

GROUPWARE AND AUTHORING
ISBN 0-12-575005-6

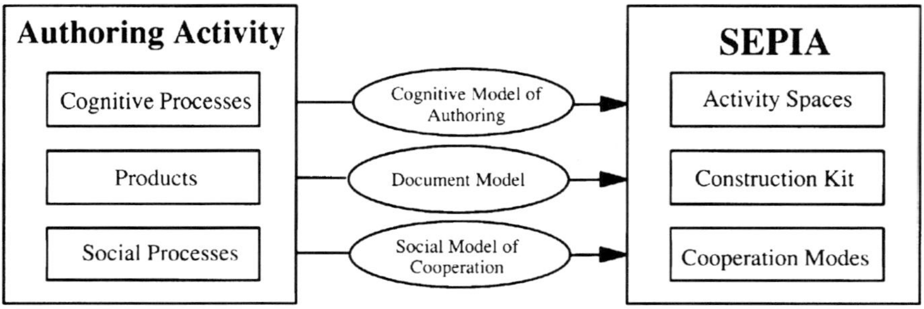

Figure 12.1 Research and development strategy for SEPIA.

(1989). We like to note that the point of view that authors of hypermedia documents need specialized support is still or even more valid than at the time of our previous publication in 1989. We also learned the lesson that one cannot develop authoring tools without being aware of what a presentation environment requires. This is reflected in our R&D strategy which addresses the cognitive processes, the product, and the social aspects of the authoring activity. Figure 12.1 shows the relationship of the activity under investigation, the theoretical basis, and the resulting components of SEPIA. Paying attention to the process aspect requires to develop and refine a model of the cognitive processes of writing and to transform these results into requirements, as e.g. in our activity space concept. Looking at hyperdocuments as a product with features of a new rhetoric (Thuring *et al.*, 1991, 1995) results in requirements for a corresponding functionality, as e.g. our construction kit in the rhetorical space. To get valid requirements. we built a large hyperdocument based on the SEPIA presentation interface (SPI) as a separate reading environment in order to test our assumptions about a new rhetoric for hypermedia (Hannemann *et al.*, 1992; Thuring *et al.*, 1995). Considering that most large and complex documents are prepared by a team (Streitz, 1995), social cooperation models had to be defined, and SEPIA had to be extended from a single-author to a multiple-author environment by providing corresponding cooperation modes (Haake and Wilson, 1992). Thus, detailed knowledge about the process, the product, and the social situation played equally important roles in the development of our user-oriented and task-driven authoring environment.

THE CHALLENGE OF HYPERMEDIA AUTHORING

Readers as well as authors have to struggle with a variety of problems arising from the net-like character of hypertext.

The reader of a hyperdocument is typically confronted with two difficulties. The first one is known as the navigation problem: Readers often ‘get lost in hyperspace’ (Conklin, 1987). Most of the research on reading hypertext has solely concentrated on the navigation problem thus overlooking a second difficulty: many readers have trouble to comprehend a hyperdocument, i.e. they often fail to grasp its overall structure or to understand the semantics of links. Disorientation and deficient comprehension probably have the same cause: readers are impeded in forming a coherent mental representation of the document. As a consequence, more and more readers complain about the low quality of hyperdocuments. To create hyperdocuments of high quality, the author must be aware of his readers' problems and view them as problems caused by him – at least to a certain degree. Especially, he is responsible for designing hypertext structures and presentation formats which increase the coherence of his document and support efficient navigation. But this is not an easy task. In contrast to writers of linear documents, authors of hyperdocuments have no guidelines telling them what their product should look like. Many rhetorical decisions must be made without the security of widely accepted conventions. Since these decisions entail activities supplementary to the processes of writing a linear text, such activities are often regarded as cognitive overhead (Conklin, 1987). The lack of rhetorical guidelines and cognitive overhead complicates the authoring of hyperdocuments and contributes to the low quality to be observed in many cases. To overcome this unsatisfactory state, the developers of hypertext systems, must be more aware of reader- and author-specific problems and the construction of writing tools must be based on a sound theoretical foundation. Applying the basic principle of cognitive compatibility (Streitz, 1987), we have translated this insight into the requirement that authoring systems which are intended to give appropriate support must be cognitively compatible to authoring activities (Streitz *et al.*, 1989).

A cognitive framework: authoring as design problem solving

Based on an analysis of the cognitive processes of writing and the features of the authoring situation, we have characterized writing as a design activity (Hannemann *et al.*, 1990). The interdependencies of extensive planning, production and revision activities are characteristic for the writing process and lead to both an external product – the text – and an internal product – a new knowledge structure. Just as readers may find it difficult to explore the hyperspace, authors find it difficult to explore the complex design space. Helping an author 'travelling' through this space, the development of an authoring environment must rely on three main features of every design process:

- Design is a complex problem solving process, which consists of different subproblems. These problems are solved by specific activities which are opportunistic, i.e. they strongly interact and build on each others' results.
- Design is the construction of an artifact which has to fulfil specific criteria and for which the designer needs adequate building blocks to compose the artifact.

- Design usually is a social process that involves a group of individuals. Therefore, facilities which support cooperation should be incorporated into an authoring environment.

Now, we describe the implications of these aspects and derive requirements for the development of SEPIA.

Supporting the design process: activity spaces for hypermedia authoring

Using results of research on writing, we have identified three closely related subproblems which an author must solve to produce a document: the content problem, the rhetorical problem, and the planning problem. According to Newell (1980), the mental representation of these three problems can be described in terms of separate but interacting problem spaces formed by different constraints, design objects and operations in which different knowledge sources are brought to bear. Applying the principle of 'cognitive compatibility', we use this decomposition of the design space into subspaces as a basis for dedicated requirements of components of the authoring environment. These (cognitive) problem spaces are 'matched' in the SEPIA system by corresponding activity spaces. Each activity space provides specific design objects and operations appropriate to facilitate the author's activities when working on the above subproblems:

- the content space,
- the rhetorical space, and
- the planning space.

Since argumentation is a crucial cognitive activity which plays an important role in writing for a large number of document types, we supplemented these three spaces by a fourth space called

- argumentation space.

To support the construction of artifacts SEPIA provides a special 'construction kit' which is integrated in the rhetorical space (for more details see Thüring *et al.*, 1991, 1995).

Supporting the social process: from single to multiple authors

A main feature of the authoring process is that it involves in many cases more than one person. This is especially true for hypermedia (Streitz, 1995) . The design of SEPIA has to reflect this by providing support for the cooperation of authors working in groups. This involves the following activities.

First of all, authors access and modify shared hyperdocuments concurrently. The environment should allow a maximum of concurrent activities by the authors whenever they work on different parts of the document. Authors working on the same part of the document should be prevented from accidentally destroying each other's work. Group authoring occurs in different modes of collaboration that we label: individual, loosely coupled, and tightly coupled work. The modes differ in the level of awareness each author has of the activities of the co-authors. In individual work, a single author manipulates a task-specific cluster of nodes and links. Even though the author works individually, there is a need to collaborate with the co-authors asynchronously, for instance, through an annotation facility. In loosely coupled work, several co-authors working on the same subtask manipulate the same cluster. In this mode, they need to be aware of each others presence and activities. In tightly coupled work, authors cooperate and coordinate their work in synchronous conference-like 'meetings'. In this mode, authors should be provided with a WYSIWIS-functionality (WYSIWIS – What You See Is What I See) and additional channels for meta-communication. Cooperative writing proceeds by shifting between these three collaboration modes. Due to the opportunistic nature of cooperative writing, one cannot foresee the sequence of the collaboration modes. Therefore, smooth transitions between the modes must be supported.

Summary of requirements

To support both individual and cooperative writing of hypermedia documents, SEPIA should therefore meet the following requirements. It should

R1. support activity spaces for hypermedia authoring, i.e.
  (a) provide task-specific objects and operations,
  (b) provide views on hyperdocument structure (network level) and content (node level),
  (c) provide a cognitively compatible user interface,
  (d) support exchange and cross-referencing of objects across activity spaces,
  (e) provide a hypermedia data model which is tailorable to activity spaces and tasks,
  (f) provide persistent storage for structure, content, and view information,
  (g) support multimedia data (text, sound, voice, graphics, pictures, etc.).

R2. support versioning of hyperdocuments.

R3. support distributed authoring of hyperdocuments including access to a shared hyperdocument database.

R4. support shared workspaces at the network and the node level. These
  (a) are shared browsers for activity spaces, resp. composite nodes in general.

(b) support different collaborative modes (individual, loosely coupled, lightly coupled),
(c) allow for smooth transition between modes.

R5. support additional channels for meta-communication (audio, video conferencing).

FUNCTIONALITY AND USER INTERFACE

Within each activity space there are two levels of operations: the network level (navigation in the graphical browser and actively editing the network) and the node level (reading and editing content).

Authoring at the network level

Activity space functionality

Figure 12.2 shows a screendump of open activity space browsers. They were opened by clicking on their initials (P, C, A, R) in the 'launcher' of the

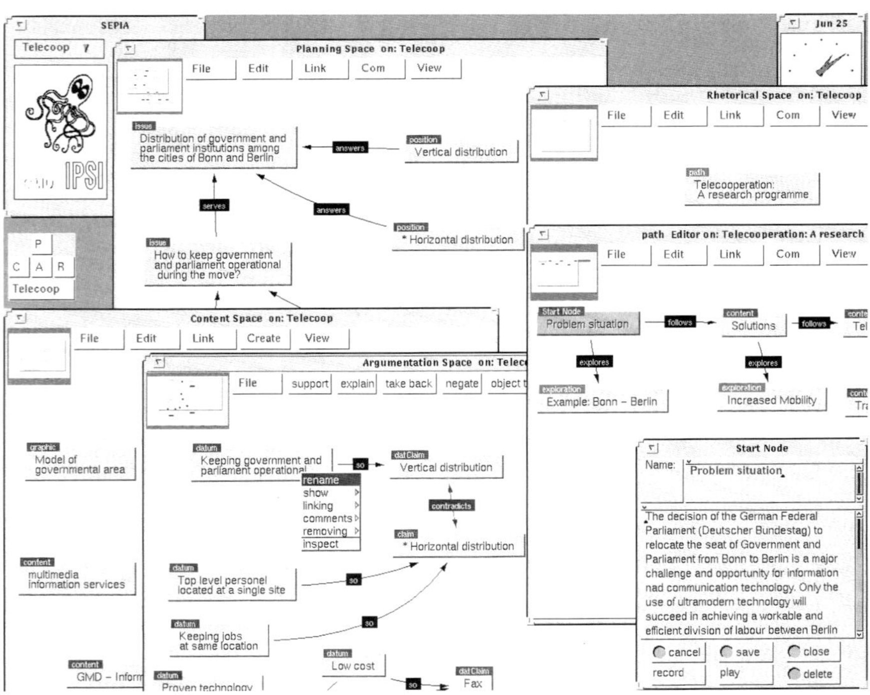

Figure 12.2 User interface of SEPIA.

'project' Telecoop. (The example was created in the context of the POLIKOM project on telecooperation support between Bonn and Berlin, Hoschka *et al.*, 1992). Users can browse in each space by activating nodes and links and scrolling if the current window does not contain all objects. A 'roaming box' (upper left corner) shows an actively manipulable presentation of the whole space (resp. composite node). Each space provides space-specific functionality (typed nodes, links, operations) available for every author independent from his cooperative work node.

The design objects and operations of the *content space* are dedicated to facilitate the development of a domain model. For this purpose, SEPIA provides the structuring facility of hypertext to support idea dumping, their grouping in topic related clusters by composite nodes and connecting them via, typed links. This can also involve access to background material either from internal (e.g. previous documents) or external sources (e.g. querying a data base).

In the *rhetorical space*, the author creates the reader-oriented, final document. This final product can be both a conventional, linear text or a hyperdocument, formed by a typical network of nodes and links. Both document types constitute a scale ranging from strictly linear to strictly non-linear documents. Notice that hyperdocuments can vary in the degree of their linearity between these two endpoints. Nevertheless, they all should satisfy one major requirement: in order to support comprehension and navigation on behalf of the readers, they must appear as coherent entities. Therefore, the rhetorical space provides a spatial 'construction kit' based on the concept of coherence consisting of design objects that are explicitly tailored to the requirements of designing artifacts (Thüring *et al.*, 1991, 1995).

In the *planning space*, an author has the opportunity to externalize his writing plans, resp. goals, to construct issues to be concerned with in the document, and to establish an agenda for the authoring activity. Consequently, this space serves as a meta space for coordinating the activities in the other three spaces and for controlling the progress of the design process.

For the development of an issue structure, SEPIA provides a set of dedicated nodes and links. We use a modification of the IBIS method (Kunz and Rittel, 1970) by extending the issue concept and introducing a new principle for linking issues (Schuler and Smith, 1990). In addition, the planning space is linked tightly to the argumentation space. 'Positions' which are formulated as 'answers' to issues in the planning space are transformed and recreated as 'claims' in the argumentation space prompting the author for providing supporting arguments (example in Figure 12.1). 'Horizontal distribution').

The *argumentation space* supports the development of an argumentation structure by providing appropriate design objects and operations based on our extension of the argumentation schema developed by Toulmin (1959). Using the argumentation space, the author can elaborate an argumentation by generating support or objections at different levels, by formulating contradictions and by constructing argumentative chains (for details see Streitz *et al.*, 1989).

When 'travelling through activity spaces', the author does not need to follow a predetermined route. At every point in the authoring process, he can decide which subspace to use next. To support the high flexibility for interaction and smooth transformation of knowledge between the activity spaces, SEPIA allows automatic transfer of design objects between specified spaces, their reuse, and the indication and control of references between activity spaces.

Multiple authors

Figure 12.3 shows the user-interface of an author who is in different composites in different cooperation modes.

When several co-authors work on the same task (i.e. each of them has an active browser on the corresponding composite node), the respective browsers initially are in loosely coupled mode (Planning Space in Figure 12.3). Authors are made aware of each other via (1) a list of all concurrent users displayed in

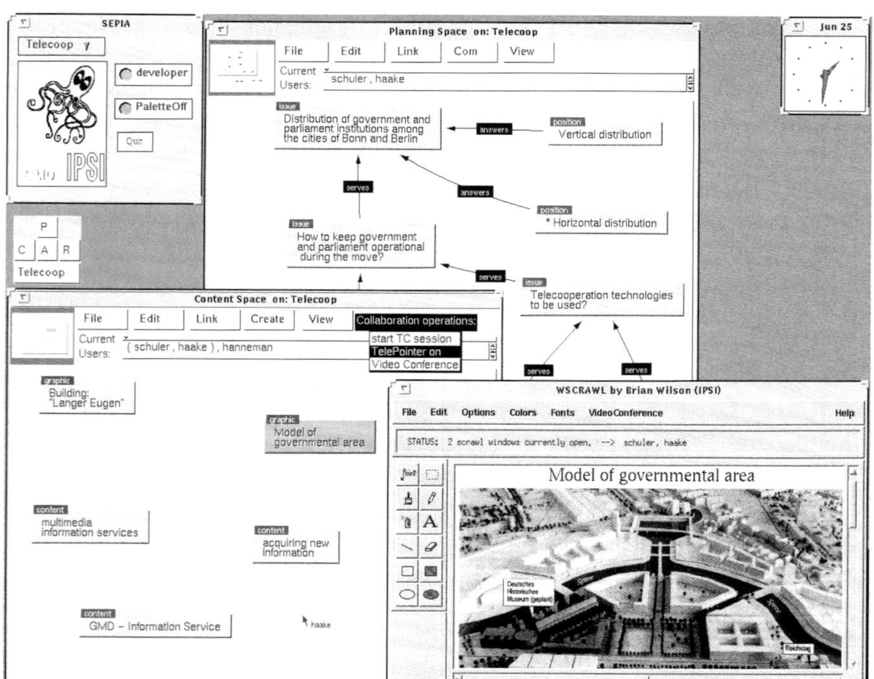

Figure 12.3 User interface of cooperative SEPIA.

the resp. browsers (e.g. schuler, haake) (2) highlighting of objects locked by other users, and (3) a relaxed WYSIWIS view. Actions affecting the view of the node are private, but manipulations of objects in the node become visible immediately to all other browsers if they affect the currently visible area. Locking at the data base level is used to prevent co-authors from simultaneously modifying the same object.

In tightly coupled mode, the coupled browsers display a WYSIWIS-view on the composite node's content. For an example see the Content Space in Figure 12.3 showing two tightly coupled users (schuler, haake) and one additional loosely coupled user (hannemann). In addition to the functionality of the loosely coupled mode, scrolling and resizing events are immediately broadcast to all tightly coupled browsers.

Awareness of the co-authors' activities is a prerequisite for smooth ad hoc transitions from one mode of collaboration to another. Currently, the transition from individual work to loosely coupled work is triggered automatically when a second author opens a composite node already 'occupied' by the first author. This is indicated by a 'door bell' sound on both workstations and the change of the user list. Being in loosely coupled mode, authors might want to join for a tightly coupled session. To start a tightly coupled session, one co-author selects all or a subset of those co-authors currently in the same node and invites them to participate in the session. The system asks each of them to confirm. The browsers of those co-authors who confirmed are shifted into tightly coupled mode. Authors can exit a tightly coupled session either by closing the composite node or by returning to loosely coupled mode (Haake and Wilson, 1992).

Node level

Beyond the structural aspects at the network level, hyperdocuments are very much characterized by the type of media which are used. All atomic (content) nodes can carry multimedia information including text, graphics, pictures, and sound. They can also be annotated by multimedia nodes. We are also working on the integration of digital video as content of a node. This use of multimedia has to be distinguished from using it for communication purposes as, e.g., in audio and video conferencing systems.

Cooperative use of hypermedia requires joint viewing and editing of the content of a node. This is facilitated by integrating WScrawl (Wilson, 1992), a group-aware, color, pixel-oriented, shared drawing tool we have also used as part of another desktop conferencing scenario (Lemke *et al.*, 1992). Here, it is used for displaying and editing the graphics and picture content of nodes (e.g. the picture of the 'Model of the governmental area' displayed for the users 'schuler' and 'haake' in Figure 12.3). Each drawing action is immediately visible on all connected displays. Users can import arbitrary information from their screens (even outside of WScrawl or SEPIA windows) using the 'SuperSelect' facility and show it to everybody currently sharing the view in WScrawl.

Meta-communication channels

Having shared browsers is only one way of supporting synchronous remote cooperation. As indicated by the 'interactive communication model' in CoLab (Tatar *et al.*, 1991), additional communication channels are required. SEPIA provides a digital audio channel for audio-only conferencing as well as an analog audio/video conferencing device enabling up to four co-authors to see and talk to each other (see Collaboration menu in Figure 12.3). In addition, SEPIA supports gesturing by providing concurrent telepointing for each tightly coupled user (e.g. haake) at the network level and within WScrawl at the node level. Each telepointer displays the name of its user. Furthermore WScrawl serves as a common scratch space for co-authors in tightly coupled sessions. Groups of authors can take meetings notes which are available immediately to any group member and which can be attached to the hyperdocument if desired.

SYSTEM ARCHITECTURE AND IMPLEMENTATION

First, we describe the single author system before we discuss the implementation of the cooperative system.

The single-author system

In order to meet the requirements R1 and R2, we chose the architecture shown in Figure 12.4 which we discuss in a bottom-up fashion.

We distinguish between an application module (SEPIA's activity spaces) and an object management module. In the latter, the hyperdocument data (nodes, links, and composites, together with their attributes) are handled by the hypermedia engine HyperBase (Schütt and Streitz, 1990) which provides a persistent storage and retrieval mechanism for hyperdocuments. These are stored in a hyperdocument database. HyperBase was extended to CHS (Cooperative Hypermedia Server, *cf.* next section).

To support versioning (R2), we integrated CoVer, a contextual version server which provides basic versioning concepts to the activity space browsers. The distinguishing feature of CoVer is that it not only maintains versions of individual objects but it also maintains the task context in which versions are created. See Haake (1992, 1994) and Haake and Haake (1993) for details.

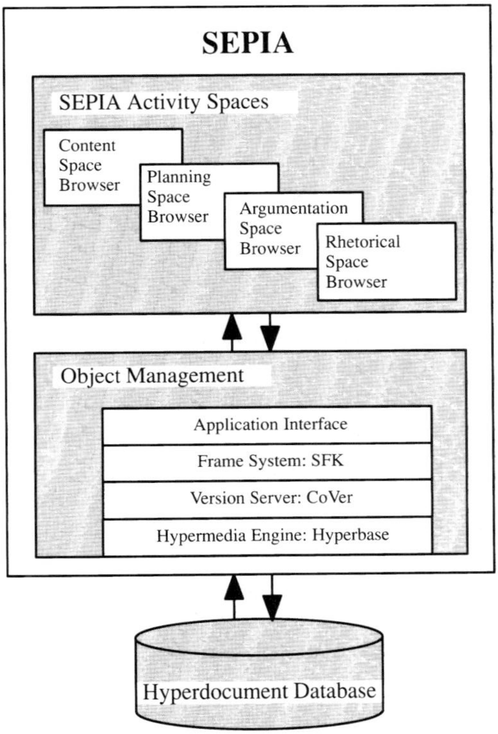

Figure 12.4 System architecture of SEPIA for single authors.

All hypermedia objects are implemented as refinements of a generic data model which was specified using the SFK frame system developed at IPSI (Fischer and Rostek, 1995). A frame-based approach is well suited for the modelling of typed hypermedia structures because it allows the declarative specification of constraints which can be checked at runtime (e.g. validity of link sources and destinations), it is easily extendible (tailorability), and it supports transactions within the authoring environment.

Our generic data model combines hypertext constructs with object-oriented frame-based representations similar to Aquanet (Marshall *et al.*, 1991) or MacWeb (Nanard and Nanard, 1991). All its entities are represented as frame objects with single inheritance. Their named and typed slots carry content, structure, and system information, as well as attributes. The basic data model objects are typed nodes and links (see Figure 12.5), where the types are realized as frame classes. The content slot of the nodes contains the hypermedia's primitive data types (e.g. text, image, sound). Links are also typed first-class objects. They represent relationships between SEPIA objects. Their type definition includes their constraint information.

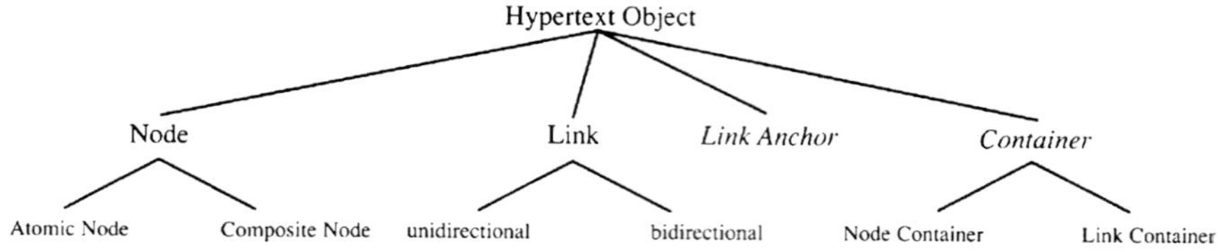

Figure 12.5 SEPIA data model hierarchy. Basic data objects are shown in normal letters, view objects in italic.

Source and destination objects of a link are link anchor objects which are associated to the basic objects of the link relation. Anchors are conceived as logical and not geometrical entities bound to a portion of text or picture. The application interface (see Figure 12.4) defines the mapping of the hypermedia data model to the data model of HyperBase.

SEPIA's basic structuring means are composite nodes which contain a partially ordered set of basic objects (nodes and links). Composite nodes are used to represent subgraphs of the hypermedia network. Activity spaces and folders used in an activity space are implemented as composite nodes. Each activity space uses an application-dependent subset of the node and link types. Activity space browsers provide activity-specific views on the hyperdocument. These views provide access to task-specific objects and operations. Activity space browsers can exchange hypermedia objects or can create reference links to objects of other activity spaces. In a hypermedia environment it is important to support persistent view information because structuring the layout of a hypermedia network is an additional important feature for authors.

For every data object (node, link, composite node) to be displayed in an activity space browser, SEPIA uses a special persistent container object which contains its view information. Thus, all display information (e.g. position, icon, style, size in a graphical net browser) of a data object to be shown in a browser is stored in a special container object which is typed according to the data object. As a result, one data object can be connected with different container objects and therefore be displayed differently in different contexts via different container objects. Example: A 'position' in the planning space can be displayed in its role as a 'claim' in the argumentation space at the same time.

The multi-author system

In order to meet the requirements for cooperative authoring (R3–R5), we extended the architecture as follows (see Figure 12.6).

The cooperative hypermedia server CHS provides shared access to hypermedia documents. We explored several ways of implementing shared hypermedia servers, such as building CHS on top of a multi-user DBMS or

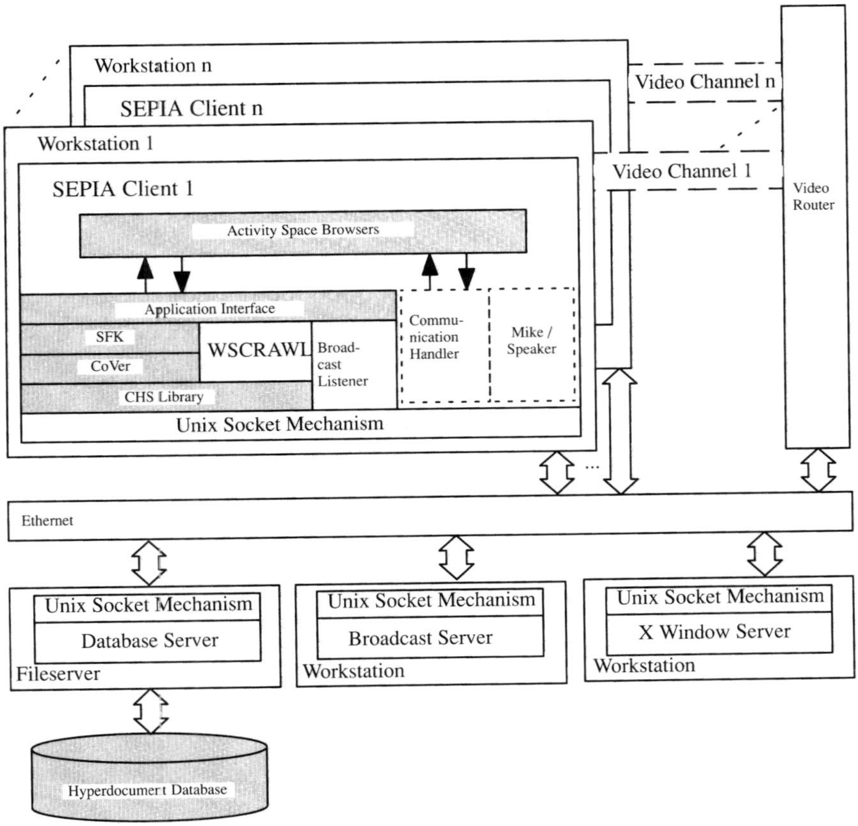

Figure 12.6 System architecture for cooperative SEPIA. Shaded areas represent components which already exist in the SEPIA system for single authors. The communication handler and the mike/speaker processes are represented as dotted lines because they are created on demand only.

using a file–system based approach. In the DBMS approach, CHS can exploit the transaction management facilities of the underlying database system for concurrency control and recovery. It captures deadlock and livelock situations and ensures that the hyperdocument database is always in a consistent state. The adopted client-server architecture enables multiple clients to access the same database server in a distributed computing environment (R3). In order to support collaboration, CHS maintains a list of users which are currently logged into the system. The data model of CHS has been extended by locks which can be assigned to objects. The application interface now not only defines a mapping from the clients' data model to the data model of CHS, but it also defines policies for transferring data between a client and the shared database (more details are found in Schutt and Haake, 1993).

Shared workspaces at the network level

Shared workspaces (R4) have been realized through application interfaces and browsers which exchange update information. In SEPIA, all changes are immediately stored in the shared database. In addition to this, change notifications are broadcast among SEPIA clients in two ways. First, the application interface broadcasts change notifications of hypermedia objects stored in the database to ensure that all clients use the same state of the shared objects. This feature is used to realize the loosely coupled mode of activity space browsers. A broadcast server is connected to all SEPIA clients which broadcasts change notifications among the clients. Every SEPIA client includes a broadcast listener process which waits for change notifications from the broadcast server.

Second, activity space browsers which are in tightly coupled mode communicate directly with each other. They exchange messages synchronizing scrolling, resizing, and telepointing. These messages are received by a local communication handler which is associated with each browser. Each browser has a session object attached to it which keeps track of cooperation modes and current users.

Shared workspaces at the node level

Sharing of information is also available at the node level. In SEPIA, we use the WScrawl shared drawing tool for that purpose. Opening a node with graphical contents starts WScrawl which provides an arbitrary number of authors with a shared whiteboard every author can write on. WScrawl uses the X window server to synchronize event handling and to exchange data among participating authors. When WScrawl is called from a browser which is in tightly coupled mode, it is also started in tightly coupled mode and displays the content of the node to be shared automatically on all users' workstations which are currently tightly coupled with this browser.

Additional communication channels

In order to provide additional communication channels (R5), we are following two technical routes: analog and digital. Digital audio is automatically set up as a bidirectional communication line – over the ethernet – among two tightly coupled users in a session. There are appropriate mike and speaker processes installed at the beginning of a tightly coupled session at each workstation, which send and receive audio packets to or from the remote partners. Only one tightly coupled session at a time can use the audio communication facility due to the limited mike and speaker resources. When finishing a tightly coupled session the corresponding audio processes are automatically shut down.

On the other hand, we integrated a video conference system installed at IPSI into the cooperative SEPIA clients. As part of the SEPIA interface, a user can ask the video router to provide an analog video and audio connection between him/her and remote partners. Initially, the video conference was limited to connections of two people but by using now a cross split video switch, simultaneous video conferencing is available for up to four people at a time.

Implementation details

The cooperative SEPIA clients are implemented in Smalltalk-80 (Parc Place Visual Works 1.0) on SUN Sparc-10 workstations running SUN OS 4.1.3 Unix and the Open Windows 3.0 window system. CHS is implemented in C on top of the relational DBMS Sybase. The audio communication feature uses the Netfone software, release 1 (Walker, 1991) written in C. The video server and WScrawl are implemented in C. WScrawl uses an X server to broadcast information. Interprocess communication is implemented by using standard UNIX sockets.

CONCLUSIONS AND FUTURE WORK

We now discuss the innovative aspects of SEPIA on the following three dimensions of a design process and compare it with other approaches having similar goals:

1. User-oriented and task-driven system design resulting in support for different subtasks of the authoring activity;
2. Support for the special requirements of hyperdocument production;
3. Support for different modes of cooperating authors.

Dedicated support for different subtasks of the authoring activity

With respect to the first dimension, we like to state that there are only few attempts to address the problem of dedicated support for hypermedia authoring. Many systems focus primarily on providing presentation and reading environments. Similar to our approach – in terms of cognitive modelling – is the development of the Writing Environment (WE) (Smith *et al.*, 1987). It supports the creation of a network of ideas (network mode) to be transformed in a hierarchical document structure which is then displayed and can be edited in a linear mode. The network mode exhibits a node-link structure but does not offer different types of nodes and links. The final document is a linear document. While WE did not support multimedia components nor collaborative writing, the successor system ABC (Artifact-Based Collaboration) (Smith and Smith, 1991) provides support for cooperative work. StorySpace (Joyce, 1991) provides an interesting interface metaphor for authoring hypertext. Other relevant approaches for the support of authoring are the MUCH system (Rada *et al.*, 1992, 1993) and the RICH system (Wang and Rada, 1995).

This overview would be incomplete without mentioning systems for argumentation support: gIBIS (Conklin and Begeman, 1988), PHIDIAS (McCall *et al.*, 1990), EUCLID (Smolensky *et al.*, 1987), Toulmin in NoteCards (Marshall, 1989). They have in common that they use either the IBIS-approach or the Toulmin model of argumentation. Aquanet (Marshall *et al.*, 1991) provides schemata to create Toulmin or IBIS-structures. Although these systems offer dedicated support for one aspect of the authoring activity (argumentation, knowledge structuring) they lack support for the other processes we have identified and realized in the four activity spaces of SEPIA.

In summary of the first dimension, we can state that SEPIA is special in so far as it provides support for a wide range of hypermedia authoring activities. It is theoretically well grounded and reflects the theory via the provision of dedicated node and link types and corresponding operations in each space. In addition, it offers interspace linking possibilities and the reuse of hypermedia structures and content across subtasks.

Dedicated support for hyperdocument production

The production of hyperdocuments requires concepts and methodologies with respect to the final product. Authors need support on different levels of hypermedia networks. Conceptually related to our construction kit (Thüring *et al.*, 1991, 1995), is HDM – the hypermedia design model – proposed by Garzotto *et al.* (1991, 1993). It utilizes a schema approach for efficiently high level structuring of large applications and subsequent instantiation. Another attempt to provide high level concepts to the author was proposed by Smith Catlin *et al.* (1991). They extended Intermedia with templates realized as a set of pre-linked documents which can contain both content and formatting information. But they do not explicitly address the problem of coherence. A related approach for providing high-level overviews is the work by You and Rada (1994) on outline manipulation in the context of the hypertext system MUCH where they exploit the potential of hypertext for creating alternative views in a dynamic fashion.

Support for different modes of cooperating authors

SEPIA realizes two roles which from our point of view (Streitz, 1994a) hypermedia can and should play for cooperative work: (1) hypermedia constitute the content of cooperation and (2) hypermedia provides a base technology and represents a medium for facilitating cooperation. This is in line with the observation of Halasz (1988, p. 848): 'Hypermedia is a natural medium for supporting collaborative work'. Comparing SEPIA with other systems on this 'cooperative' dimension yields the following observations.

The GROVE group text editor (Ellis and Gibbs, 1989; Ellis *et al.*, 1991) uses local editors and replicated documents together with a central coordinator serializing all editing operations. SEPIA is geared towards hyperdocument authoring and synchronization is done using transactions and locking of objects in the database. Instead of broadcasting operations which are difficult to sequentialize, SEPIA broadcasts update notifications which need not be sequentialized by the clients. The rIBIS system (Rein and Ellis, 1991) is based on a central server architecture providing one TC session per hyperdocument and supporting only one mouse – a group mouse – within a TC session. SEPIA is implemented following the replicated architecture approach providing multiple TC sessions per composite node and supporting a private mouse for each co-author. Switching between cooperative modes is very smooth in SEPIA. While Dewan and Choudhary's (1991) collaboration support environment requires users to tailor the coupling behaviour to their needs, cooperative SEPIA relieves users from constructing a specific coupling behaviour. Furthermore, SEPIA provides concurrency control and maintains dynamic sessions. Aquanet (Marshall *et al.*, 1991) follows also the replicated architecture approach but does not support synchronous cooperation in terms of shared views, telepointers, and audio communication. The PREP-editor (Neuwirth *et al.*, 1990, 1992) supports asynchronous collaboration addressing cooperative aspects of writing in terms of common planning and annotation activities and flexible diffing (Neuwirth *et al.*, 1992, and this volume). Although not developed as a hypertext system in the first place, it makes use of some hypertext features in an interesting fashion as, e.g. separate but linked columns for each author and for annotations.

New developments and future work

In this part, we reflect on our previous experiences with SEPIA, provide information on new developments of the system since the first publication of the original paper, and point to future work. In our early uses of the prototype system, we have been concerned with (argumentative) proposal writing, project planning, recording user feedback in SEPIA itself, and replicating the task of a science journalist writing an article on a scientific debate. Our experiences show that the system is appropriate for these tasks. In order to test SEPIA in new application domains we followed several routes.

First, we experimented with adapting existing activity spaces to new task contexts. Examples are cooperative decision making and capturing design rationale. This was achieved by focusing especially on the planning space and the argumentation space and by modifying the types of nodes and links appropriately.

Another approach was taken by using the tailorability of the activity space framework and defining new application-specific spaces. An example is the so-called MuSE–SEPIA (Haake *et al.*, 1994) which was developed in the MuSE project (Multimedia Systems Engineering). This project aims at providing a computer-based environment for the engineering of complex technical systems (e.g. trucks, aircraft). The system comprises both the validation of the system model (before it is actually built) and support for modelling techniques required by the designer. For this application, we developed new spaces, e.g. a modelling space and a validation space with new types of nodes and links derived from the requirements of the system engineers.

Quite a different route has been taken by developing the DOLPHIN system (Streitz *et al.*, 1994) which provides support for a range of collaborative activities, e.g. face-to-face meetings in electronic meeting rooms, which were outside the original scope of SEPIA. But DOLPHIN can be used in a complementary way because of its full compatibility to SEPIA. We will come back to this later on.

Finally, we have developed a number of components as extensions or enhancements starting with the original SEPIA system but to be used in most of the new, sometimes rather application-specific variations of SEPIA. This includes the reading environment SPI (SEPIA Presentation Interface), a linearizer tool, object-oriented database support, and versioning.

Although SEPIA is a hypermedia authoring environment, we have to acknowledge that we still live in the context of traditional linear documents and printed paper output. Therefore, we have developed a linearizer which transforms a hyperdocument in the rhetorical space into a linear document (Knopik and Bapat, 1994, Lakoumentas, 1995). The overall strategy is composed of substrategies at four different levels (graph traversal, insertion into the linear list of nodes, handling substructures, creation of export format). In our implementation, we allow the user to select these substrategies. For example, we offer ASCII, Interleaf, and HTML as export formats. Conversely, an Interleaf document with appropriate markup can be read in and converted to a hyperdocument which is based on our notion of paths. We will also extend the transformation process to produce documents which conform to the SGML standard (ISO, 1986). Closely related to this are enhancements in the rhetorical space building on the idea of the construction kit (Thüring *et al.*, 1995). This includes to provide special predefined document types for later use. The definitions will be based on SGML or HyTime (Newcomb *et al.*, 1991; DeRose and Durand, 1994).

Other extensions we have developed are a graphical path editor and a reading environment. The path editor allows the definition and modification of path conditions bound to nodes and links in the rhetorical space. A path interpreter is used to evaluate such conditions (which are based on a history of visited nodes and links) at run time. The reading environment provides the author with previews of the final presentation (Hannemann *et al.*, 1992). Related work on the design of user-interfaces for hypermedia applications is described in Schuler *et al.* (1995).

As mentioned before, we are working on enhancements for the DBMS support. This is part of HyperStorM, a joint project of two research divisions within IPSI. It is concerned with the integration of the SEPIA system and the VODAK system which is a distributed object-oriented DBMS developed at GMD-IPSI (Klas *et al.*, 1990). HyperStorM develops an extendable object-oriented hypermedia engine which supports the specification of application semantics as object classes in the hypermedia engine (Wäsch and Aberer, 1995). There is also related work at IPSI on storing Hy Time documents in an object-oriented database (Böhm and Aberer, 1994).

Furthermore, we have been working on the integration of versioning support into SEPIA. This is based on the contextual version server CoVer (Haake, 1992, 1994). Here, we address not only the object management but with equal importance the user-interface aspects of how to present versions of hypermedia objects to the user. A first attempt is described in Haake and Haake (1993). Versioning is being used in several application situations. While it is useful in managing different stages and intermediary products of the authoring activity for a single author it becomes more relevant and even crucial in cooperative writing situations. For example, the history cards in NoteCards (Irish and Trigg, 1989) list log of updates. But beyond this one is also interested in the content of previous versions, their properties, and their relationships to the current version. We are also looking at other applications (DOLPHIN) with a need for versioning support, e.g. for tracking the development of ideas and discussions in group meetings including the audio and video coverage of the sequence of events and their correspondences in the hypermedia structures.

While the developments mentioned before are very relevant, the most important change took place with respect to CSCW support. Here, we have extended our view to a more global perspective (Streitz, 1994a; Streitz 1994b). A comprehensive view of the overall collaboration scenario of teams of authors creating large-size documents, or of cooperating work groups in general, reveals the central and important role of face-to-face meetings, e.g. for initial planning and brainstorming activities and, later on, for review processes and editorial decisions. Thus, we built an electronic meeting room, the OCEAN-Lab, where each participant can use a notepad computer mounted in the table. The computers are connected to each other by a local network and with a large public display which is also used as an interactive electronic whiteboard (Streitz *et al.*, 1994). It was clear that these activities require a different set of tools and especially different structures than those provided by SEPIA. Similar to the use of traditional blackboards/whiteboards in meeting rooms, people need possibilities for communicating their ideas via handdrawn sketches and scribbles, making annotations, etc. This requires a wide range of structures from more informal in early phases to more formal structures in later phases (Haake, Neuwirth and Streitz, 1994). This functionality is now provided by the DOLPHIN system (Streitz *et al.*, 1994) where one can write with a cordless pen, use gestures for frequently used operations. One can also transform/develop these informal structures into more formal hypermedia structures with nodes and links. All structures can exist in coexistence with each other on the same 'page', as part of different composites, and at different levels of these non-linear networks. In order to obtain feedback on our design decisions, we ran an evaluation experiment. Details can be found in Mark *et al.* (1995). DOLPHIN is based on an improved version of the cooperative systems architecture of SEPIA. It employs a very different interaction paradigm (including gesture recognition for frequently used operations) and accommodates different types of objects as, e.g. handwritten scribbles which can be turned into hypermedia nodes.

In the case of larger groups of authors cooperating over longer periods of time, coordination becomes crucial. In this context, we are developing a coordination functionality and we are addressing work flow management support. Due to the commonalities in the underlying system architecture, users can work with SEPIA and DOLPHIN in parallel and exchange objects and structures between them without any problem. This is needed and helpful in further extensions we are currently working on (Streitz, 1994b). This concerns the coupling of several meeting rooms in different locations and external partners in remote offices by using recent advances in network technology. This project is called 'Virtual Meetings based on ATM'. While these new developments yielded significant progress, there is still a need for the evaluation of user acceptance and of scaling-up in terms of the number of users and size of documents.

ACKNOWLEDGEMENTS

We like to thank B. Bokowski, L. Kirchner, J. Schümmer, and Ch. Schuckmann for helping us to implement SEPIA and DOLPHIN.

REFERENCES

Böhm, K. and Aberer, K. (1994) Storing HyTime documents in an object-oriented database. In Adam, N., Bhargava, B. and Yesha, Y. (eds), *Proceedings of the Third International Conference on Information and Knowledge Management*, ACM Press, pp. 26–33.

Conklin, J. (1987) Hypertext: An introduction and survey. *IEEE Computer*, **20**(9), 17–41.

Conklin, J. and Begeman, M. L. (1988) gIBIS: a hypertext tool for exploratory policy discussion. *Proceedings of the ACM Conference on Computer-Supported Cooperative Work (CSCW'88)*, pp. 140–152.

DeRose, S. J. and Durand, D. G. (1994) *Making Hypermedia Work. A User's Guide to HyTime*. Kluwer, Amsterdam.

Dewan, P. and Choudhary, R. (1991) Flexible user interface coupling in a collaborative. system. *Proceedings of the CHI'91*, pp. 41–48.

Ellis, C. A. and Gibbs, S. J. (1989) Concurrency control in groupware systems. *Proceedings of the ACM SIGMOD'89 Conference on the Management of Data*, ACM Press, pp. 399–407.

Ellis, C. A., Gibbs, S. J. and Rein, G. L. (1991) Groupware – some issues and experiences. *Communications of the ACM*, **34** (1), 38–58.

Fischer, D. H. and Rostek, L. (1995) *SFK: A Smalltalk Frame Kit – Concepts and Use*. Technical Report GMD-IPSI, Darmstadt, March 1995.

Garzotto, F., Paolini, P. and Schwabe, D. (1991) HDM – a model for the design of hypertext applications. *Proceedings of the 3rd ACM Conference on Hypertext (Hypertext '91)*, pp. 313–328.

Garzotto, F., Paolini, P. and Schwabe, D. (1993) HDM – a model based approach to hypermedia application design. *ACM Transactions on Information Systems, 11* (1), 1–26.

Haake, A. (1992) CoVer: A Contextual Version Server for Hypertext Applications. *Proceedings of the European Conference on Hypertext (ECHT'92)*, ACM Press, pp. 43–52.

Haake, A. (1994) Under CoVer: the implementation of a contextual version server for hypertext applications. *Proceedings of the European Conference on Hypermedia Technology (ECHT'94)*, ACM Press, pp. 81–93.

Haake, A. and Haake, J. (1993) Take CoVer: exploiting version support in cooperative systems. *Proceedings of ACM*/IFIP Conference InterCHI'93, ACM Press, pp. 406–413.

Haake, J., Bapat, A. and Knopik, T. (1994) Using a hypermedia system for systems engineering. *Proceedings of the East-West International Conference on Multimedia, Hypertext, and Virtual Reality (MHVR'94)*, pp. 63–68.

Haake, J., Neuwirth, C. and Streitz, N. (1994) Coexistence and transformation of informal and formal structures: Requirements for more flexible hypermedia systems. *Proceedings of ACM European Conference on Hypermedia Technology (ECHT'94)*, ACM Press, pp. 1–12.

Haake, J. and Wilson, B. (1992) Supporting collaborative writing of hyperdocuments in SEPIA. *Proceedings of the ACM Conference on Computer Supported Cooperative Work (CSCW'92)*, ACM Press, pp. 138–146.

Halasz, F. G. (1988) Reflections on NoteCards: seven issues for the next generation of hypermedia systems. *Communications of the ACM*, **31** (7), 836–852.

Halasz, F. G. (1991) *'Seven issues': Revisited* Final Keynote Talk at the 3rd ACM Conference on Hypertext, San Antonio, TX, December 15–18, 1991.

Hannemann, J., Thüring, M. and Streitz, N. A. (1990) Schreiben als Designproblem: Ein integrativer Ansatz. In D. Frey (Hrsg.), *Bericht über den 37.Kongreß der Deutschen Gesellschaft für Psychologie*. Hogrefe, Göttingen.

Hannemann, J., Thüring, M. and Friedrich, N. (1992) Hyperdocuments as user interfaces: Exploring a browsing semantic for coherent hyperdocuments. In R. Cordes and N. Streitz (eds), *Hypertext und Hypermedia 1992* (S. 87–102). Springer, Heidelberg.

Hoschka, P., Butscher, B. and Streitz, N. (1992) Telecooperation and telepresence: Technical challenges of a government distributed between Bonn and Berlin. *Informatization and the Public Sector*, **2** (4), 269–299.

Irish, P. M. and Trigg, R. H. (1989) Supporting collaboration in hypermedia: Issues and experiences. *Journal of the American Society for Information Science*, **40** (3), 192–199.

ISO (1986) *ISO/IEC International Standard 8879–1986: Information Processing – Text and Office Systems – Standard Generalized Markup Language (SGML)*, International Standards Organisation.

Joyce, M. (1991) StorySpace as a hypertext system for writers and readers of varying ability. *Proceedings of the 3rd ACM Conference on Hypertext (Hypertext '91)*, ACM Press, pp. 381–387.

Klas, W., Neuhold, E. J. and Shrefl, M. (1990) Using an object-oriented approach to model multimedia data. *Computer Communications*, **13** (4), 204–216.

Knopik, T. and Bapat, A. (1994) The role of node and link types in open hypermedia systems. *Proceedings of the ECHT'94 Workshop on Open Hypermedia Systems*. Report R-94-2038, Aalborg University, Denmark, October, pp. 33–36.

Kunz, W. and Rittel, H. (1970) *Issues as elements of information systems* (Working paper 131). University of California, Berkeley, CA.

Lakoumentas, N. (1995) *Linearisierung von Hyperdokumenten im Hypermediasystem SEPIA*. Diplomarbeit (Master Thesis). GMD-IPSI and Technical University Darmstadt, March.

Lemke, A., Streitz, N. A. and Wilson, B. (1992) *WSCRAWL: The Use of a Shared Workspace in a Desktop Conferencing System*. GMD-IPSI, Technical Report. Arbeitspapiere der GMD Nr. 672.

Mark, G., Haake, J. and Streitz, N. (1995). The use of hypermedia in group problem solving: An evaluation of the DOLPHIN electronic meeting room environment. *Proceedings of European Conference on Computer-Supported Cooperative Work (E-CSCW'95)* (in press).

Marshall C. (1989) Representing the structure of a legal argument. *Proceedings of 2nd International Conference on AI and Law*, Vancouver, pp. 121–127.

Marshall C., Halasz, F., Rogers, R. and Jansen, W. Jr. (1991) Aquanet: a hypertext tool to hold your knowledge in place. *Proceedings of the 3rd ACM Conference on Hypertext (Hypertext '91)*, ACM Press, pp. 261–275.

McCall, R., Bennet, P., D'Ornozio, P., Ostwald, J., Shipman, F. and Wallace, N. (1990) PHIDIAS: integrating CAD graphics into dynamic hypertext. In A. Rizk, N. Streitz, and J. André (eds), *Hypertext: Concepts, Systems, and Applications (ECHT'90)*. Cambridge University Press, pp. 152–1654.

Nanard, J. and Nanard, M. (1991). Using structured types to incorporate knowledge in hypertext. *Proceedings of the 3rd ACM Conference on Hypertext (Hypertext '91)*, ACM Press, pp. 329–343.

Neuwirth, C. M., Kaufer, D. S., Chandhok, R. and Morris, J. H. (1990) Issues in the design of computer support for co-authoring and commenting. *Proceedings of the Conference on Computer-Supported Cooperative Work (CSCW '90)*, ACM Press, pp. 183–195.

Neuwirth, C. M., Chandhok, R., Kaufer, D., Erion, P., Morris, J. and Miller, D. (1992) Flexible diff-ing in a collaborative writing system. In *Proceedings of the Conference on Computer-Supported Cooperative Work (CSCW'92)*, ACM Press, pp. 147–162.

Newell, A. (1980) Reasoning, problem solving, and decision processes: The problem space as a fundamental category. In Nickerson, R. S. (ed.), *Attention and performance*, Vol. 8, pp. 693–718, Lawrence Erlbaum, Hillsdale, NJ.

Newcomb, S. R., Kipp, M. and Newcomb, V. (1991) The 'HyTime' hypermedia/time-based document structuring language. *Communications of the ACM*, **34** (11).

Rada, R., Wang, W. and Birchall, A. (1992) An expertext system for collaborative authoring. *Expert Systems with Applications*, **5** (3/4), 275–288.

Rada, R., Wang, W. and Birchall, A. (1993) Retrieval Hierarchies in Hypertext. *Journal of Information Processing and Management*, **29** (2), 359–371.

Rein, G. L. and Ellis, C. A. (1991) rIBIS: a real-time group hypertext system. *International Journal of Man-Machine Studies*, **34**, 339–367.

Schutt, H. and Haake, J. M. (1993) Server support for cooperative hypermedia environments. In Frei, H. P. and Schäuble, P. (eds), *Proceedings of Hypermedia '93*, Springer, Heidelberg, pp. 45–56.

Schütt, H. and Streitz, N. A. (1990) HyperBase: a hypermedia engine based on a relational database management system. In Rizk, A., Streitz, N. and André, J. (eds), *Hypertext: Concepts, Systems, and Applications (ECHT'90)*, Cambridge University Press, Cambridge, pp. 95–108.

Schuler, W., Hannemann, J. and Streitz, N. (eds) (1995) *Designing User Interfaces for Hypermedia*. Springer, Heidelberg.

Schuler, W. and Smith, J. B. (1990) Author's Argumentation assistant (AAA): A hypertext-based authoring tool for argumentative texts. In Rizk, A., Streitz, N. and André, J. (eds), *Hypertext: Concepts, Systems, and Applications (ECHT'90)*, Cambridge University Press, Cambridge, pp. 95–108.

Smith, J. B., Weiss, S. F. and Ferguson, G. J. (1987) A hypertext writing environment and its cognitive basis. *Proceedings of the First ACM Workshop on Hypertext (Hypertext '87)*, ACM, pp. 195–214.

Smith, J. B. and Smith, F. D. (1991) ABC: A hypermedia system for artifact-based collaboration. *Proceedings of the 3rd ACM Conference on Hypertext (Hypertext '91)*, ACM Press, pp. 179–192.

Smith Catlin, K., Garrett, L. N. and Launhardt, J. A. (1991) Hypermedia templates: an author's tool. *Proceedings of the 3rd ACM Conference on Hypertext (Hypertext '91)*, ACM Press, pp. 147–160.

Smolensky, P., Bell, B., Fox, B., King, R. and Lewis, C. (1987) Constraint-based hypertext for argumentation. *Proceedings of the First ACM Workshop on Hypertext (Hypertext'87)*, pp. 215–245.

Streitz, N. (1987) Cognitive compatibility as a central issue in human-computer interaction: Theoretical framework and empirical findings. In G. Salvendy (ed.), *Cognitive Engineering in the Design of Human–Computer Interaction and Expert Systems*, Elsevier, Amsterdam, pp. 75–82.

Streitz, N. (1994a) Putting objects to work: Hypermedia as the subject matter and the medium for computer-supported cooperative work. In Tokoro, M. and Pareschi, R. (eds), *Object-Oriented Programming Proceedings of ECOOP'94*. LNCS 821, Springer, Heidelberg, pp. 183–193.

Streitz, N. (1994b) From individual work and desktop-based collaboration to virtual meeting room environments. Keynote talk at the *East-West International Conference on Multimedia, Hypertext, and Virtual Reality (MHVR'94)* Moscow, September 14–16.

Streitz, N. (1995) Designing hypermedia: A collaborative activity. *Communications of the ACM*, **38** (8), 70–71.

Streitz, N., Geissler, J. Haake, J. and Hol, J. (1994) DOLPHIN: Integrated meeting support across LiveBoards, local and remote desktop environments. *Proceedings of the ACM Conference on Computer-Supported Cooperative Work (CSCW'94)*, ACM Press, pp. 345–358.

Streitz, N. A., Hannemann, J. and Thüring, M. (1989) From ideas and arguments to hyperdocuments: travelling through activity spaces. *Proceedings of the 2nd ACM Conference on Hypertext (Hypertext'89)*, ACM Press, pp. 343–364.

Tatar, D. G., Foster, G. and Bobrow, D. (1991) Design for conversation: lessons from Cognoter. *International Journal of Man-Machine Studies*, **34**, 185–209.

Thüring, M., Haake, J. and Hannemann, J. (1991) What's Eliza doing in A Chinese Room? – Incoherent hyperdocuments – and how to avoid them. *Proceedings of the 3rd ACM Conference on Hypertext (Hypertext '91)*, ACM Press, pp. 161–177.

Thüring, M., Hannemann, J. and Haake, J. (1995) Hypermedia and cognition: designing for comprehension. *Communications of the ACM*, **38** (8), 57–66.

Toulmin, S. (1959) *The Uses of Argument*, Cambridge University Press, Cambridge.

Wäsch, J. and Aberer, K. (1995) Flexible design and efficient implementation of a hypermedia document database system by tailoring semantic relationships. In *Proceedings of the Sixth IFIP Conference on Data Semantics (DS-6)*.

Walker, J. (1991) Netfone Release 1. Posted in newsgroup *comp.sources.sun*. September 12, 1991.

Wang, W. and Rada, R. (1995) Experiences with semantic net-based hypermedia. *International Journal of Human–Computer Studies* (in press).

Wilson, B. (1992) WScrawl 2.0. Available at http://www-cs-students.stanford.edu/~brianw/bw.html

You, G.-N. and Rada, R. (1994) A systematic approach to outline manipulation. *International Journal of Human–Computer Studies* **41**, 283–308.

13 Structured and Distributed Cooperative Editing in a Large Scale Network

DOMINIQUE DECOUCHANT, VINCENT QUINT
and MANUEL ROMERO SALCEDO

INTRODUCTION

Cooperative editing is an important field in CSCW. Many editors have been developed or extended to allow several users to work simultaneously on shared documents. Some of these systems are dedicated to traditional documents, other ones manipulate drawings only (Peng, 1993). Some cooperative editors have been especially designed for conferencing systems, some others are oriented towards document production. Cooperative editing constitutes a very active research domain.

At the same time, an important research activity is carried out in the field of structured documents. Researchers are interested in structured documents (Furuta *et al.*, 1988) and standards such as SGML (Goldfarb, 1990) or ODA (ISO, 1989) have inspired other research activities. Cooperative editing and structured documents share many common issues and it seems natural to take advantage of the advances in these two fields to define new tools that allow users to cooperate in producing complex structured documents.

This chapter addresses the problems posed by the combination of cooperative editing and structured editing. It shows that the structured approach to document representation may be very fruitful in the context of cooperative applications. The results presented here are based on the experience gained in developing and using Alliance, a structured cooperative editor, which has been built on top of the Grif editor (Quint and Vatton, 1986).

Alliance has been designed as a cooperative application that allows several users, distributed on a network, to work on shared structured documents. The current version of Alliance can run both in a local area and in a wide area network. This is a result of the two phases in the development of the application. In the first phase, we only focused on the main features of cooperative structured editing (document fragmentation, sharing entity, editing roles and group awareness), and intentionally we did not pay attention to problems regarding document access and storage management. So, the

GROUPWARE AND AUTHORING
ISBN 0-12-575005-6

document management layer for this first approach (Decouchant *et al.*, 1993) was only based on the Network File System (NFS). This choice is well suited to cooperative editing in the field of office work, where users are linked by a local area network.

In the second phase, we have studied the adaptation of cooperative functions to the World Wide Web (Berners-Lee *et al.*, 1994). The aim of developing and extending Alliance on the Web was to make this application more widely available, by using long-haul networks and allowing loosely coupled interconnections. For reaching this goal, evolutions of the Alliance cooperation services were needed to take into account most of the problems posed by the Internet and to obtain acceptable performances. From the implementation point of view, the document management layer, initially based on NFS, has been extended to the services provided by HTTP (Berners-Lee, 1993) on the Web.

The chapter is organized as follows. The next section presents the structured document model and the principles of structured editing. These two topics are important as they provide some features that have not been widely used in cooperative applications until now. Next are presented the main concepts on which a cooperative editor is based, taking into account and exploiting the structure of documents and the structure of the environment: basically, a document is considered as an organized set of fragments on which users can act according to the role that has been assigned to them. Then, the advantages of a structured document model for cooperative editing are discussed. Structure helps to share documents among several users, to develop efficient mechanisms for cooperation, to maintain document consistency, and to keep each user aware of the work performed by the group. The specific problems posed by the extension of Alliance to a wide area network are then presented. Typical problems of distributed applications but more specifically of distributed groupware applications are presented. Among these problems, we focus on document distribution and replication, document transfer, the issue of mobile work. Finally, we conclude and suggest future work in the domain of cooperative authoring on the Web.

STRUCTURED DOCUMENTS

The structured model of documents

With the structured approach (Furuta *et al.*, 1988), a document is considered as an organized set of typed elements which are logically related to each other. In a document such as an article, typical elements are: the title, author names, paragraphs, sections, section headings, figures, captions, bibliography, bibliographic item, etc. All these elements have various relations: a section contains a heading, some paragraphs and optionally some subsections; a paragraph follows another paragraph; a paragraph may refer to a bibliographic item, etc.

These elements with their relationships constitute the logical structure of a document. This structure is constrained by a generic structure which defines all element types that can be used in an article and their possible relationships. Then, the generic structure defines the structure of documents of type article, and all documents of that type must conform to the model of their generic structure. By defining other generic structures, it is possible to define other document types, which involve different types of elements with different relationships. This document model is the basis of standards such as ODA (ISO, 1989) and SGML (Goldfarb, 1990) (in SGML, a generic logical structure is called a Document Type Definition: DTD).

The logical structure of a document not only contains elements, but also attributes. An attribute is information associated with a logical element of a document that adds semantics to that element. Like element types, attributes are defined in the generic structure, which specifies their type (number, name, character string, list of values, reference, etc.) and the type(s) of element with which they can be associated.

As the logical structure of a document is always consistent with the model of a generic structure, it is possible to generically define the graphical aspect of documents: presentation rules are associated with element types and attributes. They specify parameters such as font, color, spacing, line length, indentation, justification, etc. Presentation rules are gathered in presentation models: a presentation model contains all rules necessary to specify the graphical aspect of all types of elements and attributes defined in a generic logical structure.

Structured editing

A structured editor uses the document type (the generic structure) for helping (or obliging, when it is needed) the user to produce a document that is an instance of that type, i.e. with a logical structure consistent with the generic structure. With that approach, a document is represented in the system by its logical structure, also called abstract tree. This structure is mainly hierarchical, with additional relationships which represent non-hierarchical links between elements, such as cross-references. With these links, a structured document may also be considered as a hypertext (Quint and Vatton, 1992).

A structured editor applies the presentation rules to the elements constituting the logical structure of a document, thus producing the graphical aspect of that document. As several presentation models may be associated with a generic logical structure, the graphical aspect of a document can be modified globally, just by changing the presentation model in use.

The Grif editor is based on the document model presented above and it follows the principles of structured editing. It also specifies different views, which present in different windows the same logical structure with different graphical aspects. For instance, the table of contents of a report is a view that shows only the elements of type SectionHeading and uses font and layout parameters different from the main view. These views show a graphical representation of documents that is very similar to a printed document: the logical structure is not directly seen by the user who interacts with the editor through the views displayed on the screen (see Figure 13.2).

With these basic functions, the services offered by Grif do not seem fundamentally different from those offered by an editor-formatter based on a simpler document model. Thus, new users get acquainted with it very shortly. But its high-level document model allows it to offer powerful editing functions and to produce a more abstract representation of documents, which makes it possible to process these documents with a number of different tools.

Another important feature of the Grif editor is that it is flexible enough to be integrated in a variety of environments. It can be driven by a program, as all functions offered to the end user (plus some additional functions) are also accessible through an Application Programming Interface (API). In addition, a mechanism called External Call Facility (ECF) allows an application to attach its own procedures to the standard editing functions, thus replacing or modifying the behaviour of these functions. The API and the ECF are described in more detail in Quint and Vatton (1994).

Cooperative structured editing

Many cooperative editors have been described, but few of them use a structured document model. Milo (Jones, 1993) is one of these editors that organize the cooperation on a structured representation of documents: users can create notes that are then combined to compose documents. The document is represented as a hierarchy that is dynamically built by users, but this structure is completely free; there is no generic structure. With that approach, Milo can be considered as a tool for idea generation; from the document structure point of view, it is very close to groupware applications based on a hypertext approach.

The hypertext approach considers that 'hypermedia is a neutral medium for supporting collaborative work' (Halasz, 1988). Such systems as Sepia (Streitz *et al.*, 1992), Quilt (Fish *et al.*, 1988), Prep (Neuwirth *et al.*, 1990), and rIBIS (Rein and Ellis, 1991) are based on that principle.

The MUCH (Wang and Rada, 1995; Zheng Min and Rada, 1994) system is also based on the hypertext approach which is enforced by the use of typed links between document nodes: the organization of the documents follows the well-known 'semantic net' principle (Conklin, 1987; Rada, 1990), and constitutes a sensible progress towards information structuring.

One of the most important aspects in a cooperative application is the structure of the shared environment and hypertext links are indeed one way of structuring documents. We propose to go further, by considering the full structure of documents built in accordance with a generic structure.

SHARED DOCUMENTS

The structured approach to document processing proves particularly advantageous for large documents involved in complex applications. That approach is for instance widely used in the domain of technical documentation. In that domain, documents are very large, they must follow some standards (hence the advantage of a generic structure), various versions must be maintained and different configurations are often generated. Technical documents are typically produced by several writers working simultaneously. The work that each person is supposed to perform is well defined; different writers play different roles, according to their skill and the current state of documents. Access to the shared documents must be controlled, to avoid conflicts and inconsistencies.

The Alliance application

Alliance has been designed as an environment for cooperative editing. Such an editing environment may be compared with a programming environment, the main difference being that it is dedicated to the production of documents, whereas a programming environment is designed for producing programs. As a first approximation, when considering only the main objective, the two environments may appear similar. However they present a number of differences, which prevent applying to document environments techniques and results brought by years of experience in developing and using programming environments (Quint *et al.*, 1990). When developing Alliance, the goals were to study and better understand the specific document requirements and to develop techniques that would allow complex structured documents to be handled more efficiently in a collaborative distributed environment.

The application has been developed for Unix workstations connected by a network. It controls several local instances of the Grif editor, running on different workstations, and allows their users to cooperate. In addition to the local editing functions inherited from Grif, it handles document storage and access to distributed documents; it offers high-level services for managing user interaction and cooperation, for defining shared document fragments, for distributing roles to users, for supporting group awareness, for updating copies of shared documents, and for controlling consistency of modifications.

The main aspects of Alliance are presented here according to its notion of users, to the roles played by users, to the structure of the shared environment and to the views presented to each participant.

User management

A groupware application can be defined as 'A computer based system that supports groups of people engaged in a common task (or goal) and that provides an interface to the shared environment' (Ellis *et al.*, 1991). In Alliance, the final version of a document can be considered as the common goal to be reached, and the Grif editor provides the view by which each user may perceive the shared document.

Obviously the notion of a user is fundamental in a groupware application. Many applications rely on the notion defined by the host operating system. The problem is then to manage a global database containing all users of a distributed application. These users are considered as physical or logical persons who can login to make actions with well specified privileges on computer resources (disks, CPU, files, display, applications, drivers, etc.). Such a user definition is fully disconnected and often not adapted to the shared environment of distributed groupware applications.

In Alliance, a user is simply a name that identifies a person. A list of users (names) is associated with each document. This list is built by the document owner and is independent of the lists associated with other documents. It indicates the users who are authorized to act on the document. The document owner can update this list at any time.

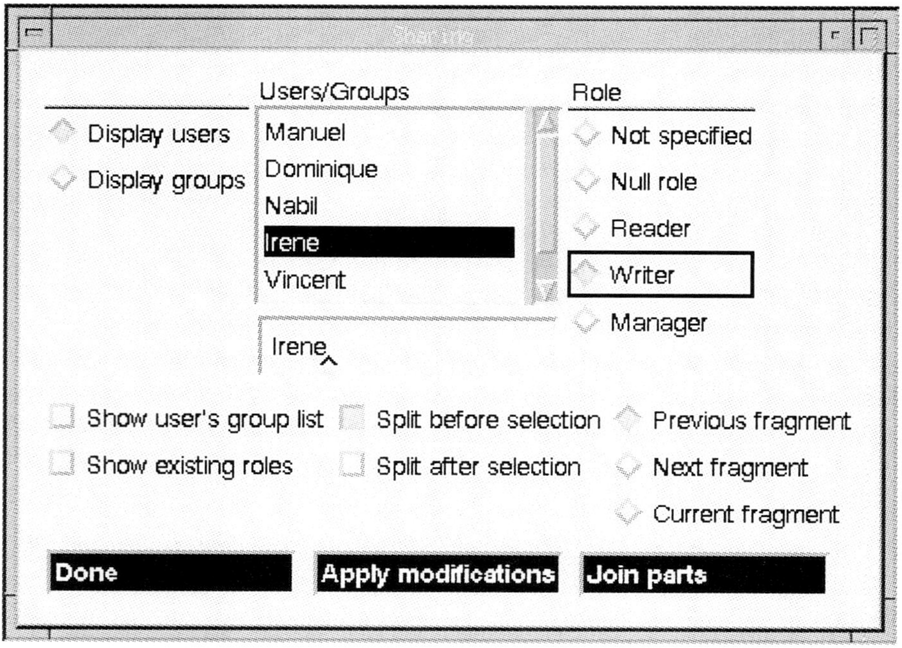

Figure 13.1 The Alliance tool to express document sharing.

The document owner is the user who creates the document or makes it available in the Alliance environment. Initially, the owner plays the role of a manager (see next section) for the whole document. He is free to assign various roles to other users.

A notion of group is also used in Alliance. A group is a name that represents several users playing the same role on documents. A user may be a member of several groups. A group can appear in the list associated with a document. It indicates that all users belonging to that group are allowed to act on the document.

All users of the list associated with a document can be involved in the commands for sharing documents. They will also be involved in future tools which are in development for negotiation, messaging or annotation. For instance, the document sharing tool (see Figure 13.1) allocates roles to the users and groups according to the list associated with the document.

An Alliance user must be registered in the host system of one site involved in the application. This site contains the information needed for managing all documents belonging to that user. As the scope of a user is restricted to the host system where it is registered, users have an external name and an internal name that contains both the identification of their site and their login name on that site. The user list associated with each document contains both the external name and the internal name for each user.

When the document owner creates or updates the list of users, he provides the following data for each entry:

- the URL (Berners-Lee, 1994) (Universal Resource Locator, in the Internet) or the machine name (in a local area network) that identifies the site of that user.
- the login name of the user on that site.

Once the list has been initialized, the owner sends a message to all users concerned by the document and gives them his URL, his login name and the local document name. Each remote user can then get a full copy of this document, and he knows the associated users and groups. Thus, all users are able to contact each other, even if they meet for the first time.

Roles of users and groups

In the development of a large document, the way people interact with each other is well defined: the work is organized and planned, and each member of the team has a different role to play in the project. Therefore a notion of role has been introduced in Alliance. For each part of a document, a user may have one of the four available roles.

- As the purpose of the application is to edit documents, the first role that appears to be necessary is the writer role. A writer is a user who can modify (i.e. change the structure or the content) of (a part of) a document.

- The second role is the one of a reader. A reader is a user who can see and read a part of a document, but who cannot modify it. The writer role includes the reader role.
- A third role, called null role, has been introduced for preventing some users from even seeing some parts of a document that is confidential for them. Obviously, a user with that role cannot modify the document either.
- The last role, called manager, is provided for people who give to other people the possibility of playing roles on documents. This manager role allows users having it not only to assign roles to new users, but also to change the role of existing users. The operations allowed by this role include that allowed to a writer.

The same user may have different roles on different parts of a document. He can then be authorized to modify some parts of the document, to only read some other parts and not even to see the rest.

Roles attached by a manager to a specified part of document are named potential roles, as opposed to current roles that users really play at a given moment. Each user can play one of the four roles on a given (part of) document at a given time. This current role of a user is assigned by the application, according to the potential role of that user and to the current activity of other users. Potential roles are stable attributes of users; they are changed only when another user, playing the manager role, decides to do so. On the contrary, the current role of a user may change dynamically, depending on the status of the application and on the will of the user himself. Of course these changes must respect the potential role of the user.

For the same document (or the same part) several users may own the same potential roles, including the writer or manager roles. This is necessary for the kind of application considered, even if it may cause conflicts. These conflicts are solved by a reader/writer policy: for each piece of document, only one user can actually play the writer or manager role at a time; the current roles of other potential managers and writers are then temporarily reduced to a reader role. In addition, the writer and manager roles are mutually exclusive at the same time.

This policy may be considered as a strong constraint imposed to users, but it is necessary for preserving the document consistency and it is made acceptable by two mechanisms: dynamic fragmentation and dynamic changes of current roles, which are presented below.

Dynamic document fragmentation

The way users want to share the documents on which they work together must be explicitly expressed. This is accomplished by a user owning the manager role which assigns potential roles to users and groups. When a user creates a new document he receives the manager role for the whole document. He is then free to complete the document and to give roles to other users.

According to the roles given by a manager, documents are automatically divided into variable-sized fragments, which are the sharing units. A fragment is a continuous part of a document on which the roles of each user or group are the same; different users or groups may have different roles, but the role of a given user or group does not change in the whole fragment. The process of fragmentation is based on that definition. This implies that whenever roles change, fragmentation may change.

As a consequence of the fragment definition, the roles may be checked, while editing, on the basis of fragments, and the consistency of user contributions can thereby be guaranteed.

Choosing the right sharing granularity

Choosing sharing granularity constitutes a major issue when designing an asynchronous groupware application. In a synchronous application the problem is very different, because concurrent modifications of the shared environment are not handled in the same way.

Synchronous applications such as Grove (Ellis *et al.*, 1991) are based on the WYSIWIS (What You See Is What I See) paradigm (Stefik, Foster *et al.*, 1987; Stefik, Bobrow *et al.*, 1987): at any moment all users see the same state of the shared environment. In these applications, concurrency is controlled by executing all editing commands in mutual exclusion and by sending each document modification to all sites. The whole document is locked for a short period of time, each time a user issues a command.

This way of controlling concurrent access to the shared document is not applicable in an asynchronous application which allows authors to work simultaneously and to modify independently from each other some parts of the shared document. For that kind of application, the document must be divided into smaller entities which are locked for a longer time by a single user. The problem is then to choose the right size of these entities.

Some projects such as Quilt (Fish *et al.*, 1988; Leland *et al.*, 1988) and CES (Greif *et al.*, 1992) propose a very restrictive and static notion of a shared entity. In an article, only sections can constitute sharing entities. The drawbacks of that notion have been considered by Mace (Newman-Wolfe and Pelimuhandiram, 1991), which allows users to dynamically split the document without any constraint: a document is simply a sequence of characters and any substring can constitute an entity. CES and Mjølner (Minor and Magnusson, 1993) consider a simple structure that divides a document into sections and sections into textual units, which can be used as sharing entities.

All these attempts have shown that structure is useful for sharing documents (sections are often involved in the systems mentioned above), but freedom is also necessary (some systems allow any part of a document to be a shared entity). An asynchronous application should work on entities of any size and type, not only sections, lines or character strings. This is the approach chosen for Alliance which provides dynamic document sharing and variable-sized fragments. A fragment can be as small as a single character string or as large as a sequence of sections or chapters if needed.

The structured approach appears as an efficient way to build asynchronous document editing applications.

Fragmenting documents

In Alliance, fragmentation is carried out by the application, so that a document manager has only to worry about the roles he wants to assign to users, not about document fragmentation. To assign new roles or to change existing roles, a manager selects any part of a document in any view of that document, and specifies the new roles that users or groups can play on that part of the document. The selected part can be chosen independently of existing fragments.

Role assignment is not strongly constrained by the hierarchical organization of the document. For example, it is possible to give a user (say, an artist) the writer role on a drawing, but not on the section that contains it. However, the hierarchical organization of documents puts some constraints on the roles assigned to a user or to a group: if a user has a writer role on a drawing, he must have at least a reader role on the section that contains that drawing, but there is no constraint on the roles of the paragraphs that precede or follow the drawing in that section.

Figure 13.2 shows how a manager can assign roles to users. He selects the second paragraph of the abstract and uses a dialog box (see Figure 13.1) for choosing a user or a group and the role to be given to that user or group. This example also shows that the logical structure may help a manager to assign roles, as a large part of a complex document may be selected very quickly: this paragraph is selected by clicking the border of its enclosing box, a whole section is selected by clicking on the section number, etc. In addition, all views displayed by the editor can be used for all editing operations, including selection: assigning different roles for all sections of an article can be done on the table of contents, without scrolling the document.

Views

Although documents are divided into fragments, this division does not affect the image presented to users. The border between two fragments does not appear on the screen and, wherever it is located, it does not alter the layout of the displayed document. Thus, users can read documents in a continuous way,

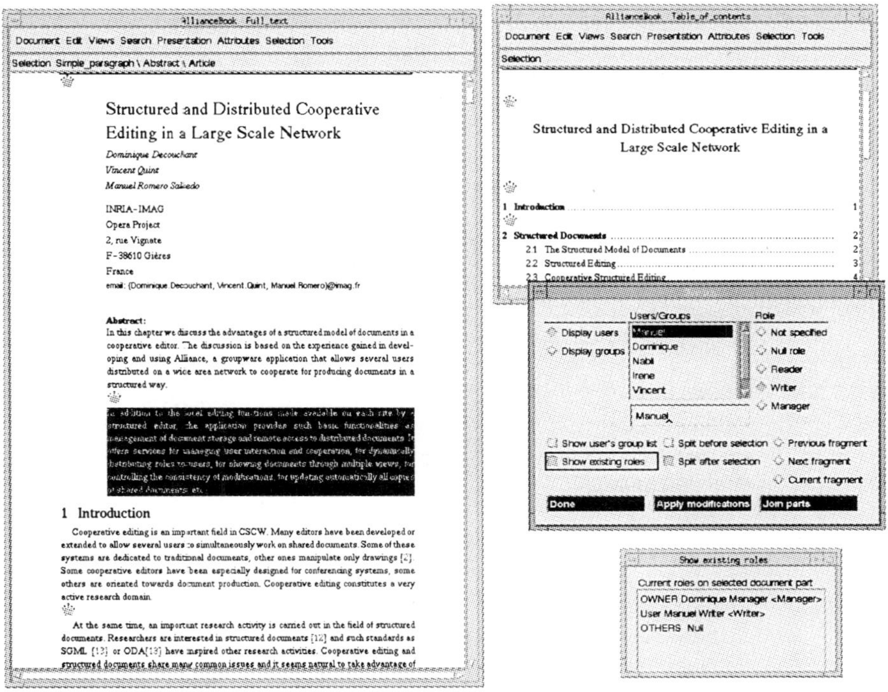

Figure 13.2 Role assignment.

independently of their fragmentation, in the same way as with a stand-alone document editor. However, if they are needed, fragment limits may be shown by specific symbols (see Figure 13.2).

Figure 13.3 shows the displays seen by two users (A and B) editing a shared document. This document is composed of three fragments. The first fragment contains the title, the author names, the affiliations and the first paragraph of the abstract. The second fragment includes the second paragraph of the abstract, the header and the first paragraph of the Introduction. The third and last fragment contains all remaining parts. For showing fragments, limits are represented in both views by various symbols, which also indicate the current role played by the user on each fragment.

The content of the second fragment only appears in the view presented to user B who plays a manager role for that fragment. This fragment is accessed with the null role by user A (information is invisible). Conversely, the first fragment can only be seen by user A. The third fragment can be written by user A, but only read by user B.

As a user may have different current roles for different parts of a document, he needs to be notified of the role he can really play on each part. This is performed by the use of colors and by the insertion of special active symbols

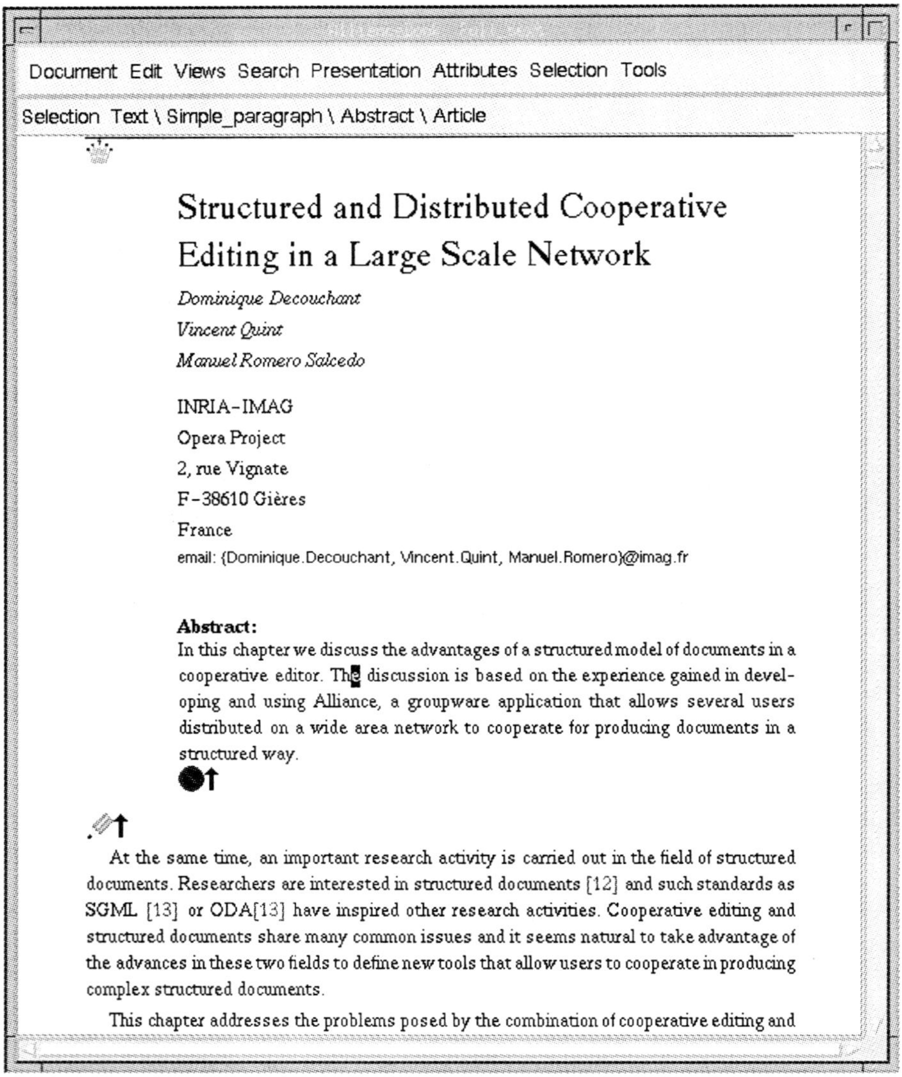
Document Edit Views Search Presentation Attributes Selection Tools

Selection Text \ Simple_paragraph \ Abstract \ Article

Structured and Distributed Cooperative Editing in a Large Scale Network

Dominique Decouchant
Vincent Quint
Manuel Romero Salcedo

INRIA-IMAG
Opera Project
2, rue Vignate
F-38610 Gières
France
email: {Dominique.Decouchant, Vincent.Quint, Manuel.Romero}@imag.fr

Abstract:
In this chapter we discuss the advantages of a structured model of documents in a cooperative editor. The discussion is based on the experience gained in developing and using Alliance, a groupware application that allows several users distributed on a wide area network to cooperate for producing documents in a structured way.

At the same time, an important research activity is carried out in the field of structured documents. Researchers are interested in structured documents [12] and such standards as SGML [13] or ODA[13] have inspired other research activities. Cooperative editing and structured documents share many common issues and it seems natural to take advantage of the advances in these two fields to define new tools that allow users to cooperate in producing complex structured documents.

This chapter addresses the problems posed by the combination of cooperative editing and

Figure 13.3 Two views of the same document: view of user A.

at each fragment limit (see section entitled 'Group awareness through document structure', below). When the user has a null role, the corresponding parts are not displayed, but the user may notice that they exist, as numbers (section number, figure number, etc.) take hidden parts into account. Parts where the user has the reader role are displayed with a specific color that each user can choose. Parts where the user has a writer or manager role are displayed with their normal color.

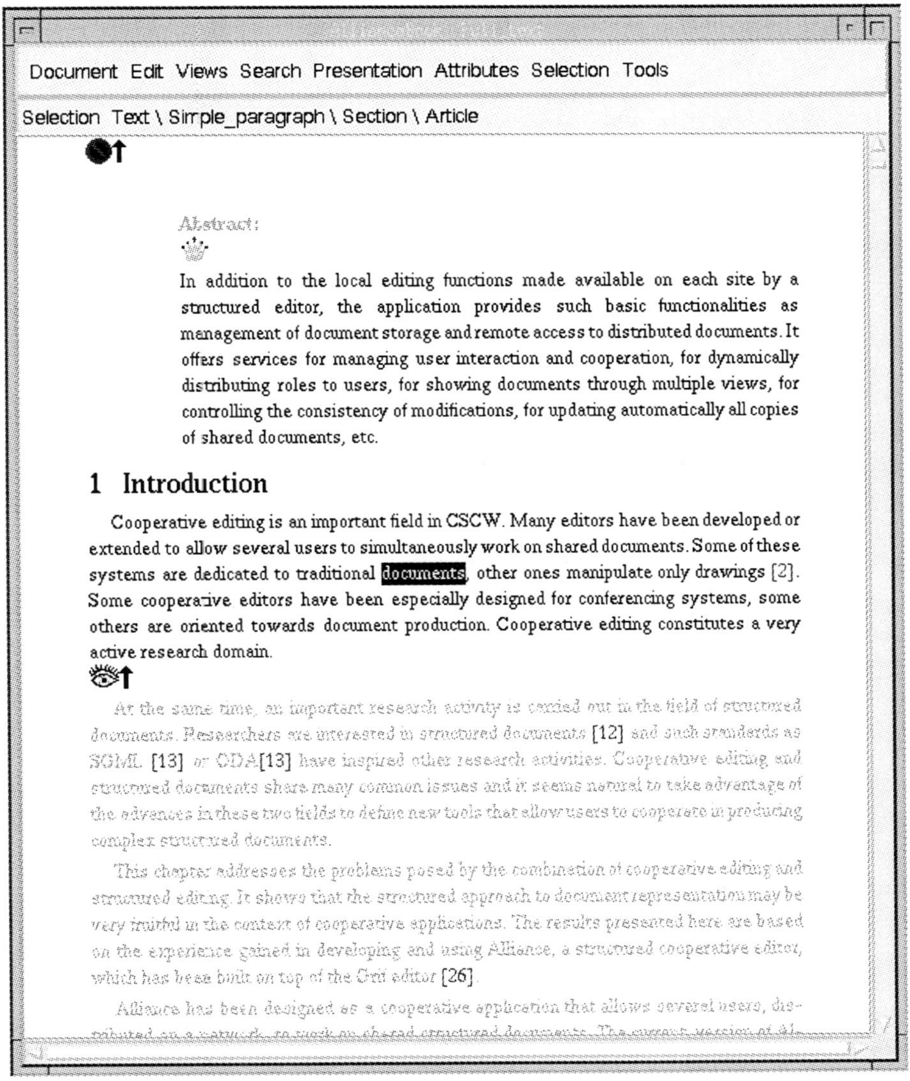

Figure 13.3 (*continued*): view of user B.

DOCUMENT STRUCTURE AND COOPERATION

This section discusses the advantages of an abstract document structure for managing cooperative editing. In particular, the principles involved in sharing a document are presented relative to the document structure (typed elements, hierarchical structure and generic structure).

One of the major issues in cooperative applications is to maintain the consistency of the data that are concurrently accessed by several users. This issue is discussed first. Then the problem of dynamic changes of roles is addressed. Some means are proposed to allow users to change their current roles at any time, independently of the fragmentation. Obviously these changes must respect the potential roles allocated by the manager. Finally, the important problem of group awareness is addressed and a solution is proposed. This solution takes advantage of document structure for notifying all users of each individual contribution.

Document consistency

Alliance allows cooperative editing on both local area networks (LAN) and wide area networks (WAN). From the user point of view, there is no difference between these two environments. The solution chosen to solve the problem of document consistency has been designed for both types of networks, taking into account their specific features (cost, delay and reliability of communications).

For maintaining document consistency in the LAN version, only one copy of each document is stored on disk, whatever the number of users working on it and the sites from which the users work; but several files are used for storing a single document, one file for each fragment. These files reside on a volume that is accessible from all workstations involved in the application. This is achieved by using NFS which presents all remote files as if they were local.

The solution developed in the LAN context is based on the uniqueness of the files storing a document. It is not applicable to a wide area network for several reasons which are discussed later in this chapter. But, despite this difference some common principles apply to both types of networks.

With both types of networks, each fragment is constituted by a set of sub-trees of the document abstract tree. These sub-trees are ordered in the order defined by the document tree. For each author who wants to work on the document, the application loads in core memory a copy of all fragments from the secondary storage, thus reconstructing the complete abstract tree of the document. All fragments are then replicated within local editors, but only in core memory.

For allowing managers to allocate roles freely, a fragment does not need to be a single sub-tree, nor a sequence of sibling sub-trees. As shown in Figure 13.4 a fragment may contain any sequence of elements that are encountered in a prefixed traversal of the document abstract tree. For instance, the second fragment of the document contains:

- the second paragraph of the abstract,
- the element representing the root of the first section,
- the section heading of the first section,
- the first paragraph of that section.

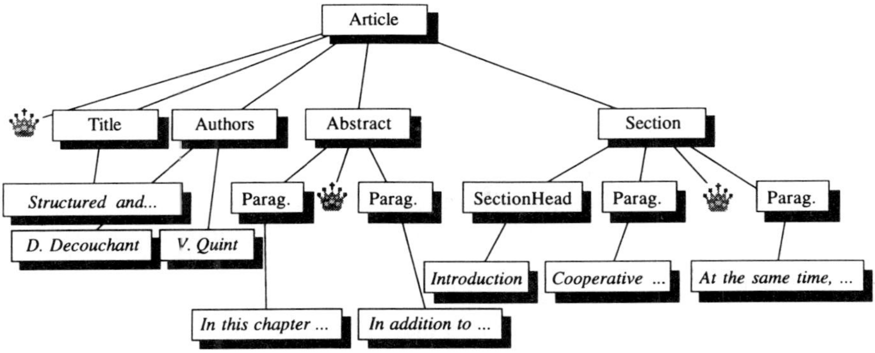

Figure 13.4 Fragmentation of document tree.

The fragment delimiters must be kept by the editor in core memory, so that the editor is able to write each fragment in the corresponding file, when saving the document. This is achieved by inserting in the abstract tree a special type of element, called delimiter, that indicates the limit between two fragments (each delimiter is represented in Figure 13.4 by one of the symbols shown in Figure 13.6). Each delimiter is the first element of the fragment.

Inserting delimiters in a structured document poses problems: according to the principles of structured editing, only elements that are declared in the generic structure can be inserted into an abstract tree. For allowing any type of document (defined by any generic structure) to be collaboratively edited, it would be necessary to define the type delimiter in all generic structures, which would be practically impossible. This problem was solved by the generic structure extensions available in the Grif editor (see Quint and Vatton, (1994) for more details). This mechanism allows a piece of generic structure (the one defining delimiters, in that case) to be dynamically added to an existing generic structure by the application that needs it. With that feature, any existing or future Grif document may be handled by Alliance, without any modification of its generic structure. In the generic structure extension, the delimiter element is defined as an inclusion (in the SGML sense), which allows it to be inserted at any place in an abstract tree.

Document fragments (pieces of an abstract tree) are stored on disk in a linear representation, in prefixed form. As each fragment does not contain a complete tree (see the example of Figure 13.4), additional information is needed in the fragment files for reconstructing the abstract tree correctly from the fragments. For that purpose, a fragment is made up of a sequence of items, which contain three parts: the relative level in the tree, the kind of the item (sub-tree: ‘T’, or single node: ‘N’) and the tree or the node itself. For instance, Figure 13.5 shows the representation of the second fragment.

The relative level is the level in the abstract tree of the current item relatively to the previous item. The first item of a fragment is considered as the

```
Level  0, kind T, <Paragraph "In addition to...">
Level -1, kind N, <Section>
Level  1, kind T, <SectionHead "Introduction">
Level  0, kind T, <Paragraph "Cooperative ...">
Level  0, kind T, <Delimiter>
```

Figure 13.5 Representation of the second fragment.

item following the last item of the previous fragment, which is always a delimiter. The example of Figure 13.5 can be interpreted in the following way: the first item is the Paragraph sub-tree that is the next sibling (relative level 0) of the second fragment delimiter (last item of previous fragment); the second item is the single element (kind N) Section, which is the next sibling of the parent element (relative level -1) of previous Paragraph; the third item is the sub-tree SectionHead, which is the first child (relative level 1) of the previous Section element, etc.

Each fragment file contains at the end the delimiter of the next fragment. This is necessary for allowing a fragment to be loaded independently of its neighbors, when the document is updated. Delimiters are constant elements that cannot be manipulated by standard editing operations. They can be created or deleted only by a user having the manager role, and these operations are not performed directly by the user, but by the application as a consequence of a change of roles.

The application knows the potential roles of all users: each fragment file has two associated files; the first one contains the potential roles of all users and groups for that fragment; the second file contains the current roles. When a document is loaded in a local editor, the application associates a current role with each fragment in such a way that only one user can access a fragment with the manager or writer role at a given time. Then, the application must take into account:

- the user who loads the document, and the groups to which he/she belongs,
- the potential role of that user for that fragment,
- the current roles of other users for the same fragment: if another user already has the writer or manager role, the current user cannot have it.

The current roles assigned to the user who loads the document are associated with each logical element in the document abstract tree. These roles are represented in the abstract tree in the terms of the editor. The Grif editor can associate an access right attribute with any element in an abstract tree. That attribute can take one of the three values: read/write, read only and hidden. The editor takes that attribute into account for allowing or preventing the user from performing some editing functions. All functions are allowed for elements in read/write mode; elements in read only mode cannot be modified; elements in hidden mode cannot be manipulated in any way. The editor also uses this attribute when displaying an element on the screen: elements in read/write mode are displayed with their normal color, elements in read only mode are displayed in a special color, and hidden elements are not displayed at all.

In the above example, suppose that a user (user A in Figure 13.3) has no access to the second fragment of the document (null role). When that fragment is loaded for him, all its elements are set in hidden mode, and that information is not displayed on the screen.

The user cannot access or modify the access right attributes; there is no command for that purpose. Only an application can read or change these attributes through the API. As Alliance is an application that drives the local editors through the API, it can access the access mode attributes.

Due to the ECF mechanism, the application can be notified of all changes made by the editor. Thus, it knows what fragments have been modified by the local user. When the user decides to validate the last changes he has made in a document, the application saves on disk only the fragments for which the user has the writer or manager role and that have been modified.

Controlling and changing roles

Most functions of the collaborative editor are based on the roles played by users. The operations that a user can perform on a document are not only limited by his potential roles, but also by the current roles of other users. Therefore, it is important for users to be able to change their current role while they are working on a document; that allows other users to work as freely as possible on the same document. Obviously these changes of role are controlled by the application, in order to check that the new current roles are consistent with the potential roles and with the principle of a unique writer at a time for each fragment.

When a user owns the potential role of a manager or a writer for a part of a document that he only wants to read, he can declare that he temporarily restricts his role for that part. Then, another user can get the writer role for the same part. It is also important that a user who has temporarily reduced his role can recover his full role, when this is allowed by the current roles played by other users. Dynamic changes of roles are not only caused by users changing their own roles, but also by a user acting as a manager, who assigns new roles to users or groups.

A user must be able to change role for any part of a document, even parts that do not correspond to existing fragments. Then, there are two kinds of role changes: some changes just modify the roles associated with existing fragments, some others modify document fragmentation.

Fragmentation modifications occur during an editing session when two successive fragments are merged (because they receive the same roles) or when a unique fragment is split into two fragments (because the roles are no longer the same for the whole fragment). Thus, the sharing granularity can change according to users needs and the application does not put any restriction on the number nor on the size of fragments.

Fragments are merged by removing a delimiter element in the abstract tree. Fragments are split by inserting a delimiter element. For example, if a role manager decides to give different roles on the second paragraph of the abstract and on the beginning of the introduction, the application inserts a new delimiter between the Abstract and Section elements (see Figure 13.4), and this is done in all local editors working on the document.

If this kind of modification is supposed to be permanent (change made by the manager), it must also be done on disk, which causes fragment files to be deleted or created.

Group awareness through document structure

As in any groupware application, group awareness is a key issue in a cooperative editor (Dourish and Bly, 1992; Lauwers and Lantz, 1990). Group awareness allows each user to be informed of the work done by the others; it also allows him to decide how and when his own contribution should be shown to others. In a cooperative editor, users who work together for producing a common document are faced with the problem of keeping each other aware of their current activity. Each user needs answers to questions such as:

1. 'What is my current role on this part of this document?'
2. 'Could I act with a role giving more privileges on this part?'
3. 'How may I transmit my contribution to other users?'
4. 'How may each user be aware of my contributions?'
5. 'May I control the way my document is updated by other users?'
6. 'What do my colleagues do? On what parts of the document?'
7. 'May I negotiate my contribution with other users?'

Few papers have been published on the crucial problem of group awareness. Most contributions (Nastos, 1992) propose to keep users aware of the common task by several ways, such as color, shared scrollbars, observation views, audio bips, multimedia communication, etc. These solutions are different for synchronous and asynchronous applications (Ellis *et al.*, 1991; Stefik, Bobrow *et al.*, 1987).

Alliance is based on asynchronous group awareness: a user can see the contributions made by writers after a delay that depends on the decisions made by him and by the writers themselves. Each writer explicitly validates his contribution in order to allow other users to see it. At any time, each user may decide to accept or not that the latest version be displayed on his screen. This is achieved by the special active symbols (delimiters) that are inserted in the document at each fragment limit. These symbols show to the user his current role for the following fragment and the status of this fragment. As they have different roles, different users see different symbols at the same time (see Figure 13.3).

The set of symbols representing user's role (see Figure 13.6) has been extended with additional symbols that show the status of the following fragment. These symbols are active: by clicking on them, the user can change the status of the associated fragment.

When a user acts as an attentive reader for a fragment, each time a new version of that fragment is made available by its current writer, the symbol changes to the state modified fragment. Then, the user may decide to get an up-to-date copy of the fragment by clicking on the symbol, which comes back to the state attentive reader.

The locked reading symbol indicates that the user does not want to be aware of new versions of the corresponding fragment, and the automatic update symbol means that he wants the fragment to be automatically updated as soon as a new version is validated by the current writer. Transitions (see Figure 13.6) between the three states of a read-only fragment (locked reading, attentive reading and automatic update) are made by clicking on symbols.

When a user acts with the null role (masked fragment) on a fragment, that fragment is masked. This may be a consequence of the role that has been assigned to him by a manager, but it may also be the result of his own decision: the user may temporarily reduce his role for a given fragment to focus on other fragments. As with the reader role, a user who acts with the null role must be aware (modified masked fragment) as soon as the fragment or some included parts (in case of creation of new fragments) becomes readable or even writable.

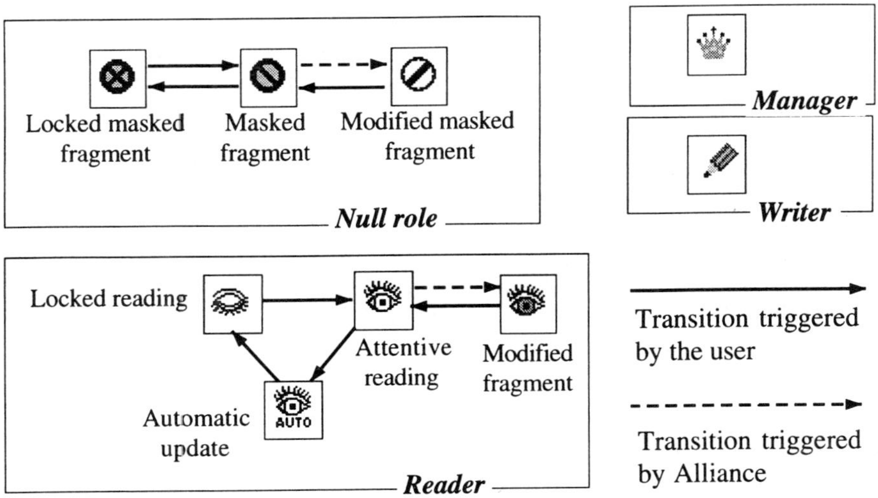

Figure 13.6 Group awareness automata.

The locked masked fragment symbol indicates that the user does not want to be aware of new editing possibilities on the corresponding fragment, such as fragment splittings and role modifications.

In addition, an up arrow is added (resp. removed) to a symbol to indicate that the user can play a higher (resp. lower) role (see Figure 13.3).

Group awareness in collaborative editors is often based on the following principle: in asynchronous systems, each editor records all editing commands performed by the local writer and, when the writer validates the modifications, these commands are transmitted to all editors, which must replay them. Replaying commands is often tedious and time consuming. The synchronous solution consists in sending each command as soon as possible and replaying it immediately in the other editors.

In Alliance, the asynchronous solution is used (writers explicitly validate their changes), but without sending to each local editor a long sequence of editing commands at validation time. When the writer validates the last changes he has made, all modified fragments are first written into the corresponding files, then the references of the modified fragments are transmitted to all other editors working on the document, and each editor updates its copy of the abstract tree, when it has to do so, in two steps:

1. All elements belonging to the fragment are removed from the abstract tree.
2. The updated fragment is read (eventually remotely) from its file, and the corresponding elements are inserted in the abstract tree. The image of the new elements is then redisplayed in all views.

Each updated fragment is globally replaced, without taking care of the number and the type of modifications done by the writer. Only the notifications of fragment change are sent automatically to all editors. They are used for updating the symbols that represent fragment delimiters on the screen. Fragments themselves are transmitted only when an editor needs them.

Although fragment replacement in an abstract tree implies some tree manipulations, its cost has been considered lower than the cost of replaying a sequence of editing commands. A typical editing session implies a large number of basic modifications but less validations and then less tree updates.

The group awareness mechanism presented here is simple and well integrated in the process of structured editing. It is easy to use, as it always reflects the state of fragments. It is also nonintrusive and controllable, as it lets users control display updates.

COOPERATIVE EDITING ON A WIDE AREA NETWORK

In this section, we present the main issues that have been addressed when extending Alliance to a wide area network. We focus first on the problems posed by the delays and failures that can occur in such networks and we discuss the impact of these problems on the architecture.

Then, we describe the document storage mechanism that allows each user to work on shared documents when all sites can communicate and exchange information, but also when some users are isolated by some network failures.

Finally, we show how Alliance addresses the problem of mobile cooperative editing.

The Alliance architecture

Architecture for a local area network

Basically, Alliance allows each user to edit locally an instance of a shared document and it allows all users sharing a document to communicate in order to be aware of the work performed by others. Therefore, two main functions can be identified in this application:

1. *The editing function* allows users to process documents locally, in the core memory of their workstation,
2. *The document management function* provides support to the editing function for document naming, document storage, control of access concurrency, document replication, and group awareness.

   For instance, group awareness requires that, at any moment, all local instances of Alliance that are editing a given document be known, in order to notify them of fragment changes.

The distributed application is constituted by several instances. An instance of Alliance is the piece of software that runs on a workstation for a single user. In the LAN version, an instance involves a single process. This process encapsulates both main functions (editing and document management). If several users share the same workstation, this process is replicated for each user.

As shown in Figure 13.7 an instance of Alliance may be viewed as a main module that controls the functions performed by other modules.

The main module controls the editing module via the Grif API. It can update a fragment for which a new version has been sent from another instance; it can ask the editor to store a local fragment in a file; it can ask the editor to prevent the user from modifying some parts of the edited document, etc.

Editing events are transmitted via the ECF by the editing module, to inform the main module about some commands performed by the user. For instance, that is the way the main module knows what part of the document is currently selected, when the user changes the roles of other users for the selected part.

The main module also receives events (callbacks) from the user interface module (Motif), when the user issues commands that do not concern editing, but cooperation, such as changing the role of other users.

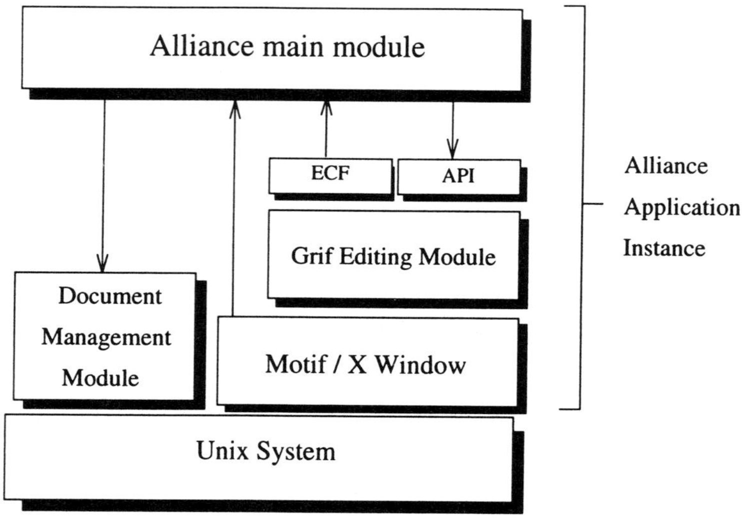

Figure 13.7 Architecture for a local area network.

Finally, the main module calls the document management module when it needs to access the fragments stored in files.

From a local area network to a wide area network

Porting Alliance to a wide area network implies to take into account the specific features of such networks. In the LAN environment, documents are shared using NFS. Then, they are (almost) always available from any workstation and there is no transmission delay, at least from the user point of view. There is no difference in the way local and remote documents or fragments are accessed and managed.

A WAN, such as the Internet, is composed of many sub-networks that communicate via gateways. The WAN is inherently unreliable because of unpredictable communication delays, link failures or computer crashes. In those cases, the WAN can be temporarily partitioned leading to disconnection of sub-networks. For an application such as Alliance, these failures make some remote files unreachable and transmission delays cannot be ignored. All actions involving remote resources can cause long delays or even locks if these remote resources are treated as if they were local.

Therefore the communication support of Alliance has been separated from the part that is in charge of user interface and local editing. A two-process architecture allows a user to edit documents independently of network failures or communication delays.

Another issue in a WAN is remote file access. We have first considered a simple solution, which would avoid to change the way files are accessed. The same service as NFS is offered in WANs by other systems, such as the Andrew File System (AFS), which hide distribution and present remote files in the same way as local files. Although it would not change the architecture of Alliance, this solution has been rejected, because we were looking for a file system that is widely available and used, and that would make the installation of Alliance on any site a simple task, even for an occasional usage.

The World Wide Web satisfies these conditions. It is constituted by a number of servers that provide remote file access. A Web server can be easily installed on any computer and the software is widely available.

Architecture for a wide area network

Web servers are based on the HTTP protocol (Berners-Lee, 1993). HTTP is an application-level protocol suitable for distributed, collaborative and multimedia systems. It allows on-line access to distant information using a request/ response paradigm according to the client/server model. In the WAN version, Alliance fully exploits this model for allowing instances of the application to cooperate: each instance acts as a client and each site acts as a server. Clients send requests to servers in order to:

- obtain information about shared documents (list of users, effective role played by a user in a fragment, etc.);
- get a new version of a fragment.

On the server site, the work is carried out through the Common Gateway Interface, by executing scripts.

Basically, a script is a program that can be executed for an HTTP client to perform some specific work on a server site. A script can receive information through input parameters and it can send results back to the calling client. Alliance implements a set of scripts that allow clients to get information about shared documents, or about fragments.

HTTP proposes three methods: Get, Post and Put. Get allows a client to request a document identified by its URL. Post is used to trigger execution of an existing script; a Post request is composed of the script URL and a list of input parameters to be provided to the script. Put is supposed to allow a client to write a file remotely, but very few servers implement this method. Get and Post return their result through the standard output.

As the Put method is not available, a client must combine two methods for writing a file remotely (see Figure 13.8). It sends to the server a Post which starts a script sending back a Get message to the client. Then the client returns the file as the result of the Get message and the script that issued the Get

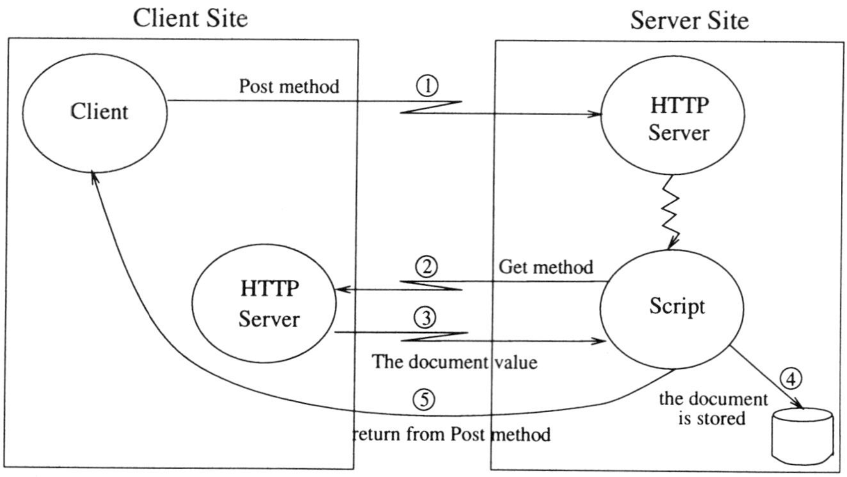

Figure 13.8 Implementation of the Put method.

message writes this file locally on the server. Due to the lack of the Put method, an HTTP server is also required on the client site.

The following example explains how a client can obtain the list of documents owned by a remote user. First, the client builds a request containing the URL of the script GetUserDocumentList, with the login name of the remote Unix user as parameter. Then, it invokes the HTTP Post method and the script is executed on the server site. The script first checks that the user is registered on the server, then it loads the list of documents belonging to that user. Finally, the list is returned to the client through the standard output. On error, the script returns an appropriate diagnostic.

Executing scripts on a remote server poses several problems concerning message security and authentication of users and applications. These security issues are addressed by several teams (see for instance Lewontin, 1995; Anderson and Garvin, 1995; Hallam-Baker, 1994; Hickman, 1994; Rescorla and Schiffman, 1994; Spero, 1994) and the solutions they propose should be integrated into Alliance.

In order to cope with the specific constraints of the Internet, each instance of Alliance is now divided into two processes (see Figure 13.9):

- All editing functions for which the user is expecting an immediate feedback, and that do not depend on remote resources are performed by the Editor.
- All functions that can cause transmission delays or locks are performed by the Assistant. These functions are almost the same as those performed by the document management module in the LAN version. The Assistant takes in charge all functions regarding the client side of remote access.

Each user on a site is served by an Editor process and an Assistant process. In

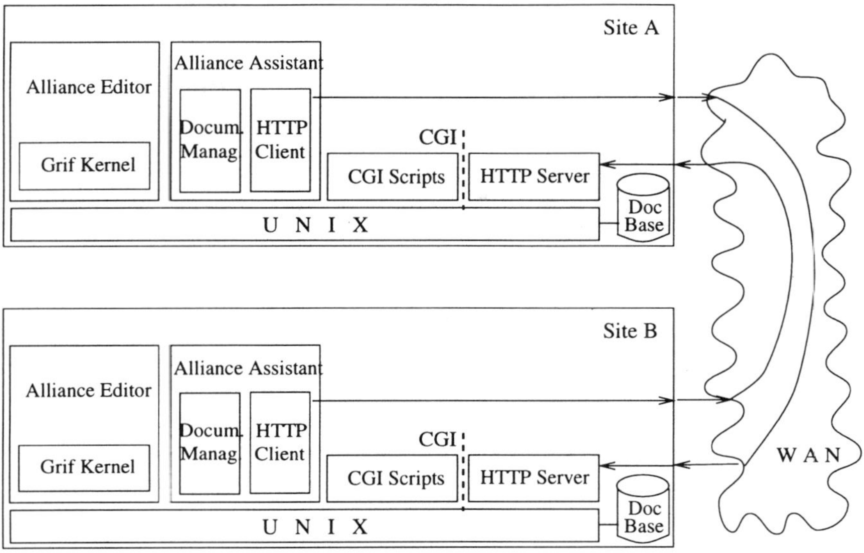

Figure 13.9 Architecture for a wide area network.

addition to these processes, which are in charge of the local users, each Alliance site runs a daemon, even if no local user is active. This process is an HTTP server that contains the Alliance scripts implementing all operations required by the remote Alliance Assistants. Each Alliance script is executed in response to an Alliance client request.

An Alliance site can be in two distinct modes:

- Editing mode: in this mode, Alliance can not only process remote requests, but it can also send requests to other sites and forward event actions related to fragment updates for instance. A single site can run several instances of the application at the same time, one for each active local user.
- Absented mode: in this mode, no instance of the Alliance application is running neither as the Editor nor as the Assistant. This mode allows Alliance to be able to manage incoming requests and update fragments even if no user is active locally.

Document distribution and replication

In Alliance, a document is represented by a set of files (see section on Shared documents, above) which contain document fragments, user roles for each fragment, the order of all fragments in a document, and the current state of each fragment.

In order to allow each user to work on a shared document, even in case of network failure, documents are copied on each site where they are needed. All document fragments and the corresponding management information are replicated among different sites (see Figure 13.10), where they are stored in local files. Each user can then work independently. In order to allow cooperation and group awareness, local copies must be updated when remote users have made modifications. But, as Alliance is based on an asynchronous model of cooperation, these updates do not need to be done in real time. Nevertheless, a mechanism is required for maintaining the consistency of all those copies.

Document consistency is based on a simple principle. In the whole system, there always exists one master copy for each fragment, which is the reference; there are as many slave copies as needed. On a given site where at least one user works on the document, all fragments of that document are available in local files and each fragment copy is either the master copy for that fragment or a slave copy. These two types of copies allow different effective roles to be played by the local user:

- The master copy (in grey in Figure 13.10) allows the user to act on it with the writer or manager role. As the master copy is unique, only one user can play these roles for a given fragment, which enforces the assumption made earlier in this chapter.
- A slave copy only allows the reader or null roles, even if a higher potential role is assigned to the user.

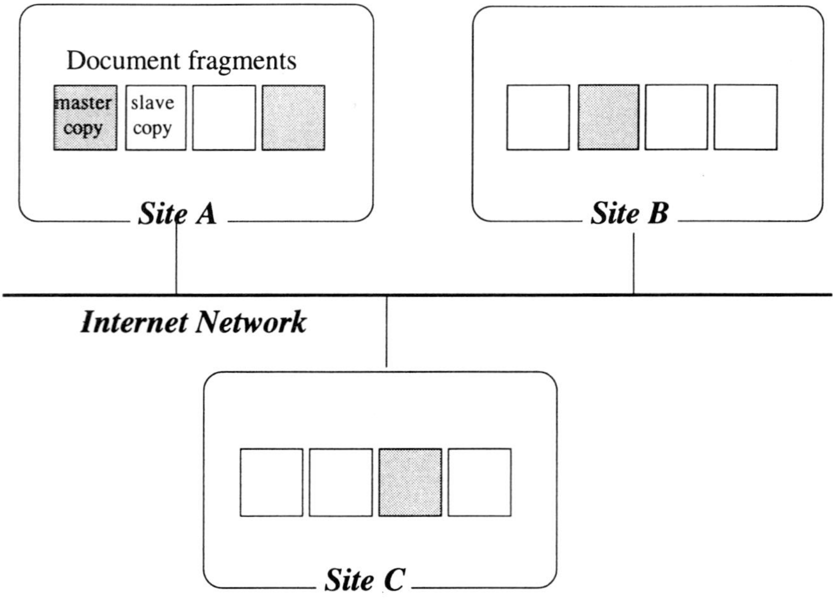

Figure 13.10 Distribution of the fragment copies of a document.

According to this principle, the set of all master copies constitutes the current document state. As a site usually does not own the master copies of all fragments of a given document, each site, and then each user may have a delayed perception of the document state. However, these different perceptions of the document are regularly corrected by asynchronous transmission of updating messages, when a site owning the master copy of a fragment produces a new version of that fragment.

Master copies can migrate from one site to another. This operation is based on a transaction mechanism in order to avoid loss or duplication of the master copy that could be caused by communication failures. The possibility of moving the master copy of a fragment is evaluated each time a user tries to act on a fragment with the writer or manager role, in accordance with his potential role. The transaction fails if the master copy is unreachable or is already locked in reader or manager mode by its current owner. If no user is currently playing the writer or manager role on the site of the master copy, or if the user playing these roles accepts to change role, the master copy can move.

As explained in the section on group awareness, when a fragment is updated by a user acting as a writer, this fragment is not automatically sent to all sites working on the document. Only a short message is sent: it informs the remote sites that an updated version of the fragment is available. With the replication policy presented above, communication between sites is needed only to transmit these short messages, to transfer updated copies to the sites which ask for it, and to get remote user lists.

Disconnected and mobile cooperative editing

An advantage of document replication is that it allows nomadic cooperative work. We might think for instance of a user accessing the network and working in a collaborative way on a document. When he leaves his office, he disconnects his workstation, with the full editing environment, and continues to work in disconnected mode. When the station is connected again to the network, Alliance automatically takes in charge all document fragment updates. This kind of operation mode is the result of an intended disconnection. In case of any network failure, users can work on their documents in the same way.

CONCLUSION AND PERSPECTIVES

Alliance is a cooperative application that allows several users to simultaneously edit shared structured documents over a local or a wide area network. The application fully exploits the intrinsic possibilities of structured editing to manage document sharing.

Many of the advantages of structured editing enhance the functionality of a cooperative document editor. Large and complex documents can be processed. These documents can include a variety of components such as graphics, tables and equations, which can be shared in the same way as the rest of the document. The rich logical structure allows managers to handle document sharing efficiently. It also allows to dynamically change sharing granularity, thus permitting users to change role easily. As sharing is based on a well-defined structure, document consistency can be guaranteed by simple ways.

The current implementation of Alliance includes all functions presented in this paper. Additional services are under development for helping users to communicate with each other through an annotation mechanism and additional dialog options. Annotations will permit users to associate some comments with the document parts for which they have only the reader role. Private and shared annotations will be available.

The wide area version of Alliance uses only one part of the services provided by the Web, the HTTP protocol and servers. It does not take advantage of all the possibilities offered by the World Wide Web. For the moment, document fragments are stored in a specific format, not in HTML (Berner-Lee, 1994b), which is the usual document format on the Web. The next version of Alliance will also integrate HTML. In fact this work is in progress. The Grif editor has already been adapted to the Web and the result of this adaptation, Symposia, can handle HTML documents (Quint *et al.*, 1995). Alliance and Symposia are converging in order to provide Web users with a collaborative tool for producing HTML documents on the Web.

BIBLIOGRAPHY

Anderson, S. and Garvin, R. (1995) Sessioner: flexible session level authentication with off the shelf servers and clients. *Proceedings of the Third International World-Wide Conference*, edited by *Computer Networks and ISDN systems*, *The International Journal of Computer and Telecommunications Networking*, **27**, 1047–1053.

Peng, C. (1993) Survey of collaborative drawing support tools. *Computer Supported Cooperative Work*, **1** (3), 197–228.

Berners-Lee, T. (1993) *Hypertext Transfer Protocol: A Stateless Search, Retrieve and Manipulation Protocol*, Internet draft, CERN, November.

Berners-Lee, T. (1994a) *Uniform Resource Locators – A unifying syntax for the expression of names and addresses of objects on the network*, Internet draft, CERN, January 1994.

Berners-Lee, T. (1994b) *Hypertext Markup Language Specification – 2.0*, Internet draft, CERN, November.

Berners-Lee, T., Cailliau, R., Luotonen, A., Frystyk Nielsen, H. and Secret, A. (1994) The World-Wide Web. *Communications of the ACM*, **37** (8), 76–82.

Conklin, J. (1987) Hypertext: an introduction and survey. *Computer*, **20** (9), 17–41.

Coulouris, G. and Dollimore, J. (1994) *Distributed Systems: Concepts and Design*, Addison-Wesley.

Decouchant, D., Quint, V., Riveill, M. and Vatton, I. (1993) *Alliance: A Cooperative, Structured, Distributed Document Editor*, (R.R. 20), Bull-IMAG, Grenoble.

Dourish, P. and Bly, S. (1992) Portholes: supporting awareness in a distributed work group. *Proceedings of CHI'92 on Human Factors in Computing Systems*, Bauersfeld, P., Bennett, J. and Lynch, G. (eds) Monterey, California, pp. 541–547.

Ellis, C. A., Gibbs, S. J. and Rein, G. L. (1991) Groupware: some issues and experiences. *Communications of the ACM*, **34** (1), 38–58.

Fish, R. S., Kraut, R. E., Leland, M. D. P. and Cohen, M. (1988) Quilt: a collaborative tool for cooperative writing. *Proceedings of Conference on Office Information Systems*, ACM Press, pp. 30–37.

Furuta, R., Quint, V. and André, J. (1988) Interactively editing structured documents. *Electronic Publishing – Origination, Dissemination and Design*, **1** (1), 19–44.

Goldfarb, C. F. (1990) *The SGML Handbook*, Oxford University Press, Oxford.

Greif, I., Seliger, R. and Weihl, W. (1992) A case study of CES: a distributed collaborative editing system implemented in Argus. *IEEE Transactions on Software Engineering*, **18** (9), 827–839.

ISO (1989) *Information processing – Text and office systems – Office Document Architecture (ODA)*, ISO 8613.

Halasz, F. G. (1988) Reflections on NoteCards: seven issues for the next generation of hypermedia system, *Communications of the ACM*, **31** (7), 836–852.

Hallam-Baker, P. M. (1994) Shen: a security scheme for the World-Wide Web. *Internet Draft*, http://info.cern.ch/hypertext/WWW/Shen/ref/shen.html.

Hickman, K. (1994) The SSL protocol, Netscape Communications Corp., November, http://home.mcom.com/info/SSL.html.

Jones, S. (1993) Milo: a computer-based tool for (co)-authoring structured documents. *Computer Supported Collaborative Writing*, Sharples, M. (ed.), Springer Verlag, pp. 185–202.

Lauwers, J. C. and Lantz, K. A. (1990) Collaboration awareness in support of collaboration transparency: requirements for the next generation of shared window systems. *Proceedings of CHI'90 on Human Factors in Computing Systems*, Carrasco Chew, J. and Whiteside, J. (eds) Seattle (Washington), April, pp. 303–311.

Leland, M. D. P., Fish, R. S. and Kraut, R. E. (1988) Collaborative document production using Quilt. *Proceedings of the Conference on Computer Supported Cooperative Work*, ACM Press, Portland, OR, pp. 206–215.

Lewontin, S. (1995) The DCE Web toolkit: enhancing WWW protocols with lower-layer service. *Proceedings of the Third International World-Wide Conference*, edited by Computer Networks and ISDN systems, *The International Journal of Computer and Telecommunications Networking*, **27**, April 765–771.

Minör, S. and Magnusson, B. (1993) A model for semi-(a)synchronous collaborative editing. *Proceedings of the Third European Conference on Computer Supported Cooperative Work – ECSCW'93*, de Michelis, G., Simone, C. and Schmidt, K. (eds), Kluwer Academic Publishers, Milan (Italy), 13–17 September, pp. 219–231.

Nastos, D. (1992) *A Structured Environment for Collaborative Writing*, Thesis for the Degree of Master of Science, University of Toronto (Canada).

Neuwirth, C. M., Kaufer, D. S., Chandhok, R. and Morris, J. H. (1990) Issues in the Design of Computer Support for Co-authoring and Commenting. *Proceedings of the Conference on Computer Supported Cooperative Work*, ACM Press, October, pp. 183–195.

Newman-Wolfe, R. E. and Pelimuhandiram, H. K. (1991) MACE: a fine grained concurrent editor. *Proceedings of the Conference on Organizational Computing Systems*, ACM Press, November, pp. 240–254.

Peng, C. (1993) Survey of collaborative drawing support tools. *Computer Supported Cooperative Work*, **1** (3), 197–228.

Quint, V., Nanard, M. and André, J. (1990) Towards document engineering. *EP'90*, Furuta, R. (ed.), Cambridge University Press, pp. 17–29.

Quint, V., Roisin, C. and Vatton, I. (1995) A structured authoring environment for the World-Wide Web. *Proceedings of the Third International World-Wide Conference*, edited by *Computer Networks and ISDN systems, The International Journal of Computer and Telecommunications Networking*, **27**, April, 831–840.

Quint, V. and Vatton, I. (1986) Grif: an interactive system for structured document manipulation. *Text Processing and Document Manipulation, Proceedings of the International Conference*, van Bliet, J.C. (ed.) Cambridge University Press, pp. 200–213.

Quint, V. and Vatton, I. (1994) Making structured documents active. *Electronic Publishing – Origination, Dissemination and Design*, **7** (1), 55–74.

Rada, R. (1990) Hypertext writing and document reuse: the role of a semantic net. *Electronic Publishing – Origination, Dissemination and Design*, **3** (3), 3–13.

Rein, G. L. and Ellis, C. A. (1991) rIBIS: a real-time group hypertext system, *International Journal of Man–Machine Studies*, (34), 349–368.

Rescorla, E. and Schiffman, A. (1994) The secure Hypertext Transfer Protocol. *Internet Draft*, http://www.comerce.net/information/standards/drafts/shttp.txt, December.

Spero, S. (1994) HTTP-NG: Status Report, *Internet draft*, November.

Stefik, M., Foster, G., Bobrow, D. G., Kahn, K., Lanning, S. and Suchman, L. (1987) Beyond the chalkboard: computer support for collaboration and problem solving in meetings. *Communications of the ACM*, **30** (1), 32–47.

Stefik, M., Bobrow, D. G., Foster, G., Lanning, S. and Tatar, D. (1987) WYSIWIS revised: early experiences with multiuser interfaces. *ACM Transactions on Office Information Systems*, **5** (2), 147–167.

Streitz, N., Haake, J., Hannemann, J., Lemke, A., Schler, W., Schütt, H. and Thüring, M. (1992) SEPIA: a cooperative hypermedia authoring environment. *Proceedings of the European Conference on Hypertext and Hypermedia ECHT'92*, Lacarella, D., Nanard, J., Nanard, M. and Paolini, P. (eds) ACM Press, pp. 11–22.

Wang, W. and Rada, R. (1994) Experiences with semantic net based hypermedia. *International Journal of Human–Computer Studies*, June.

Zheng, Min and Rada, R. (1994) MUCH electronic publishing environment – principles and practices. *Journal American Society Information Science*, **45** (5), 300–309.

14 A Three-level Binding for Collaborative Editing Semantics

DAVID STOTTS, PRASUN DEWAN, JONATHAN MUNSON and JAIME NAVON

INTRODUCTION

Group interactions for collaborative authoring are 'burned into' most collaborative software systems. The allowed actions of users, individually and collectively, are decided by software designers, and users must adapt to these decisions. Collaborations, though, often are long-lived, and a more dynamic technique is needed for software to adapt to changing circumstances during collaborative work.

Suite (Dewan and Choudhary, 1991, 1992; Shen and Dewan, 1992) is a system that allows construction of group tools, including authoring environments. Suite partially solves the dynamic group interactions problem by allowing collaborating users to set coupling parameters, custom tailoring the granularity of information and synchronization of actions shared among users. Group interactions are specified by a collection of constraints; values for the constraints are selected dynamically by the collaborators, choosing from ranges for each constraint. The basic constraint set, though, is fixed. Addition or deletion of basic constraints requires recompiling the system.

Trellis (Stotts and Furuta, 1989, 1990; Furuta and Stotts, 1989, 1994a) is a collaboration specification/support system in which group interactions are specified as a separate, interpreted protocol engine. The protocol can be changed dynamically without recompiling applications using the engine – indeed, without ending execution of any applications using the engines.

We have modified Suite to use the Trellis engine for collaboration protocol information. The result is Sui'tre (pronounced 'sweeter'), a system for building collaboration software in which the definitions of group interactions can change, even during system use. We illustrate our hybrid system by showing a group authoring tool and giving examples of situations in which the dynamically altered group protocols are useful. We next present the different aspects of defining and controlling group actions and interactions in collaborative software. We then motivate in detail the idea of three-level binding, giving a variety of scenarios showing flexibility in allowing users to define their

GROUPWARE AND AUTHORING
ISBN 0-12-575005-6

interactions. The implementation of Sui'tre is explained and a user-oriented tour of its facilities given. We discuss research into expressing collaboration protocols – concurrency and synchronization – in the World Wide Web (WWW), and finally give conclusions and directions for future work.

SEMANTICS OF GROUP INTERACTIONS

Collaborative editing involves several distinct tasks. In top-down construction, for example, initial outline generation is followed by fleshing out of outline items, and the process concludes with a pass for coherence of the text as a whole. There are other processes one can imagine that are not top-down; for example, individual generation of paragraphs, sections, or other chunks is followed by integration and pruning.

Our research is examining this question: when should the semantics of these different tasks and processes be bound by collaborative editing systems – both applications and infrastructures? Our investigations into this problem have led to this three-level characterization of semantic bindings:

- Some systems, like Xerox's Colab editor, and Shared Window Systems, completely bind the semantics of group interaction at program writing time (i.e. software engineers design and define the rules of collaboration).
- Others systems, like Suite (Dewan and Choudhary, 1991, 1992; Shen and Dewan, 1992) and PREP (Neuwirth and Kaufer, 1989; Neuwirth *et al.*, 1990; Cavalier *et al.*, 1991), bind parameterized functions to these tasks and allow users to set values for their parameters at runtime. Thus the range of collaboration semantics is bound at program writing time, but the exact semantics is not bound until time of system use.
- Still others like Trellis (Stotts and Furuta, 1989, 1990; Furuta and Stotts, 1989, 1994a) have built-in facilities for defining/interpreting collaboration semantics. Few, if any, specific collaborations are designed in by the builders of such a system; instead, collaboration specialists, or the users themselves, must bind specific semantics at runtime.

A collaboration support system must make tradeoffs between these kinds of bindings. Earlier binding is more efficient, puts less burden on the users since they are required to do less work, and is simpler to use (all collaborators have a better idea of what is going on, the semantics don't change on them dynamically). Later binding increases flexibility – there is considerable evidence showing collaborative work is situational – as it allows changes based on the situation (Kaplan *et al.*, 1992). Fully dynamic semantics seem to be most natural and most effective for very unstructured, or very long-lived collaborations.

Therefore, the idea of developing collaboration systems that support all three kinds of binding is attractive. We hypothesize that systems built to directly deal with each level – making specific decisions for what capabilities to provide (or exclude) at each level – will be clearer to build and more natural to use. We have done some preliminary work on this idea by developing a collaborative outline editor, called Sui'tre (combining Suite and Trellis), to support this idea. In this chapter we motivate the concepts of fully dynamic collaboration semantics, as well as describe and illustrate Sui'tre.

STATIC VS DYNAMIC BINDING: A CLOSER LOOK

Ideally, binding of group interaction semantics should be done very early in a collaborative software system. Early binding has several advantages:

1. It makes less work for the user (since the system developers make the design choices).
2. It is more efficient at run time, since an interpreted language is not needed.
3. It is more understandable, since the user need not learn any definition notations.

Later binding of collaboration semantics, though, has two advantages of its own:

1. *Evolving functions*: at this state, we do not have enough experience with collaborative applications to 'burn in' all the right choices, so (for now at least, and for the near future) we need systems that support the easy creation and testing of new collaborative processes.
2. *Situational collaboration*: collaboration is situational; for some domains there will never be one right choice for rules of group interaction.

This seems to imply that we need a two-level binding structure: static and dynamic. We are proposing a three-level structure, though, by further dividing dynamic binding into two forms. One solution, adopted by Suite, is to support parameterized functions, giving flexible customization of otherwise pre-defined collaborative processes. The other solution, adopted by Trellis, is to support the programming of interpreted collaboration protocols. Rather than choosing one approach or the other, we believe groupware designers should include both dynamic forms in a fully functional system:

- Parameters we expect to be used in accommodating situational collaboration.
- Parameters alone are not always sufficient, as creating them means understanding enough of the design space to accurately or effectively parameterize it. This is currently not the case for many collaborative task domains – domains (like collaborative editing) in which we have been building groupware for some time, but in which the jury is still out on the 'best' processes. It is especially not the case for work domains not yet supported with collaborative software.

- We need programming/definition methods to support evolving collaborative processes. In the absence of such facilities, one must recompile a system repeatedly as alterations are made to its basic group functions. Problems with this approach include: slow (or no) development of additional functions; source code may not be available for modifying; and source code may not be understandable by users.

Three-level semantic bindings can then provide several useful services. For clarity, we can term these levels:

1. static bindings (as in most groupware)
2. parameter bindings (dynamic as in Suite)
3. process bindings (dynamic as in Trellis)

Binding usage scenarios

Consider now some scenarios in which different design decisions are made for the three binding levels.

- First, different tasks in a system can be bound at different levels. With static binding the data types and user-interface commands are fixed. Data types include name and contents of recursive sections of a document outline, for example. Commands include editing actions like insert, delete, replace name, replace contents. With dynamic parameter binding we can determine specifics of access control to the document data – who can do what to the document, based on user/role identity. User 'Dewan' might be given Read-Only rights at all times, whereas others might be given Complete-Access. The system would allow these privileges to be easily changed during editing by selecting new rights from a palette of choices. However, the concept of access right is designed into the system as a parameterized structure. With dynamic process binding we can 'program' a control structure that determines which of the commands defined above can be activated, in what order, and by what class of users. Processes can be structured to allow some actions to be initiated in parallel, or to be synchronized to the completion of earlier actions.

As an example, consider an editing process having three phases of editing activity, with no feedback from one back to an earlier one. For example, we might design the editing process to have an initial brainstorming phase in which all users add items to a document outline; no one is allowed to delete items added by others. After this, the process might progress to the refinement phase, in which all users are allowed to expand on the outline, adding, deleting, or altering outline items without regard to which user initiated an item. Finally, the process would progress to the development phase in which paragraphs are added to the outline item to produce a fully fleshed document.

Once the group proceeds from one phase to the next, there is no going back to an earlier phase.

In this example, the set of editing activities is statically bound; the tool would have 'burned in' the concept of an outline, an outline item, a hierarchy of items, and content paragraphs. It would also have statically bound actions like 'add item' and 'delete item'. Classes of users and access privileges would be designed in, but specific classes and values are determined during use by parameters. The editing process itself, as described, would be defined for the task at hand; as editing progresses, if the users determined that they needed to go back to the brainstorming phase from development phase, then the process definition could be altered to allow this. Correspondingly, if there were a real reason to not allow such, the tool would enforce the process as defined. Consider another scenario:

- Different aspects of the one task (for example, Suite's view coupling) can be bound differently. With static bindings, we can define three levels of coupling at application development time: high, medium, and low. With parameter bindings, users could explicitly select during editing the level desired. This is the manner in which Suite applications behave now. With process bindings an editor can use a process definition to decide the situations under which coupling should change, or allow different parameter ranges under different circumstances. For instance, during early mornings allow high couplings only; in afternoons, allow high or medium, in evenings, only low. Again, these time-based changes are determined by each group doing editing, and defined in a process description.

Process is the point

We can summarize the point of the Sui'tre system in a single word: process. Earlier full-function collaborative software development systems (like Suite and Kaplan's Conversation Builder) have recognized the need for flexibility in collaborative support, but they have primarily taken a specific collaborative process, such as editing or teleconferencing, and developed instances of systems embodying those processes. Experimentation with flexibility has been largely in allowing each user to customize the manner in which he perceives the interactions and the group product. The Trellis approach is to allow the collaboration process itself to be a parameter, if you will, of the system. Trellis, though, lacks well-done user interface facilities so cannot be used on its own for serious system development.

Sui'tre overcomes the shortcomings of both Suite and Trellis, resulting in a significant tool for developing real systems that support variable and dynamic collaborative processes. In the remaining sections, we present its architecture and applications.

SUI'TRE: COMBINING TRELLIS AND SUITE

The Sui'tre collaborative editing system is a combination of the best features of the Suite multi-user interface development system with Trellis collaborative protocol engines. The resulting system allows users to specify and dynamically change the manner in which a collaboration, such as group editing of documents, will proceed. Before detailing the features and operation of Sui'tre, we will recap the structure and function of the component technologies – Suite and Trellis. If you are familiar with the basic premises and functioning of both Trellis and Suite, you should skip to the section entitled 'Details of Sui'tre implementation' to continue reading about Sui'tre itself.

Overview of Suite

Suite has been explained in detail in earlier reports (Dewan and Choudhary, 1991, 1992; Shen and Dewan, 1992). For completeness here, though, we briefly discuss the main features of the system. Our discussion is drawn from a digital library project called the Repository for Patterned Injury Data (RPID) (Stotts *et al.*, 1994; Dewan *et al.*, 1995) under development in the UNC Colab. This system is a database of medical information for supporting collaboration among forensic pathologists. We have assembled an initial prototype using Suite for the multi-user interface. Our example here shows two users collaboratively editing an autopsy report.

An important abstraction in a digital library is the notion of a shared workspace. A shared workspace is a window on the screen that gets updated in response to actions of several other users. In Suite, a shared workspace is designed to have flexible sharing semantics based on abstract data objects defined in the implementation code. Flexibility comes from allowing users to select values for the parameters of the collaboration, thereby customizing their interactions.

Shared workspaces, roles, and rights in Suite

In general, the RPID library helps pathologists resolve cases by producing autopsy reports on them. These reports are represented internally as linked data, amenable to printing or to browsing as hypermedia documents. Using Suite, we create roles for the people involved in creating and using data in each case, and we assign access privileges based on roles. Suite manages the administration of these privileges as well as basic concurrency control on the database.

The Suite-based implementation provides each user with a window on the data contained in each case. The overall structure and substructure of the data (object/field names and types) is shown, and according to the privileges of the specific user, values for the data are shown with appropriate levels of detail.

The designer of each case must specify access rights on a substructure basis, determined according to the roles played by the users. Examples of roles in RPID include pathologist, examiner, data entry, manager, judge, etc. The existence of different substructures can be revealed or hidden on a role-by-role basis; for revealed substructure, the values can be hidden, fully displayed, or partially displayed with various levels of detail.

Each case is assigned to an examiner, who is responsible for its final contents. The New Case object in the windows of Figure 14.1 contains an outline of the general structure of such a report. The report identifies the subject, examiner, assistant, and toxicologist on the case, describes the wounds and evidence found, and contains the results of the toxicology tests.

In our hypothesized scenarios, several people, playing different roles, collaborate with the examiner in the production of the report. A secretary helps enter most of the information in the report. A toxicologist produces the results of the toxicology tests. The assistant signs the report once it is completed. Finally, one or more consultants help the examiner reach a verdict on the manner of death by entering consultation comments.

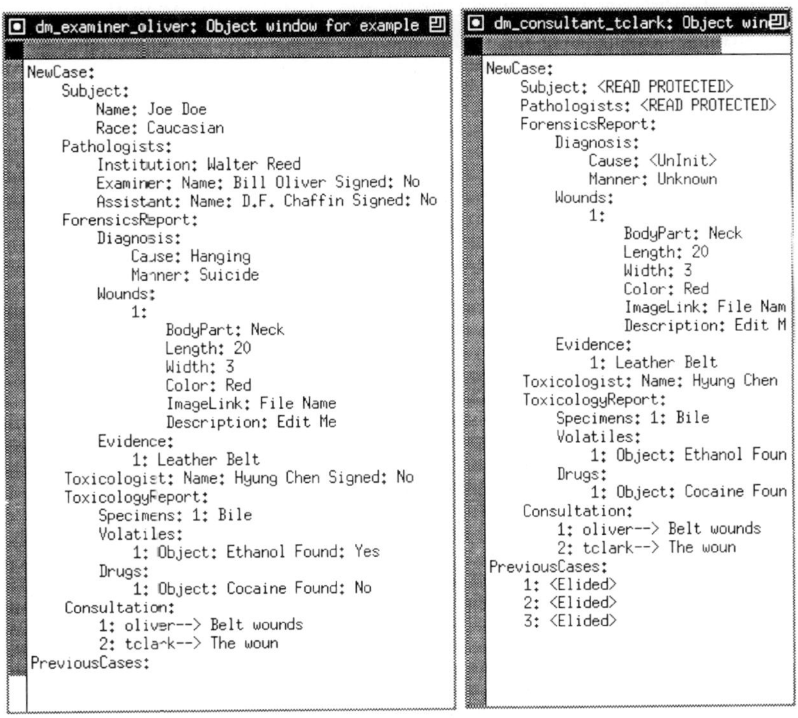

Figure 14.1 Examiner and consultant share autopsy report and list of previous cases; they have different access rights to, and views of, the information.

Coupling of operations among users

Shared workspaces provide high-level support for collaboration among distributed users. In general, each collaborator manipulates a set of fields shown in his workspace. The workspaces of the different users are coupled by a set of coupling constraints defined by the library. These constraints ensure that users automatically receive information in which they are interested in a timely manner. Most of the previous work in shared workspaces constrain all coupled workspaces to be identical, thereby supporting WYSIWIS (What You See Is What I See) collaboration. The coupling constraints defined for this application, however, are more complex and depend on the roles of the users and the fields they are editing. For instance, the MANNER field of the forensics report entered by the examiner is sent to others when he executes the TRANSMIT command, while every character typed by a consultant in the CONSULTATION field is immediately sent to all other consultants on the case (Figure 14.1).

In addition to the values of the objects in the workspace, the application can also couple the views of these objects. A view of an object selects the set of fields of the object that are displayed to the user. For instance the view of the object Previous Cases determines which of the previous cases are shown to the user. The digital library currently provides users with several commands to change the view of this object. For instance, it allows them to select all previous cases, none of the previous cases, all cases that involve wounds to a particular part of the body, and all cases in which the wound length is greater than, equal to, or less than a specific length. The application allows consultants working on the case to browse through previous case information separately (Figure 14.1) or together (Figure 14.2).

As potentially sensitive information becomes available to multiple users, it is important to ensure that it be protected from unauthorized access. Several access control schemes have been devised for objects managed by file systems and database systems. Some of these concepts apply directly to our library. For instance the list of previous cases is associated with a Write right, which ensures that a previous case cannot be updated. Several additional access concepts, not found in traditional systems, are supported in this application to support the desired protection. Rights are associated with fine-grained objects, which override those defined in the parent objects. For instance, the Assistant field is associated with its own Write right, which is used to ensure that only an assistant can sign his name. The Read right must be interpreted differently, since users do not explicitly request reads. A read protected object is made opaque in the display by replacing the display of its contents with a special string indicating that the item is read-only (Subject and Pathologists fields of Figure 14.1). In addition to the traditional Read and Write rights, a large number of other rights are supported. For instance, an Update right ensures that only the examiner can commit the current case to the database and the View Coupled right ensures that only a consultant can couple his view with the

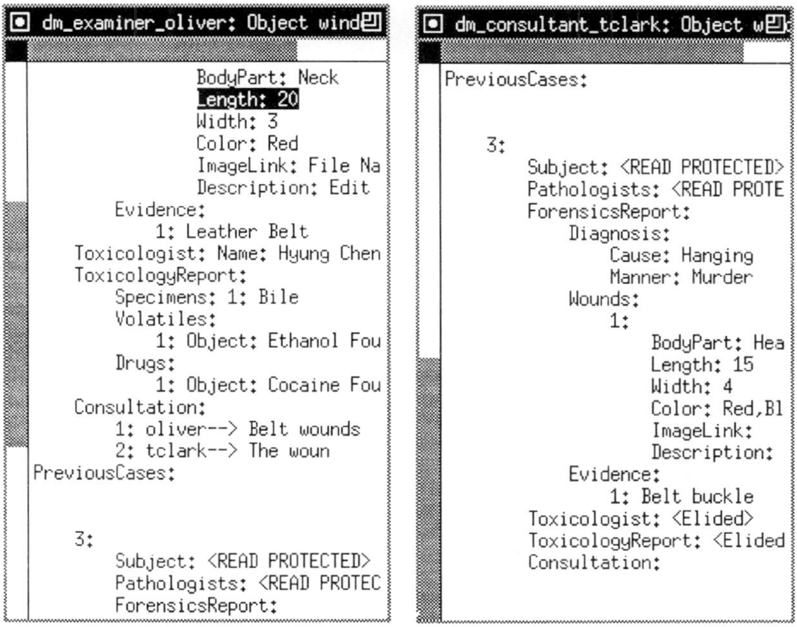

Figure 14.2 Examiner and consultant share view showing all previous cases with wounds of length < = 20.

views of other consultants. In general every operation that can be shared with another user is associated with its own right. We have a large number of such operations (over 50), and the rights to these operations are arranged in right groups such as Data Rights and Coupling Rights. A right group allows access to whole group of operations to be given by one specification. Rights are given not to individual users but to roles such as Examiner, Assistant, Secretary, and Consultant. Moreover, these roles are arranged in a DAG, which allows a role to inherit rights from its parent roles. For instance, an Examiner is a Consultant, and thus inherits the rights of a Consultant, which it can override.

All of the capabilities mentioned here have been implemented using the Suite system (Dewan and Choudhary, 1992). Individual papers on coupling (Dewan and Choudhary, 1991), access control (Shen and Dewan, 1992), and merging (Munson and Dewan, 1994) describe these capabilities in more detail.

Sui'tre goes beyond our RPID prototype in an important way. In RPID, with Suite, the access control precedences, work flow, and roles were all defined in the C data structures of the Suite-built editor; with Sui'tre, we now have Suite communicating with the Trellis engine to get process information related to collaboration groups and group behavior. This gives the ability to alter dynamically the interaction rules for collaborations without recompiling the system. We explain this in more detail after an overview of Trellis.

Overview of Trellis

The Trellis project is an ongoing effort to create interactive linked information systems that have a formal basis and that support analytical techniques. The first such effort was a hypertext model (Stotts and Furuta, 1989), with a follow-up framework for highly-interactive time-based programming (termed temporal hyperprogramming (Stotts and Furuta, 1990)). The current model is an extension of these earlier designs that explicitly distinguishes the various agents acting within a linked structure, and that provides an analyzable mechanism with which agents may exchange data.

The Trellis model treats a hyperprogram as an annotated, colored, timed, place/transition net (Petri net).[1] In Trellis, the places of a net are annotated with fragments of information (text, graphics, video, audio, executable code, other hyperprograms); these annotations are termed the content elements of the hyperprogram. A hierarchy is created by allowing the content element of a place to be itself an independent hyperprogram.

In addition to many goal-oriented applications for the Trellis engine, we have adapted a concurrent program verification technique called model checking (Clarke *et al.*, 1986) to produce analysis methods for hyperprogram verification, that is, for demonstrating that Trellis nets exhibit, when browsed, the reader-document interactions that are desired by their authors (Stotts *et al.*, 1992).

Clients: Browsing a net

To use a Trellis model (as hypertext, for example) we provide visual interfaces (clients) to give a user a tangible interpretation of the net and its annotations. When a token enters a place during execution of the engine, the content element for that place is presented for viewing or for other consumption in the client.

Any enabled transitions leading out of that place are shown to the user as selectable hypertext links, or as other hot spots in the client interface. Selecting a button (with a mouse, say) will cause the engine to fire the associated net transition, moving the tokens around: this leads the client to display new content information, and so on.

Figure 14.3 shows the high-level client/server architecture of a Trellis-based implementation. Trellis clients and engines execute as independent Unix processes, communicating via RPC. The Trellis engine determines the static structure and dynamic collaborative behavior of a hyperlinked information base; the individual clients determine the context-dependent and user-directed

[1] We assume some familiarity with basic net theory; an overview can be found in Murata's survey (1989) or Peterson's survey (1977).

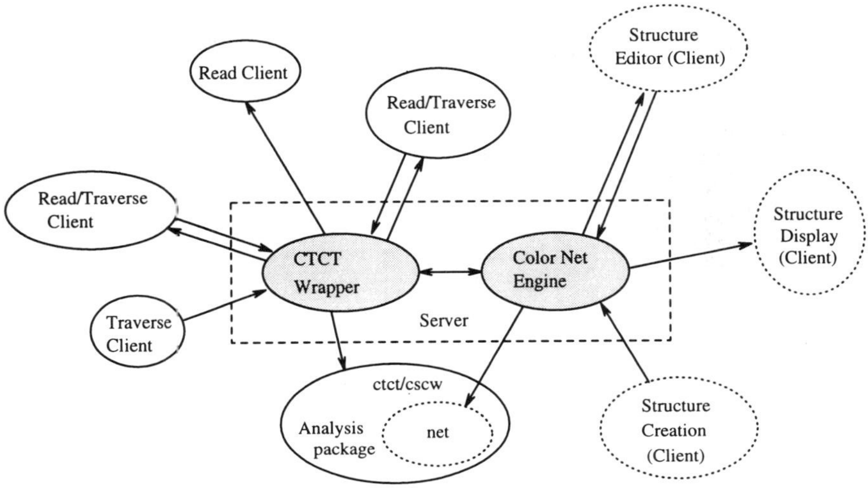

Figure 14.3 Trellis client/server system architecture. Arrows show information flow; clients with arrows out of the model only are 'observers', that is, they cannot affect the progress of the collaboration.

presentation of that information. Clients can be written for different platforms or window systems.

The current Trellis prototype, χTrellis is written for X-windows and Unix. A central server process (the engine) implements the semantics of the colored net, providing the specification of the collaboration protocol, but it has no user-visible interface of its own. One or more (possibly distributed) client processes must communicate with the server to give users some visible (or consumable) representation of the information annotated on the net engine. Figure 14.4 shows several χTrellis clients executing concurrently, including the net editor χTed and two instances of the text browser χtb. The specific net structure shown is explained in the following section on collaboration protocols.

Colors on tokens

The Trellis engine depends on colored Petri nets for expressing collaborative interactions, so more detail on how colors work is in order. Colors are associated with tokens, giving a simple typing system; colors can be used to distinguish one individual from another, one group from another, one task from another, or for other distinctions. A color expression appears on each arc entering and leaving a transition; when the transition is to be fired, the tokens in the input places are examined to see if their colors satisfy the color expressions. An appropriate set of input tokens is chosen, the transition is fired, and tokens with colors matching the output arc expressions are generated into the output places.

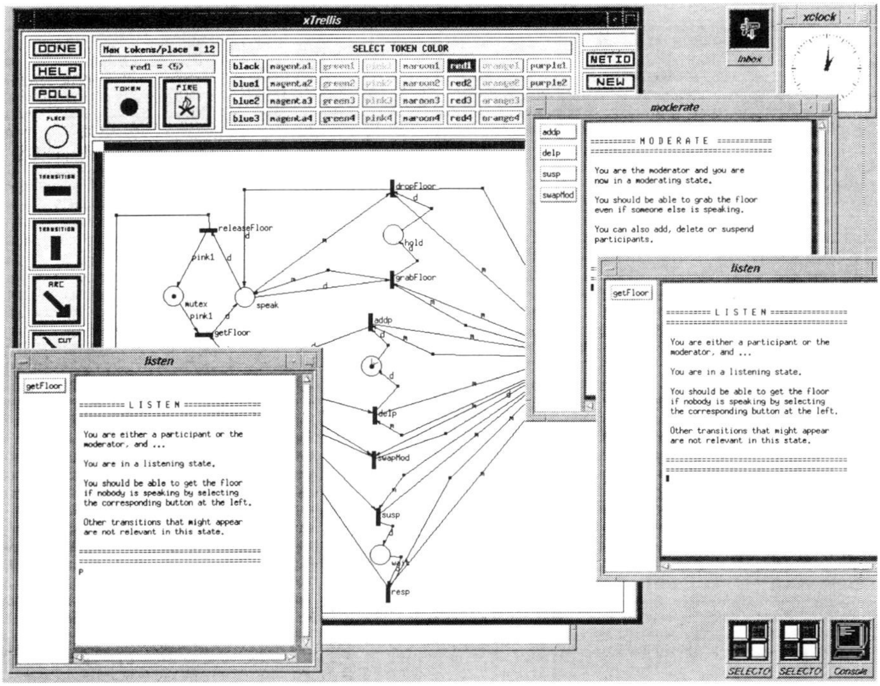

Figure 14.4 Prototype of moderated meeting in Trellis.

Consider the example shown in Figure 14.5. The color expression a + b on the left arc specifies two tokens of arbitrary colors, with the two colors being different. The expression 2b on the right arc requires two tokens of one color, and it must be the same color as selected for 'b' from the left place. The expression 3a indicates that when fired, the transition will place three tokens of the color selected for 'a' into its output place. Given the colors shown in the input places, there are two possible color substitutions:

substitution 1: a is red, b is green
substitution 2: a is blue, b is green

Figure 14.6 shows a Trellis net for directing a moderated meeting. This protocol is discussed in detail in an earlier paper (Furuta and Stotts, 1994b), so the current discussion will just touch on some general points.

In this collaboration protocol, we use colors to distinguish individual participants (as opposed to classes of participant). The moderator has one color token, and each other participant has a different color token. There is a pool of new colors to select from when new participants are added by the moderator. In addition, one color (different from all participants) is used for mutual exclusion in floor control.

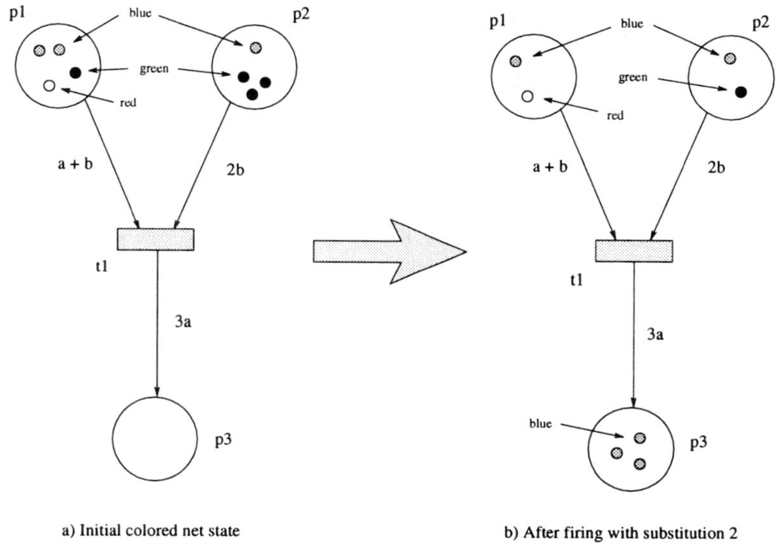

Figure 14.5 How colored place/transition nets work.

The meeting protocol is designed to limit some operations to the moderator and to permit the moderator to override participants if desired. It even has a section that implements swapping the moderator job with one of the current participants. Notice that a moderator-colored token appears in both the 'moderator' place and the 'listen' place; thus, in this protocol, the moderator is also a participant in the discussion.

The screen shown previously in Figure 14.4 illustrates a multi-user simulation of this meeting in Trellis. The editor client χTed shows the structure of the meeting protocol. The browser window on the left is the view of one of the participants; the windows on the right are collectively the moderator's view. Two different browser processes are executing concurrently, interacting with the engine. Note that the moderator's view is a superset of the normal participant's, since in this protocol the moderator may also participate in the meeting. Buttons are visible next to the text windows to allow invocation of the engine actions hypertextually.

Dynamic protocols

Since Trellis protocols are interpreted, dynamic modifications can be made to the net. If the functionality already programmed in a net is not sufficient, a person editing the specification 'on the fly' can add new functionality without terminating the current use of the net. For example, if a meeting is going on under control of the previously examined protocol, and if it is decided that two people should

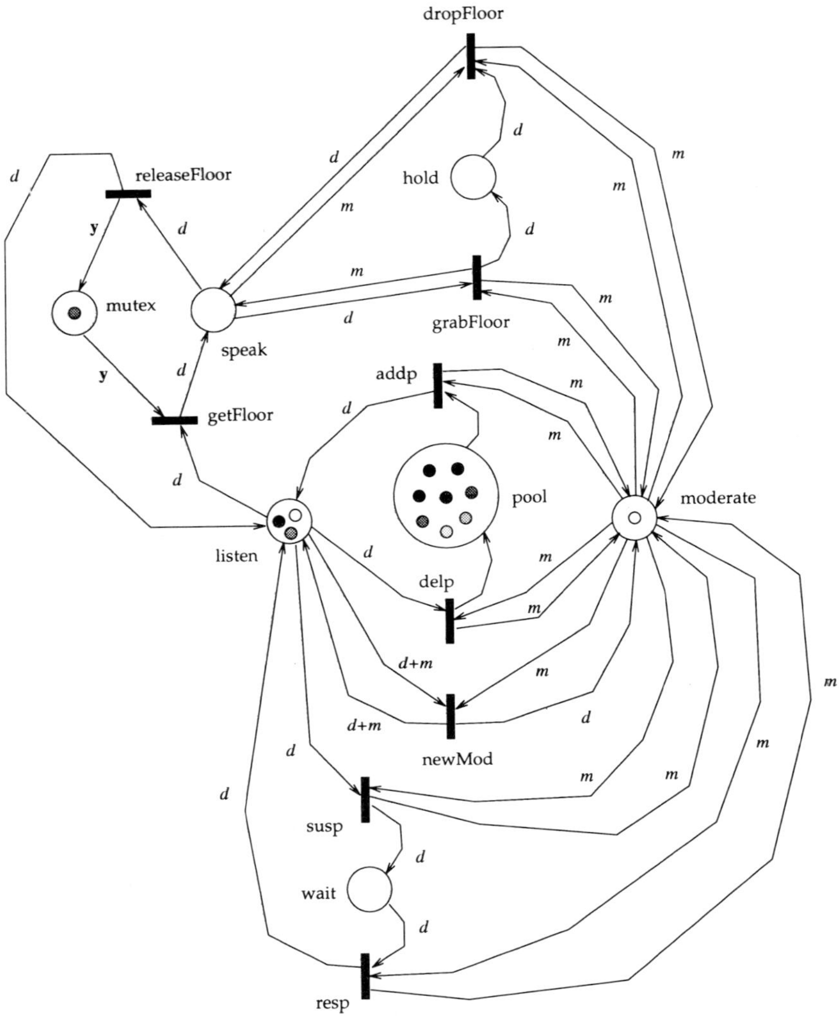

Figure 14.6 Meeting protocol implementation.

be able to get the floor and speak at one time (!!!), the Trellis editor can be used to drop another token (of the correct color) into the 'mutex' place without ending the meeting. Further, if voting needs to be added to the activities participants can perform (along with 'listen' and 'speak'), the proper net links to create a voting function can be edited together and linked into the protocol structure while the meeting progresses. In addition to human editing, changes can be made through the actions of a decision-making program (a 'silent' client, so to speak). Any process written to communicate with the engine via its RPC interface can request that its actions (like 'add arc' or 'fire transition') be executed.

Details of Sui'tre implementation

In terms of the Trellis architecture (shown previously in Figure 14.3), the Sui'tre application is a Trellis interface client that has been produced using the Suite multi-user interface development system. A schematic of Sui'tre is shown in Figure 14.7. It illustrates the relationships among the Trellis engine, the Suite applications, the Suite dialog managers, and the collaborating users. Communication between Trellis and Suite is implemented as follows:

- The different places in the colored Petri-Net describing the collaborating protocol can be thought of as different states or phases within the collaboration protocol. Each place in the net is associated with a set of permissions. There is a special place attribute called suitePermissions whose value is a string with the relevant collaborative suite attributes (access, coupling, etc.).
- Each participant is associated with a token color in the net. When suite finds a token of color x in place p, it sets the attributes for user X to the values specified in the suitePermissions attribute for that place.
- Moves from one state of collaboration (place) to another are carried out by the participants but they are restricted by the structure of the net. The Suite application asks the Trellis engine for list of valid transitions for one user and then Trellis finds all firable transitions from places with tokens of the corresponding color. A list of operations (which is a special attribute of the

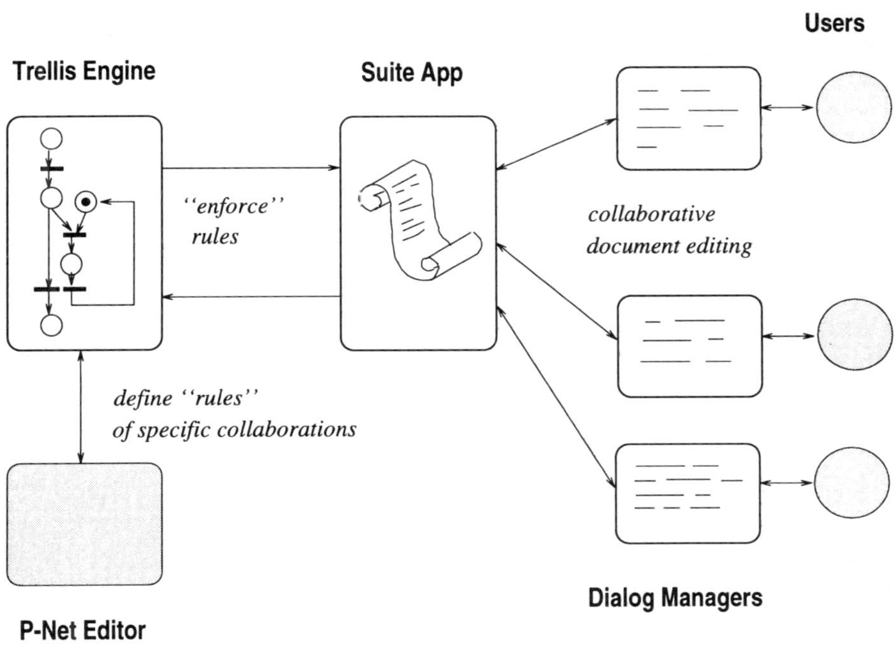

Figure 14.7 Sui'tre system architecture.

transitions) is returned to the application and the user can now move to any of the states that are allowed.

- After a user selects an operation, the Suite application sends back to the Trellis engine the selected operation and Trellis fires the corresponding transition. The new marking is returned to Suite in order to reset the permissions of the different users.

Communications between the Suite components and the Trellis engine is via RPC. The engine has more than 60 methods that can be invoked by client processes. The operations include changing the net structure, changing the information annotated on the net components, firing transitions, reporting net state, and reporting net annotations. In essence, the Trellis engine serves as a blackboard for the Suite components. In terms of our three-level binding structure, the static and parameter bindings for group editing are contained in the Suite application: the process bindings are contained in the Trellis engine, and may be altered during document editing (with the Trellis editor xTed, or via other clients).

Evolving process nets

An example will help illustrate this notion of changing the process during use of Sui'tre. Consider the simple and ubiquitous collaborative application of conferencing. We might build (with Sui'tre) a group chat tool with one common window where anybody can write at any time. There is tight coupling and no need for access control. Schematically, this trivial process is shown by the net in Figure 14.8.

As also occurs with people chatting in a room, this scheme works pretty well for a relatively small number of participants. When this number increases, a more manageable process would involve some floor control, where only the one who 'has the floor' has the right to speak (i.e. to write into the shared window).

Operating under the dynamic protocol binding of Sui'tre, our chat tool would change its behavior to have floor control when the simple net from Figure 14.8 is altered to the more complicated one shown in Figure 14.9. This new process has synchronization, allowing only one person at a time to have access to the 'speak' phase of the process: the remainder of the participants would be in the 'wait' phase (presumably listening to the speaker). The natural

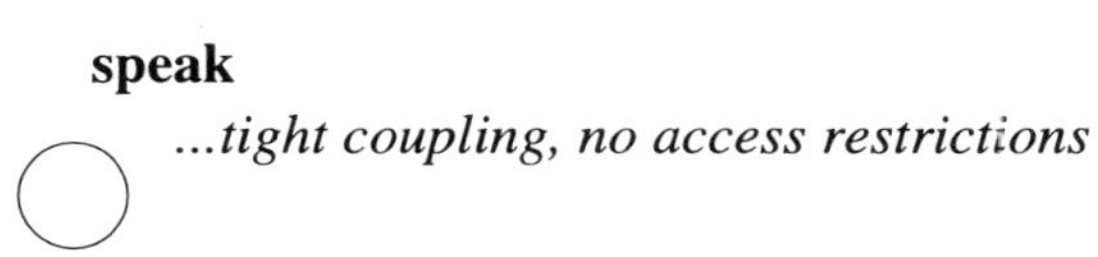

Figure 14.8 Trivial net for group chat process.

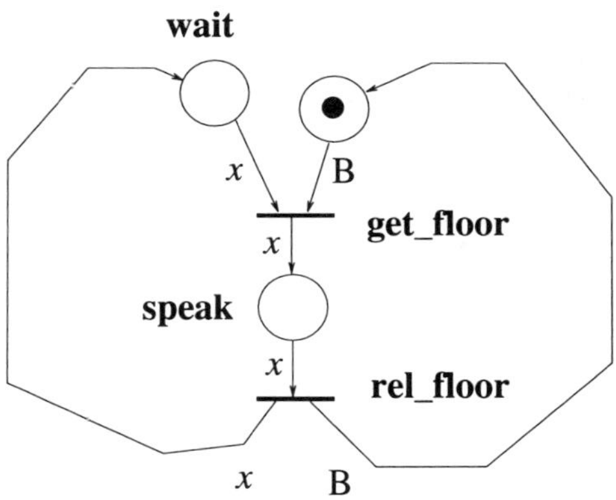

Figure 14.9 Floor control added to group chat process.

progression of this example will lead to the fully moderated meeting protocol shown earlier in Figure 14.6. As previously mentioned, alterations can be done to the process nets without having to end execution of the chat tool.

COLLABORATIVE EDITING IN SUI'TRE

In this section we illustrate the ideas presented above with an outline editor we have built with Sui'tre. Before explaining the system in action, we present the collaboration process used in the editor, and discuss dynamic alterations to it.

As mentioned earlier one way a group might create an outline is with a three-phase process: brainstorming, refinement, and development. Each one of these phases requires a different mode of collaboration. During the first phase (brainstorming) the participants working under a tight coupling can only add new items to the outline. In the next phase (refinement) participants are

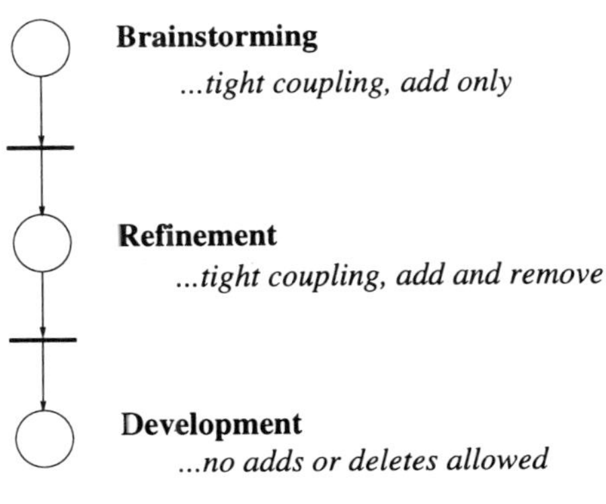

Figure 14.10 Simple group editing process.

allowed to insert and also delete elements. This second phase works also in a tight view-coupling fashion (i.e. WYSYWIS). In the last phase no new items can be inserted and no items can be deleted, and a tightly view-coupled scheme is no longer needed.

This three-phase process can easily be modelled by a colored Petri-Net with three places, one for each phase of the process as shown in Figure 14.10. Each place has been annotated with Suite attributes appropriate to the mode of collaboration required in that phase. One variation of this process is to add a floor control mechanism (similar to the one we discussed previously), but just for the refinement phase (see Figure 14.11). Finally, we could also add feedback arcs so users are allowed to go back to previous phases if they so desire (see Figure 14.12).

Figure 14.13 shows the view of one Sui'tre user, participating in a two-person editing session. The Trellis editor is running on the left, showing the simple three-phase process. The large window on the right is the Sui'tre editor window, and the Suite dialog manager window appears above that. The net shows two participants in the editing session, as two tokens appear in the place labeled 'Brainstorming'. In this case, both users are in the same phase of the editing process. The Sui'tre window shows an outline they have built, having six items, some of which have subitems. At this point, there are no contents for the items (since the process is still in brainstorming). Sui'tre will not allow the users to add contents to the items in the editor window until they have advanced to 'Development'.

The view of the other user is shown in Figure 14.14. This user is not viewing the process with the Trellis editor, but he has displayed the Suite coupling parameter window to the left of the Sui'tre editor window. The users are tightly coupled at this point, so each sees the same view of the outline being edited. Tight view coupling is in effect at this point because the designer of the Trellis

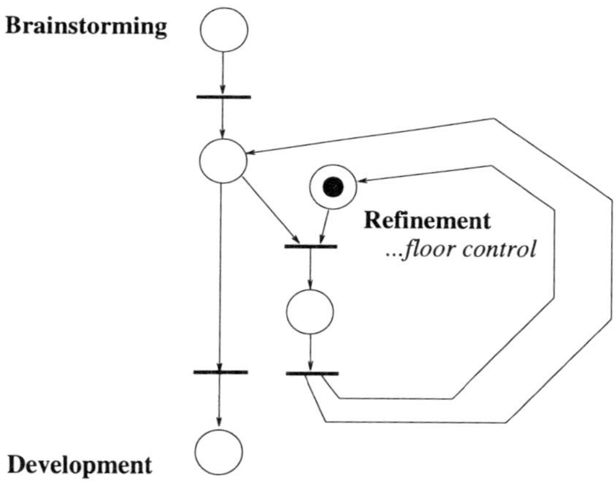

Figure 14.11 Adding feedback to the process.

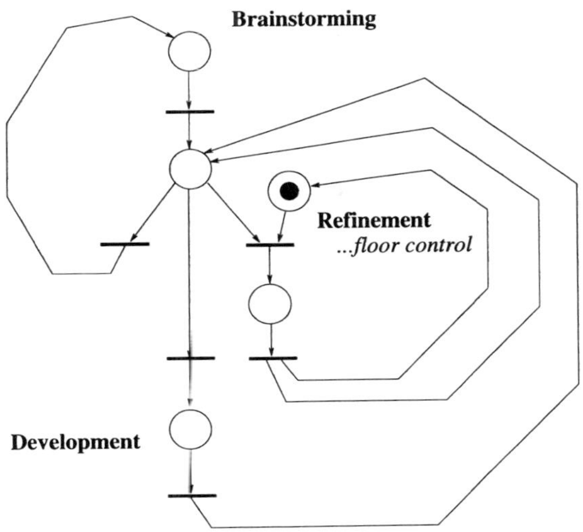

Figure 14.12 Example net for editing process.

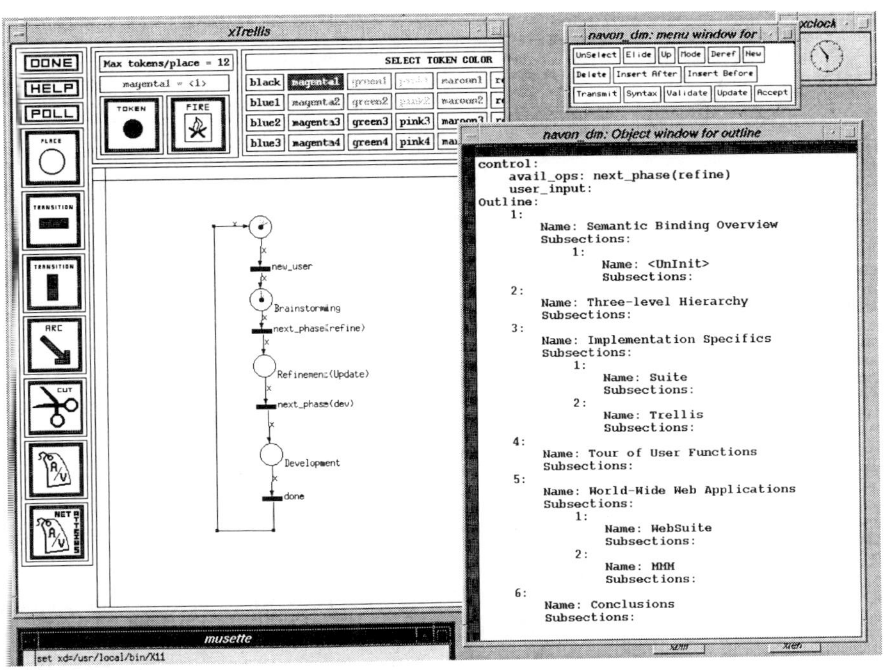

Figure 14.13 Screen showing Sui'tre: Trellis net and Suite client.

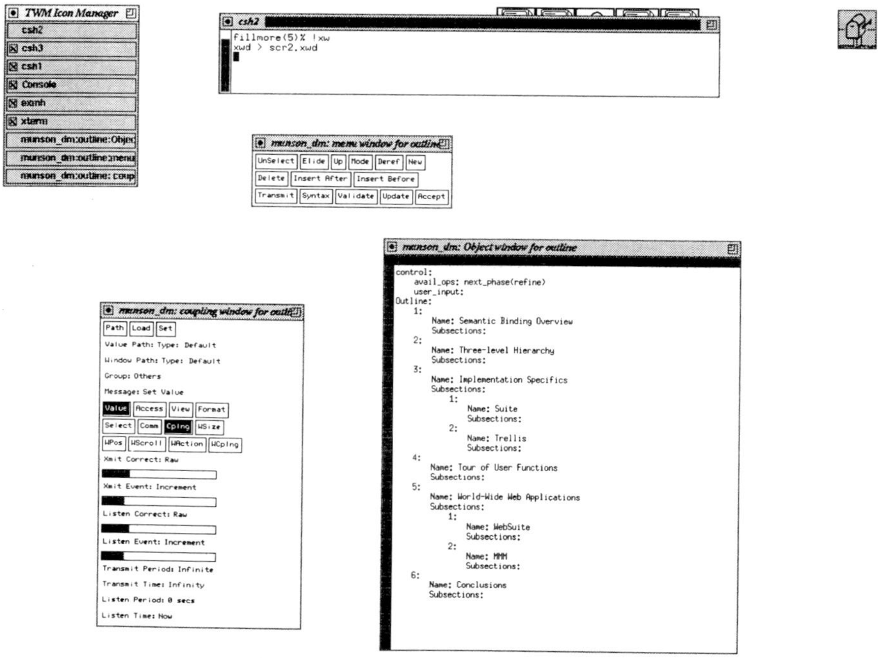

Figure 14.14 Another Sui'tre screen: second user with Suite client.

process net gave 'tight' as the value of the view coupling attribute; the Sui'tre client reads this information from the net and will not allow (at this point in the process) users to change the parameters through the normal Suite interface. If a user were to employ the Trellis editor to alter (or eliminate) the value of the view-coupling attribute, then the process would not control the editing in the same way, and users would be free to select their own coupling parameters.

The users can advance in the process by typing 'next-phase' on the 'user-input' line at the top of the editor window. The Sui'tre client would then contact the Trellis engine, and fire the 'net-phase(refine)' transition. New values for the various coupling attributes would be retrieved from the engine, and the editing would proceed under (perhaps) new conditions.

The manner in which the process information from the Trellis engine is used is a function of the design of the Sui'tre client. In the example given, users advance from one phase to the next individually. If desired, the Sui'tre editor client could require all users to move from one phase to the next as soon as any requests a move. In this case, a voting procedure could be added to the net structure to make users happier about being 'forced' to move to the next phase.

The designer of a Sui'tre editing client could design several behavioral dimensions that the process net could address through attributes. We have already mentioned examples in which various Suite editing operations are enabled or disabled phase-by-phase. Users could also be limited in the form of the outline they can construct at various phases. For example, depth and breadth of the tree: users could be prevented from going more than two or three levels deep in the item/subitem hierarchy in early phases, or they could be allowed to make only a certain number of subitems for each item.

WWW APPLICATIONS

We have several applications under development designed to move the results of our research to use on the World Wide Web. We briefly discuss here two of them – one from the Trellis project, and one from the Suite project.

WebSuite: Suite Multi-user interfaces in Mosaic

One project at UNC has resulted in a new, Web-based interface for the traditional Suite functionality. The result, called WebSuite, allows a group of users to open a collaborative editing session through Mosaic. Each user gets a Mosaic window. Forms are used to collect information about which collaboration a user wishes to join. Once attached to a Suite dialog manager for the requested conversation, the information contributed by the collaborating users is converted to HTML for rendering on the screen. The prototype is still undergoing experimentation, and will be discussed in detail in a later report.

MMM: Trellis protocols in the Web

We have been working on moving the lessons learned from Trellis research into practice in the World Wide Web.[2] The result is Web-based hypermedia for expressing and simulating collaboration protocols like those shown previously (Figure 14.6). Called Multi-Head/Multi-Tail Mosaic (MMM), the current prototype consists of extensions to HTML and a modified version of Mosaic to recognize and interpret them. Full details can be found at URL

http://www.cs.unc.edu/ ladd/mmm/mmm.html

as well as a download point for Sparc binaries (experimental use).

One main contribution of Trellis is the generalization of a hypermedia link to allow multiple source nodes and/or multiple destination nodes. We call this a multi-head/multi-tail link, or MHMT. In Trellis several interpretations have been explored for MHMT links, most notably the Petri net structure. Other

[2] We wish to acknowledge Michael Capps and Brian Ladd for their work in implementing the MMM browser and generating the example seen here.

interpretations are as natural, though; for example, the MHMT links can be viewed as defining parallel finite automata (Stotts and Pugh, 1994), which allow definition of concurrency and synchronization but do not count tokens at nodes. The point is that MHMT links allow the link structure of a hyperdocument to define the transition diagram of an automaton involving concurrency and synchronization; the specific semantics of this automaton are design issues for system builders and authors.

To realize MHMT links in the Web, we created the <MHMT> tag for HTML. Following is the definition of a single link with two source nodes and three destination nodes. We will first explain the syntax:

```
<MHMT text = "Continue to Neck" display_text = "Show Neck">
  <A HREF = "http://www.abcMed.com/head-neck.html">X-Rays</A>,
  <A HREF = "http://www.xyz.org/neck.html">Neck Photos</A> and
  <A HREF = "http://www.abcMed.com/neck-desc.html">Neck Description</A>.
  <IREF HREF = "http://www.cs.unc.edu/~capps/mmm/casePlan.html">
<MHMT>
```

All links in the Web implicitly have one source node – specifically, the HTML file containing the <MHMT> tag itself. In this case, the <IREF HREF="..."> tag defines a second source node. The normal <A HREF="..."> anchor tag is used to define destination nodes; in this case, there are three.

When read with the MMM browser, MHMT links create and synchronize concurrent browsing threads. This example will spawn three concurrently active Mosaic windows, each showing one of the destination nodes – this is creating concurrent browsing activity. The link itself will not be available to be followed in any Mosaic window until both of the source nodes are active – this is synchronization of two concurrent threads. Since all the destination nodes must be represented as coming from one link, text strings appearing inside the individual <A HREF="..."> </A> tags are ignored by MMM. The multi-link is rendered on the screen as the text string 'Continue to Neck', which appears as a parameter in the <MHMT> tag; the link will appear in the Mosaic window displaying the HTML file that contains the <MHMT> definition.

Note that we designed the semantics of <MHMT> tags to give reasonable behavior when browsed with the normal Mosaic (or Netscape) browser. In the example given, the <MHMT> tag and the <IREF> tag is ignored, so Mosaic sees essentially three <A Href = "..."> anchor tags. It will present to the reader three anchors on one page, available for normal one-at-a-time selection. No concurrent windows are opened, and no synchronization with other nodes takes place.

An example of browsing with MMM

Figure 14.15 shows the MMM browser displaying the first node of a document containing MHMT links. Notice that a single link called 'Continue' appears at

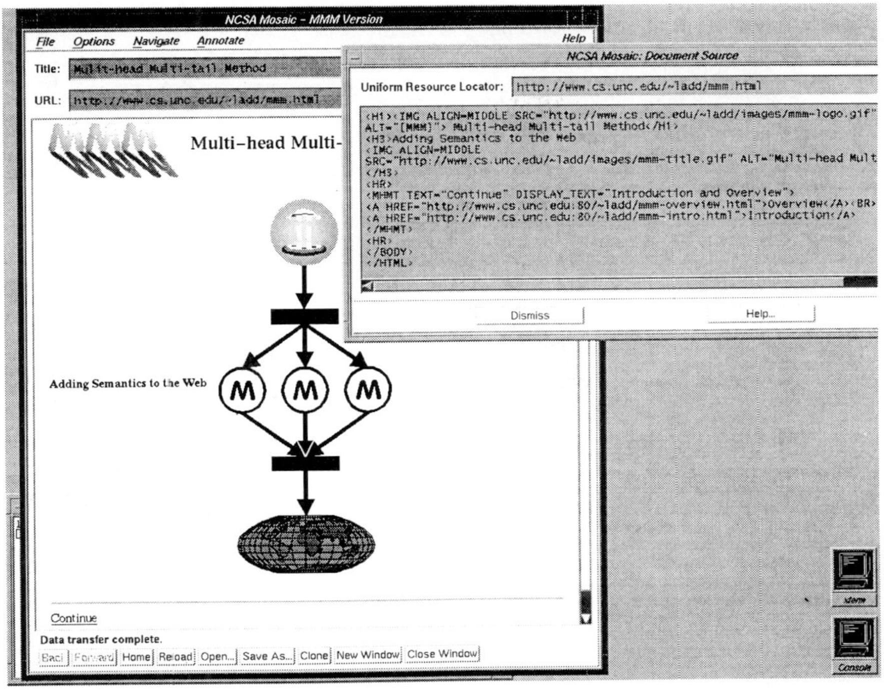

Figure 14.15 MMM screen showing definition of an MHMT link.

the bottom of the screen. The source windows show that this link is defined by an <MHMT> tag with one source page and two destination pages. Selecting the link results in the screen image shown in Figure 14.16. Here, two MMM windows have been activated, each showing one of the destination pages defined previously. One of these pages shows a diagram of the net structure we have encoded in HTML with MHMT links; the other page gives a brief description of MMM.

Note that in Figure 14.16 a selectable link called 'Continue' appears, at the bottom of the text window; at the bottom of the diagram window appears a selectable link called 'Continue to Implementation' and an inactive link called 'Continue to Conclusion'. The HTML source for the diagram page is shown, containing two <MHMT> tags defining these two multi-links. The 'Continue to Implementation' link is defined with two source pages and two destination pages. Its two source pages are, in fact, the diagram and the text shown in the figure; since both are active, the link is active. Note also that this one multi-link appears as a selectable anchor in both its source pages; the HTML source for each page contains an appropriate <MHMT> definition. The 'Continue to Conclusion' link in the diagram page is not selectable; only one of its three required source pages is active.

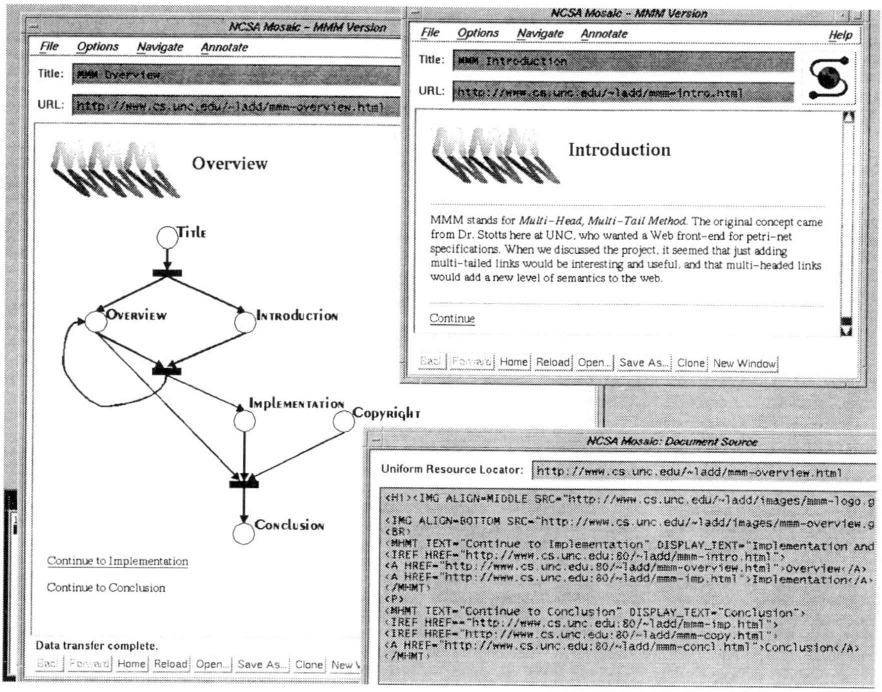

Figure 14.16 MMM screen showing concurrent browsing windows.

As the diagram suggests, selecting the 'Continue to Implementation' link (in either window) will cause the 'Introduction' and 'Overview' pages to go away; the page called 'Implementation' will then be activated, and the 'Overview' page will be reactivated. The net result is shown in Figure 14.17. Notice in the diagram that the link to the page called 'Conclusion' has three input pages. In this case, only two are active; the page called 'Copyright' is not active. The link 'Continue' in the implementation page, and the link 'Continue to Conclusion' on the diagram page, are therefore not selectable.

If the readers were to activate the Copyright page, then those links would become selectable as well. The diagram shows no links coming into the Copyright place in the net, but the page can be activated with one of the special features of Mosaic. By clicking on the link 'View Copyright' (in the implementation page) using the middle mouse button, a new Mosaic window is popped up with that page in it. All three inputs to the last link are then active, and the link becomes selectable. Figure 14.18 shows this situation.

Readers may review these screen examples at URL

http://www.cs.unc.edu/ stotts/MMM/index.html

This page also has links to a more detailed explanation of MMM and MHMT

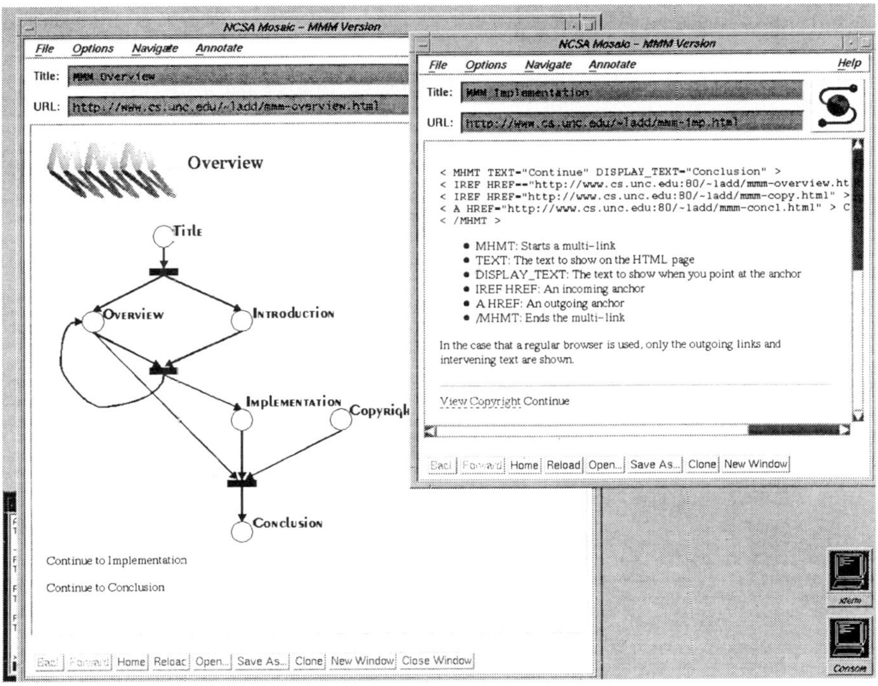

Figure 14.17 Synchronization of multiple windows in MMM.

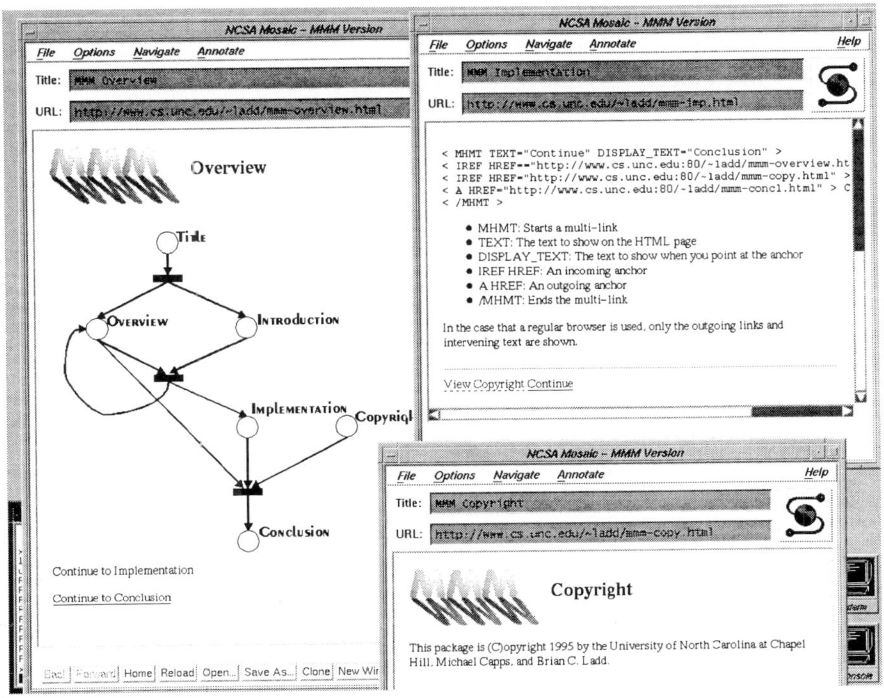

Figure 14.18 Final link becomes available.

links, as well as a link for downloading Sparc binaries for experimental use of the MMM browser.

CONCLUSIONS AND FUTURE WORK

We have presented Sui'tre, a group editing system with a three-level binding of collaboration semantics to its user interface. The interpreted component of Sui'tre provides maximum flexibility in defining group behavior, allowing users to alter their interactions while a collaboration is taking place. The pre-compiled components of Sui'tre allows casting well-known, or fairly well-developed collaboration processes to be implemented in non-interpreted form, giving better performance at run-time. These processes can be either fully static, or parameterized in Suite-fashion for customization by users.

More scenarios and experiments are need to better characterize the utility of the Sui'tre approach. We hope to report on such usage in future papers.

We are extending this work in several directions. First, we are experimenting with the use of the Trellis engine for collaboration definition on multi-user virtual environments. Our early systems allow different users to explore a common model of, say, a building. The common model is stored in each local copy of the program, rather than in a central database. Users see representations of each other, but in the first prototype there are no rules for how they may (or may not) interact. We are combining a Trellis engine with this distributed system to encode the same collaboration protocols discussed here (like moderated meetings) into virtual worlds.

Another line of investigation is a generalization of the heterogeneity we deal with in Sui'tre. Called the collaboration bus, we are designing a software framework for interconnecting different collaborative systems. One goal of the bus is to be able to create new collaborative environments using existing systems as components. For example, if we have a single-user building walkthrough virtual environment, and we also have a meeting tool for managing meetings among non-colocated people, then we have all the functionality we need to have a group building walkthrough; the combined system would allow groups of non-colocated people to explore a building design and to discuss their explorations with each other. Such a combined software system should be easier (and cheaper) to build with an interconnection bus than it would be with ground-up new development. Another line of investigation is best summarized with this scenario: I use conferencing tool X; you use conferencing tool Y; why can't we have a conference? With current collaboration technology one of us would have to obtain and learn the other's system. With the collaboration bus, we simply interconnect X and Y, have the bus perform translations between the different operations of each system, and to each of us it appears the other is using our system.

Bus-based translations are possible now for domains in which systems have similar abstract functions (like teleconferencing) and differ only in technical details of implementation. Further down the road are translations among systems that are less abstractly similar, such as the building walkthrough and group conferencing combination mentioned previously.

REFERENCES

Cavalier, T., Chandok, R., Morris, J., Kaufer, D. and Neuwirth, C. (1991) A visual design for collaborative work: Columns for commenting and annotation. *Proceedings of the 24th Hawaii International Conference on System Sciences*, pp. 729–738.

Clarke, E., Emerson, E. A. and Sistla, S. (1986) Automatic verification of concurrent systems. *ACM TOPLAS*, **8** (2), 244–263.

Dewan, P. and Choudhary, R. (1991) Flexible user interface coupling in collaborative systems. *Proceedings of the ACM CHI'91 Conference*, pp. 41–49.

Dewan, P. and Choudhary, R. (1992) A high-level and flexible framework for implementing multi-user user interfaces. *ACM Transactions on Information Systems*, **10** (4), 345–380.

Dewan, P., Jeffay, K., Smith, J., Stotts, D. and Oliver, W. (1995) Early prototypes of the repository for patterned injury data. *Proceedings of Digital Libraries '95*, pp. 123–130.

Furuta, R. and Stotts, P. D. (1989) Programmable browsing semantics in Trellis. *Hypertext '89 Proceedings*, ACM, New York, pp. 27–42.

Furuta, R. and Stotts, P. D. (1994) Interpreted collaboration protocols and their use in groupware prototyping. In *Proceedings of the 1994 ACM Conference on Computer Supported Cooperative Work (CSCW'94)*, ACM, New York, pp. 121–131.

Furuta, R. and Stotts, P. D. (1994) *Interpreted Collaboration Protocols and their Use in Groupware Prototyping*, Internal Report.

Kaplan, S., Tolone, W., Bogia, D. and Bignoli, C. (1992) Flexible, active support for collaborative work with conversation builder. *Proceedings of the ACM 1992 Conference on Computer Supported Cooperative Work (CSCW'92)*, ACM, pp. 378–385.

Munson, J. and Dewan, P. (1994) A flexible object merging framework. *Proceedings of the ACM Conference on Computer Supported Cooperative Work (CSCW'94)*, pp. 231–242.

Murata, T. (1989) Petri nets: Properties, analysis and applications. *Proceedings of the IEE*, **77** (4), 541–580.

Neuwirth, C. M. and Kaufer, D. S. (1989) The role of external representation in the writing process: Implications for the design of hypertext-based writing tools. *Proceedings of Hypertext '89*, pp. 319–341.

Neuwirth, C. M., Kaufer, D. S., Chandok, R. and Morris, J. H. (1990) Issues in the design of computer-support for co-authoring and commenting. *Proceedings of the 3rd Conference on Computer-Supported Cooperative Work*, pp. 183–195.

Peterson, L. (1977) Petri nets. *ACM Computing Surveys*, **9** (3), 223–252.

Shen, H. and Dewan, P. (1992) Access control for collaborative environments. *Proceedings of the ACM Conference on Computer Supported Cooperative Work*, pp. 51–58.

Stotts, P. D. and Furuta, R. (1989) Petri-net-based hypertext: document structure with browsing semantics. *ACM Transactions on Information Systems*, **7** (1), 3–29.

Stotts, P. D. and Furuta, R. (1990) Temporal hyperprogramming. *Journal of Visual Languages and Computing*, **1** (3), 237–253.

Stotts, P. D., Furuta, R. and Ruiz, J. C. (1992) Hyperdocuments as automata: trace-based browsing property verification. In Lucarella, D., Nanard, J., Nanard, M. and Paolini, P. (eds) *Proceedings of the ACM Conference on Hypertext (ECHT'92)*, ACM Press, pp. 272–281.

Stotts, P. D. and Pugh, W. (1994) Parallel finite automata for modeling concurrent software systems. *Journal of Systems and Software*, **27**, 27–43.

Stotts, D., Smith, J., Dewan, P., Jeffay, K., Smith, F. D., Smith, D., Weiss, S., Coggins, J. and Oliver, W. (1994) A patterned injury digital library for collaborative forensic medicine. *Proceedings of Digital Libraries '94*, pp. 25–33.

Part 5

Commercial Systems and Experiences

15 SAGE: A High Structure System for Helping Teams Find Wisdom (within themselves)

MICHAEL CAPRON, JACQUELINE DESIMONE and KAREN LACOMIS-COTE

INTRODUCTION

Most collaborative writing tools are designed to be used by authors in disparate locations, often asynchronously (the authors infrequently do simultaneous edits). By contrast, Xerox's SAGE (Software Assisted Group Enablers) WorkRight system is a suite of programs intended to be used by groups in face to face meetings. The group works together through a structured process and the resultant document represents the fruits of their collaboration. The primary components of the system are:

- *Meeting Management*: A general meeting support application for setting agendas, keeping track of time used and tracking action items.
- *Problem Solving*: An application implementing Xerox's total quality process for structured problem solving.
- *Brainstorming/Drawing*: Group-oriented tools for brainstorming and flowcharting business processes.

In many ways the problem solving application is the central application. It is a total quality structured problem solving methodology which groups use during a meeting or over the course of many writings. While Meeting Management is often used by groups for general meetings (weekly staff meetings, etc.), it is also used to support writings of groups using the Problem Solving Process. Also as part of the Problem Solving Process, tools for brainstorming and drawing are used.

Figure 15.1 shows some of the essential elements of computer supported meeting environments. Below, the relationship of the SAGE system to the four main categories is shown:

- *Media*: SAGE currently supports same place, same time meetings. Unlike systems such as Ventanna Corporation's GroupSystems V, in which every participant has their own computer. SAGE uses only one computer with a

GROUPWARE AND AUTHORING
ISBN 0-12-575005-6

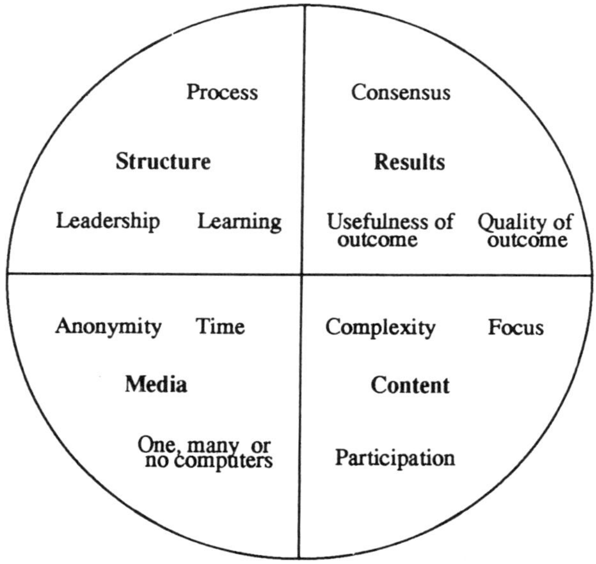

Figure 15.1 *Elements of computer-mediated meetings.*

large display device, such as a projectable LCD panel. The two primary reasons for this are cost and the fact that many team members may not be computer literate or have adequate typing skills. There is no anonymity of participation; but this does leave teams free to use ordinary verbal communication, which has a higher bandwidth than pure computer based interaction.

- *Content*: GDSS (Group Decision Support System) literature indicates that such systems are much more useful with problems of higher complexity and our system is no exception. The use of one computer screen appears to help the group stay more focused on what is occurring in the meeting.
- *Structure*: Many meeting support systems take a 'bag of tools' approach where computers and software are available for groups to use at their whim. EDS's Capture Lab (Horton *et al.*, 1991; McLeod and Liker, 1992) is a prime example of such a low structure system. It is a conference room where every participant has a Macintosh computer and conventional software such as HyperCard, Microsoft Word, etc. In contrast, SAGE is a process based, high structure system. McLeod and Liker explain the motivation well:

'The small group literature has repeatedly found that when left to their own devices, task-oriented groups often evolve structures that are sub optimal and sometimes even dysfunctional to task accomplishment (Hackman and Kaplan, 1974; Hall and Watson, 1970; Steiner, 1972); A number of studies have shown that providing specific rules and resources for task interaction (i.e., attempting to influence group structures), can lead to improved group performance along a number of dimensions . . .'.

The Xerox total quality community has established specific high structure processes for employees to use during meetings and group-based problem solving. These are intended to be used without any form of computer support and all employees have been trained in their usage. It has been found that employees forget what they learned in the training classes and do not retain command of the processes over time. An advantage of the WorkRight software is that groups using the computer support for process use, learn and retain knowledge of the process. We call this benefit transparent learning, meaning that process-learning occurs without conscious user knowledge during task accomplishment.

Results

One measure of the utility of electronic meeting support (EMS) systems is the quality of the resulting output. Numerous studies have found that EMS supported groups had better or at least equivalent results when compared with non-EMS supported groups. However, usability of results is rarely an issue in academic studies. For usability, two things are required: documentation of the group decision (and the process by which it was arrived at) and implementation of their findings. One of the chief benefits of the WorkRight system is transparent documentation, where the system automatically generates a document based on the group's use of the problem solving process. In other words, using the process is the same thing as creating the document. This is a significant improvement over the traditional method of having a group member collect notes, flip-chart pages, etc. and asynchronously generate documentation which is completed long after the fact, if at all. Worse yet, a third party (usually a secretary) who was not even in the meeting may be the one documenting the results.

Another measure of results is group consensus, or the group's overall satisfaction with the results of the meeting(s). Existing literature is inconclusive as to the effect EMS has on this variable.

SETUP

Groupware may be defined in four categories and as having both a time dimension and a space dimension. The matrix looks as follows (Ellis *et al*, 1991):

	Same Time	Different Times
Same place	face to face interaction	asynchronous interaction
Different places	synchronous distributed interaction	asynchronous distributed interaction

Table 15.1 Advantages and disadvantages of using one computer.

Pros	Cons
Only one person needs to know how to use the system.	Input is not anonymous.
The single point of focus encourages team members to work together (instead of individually at their own station).	Possibly slower: If the operator is not a fast typist, ideas may have to be held while scribe catches up – possible loss of some ideas due to reduced speed of input.
Most of the group is not distracted by having to key-in information.	

SAGE focuses on the synchronous, face-to-face meeting scenario (same time, same place) for a number of reasons which include: cost, lack of computer literacy of participants, and a reduced number of people to train on the software. We felt that face-to-face meetings were more important than distributed meetings because face-to-face meetings allow real time communication and interactions between the participants. Behaviors such as clarification of ideas, discussion of ideas, negotiation, decision making, feelings of accomplishment etc. are very important for reaching group consensus. These are more easily achieved in same time, same place meetings.

The system employs one computer in a 'chauffeured' approach where one meeting participant functions in a facilitator role while operating the software. An appropriate metaphor would be whiteboard where only one person at a time (usually) has the marker and is writing on the white board. Other people in the room suggest additional ideas, corrections, etc.

This decision to use only one computer has several advantages and disadvantages (Table 15.1). The system is designed to be low-profile – there is only one point of input, the operator of the software. This person (either a trained group member or a professional facilitator) acts as the group's facilitator by keeping the team on track in terms of process use and by suggesting pertinent tools to help the group at specific points. This person also functions as the scribe for the group by capturing all of the relevant information in real time. Group participation is high because team members can see their own words (printed neatly and readably) projected on the screen. The information is editable so that the group can fine tune their statements. The end result is a higher quality output as compared to a scribbled statement on a flip chart. The group also reaches consensus more easily since all members have had a chance to contribute to the final result. There is more 'buy-in' by the participants.

MEETING MANAGEMENT

The first thing that typically occurs in a supported meeting is creation of an agenda. The group agrees on topics and format, and assigns an expected duration to each agenda item. Agenda items may consist of any type of action. Examples include breaks, announcements, discussions, use of the Problem Solving Process, etc. If the team has previously used the SAGE system, an early agenda item is usually 'Review status of actions items from last meeting'.

The group then executes each agenda item in sequence, and the results are recorded. Participants are asked for specific inputs on status, issues/agreements and a general summary. If the resolution of an item requires that action be then outside of the meeting, that action is especially noted as an 'Action Item', and is included in the generated minutes.

Action items may be generated at any time during a meeting. The software requests specific inputs from the team to create an action item to ensure that the resulting assignment is actionable by the designated completer. A sample action item input screen from the meeting management software is shown in Figure 15.2.

While the fields may appear innocuous, the desired effect is achieved when the team is confronted with the necessity of entering the requested data. It requires more thought to complete the form than is apparent at first glance. In fact, even a decision not to fill in a field has at least forced the group to

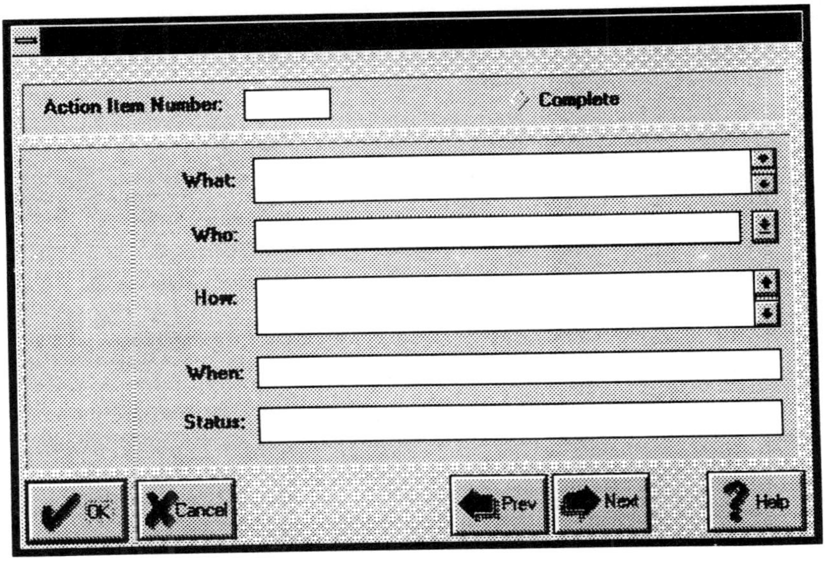

Figure 15.2 Example screen from meeting management.

consider the requested piece of information. Action items in the meeting minutes are sorted by assignee, marked as NEW when first created, and highlighted when overdue. Team members are highly motivated to complete their action items to avoid getting the 'fickle finger' icon which marks overdue items.

Meeting Management also provides a time-keeping function which generates messages (and tones) if an agenda item runs over its allotted time. The group may choose to add time to their meeting or finish at the initial time, prorating other agenda topics to allow the meeting to stay on track. In either case, the group is forced to take charge of their own time management.

At the end of the meeting, a set of minutes is printed for each attendee along with a copy for general distribution. It is a formatted compilation of the inputs of the group process for this meeting. Attached to the end of this paper are an example meeting notice and set of meeting minutes generated by the system for one of the team members.

PROBLEM SOLVING PROCESS

A number of organizations furnish their employees with structured problem solving techniques. These generally divide the process into a series of similar steps: identify a problem, analyze it, determine a solution, and implement that solution. The Problem Solving Process implemented in the WorkRight system takes this sequence into greater depth by providing discrete steps within each of the categories defined above. The discrete steps are designed to focus a team on a problem, and deal with issues such as making sure that the problem is within the team's scope of influence, that it is solvable within reasonable bounds, and that there is management support for the effort. The intent is to eliminate time wasted in trying to solve world hunger when the real problem is that the candy machine eats nickels.

Following a flowchart-like approach, teams are guided down a path of individual steps (each with associated tools to assist the process). Within the framework, there is considerable flexibility – teams may choose the tools they wish to use to complete a step, and recognition of step completion is at the discretion of the team. On a broader level however, use of the tool causes all teams to proceed at their own pace *down the same path*. Documentation is automatically generated based on the inputs of the team members, but the resulting documents all contain the same basic sections and layouts. This consistent format allows teams to compare their results with those of other teams, and avoids redundant work, since any team can read and understand any other team's outputs.

We must be careful to avoid semantic confusion with the word process. The Problem Solving Process (PSP) is the total quality process which the application implements. The PSP begins with group creation of a flowchart of the current work process (not the PSP) in which the problem resides. This flowcharting activity encourages convergent thinking and focuses the group so that all members have the same vision to work from. The drawing tool is used for this purpose, and its outputs flow into further PSP steps down the line. The group uses the brainstorming tool to create potential solutions for their problem, which are then passed along to other points in the PSP for evaluation and failsafing. Tools from the integrated toolset are suggested (through the use of a variable toolbar) at appropriate points in the PSP, and once a tool is used, the information is carried forward to later steps and also included in the final printouts. All work is captured and reported upon in one document – it is not necessary for the group to track drawings and spreadsheets from other tools and remember to print each component individually.

The PSP also continues past the point that many traditional approaches leave off – implementation and evaluation of a solution is necessary for closure of the PSP. This approach requires teams to try their solution – therefore, the solution that is presented must be actionable. Presentation of a solution also follows only after a detailed plan for implementation is conceived and failsafed (possible failure points identified and accounted for).

The application prints a report of the group's use of the PSP. Note that this is independent of the meeting minutes, because problem solving may be a portion of one meeting or may span many meetings.

In addition to its support at meeting and problems solving processes. SAGE provides a number of tools for use at any time during a meeting. Chief among these are tools to support brainstorming and flowcharting. During brainstorming, group members contribute ideas relating to a defined topic and the facilitator types them into the tool. In brainstorming, no idea is considered too wild and discussion of the merits of ideas is not permitted. Only when this phase is complete, are ideas grouped into categories and refined. Figure 15.3 shows a sample brainstorming session. Items are first typed into the Unassigned Topics window. Other windows are then created for category groupings (Desserts and Main Dishes in the example). Items may be deleted or moved between groups or groups may be added, deleted or retitled. Brainstorming may be used in areas such as the generation of potential problem solutions, agenda items or possible process steps to be used in flowcharting a work process.

Most flowcharting/drawing tools are what might be defined as 'output-oriented', meaning that the objective is to produce a drawing that has a certain appearance. SAGE's drawing tool is different in that it is input-oriented. The primary objective is to allow an operator to rapidly formulate a diagram conforming to flowcharting standards in response to group input. By this we mean that the group is generating ideas about how the flowchart should look and the person in the facilitator role is attempting to keep up with them. The features of the tool are designed to enable the operator to successfully do this; the aesthetic beauty of the resulting diagram is not ignored, but is certainly secondary.

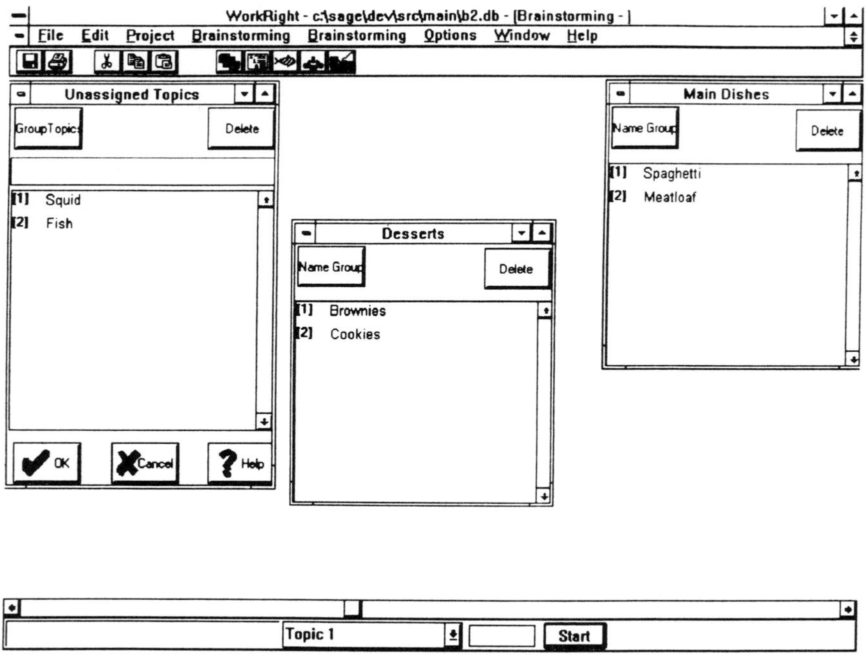

Figure 15.3 Brainstorming session.

This input-oriented approach was developed as a result of observing groups creating flowcharts and other diagrams using existing PC and Macintosh drawing tools or Post-it™ Notes on large sheets of paper. While watching these groups we were looking for attempted or imagined drawing functions which they were incapable of performing with their existing artifacts.

One of the most obvious needs was general speed of input. Group ideas would come in bursts and if the person in the coordinating role could not keep up, ideas were sometimes lost. This was most evident when using conventional software packages where adding new objects required many operations (select text mode, type text, select object type, place and size object, group object and text). SAGE's drawing tool is optimized to permit input of new flowchart objects and new connections with the minimum amount of user action. Correspondingly, reorganization of existing items and connections is also optimized.

The second category of desired features was the need to perform macro spatial operators on all or part of the diagram. There were three types of these needs. First, the ability to make space in a crowded section of the diagram was needed so that new objects could be added to that logical area. Second the group would sometimes want to compress the diagram so that most connections (lines) became short and obvious, eliminating convoluted lines. Lastly, groups wanted to sort drawing objects based on some criteria. Sometimes this involved content, such as date or person responsible. On other occasions, it involved form, such as wanting all leaf objects pushed to the extreme right of the diagram.

The final category of functionality was speed of location. Groups clearly spent a large amount of time looking for data on large diagrams, with dozens or even hundreds of objects. This usually entailed searching for some half-remembered object or trying to find the other end of a convoluted line. Again, features to enable these activities are included in the application.

OBSERVATIONS FROM TEAM SUPPORTED BY SAGE

Much of the data from computer supported meeting research comes from students who are brought together for the specific purpose of trying the technology. They may or may not already know each other. They are probably not from the business world and they are working on an artificial situation conceived solely for the experiment. Often this situation is of a crisis nature, like Arctic survival; this is not a scenario representative of corporate America. Lastly, they are probably not bringing hidden agendas to the meeting, such as departmental turf concerns or personal career ambitions. The data we present here is appealing because it comes from standing groups of real business people attempting to solve real problems. The down side of this is that there is no control group to compare against and that every group is working with a unique situation, so even supported groups may not be objectively compared. The observations reported here come from some 85 teams who have used various versions of the software. It is recorded through surveys, interviews with expert facilitators and anecdotal reporting.

The first reaction of most users exposed to the system is: 'What are computers doing in conference rooms?' After this initial reaction, the group's comfort level increases and they find that they can sit back, relax and enjoy their meeting without worrying about time, process, tools, or taking notes – all factors which are necessary to hold an effective meeting, yet take away from the group's main focus by having members perform dual roles during the meeting. It is difficult to concentrate on content when one is trying to follow a process. Having the chauffeured approach puts the group's mind at ease; the group members are open to new ideas, new processes and new tools. Teams are able to solve real problems while at the same time learning new approaches to problem solving. The team is then able to apply these new methods to solve other problems.

Teams using the system tend to become more 'jelled', or integrated. This results in more social interaction by team members. The members come to realize that they are working together to provide inputs to the end-result document.

Documentation is accurate and timely. The group has already seen the contents on the screen, has already agreed to it, and can walk away at the end of the meeting with the necessary information in their hands. This feature is immensely popular.

Use of the system increases participation of the total group – when members see their own words on the screen, they tend to like the system and become more active. Since the facilitator tends to be neutral (this is necessary in order to capture all of the input), team members are more confident that their ideas won't be lost in the shuffle or misinterpreted by later translation.

Documentation is consistent and complete. The output looks the same way for each tool or process used, and the format is designed to make the most important information the most easily recognized. Teams get used to reading the documents quickly because they will always find the same information in the same places.

The documents constitute a central repository of completed reports for use by other teams. All team outputs are stored in one place in a library and other teams can browse through the library before working on their project. This eliminates redundant work.

SAGE cuts the time spent in meetings accomplishing a task by half. In addition to the focusing effect and time management features of the software, the process is provided by the system and the team is free to concentrate on content.

Teams use the total quality processes more accurately and completely. There is also a tendency within the group to fill in any fields they are presented with. It seems awkward to leave unfilled boxes on a screen, and this usually results in a discussion as to whether or not the information is needed. Even if the end result is an unfilled box, the issue achieves closure, and the team has addressed all the necessary points (even if they never realized it). This is in contrast to the tendency in unsupported groups to stop at odd points in the process, whenever they happen to run out of paper or whiteboard space.

It is clear that groups do transparently learn both the software and the process. Team members have actually risen from their seats and pointed to the screen saying 'I know what step comes next in the process, and I know what screen you need next, and I know how to find the screen!' Team members find the system so user friendly that they want to sit in the driver's seat and take charge of the meeting. In fact several teams have actually rotated team members through the facilitator role as the group became more comfortable using the processes and the system.

Another strong asset of system use is high accountability for action items. When a team member sees his or her name appear on the screen associated with an action item and a due date, they know that at the next meeting the action item will be reviewed for completeness. There is a strong motivation to complete the assigned task. Minutes are personalized – each individual's copy has his or her action items highlighted. This enables people to work on their own assignments immediately. In unsupported groups, the excuse: 'I couldn't get my action item done on time because I just got the meeting minutes yesterday' is sometimes heard.

The system allows team members to assume all the normal meeting roles: facilitator, scribe, timekeeper, etc., but provides a fail-safe mechanism for the more difficult pieces of the roles themselves. For example, while anyone is capable of keeping track of time with their wristwatch, it is an uncomfortable task to have to interrupt a speaker to call time, particularly if the speaker being interrupted happens to be one's superior. The system provides a neutral mechanism for doing this. While SAGE is relatively simple technology, such simplicity may itself often be a virtue (You and Rada, 1994).

THE EVOLUTION OF THE SAGE SYSTEM

As a byproduct of organizational restructuring, Xerox made the decision to move toward a PC-based environment early in 1994. This decision caused the reimplementation of the SAGE product under Microsoft Windows. Removal of SAGE from a multitasking environment caused several dramatic changes in the overall architecture. The system is no longer networked, removing the central repository of historical information that was available in the Unix version. The resulting rewrite also removed some of the power of the product, particularly in the area of the drawing tool. Where the previous incarnation supported spatial operations such as dynamic reorganization of the drawing and automatic generation of connections, the new version produces a static drawing from data input during the brainstorming session. The format of the drawing was also changed to reflect an Ishikawa (fishbone) diagram at the request of the users, since they were most familiar with the Ishikawa tool.

Despite or perhaps because of these changes, the application was also released commercially, and is available under the name of WorkingRight. There are two different components, MeetingRight and SolvingRight, which are available individually. Most users within Xerox have migrated to the PC version, although a few have remained with the Unix application, preferring its expanded drawing flexibility. Several independent consultants within the Rochester area have adopted the WorkingRight software and carry it with them to the meetings they facilitate. A few corporations have also purchased multiple copies for use within their organizations. The actual level of use and customer reaction has not been documented.

REFERENCES

Ancona, D. and Caldwell, D. (1990) Information technology and work groups: The case of new product teams in *Intellectual Teamwork: Social and Technological Foundations of Cooperative Work.* Lawrence Erlbaum Associates, Hillsdale, NJ.

Argyris, C. (1989) *Reasoning, Learning and Action*, Jossey-Bass, San Francisco.

Ellis, C. A., Gibbs, S. J. and Rein, G. L. (1991) Groupware: some issues and experiences. *Communications of the ACM*, **34** (1), 39–58.

Elwart-Keys, M., Halonen, D., Horton, M., Kass, R. and Scott, P. (1990) User interface requirements for face to face groupware. *CHI'90 Proceedings*, pp. 295–301.

Galegher, J. (ed.) (1980) *Intellectual Teamwork*. Lawrence Erlbaum Associates, Hillsdale, NY.

Gallupe, R. B., DeSanctis, G. and Dickson, G. W. (1988) Computer-based support for group problem-finding: an experimental investigation. *MIS Quarterly*, **2**.

George. J. F., Easton, G. K., Nunamaker, J. F. and Northcraft, G. B. (1990) A study of collaborative group work with and without computer-based support. *Information Systems Research*, **1**, 440–457.

Green, S. G. and Taber, T. D. (1980) The effects of three social decision schemes on decision group process. *Organizational Behavior and Human Performance*, **25**, 97–106.

Greenbaum, J. and Kyng, M. (1991) *Design at Work: Cooperative Design of Computer Systems*. Lawrence Erlbaum Associates, Hillsdale, NJ.

Gutek, B. A. (1990) Work group structure and information technology: a structural contingency approach, in *Intellectual Teamwork: Social and Technological Foundations of Cooperative Work*, Lawrence Erlbaum Associates, Hillsdale, NJ.

Hackman, J. R. (ed.) (1989) *Groups That Work: And Those That Don't*. Jossey-Bass, San Francisco, CA.

Hackman, J. R. and Kaplan, R. E. (1974) Interventions into group process: an approach to improving the effectiveness of groups. *Decision Sciences*, **5**, 459–480.

Hall, J. and Watson, W. H. (1970) The effects of a normative intervention of group decision performance. *Human Relations*, **23**, 299–317.

Hymes, C. M. and Olson, G. M. (1992) Unlocking brainstorming through the use of a simple group editor. *CSCW'92 Proceedings*, pp. 99–106.

Kayser, T. A. (1990) *Mining Group Gold: How to Cash In On the Collaborative Brain Power of a Group*. Serif Publishing, El Segundo, CA.

Kraemer, K. L. and King, J. L. (1986) Systems for cooperative work and group decision making: Status of use and problems in development. *CSCW'86 Proceedings*, pp. 353–375.

Krasner, H., McInrow, J. and Walz, D. B. (1991) Groupware research and technology issues with application to software process management. *IEEE Transactions on Systems, Man, and Cybernetics*, **21** (4), 704–712.

Kuutti, K. and Arvonen, T. (1992) Identifying potential CSCW applications by means of activity theory concepts: a case example. *CSCW'92 Proceedings*, pp. 233–240.

McGrath, J. E. (1984) *Groups: Interaction and Performance*. Prentice-Hall, Inc., Englewood Cliffs, NJ.

McGrath, J. E. (1990) Time matters in groups, in *Intellectual Teamwork: Social and Technological Foundations of Cooperative Work*, Lawrence Erlbaum Associates, Hillsdale, NJ.

McLeod, P. L. and Liker, J. K. (1992) Electronic meeting systems: evidence from a low structure environment. *Information Systems Research*, **3** (3), 195–223.

Olson, J. S., Olson, G. M., Storrosten, M. and Carter, M. (1992) How a group-editor changed the character of a design meeting as well as its outcome. *CSCW'92 Proceedings*, pp. 91–98.

Opper, S. and Fersko-Weiss, H. (1992) *Technology for teams: Enhancing Productivity in Networked Organizations*. Van Nostrand Reinhold, New York, NY.

Putnam, L. (1983) Small group work climates: a lag-sequential analysis of group interaction. *Small Group Behavior*, **14** (4), 465–494.

Senge, P. M. (1990) *The Fifth Discipline: The Art and Practice of the Learning Organization*. Doubleday, New York, NY.

Stefik, M., Foster, G., Bobrow, D. G., Kahn, K., Lanning, S. and Suchman, L. (1987) Beyond the chalkboard: Computer support for collaboration and problem solving in meetings. *Communications of the ACM*, **30** 6, 32–47.

Whiteside, J. and Wixson, D. (1988) Contextualism as a world view for the reformation of meetings. *CSCW'88 Proceedings*, pp. 369–376.

You, G.-N. and Rada, R. (1994) A systematic approach to outline manipulation. *International Journal of Human–Computer Studies*, **41**, 283–309.

Meeting Notice

The QTs
March 15, 1993
8:00 am - 9:25 am

PURPOSE: **Customer Satisfaction QIT**
MEETING LOCATION: War Room, Fairport Bldg 1100

MATERIALS REQUIRED: Current Practices pre-reading
PROJECT STATUS: Team has met 22 times to date and has just completed a QIP and PSP with trained facilitation.

Lunch will be provided.
Please park behind the building and use the second entrance.

Agenda

ITEM	PRESENTER	DURATION	EXPECTED OUTCOME
Review Agenda	Team	8:00 - 8:05	Agenda Reviewed
Review Action Items	John D.	8:05 - 8:10	Items reviewed
Status of Data Collection	Brenda	8:10 - 8:40	Copies distributed and results discussed
Prepare Presentation	David	8:40 - 9:10	Presentation completed
Process Check	John	9:10 - 9:15	Check completed
Create Next Agenda	Team	9:15 - 9:25	Agenda Created

Participants

NAME	MAIL STOP	PHONE	ORG	ADDRESS
Benson, David	801-01C	x71498	D&M	Dbens:henr801c
Dixon, John	147-32A	x28768	BPIM	Jdixo:wbst147
Johnson, Robert	845-20B	x25154	OCS	Rjohn:wbst845
Mitchell, Fred	810-04F	x37662	NQT	Fmitc:fairport 810
Myers, Brenda	208-06F	x24887		Bmyer:wbst208

The QTs • March 15, 1993 Meeting Notice

Meeting Minutes for Brenda Myers

The QTs
March 15, 1993
8:00 am - 9:25 am

PURPOSE: **Customer Satisfaction QIT**
MEETING LOCATION: War Room, Fairport Bldg 1100

PROJECT STATUS: Team has met 22 times to date and has just completed a QIP and PSP with trained facilitation.

Distribution List (Attendees)

	NAME	MAIL STOP	PHONE	ORG	ADDRESS
☺	Benson, David	801-01C	x71498	D&M	Dbens:henr801c
☺	Dixon, John	147-32A	x28768	BPIM	Jdixo:wbst147
	Johnson, Robert	845-20B	x25154	OCS	Rjohn:wbst845
☺	Mitchell, Fred	810-04F	x37662	NQT	Fmitc:fairport 810
☺	Myers, Brenda	208-06F	x24887		Bmyer:wbst208

☺ - Present

Outstanding Action Items

	NUMBER	WHO	WHAT	HOW	WHEN
	3	*Brenda*	*Check with customers about survey results*	*By phone*	*April 1, 1993*
NEW	*35*	*All Team Members*	*Distribute customer follow-up tools surveys to each Sales Rep*	*Send through internal mail*	*April 2, 1993*
NEW	12	David	Collate survey results	Computer	April 15, 1993
☛	20	John	Bring Donuts	By car	March 1, 1993

☛ - Overdue items

Minutes

	ITEM	STATUS	SUMMARY	ISSUES
√	Review Agenda	Agenda was approved and no changes were made		
√	Review Action Items			
√	Status of Data Collection	Team members distributed copies and discussed results	More data needs to be collected before and assessment can be made	
	Prepare Presentation	Format agreed upon and contents started		Missing data stopped completion of output
√	Process Check			
√	Create Next Agenda			

√ - Expected Outcome Satisfied

Notes

All team members:

Please remember to put all survey results in the teams file drawer, and to discard old copies of the same information.

****

Definitions:

CSMS - Customer Satisfaction Measurement Survey

The QTs • 15 March 1993 Meeting Minutes 2

Meeting Process Check

POSITIVES	AREAS FOR IMPROVEMENT
• Very informative - learned about other business functions • Good participation • Good interactive skills • Customer satisfaction was the total focus of the meeting	• Exceeded time units on the agenda • Not all groups are sending reps to every team meeting.

Original Agenda

ITEM	PRESENTER	DURATION	EXPECTED OUTCOME
Review Agenda	Team	8:00 - 8:05	Agenda Reviewed
Review Action Items	John D.	8:05 - 8:10	Items reviewed
Status of Data Collection	Brenda	8:10 - 8:40	Copies distributed and results discussed
Prepare Presentation	David	8:40 - 9:10	Presentation completed
Process Check	John	9:10 - 9:15	Check completed
Create Next Agenda	Team	9:15 - 9:25	Agenda Created

16 Multimedia and Multi-Party Desktop Conference System: MERMAID as Groupware Platform

SHIRO SAKATA, KAZUTOSHI MAENO, HIDEYUKI FUKUOKA, TOYOKO ABE and HIROMI MIZUNO

INTRODUCTION

In the past few years, the term 'groupware' has been emerging in an interdisciplinary field of multimedia-involved computer and communication technologies. Groupware, also called CSCW (Computer Supported Cooperative Work) which shares a similar concept, means support for group (multiuser) collaborative work in a geographically distributed environment. Typical groupware applications, in which high-speed computers and broadband networks play vital roles, are remote multimedia conferencing, joint document creation and editing, remote education and instruction, remote medical treatment and diagnosis distributed software development, group decision-making, telecommuting and so forth (Ellis *et al.*, 1991; Sakata, 1993, 1994).

This chapter describes the configuration, service functions, usage examples and evaluation results of a multimedia and multi-party desktop conference system called MERMAID (Multimedia Environment for Remote Multiple-Attendee Interactive Decision-making). This system was developed in early 1988 for the first and the most advanced system in the world, through the effective integration of computer and communication technologies. MERMAID serves as a multimedia groupware platform supporting a wide range of cooperative work in a distributed environment.

It allows a group of any number of widely dispersed users to conduct a meeting from their desktop workstations and personal computers. Participants can jointly view and process multimedia information including text, graphics, image (pictures, paintings, etc.) and handwriting they are sharing, and they can simultaneously interchange voice and video. Thus, they can make a presentation and hold a discussion while interactively interchanging full-media

Reprinted from the *NEC Research & Development* **35** (4) 382–391, October 1994.

GROUPWARE AND AUTHORING
ISBN 0-12-575005-6

information in real time. This system has already been used for daily research work, such as remote technical discussions, distributed software development, cooperative remote simulations, remote lecture and presentation, remote system maintenance, joint system design, joint document editing, etc., for more than eight years. Since MERMAID was commercialized in 1993, more than 1500 systems have been used for various applications outside NEC (Sakata, 1988, 1990, 1992, 1994b, 1994c; Sakata *et al.*, 1990, 1991a, 1991b; Maeno and Sakata, 1991; Maeno *et al.*, 1991). Typical usages are distant lectures in and among universities, joint design of cars, houses, clothes, etc. and international communications. In one case for international use, MERMAID is used for hot lines for ambassadors and diplomats connecting Washington D.C., New York (United Nations), London, Paris, Beijing, Tokyo and other cities.

This chapter first introduces MERMAID system configurations, its functionalities and application examples, and then provides evaluation results based on five-year-long user experiences.

MERMAID SYSTEM OVERVIEW

MERMAID consists of multiple workstations (NEC EWS4800, UNIX™) and personal computers (NEC PC-9800, Windows™ 3.1/NT/95), each of which has a keyboard, a mouse device, a writing pad, an image scanner, voice communication equipment with the same interface as a telephone and a video

Figure 16.1 Global discussion through MERMAID exhibited in Telecom '91.

camera. MERMAID can accommodate various kinds of networks like N-ISDN, B-ISDN, leased data lines, satellite links and LANs (Ethernet™, FDDI (Fiber Distributed Data Interface)-I, ATM-LAN, etc.).

Currently inside NEC, more than twenty remote locations across Japan (Fukuoka, Kobe, Osaka, Kawasaki, Tokyo, Tsukuba, Sapporo, etc.), two locations in the US (Princeton, New Jersey and San Jose, California) and one location in Singapore are connected and have been used for global communication and collaboration.

MERMAID was exhibited and demonstrated in Telecom '91 and '95 held in Geneva. In the Telecom '91 demonstration, eight remote workstations were connected, in which five were in Geneva (Switzerland) linked through an ATM switch and the other three were in London (UK), Munich (Germany) and Tokyo (Japan). World-wide real-time discussions during full-media information interchange and sharing were successfully achieved (Figure 16.1).

MERMAID AS GROUPWARE PLATFORM

Network configuration

Figures 16.2 and 16.3 show the current MERMAID network environment and network configuration. MERMAID can accommodate a wide area leased data network and multiple LANs such as Ethernet, FDDI-I and ATM-LAN which are connected to each other using router equipment via the data network. For transmitting voice and video throughout a wide area, N-ISDN (23B + D, 6B + D, 2B + D, etc.) is currently used inside Japan and Singapore, while AT&T Accunet (56 kbps) is used in the US. When a wide area B-ISDN service

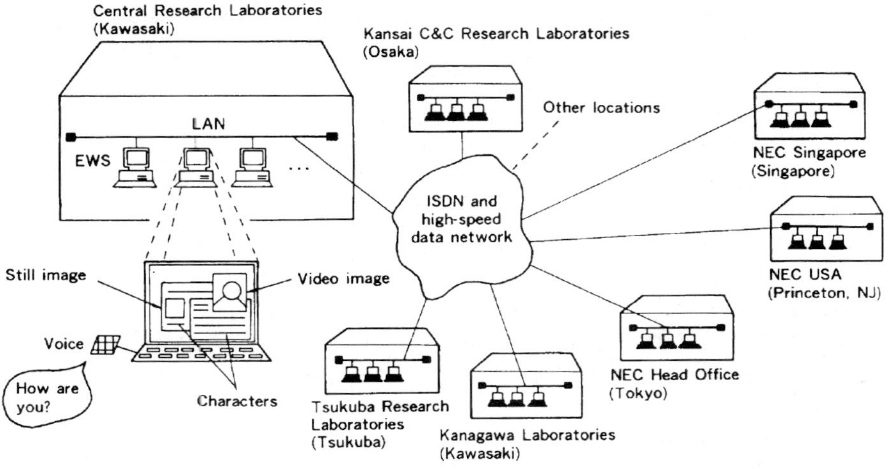

Figure 16.2 MERMAID network environment.

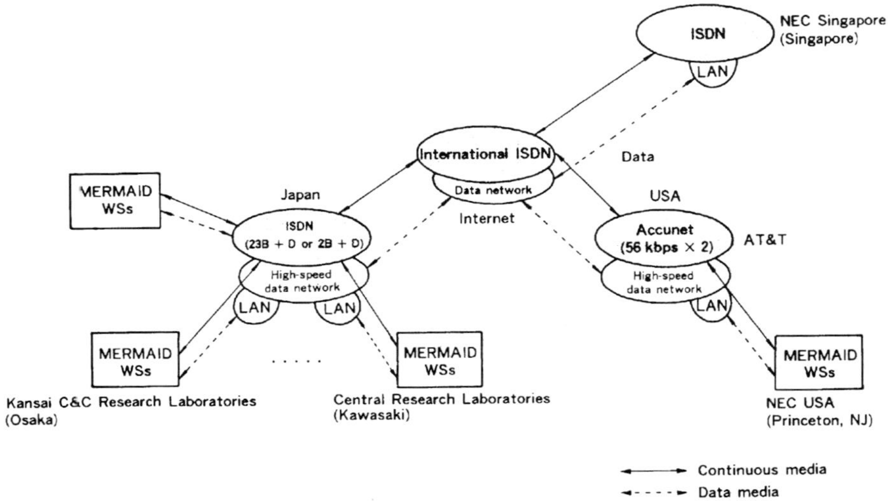

Figure 16.3 MERMAID network configuration.

becomes available, MERMAID is available in a full-ATM environment by connecting with ATM-LANs. Inside Japan and Singapore, all media can be flexibly accommodated in N-ISDN, for example, 6B (384 kbps) for video, 1B (64 kbps) for voice, while other B channels are for data (text, graphics, image, handwriting and telepointing).

Wide area full-media and multi-party real-time communication

MERMAID can link together any number of individual locations managing from a local area to a wide area network, and can provide multi-party real-time communication.

Participants can create and deliver multimedia documents to all other participants in real time. They can add hand-drawn comments, with pen-writing and mouse cursor manipulation and give editorial emphasis (telepointer) to the document currently being shown. Participants can also have live interactions using video and voice, which accelerate understanding in discussions and presentations. All the modifications to the documents made by each participant are transmitted to all other participants at the same time.

Currently, TCP/IP (Transmission Control Protocol/Internet Protocol) are used as network and transport layer protocols for data transmission. ODA (Open Document Architecture)-like protocol, which is extended from the original to accommodating video, voice, handwritten and telepointing information, is defined and implemented for real-time multimedia document communication in application layer.

Figure 16.4 Exterior view of MERMAID.

Figure 16.5 Display example in a five-party conference connecting US and Japan.

USER-FRIENDLY AND EASY-TO-USE VISUAL MULTI-WINDOW INTERFACE

Users are assumed to be ordinary office personnel: managers, engineers, clerks and secretaries. MERMAID provides a mouse based operations interface using multi-window systems, X Window System™ for workstations and Windows for personal computers, with pull-down and pop-up menus, which are easy for even computer novices to handle.

Figure 16.4 is an exterior view showing how the system is used. Figure 16.5 shows a display example in a five-party remote conference, where four are in Japan and one is in the US. Figures 16.6. and 16.7 are an exterior view and a display examples in a four-party conference connecting three nations, Singapore, US and Japan (Tokyo and Osaka). Participants discuss while jointly retrieving multimedia database and handling the retrieved and shared information.

Figure 16.8 shows a display example of remote lecture and presentation from Japan to Singapore. In this usage, productive technical discussions were held between people from a university in Singapore and NEC's research engineers in Japan. Such remote lectures are constantly conducted between universities and research laboratories in US, Singapore and Japan using MERMAID.

Figure 16.9 shows how MERMAID is used for regular US-Japan technical meeting where over 100-inch high-resolution projectors are connected to MERMAID terminals at both sides for supporting group-to-group live multimedia presentation and discussion.

Figure 16.6 Exterior view of international use connecting Singapore, US and Japan.

Figure 16.7 Display example in a four-party conference connecting Singapore, US and Japan.

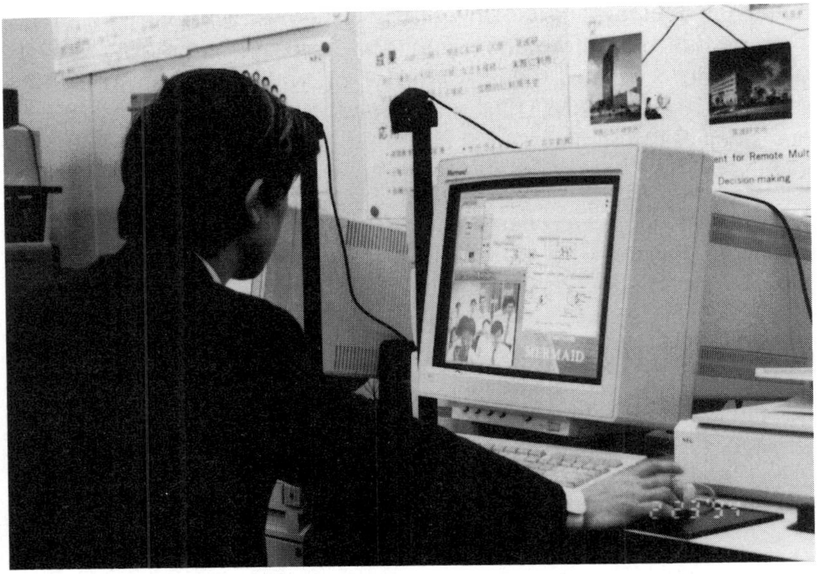

Figure 16.8 Remote lecture from Japan to Singapore.

Figure 16.9 US–Japan regular technical meetings through MERMAID.

Floor-passing control for sharing multimedia information

The notion of a floor-holder is employed for maintaining the consistency of multimedia documents viewed and processed among participants. Floor-passing control is essential in groupware or CSCW for smooth interaction and collaboration. A floor-holder has the right to manipulate shared windows, on which the documents are shared among all the participants. He can make such operations as opening and closing shared windows, scrolling documents and creating multimedia information into documents. This information sharing through windows (called shared window or whiteboard) is available even between WS-based MERMAID terminals and PC-based MERMAID terminals.

Four floor-passing modes can be freely selected and changed during a conference for supporting flexible interactions.

- *Designation mode*: The chairperson defined through a conference selects the next floorholder.
- *Baton mode*: The former floor-holder designates the next floor-holder.
- *First-come-first-served mode*: The floor is passed in the order of the requests for the floor.
- *Free mode*: All participants can simultaneously and freely manipulate the shared windows. In this mode, consistency is not completely assured.

MERMAID APPLICATIONS AND USAGE EXAMPLES

Potential MERMAID applications are listed as follows. Some applications, such as (1); (2); (4) and (6), have already been operational even outside NEC.

1. Distributed software development, simulation, CAD

2. Remote education, instruction, training
3. Joint document creation and editing
4. Financial trading support
5. Medical imaging (treatment and diagnosis)
6. Satellite office or telecommuting
7. Group decision support
8. Cooperative design, e.g. VR (virtual reality, see next section).

Figure 16.10 shows an example of distributed cooperative software development for molecular structure analysis, using MERMAID, which is in operation in a distributed research environment. In this example, research engineers X and Y, about 50 miles away from each other, develop a simulation program analyzing new molecular structures by sharing multimedia document windows and video windows. In the multimedia document windows, the program list, the program specifications and flowcharts are displayed. The video window shows the simulation results, moving colored molecular structures such as red as carbon, blue as hydrogen, green as nitrogen, yellow as oxygen and so forth, which are output from a supercomputer (NEC SX-3). They modify the source program and execute it from both sides with a remote log-in facility. While viewing the video window, research engineers discuss using voice 'how to proceed with the simulation and how to fix the program'. The engineers do not have to gather in the same place, and do not have to prepare another graphic display terminal.

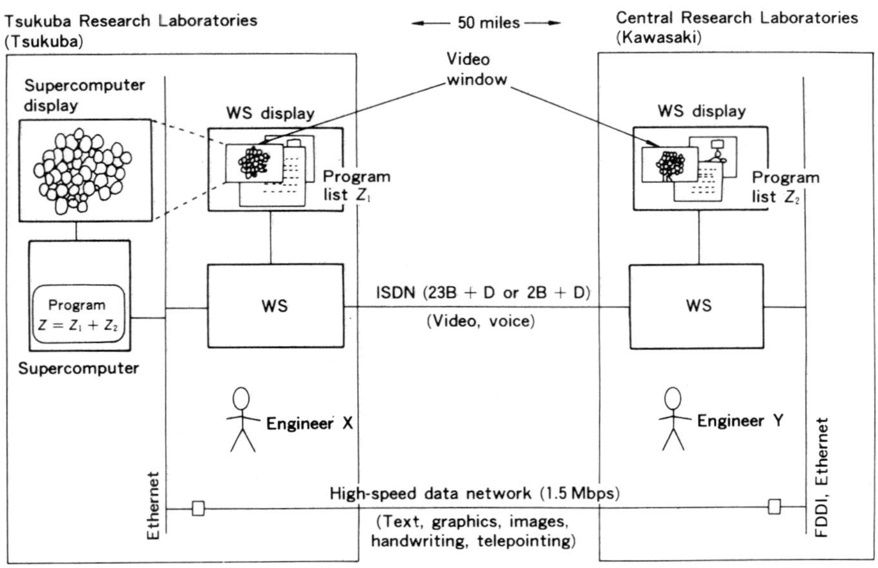

Figure 16.10 Distributed cooperative software development through MERMAID molecular structure analysis.

This software development and simulation using MERMAID enables remote engineers to conduct highly efficient joint research.

COOPERATIVE APPLICATION CONTROL BASED ON MERMAID

The cooperative application control or sharing applications in a distributed environment is recognized as an essential function to support group activities more effectively and flexibly. This function was developed as one of the outstanding extended features of MERMAID. Cooperative application control means that when application programs execute any inputs from participants, such as keyboard, image scanner and handwriting at distributed sites, executed results at all sites become identical in real time. That is, executed results are shared among all participants at the same time. This control allows any existing application programs to be extended to the remote multi-user environment with no modification.

There are two schemes for the cooperative control, distributed (or replicated) and centralized. The difference lies in where the applications are located and executed (Table 16.1). With a centralized architecture, a single copy of the shared application runs at a single site. All input events from each participant to application are forwarded to the site, and the application's output or executed result is distributed to all sites. With a replicated architecture, a copy

Table 16.1 A comparison between application sharing architectures.

Scheme	Advantages	Disadvantages	Location of AP (applications)
Replicated architecture	• Low network traffic, since only input events are distributed among the sites. • Superior response time, since all participants get output from local copies of the application.	• The same execution environment (including hardware), for the application at each site. • Difficulty in maintaining consistency, since equivalent input events are independently executed at each site.	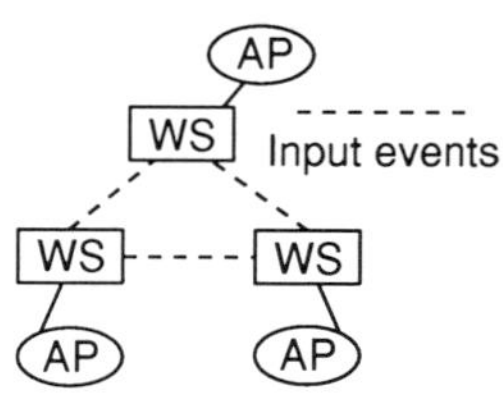
Centralized architecture	• Easy consistency maintenance, since copies of output data are distributed among the sites.	• High network traffic, since the body of output data is distributed among the sites. For some graphics and image-oriented applications, the output data traffic is significant. • Wide-band network needed.	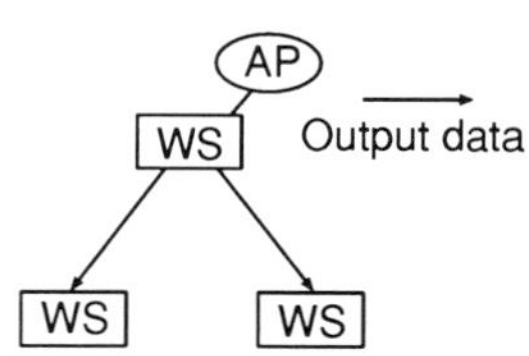

of the shared application runs locally at each site. Input events or execution commands to the application are distributed to all sites, and each copy of the shared application is executed individually at each site.

Considering the superior response time, lower network traffic and the flexibility for the system extension, the distributed scheme was chosen using MERMAID-provided functions, such as real-time multicasting and floor-passing control. Applying the distributed scheme, MERMAID has been extended from mere information interchange and sharing by participants to processing sharing by application programs as well as information interchange and sharing by participants. Figure 16.11 shows how MERMAID is extended to providing the cooperative application control function (Sakata *et al.*, 1992; Ohmori *et al.*, 1992a, 1992b, 1993).

In Telecom '91 held in Geneva, MERMAID was demonstrated with this cooperative application control scheme for hypermedia database access application. This application was developed by a third-party software house outside NEC. Connecting Geneva's five workstations through an ATM switch, London, Munich and Tokyo, international heated discussions were conducted while jointly retrieving information from the database and jointly manipulating the retrieved shared information.

Figure 16.12 shows a display example in which an application program package called micro-RESEARCHER II, already marketed as decision-support and technical office work-supported tool, runs on MERMAID. The sharing document editor application allows multiple users to co-edit documents

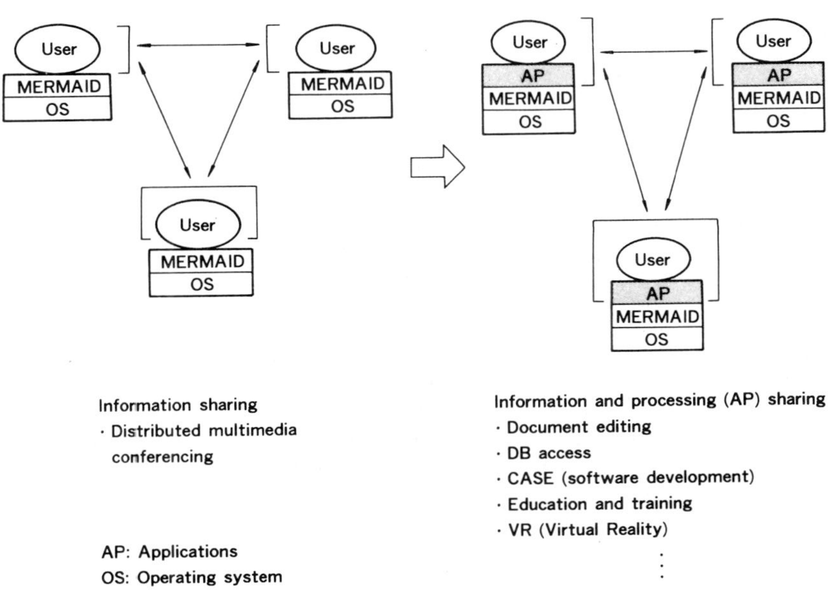

Figure 16.11 Cooperative application control using MERMAID.

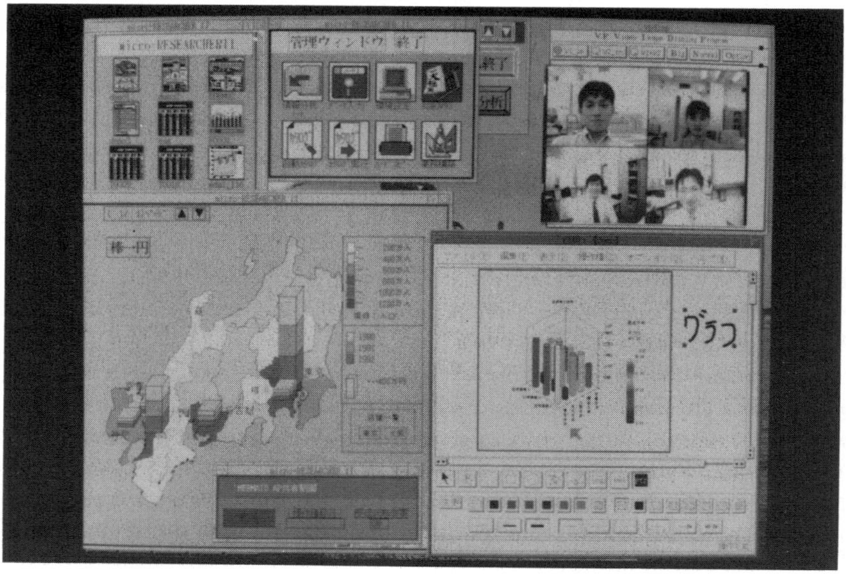

Figure 16.12 Display example of cooperative control of micro-RESEARCHER II using MERMAID.

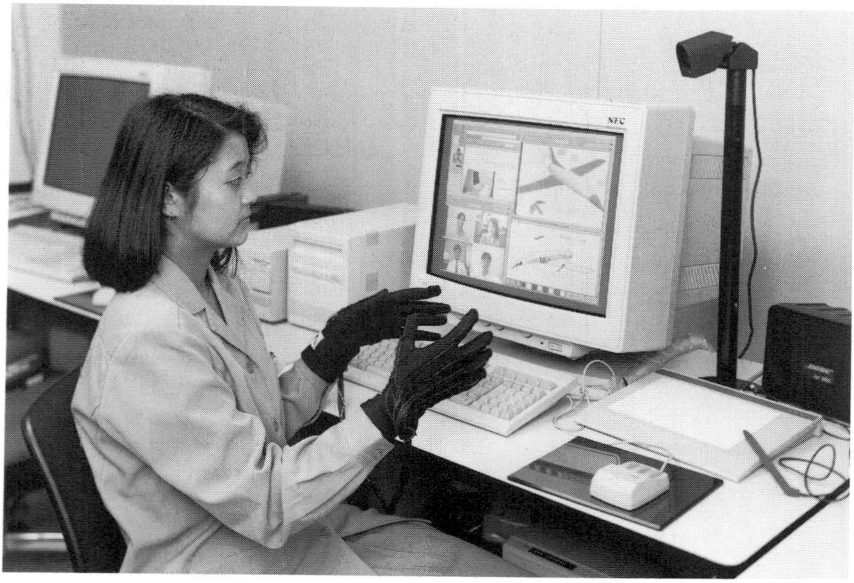

Figure 16.13 Exterior view of distributed multimedia and multi-party VR system using MERMAID.

Figure 16.14 Display example of MERMAID-supported distributed multimedia and multi-party VR system.

(materials, publications, etc.), while talking and viewing a draft document in real time. This achieves an effective, remote and cooperative document processing.

Figures 16.13 and 16.14 are photographs showing how the cooperative control scheme using MERMAID is applied to the VR (Virtual Reality) system. Although the conventional VR system has been designed as a single user (stand-alone) and a single media (graphics) application, such a VR system can be enhanced into a remote multi-user and multimedia environment. That is, a VR system as a group collaborative design tool is achieved by applying this MERMAID-based application control scheme.

USER EXPERIENCES AND EVALUATION RESULTS

Numerous evaluation results from various points of view have been obtained from experiences compiled by around 400 users for more than eight years since prototyped in early 1988.

Information media

Concerning the degree of importance of information media, almost all users so far rank voice first, data media including handwriting second, and video the last. The video has not necessarily been regarded as essential in real-time computer-supported effective collaboration. It has, however, been evaluated that the higher the video quality becomes, the higher the video is ranked. Nearly 80% of users point out that at least 1.5 Mbps bandwidth for video is necessary for smooth interaction. Since ATM-LAN became available in an in-house environment, the use of the system as a visual communication facility has been significantly increasing.

Floor-passing control

The use of the system is divided into two types. One is the use for centralized broadcast based on a chairperson-controlled floor shifting (designation mode), and the other is for intensive and brainstorming-style information exchange and discussion. The former case is rather formal meetings consisting of seniors and subordinates. In the latter case where job-rankings of participants are rather flat, free mode with no floor control is usually chosen.

Cooperative application control

Many applications have been developed adopting the cooperative control mechanism provided by MERMAID. Some were newly developed for distributed multi-user collaboration, and some, originally developed for stand-alone use including the VR system, were effectively extended to multi-user environment. In particular, cooperative control for different programs in the same application, e.g. teacher's program and students' programs in the remote education or distance learning, has achieved much higher productivity than the case where other facilities are used.

CONCLUSION

This paper has presented the configuration, service functions, usage examples and evaluation results of the world first multimedia and multi-party desktop conference system called MERMAID.

MERMAID was developed through the effective integration of multimedia computer and communication technologies. It has proved feasible for supporting a wide range of group activities including international collaboration. Since being commercialized in 1993, MERMAID has already been installed and effectively used by more than 1500 customers, e.g. universities, government organizations, software houses, CAD manufacturers, education industries and so forth, outside NEC.

Groupware is regarded as the most promising application field for B-ISDN and mobile computing environment. The authors have been working toward applying the system to ATM-LAN and WAN environments for providing higher quality multi-media communication capability and for supporting broader group collaborative applications. MERMAID function implementation on a portable terminal has also been conducted to achieve more flexible and more highly sophisticated multimedia network utilization in the near future.

ACKNOWLEDGEMENTS

The authors thank Mr Shin-ya Kubo, Mr. Hiroshi Azuma and Mr Tsuguo Nakajima for their continuous support for the system development and evaluation.

REFERENCES

Ellis, C. A., Gibbs, S. J. and Rein, G. L. (1991) Groupware – some issues and experiences. *Commun. ACM*, **34** (1), 39–55.

Maeno, K. *et al.*, (1991) Multimedia desktop conference system Mermaid based on integrated group communication architecture. *IEICE Trans. on Commun.*, **E74-B** (9), 2765–2771.

Maeno, K. and Sakata, S. (1991) Distributed multimedia conference system based on group communication architecture. *Proc. ICC*, pp. 18.3.1–6.

Ohmori, T., Maeno, K. and Sakata, S. (1992a) Distributed control for sharing applications based on multimedia and multiparty desktop conference system: MERMAID. *Proc. ICC*, pp. 337B.1.1–1.7.

Ohmori, T., Maeno, K. and Sakata, S. (1992b) Distributed cooperative control for sharing applications based on multimedia and multi-party desktop conference system: MERMAID. *Proc. ICDCS*, pp. 538–546.

Ohmori, T., Maeno, K. and Sakata, S. (1993) Distributed cooperative control for sharing applications based on multimedia and multi-party desktop conference system MERMAID. *NEC Res. & Develop.*, **34** (1), 122–131.

Sakata, S. (1988) Multimedia desktop conference system based on integrated group communication architecture. *Proc. Int. Digital Commun.*, pp. 24–32.

Sakata, S. (1990) Development and evaluation of an in-house desktop multimedia conference system. *IEE J. SAC*, **8** (3), 340–348.

Sakata, S. (1992) B-ISDN multimedia and multi-party desktop conference system (MERMAID): platform for groupware. *Proc. 2nd B-ISDN Workshop*, April.

Sakata, S. (1993) B-ISDN multimedia workstation architecture. *IEEE Commun.*, **31** (8), 64–67.

Sakata, S. (1994a) Multimedia communication protocols and services for private broadband networks. *IEICE Trans. on Commun.*, **E77–B** (3), 283–293.

Sakata, S. (1994b) Multimedia and multi-party desktop conference system (mermaid) as groupware platform. *Proc. IFIP Congr. '94*, pp. 63–68.

Sakata, S. (1994c) Multimedia computer and communication (C&C) architecture for global group collaboration: multimedia and multi-party desktop conference system MERMAID as groupware platform. *Proc. IEEE TENCON*, pp. 74–79.

Sakata, S. and Fukuoka, H. (1990) Distributed multimedia and multi-party desktop conference system MERMAID: Platform for groupware. *Proc. CSCW'90*, pp. 27–38.

Sakata, S., Maeno, K. and Fukuoka, H. (1991a) Distributed multimedia and multi-party desktop, conference system MERMAID. *NEC Res. & Develop.*, **32** (1), 158–167.

Sakata, S. and Fukuoka, H. (1991b) Distributed desktop conference system MERMAID with multimedia and multi-user interface. *IEEE J. SAC*, **9** (4), 531–539.

Sakata, S., Ohmori, T. and Maeno, K. (1992) Cooperative control for sharing applications based on distributed multimedia and multi-party desktop conference system: MERMAID. *Proc. Multimedia Commun.*, pp. 122–131.

Index